DESMOND LYNAM'S
1988 OLYMPICS

DESMOND LYNAM'S
1988 OLYMPICS

THE COMPLETE GUIDE TO THE SUMMER GAMES IN SEOUL

SIDGWICK & JACKSON

LONDON

First published in Great Britain in July 1988 by
Sidgwick & Jackson Limited

First Reprint July 1988

ISBN 0-283-99592-0

Designed by Linde Hardaker/Roger Walker Design

Typeset in Linotron 202 Plantin by
Rowland Phototypesetting Limited
Bury St Edmunds, Suffolk

Printed in Great Britain
by Butler and Tanner Limited
Frome and London
for Sidgwick & Jackson Limited
1 Tavistock Chambers, Bloomsbury Way
London WC1A 2SG

CONTENTS

TIMETABLE OF EVENTS

Sport		September														Oct.	
		17	18	19	20	21	22	23	24	25	26	27	28	29	30	1	2
Archery												★	★	★	★	★	
Athletics								★	★	★	★		★	★	★	★	★
Basketball		★	★	★	★	★	★	★	★	★	★	★	★	★	★		
Boxing		★	★	★	★	★	★	★	★	★	★	★	★	★		★	★
Canoeing												★	★	★	★	★	★
Cycling			★		★	★	★	★	★	★	★						
Equestrian				★	★	★	★	★	★	★	★	★	★		★		★
Fencing					★	★	★	★	★		★	★	★	★	★		
Football		★	★	★	★	★	★		★	★		★			★	★	
Gymnastics			★	★	★	★	★	★	★	★			★	★	★		
Handball					★	★	★	★	★	★	★	★	★	★	★	★	
Hockey			★		★	★	★	★	★	★	★	★	★	★	★	★	
Judo											★	★	★	★	★	★	★
Modern Pentathlon			★	★	★	★	★										
Rowing					★	★	★	★	★	★	★						
Shooting					★	★	★	★	★	★	★						
Swimming	Swimming				★	★	★	★	★	★	★	★					
	Diving	★	★	★	★							★	★	★	★		
	Synch.Swim.											★	★	★		★	★
	Water Polo					★	★	★				★	★			★	★
Table Tennis								★	★	★	★	★	★	★	★	★	
Tennis					★	★	★	★	★	★	★	★	★	★	★	★	
Volleyball		★	★	★	★		★	★	★	★	★	★	★	★	★	★	★
Weightlifting				★	★	★	★	★		★	★	★	★	★	★		
Wrestling				★	★	★	★	★				★	★	★	★	★	
Yachting					★	★	★	★				★	★	★			

INTRODUCTION

by Brendan Foster MBE

Faraway places with strange sounding names, Tokyo, Montreal, Moscow, Los Angeles, Calgary and now Seoul, Korea. The Olympic flame settles for its brief stay and sporting history will be made in this great city of the Far East.

Believe it or not, the best place to be for the Olympics is at home watching on BBC-TV and this book is the ideal companion to help simplify what is becoming a more and more complicated business. After all, there are now no fewer than twenty-three sports in the summer games.

Britain's best sports presenter, my friend and colleague, Des Lynam, has now translated his extensive knowledge onto paper and you shouldn't be without it. Small bore shooters, coxless pairs, épées and foils, Des has worked it all out.

There's so much to look forward to, but personally I'm most excited about one of the great confrontations in Olympic history which will take place on the track in the mens 100 metres. Carl Lewis, the reigning Olympic champion against Ben Johnson, the World Champion and current holder of the world record. A tremendous clash resulted when they met in Rome last year which resulted in Johnson setting that staggering new mark of 9.83 seconds, an unbelievable 1/10th of a second off the previous record.

Like millions, I marvelled at the race but for me the magic of the Olympic games is that the return will be unforgettable since it will take place in contest for the ultimate prize in sport – *an Olympic gold medal*.

Brendan Foster
10.3.88.

AUTHOR'S NOTE

This book is not intended to be a complex rule book. Indeed had I tried to detail the rules of all twenty-three sports in the 1988 summer games, the book would extend to several volumes and be about as interesting to read as the telephone directory.

What I have attempted to do is break down each sport, and the events within it, into an easily understood description of what actually takes place in Olympic competition, so that your enjoyment may be heightened as you watch the action on television. For some sports, which might only be viewed at the time of the Olympics, such as judo, fencing, handball and others, this may be particularly useful.

I hope you will find details of past medal winners, the stories of the heroes and heroines, and the unusual facts and figures to emerge from the modern Olympics both interesting and stimulating. I have attempted, where possible, to give general form guides to the events in Seoul which is particularly difficult bearing in mind that these words were necessarily prepared some eight months before the games begin and many months before teams are selected.

Such a book is only useful if the information is accurate. Suzi Ross Browne, formerly of Guinness Book of Records, has worked ceaselessly and selflessly to this end.

I can only apologize to her husband Mike and three beautiful daughters for the slight reduction in quality of home comforts during preparation of this book. Normal service will now be resumed.

I thank Suzi for her expertise, friendship and fun.

Here's to a safe and highly successful 1988 games.

Desmond Lynam

ABBREVIATIONS

AFG	Afghanistan	ECU	Ecuador	KUW	Kuwait
AHO	Netherlands Antilles	EGY	Egypt	LAO	Laos
ALB	Albania	ESA	El Salvador	LBA	Libya
ALG	Algeria	ESP	Spain	LBR	Liberia
AND	Andorra	ETH	Ethiopia	LES	Lesotho
ANG	Angola	FIJ	Fiji	LIB	Lebanon
ANT	Antigua	FIN	Finland	LIE	Liechtenstein
ARG	Argentina	FRA	France	LUX	Luxembourg
AUS	Australia	FRG	Federal Republic of	MAD	Madagascar
AUT	Austria		Germany	MAL	Malaysia
BAH	Bahamas	GAB	Gabon	MAR	Morocco
BAN	Bangladesh	GAM	Gambia	MAW	Malawi
BAR	Barbados	GBR	Great Britain	MEX	Mexico
BEL	Belgium	GDR	German Democratic	MGL	Mongolia
BEN	Benin		Republic	MLI	Mali
BER	Bermuda	GEQ	Equatorial Guinea	MLT	Malta
BHU	Bhutan	GHA	Ghana	MON	Monaco
BIR	Burma	GRE	Greece	MOZ	Mozambique
BIZ	Belize	GRN	Grenada	MRI	Mauritius
BOL	Bolivia	GUA	Guatemala	MTN	Mauritania
BOT	Botswana	GUI	Guinea	NCA	Nicaragua
BRA	Brazil	GUY	Guyana	NEP	Nepal
BRN	Bahrain	HAI	Haiti	NGR	Nigeria
BRU	Brunei	HKG	Hong Kong	NGU	Papua New Guinea
BUL	Bulgaria	HOL	Netherlands	NIG	Niger
CAF	Central Africa	HON	Honduras	NOR	Norway
CAN	Canada	HUN	Hungary	NZL	New Zealand
CAY	Cayman Islands	INA	Indonesia	OMA	Oman
CGO	Congo	IND	India	PAK	Pakistan
CHA	Chad	IRL	Ireland	PAN	Panama
CHI	Chile	IRN	Iran	PAR	Paraguay
CHN	People's Republic of	IRQ	Iraq	PER	Peru
	China	ISL	Iceland	PHI	Philippines
CIV	Ivory Coast	ISR	Israel	POL	Poland
CMR	Cameroon	ISV	Virgin Islands	POR	Portugal
COL	Colombia	ITA	Italy	PRK	Democratic People's
CRC	Costa Rica	IVB	British Virgin Islands		Republic of Korea
CUB	Cuba	JAM	Jamaica	PUR	Puerto Rico
CYP	Cyprus	JOR	Jordan	QAT	Qatar
DEN	Denmark	JPN	Japan	ROM	Romania
DJI	Djibouti	KEN	Kenya	RWA	Rwanda
DOM	Dominican Republic	KOR	Korea	SAM	Western Samoa

SAU	Saudi Arabia	SWZ	Swaziland	URS	USSR
SEN	Senegal	SYR	Syria	URU	Uruguay
SEY	Seychelles	TAN	Tanzania	USA	United States
SIN	Singapore	TCH	Czechoslovakia	VEN	Venezuela
SLE	Sierra Leone	THA	Thailand	VIE	Vietnam
SMR	San Marino	TOG	Togo	VOL	Upper Volta
SOL	Solomon Islands	TON	Tonga	YAR	Yemen Arab Republic
SOM	Somalia	TPE	Chinese Taipei	YMD	Yemen Democratic
SRI	Sri Lanka	TRI	Trinidad & Tobago		Republic
SUD	Sudan	TUN	Tunisia	YUG	Yugoslavia
SUI	Switzerland	TUR	Turkey	ZAI	Zaire
SUR	Surinam	UAE	United Arab Emirates	ZAM	Zambia
SWE	Sweden	UGA	Uganda	ZIM	Zimbabwe

THE 24TH MODERN GAMES

SEOUL – THE HOST CITY

The summer games come to the Far East for only the second time. The first was in 1964 when Tokyo was host city.

The capital of South Korea is one of the five most densely populated cities in the world with over 10 million inhabitants. It was virtually rebuilt after the Korean War (1950–53).

Korea was divided into North and South in 1945 after the defeat of Japan in the Second World War. The North (Peoples Republic of Korea) which is under communist control will take no part in the games by their choice. Indeed, in theory, a state of war still exists between the two countries.

Since the Korean War, South Korea has continued to grow in prosperity and is now one of the world's most successful industrial nations.

The country is situated between China and Japan and the climate is temperate. Temperatures during the games should range between 18°C and 27°C (middle 60's to upper 70's fahrenheit).

Seoul is nine hours ahead of British Summer Time.

Seoul was awarded the 1988 games by the International Olympic Committee in 1981.

Thirty-four competition venues are ready for the games. Seventy-two training facilities will be available for athletes. Most of the facilities were in use for the 1986 Asian Games.

A new Olympic village housing 13,600 competitors and officials plus 6000 media representatives has been built.

The Korean National Flag is called T'aegukki.

The Mascot for the games is a friendly Korean tiger cub called Hodori.

The Motto for the games is 'Harmony and Progress'.

POLITICS

At the time of writing, only North Korea and Cuba of potential medal-winning nations have refused invitations to attend the games.

The North Korean complications have been well documented elsewhere. Cuba has sided with the North Koreans' view that they should have been awarded half of the sports. However, the International Olympic Committee points out that games are awarded to cities, not countries.

Thankfully, for the first time since 1976, it looks as though the major competing nations will all be present, including the USA, the Soviet Union, East Germany and China.

PROFESSIONAL OR AMATEUR?

The modern Olympics founded towards the end of the last century were totally amateur in ideal.

In the early games, an athlete who was coached was thought to be at least bending if not breaking the amateur code. Sport in those years was seen very much as a part time occupation. The man who put down his tools every four years and put on his running vest or unwrapped his shooting pistol or sword was the true Olympian.

As time went by, some nations, recognizing the international status to be gained from success in the Olympics, made it possible for their athletes to concentrate on their sports to the exclusion of almost everything else.

The communist countries in particular followed this course. Strictly, they did not break the amateur code. Their sportsmen were not paid, but their army officers who concentrated on sport, were. The Americans in turn perfected the 'college' system, where their sportsmen had nothing to do but train. The amateur ideal was being broken in everything but name by the major competing nations.

Now, there are anomalies galore. Track and field stars compete despite being paid. Footballers who earn fat salaries in the West German Bundeslig or the Italian first division can play in the Olympic football competition as long as they have not taken part in the world cup.

Boxers, however, cannot take part in the games if they are paid, otherwise Mike Tyson would be a certain Olympic champion. But John McEnroe, a rival to Tyson as one of America's greatest earners from sport could be competing in Seoul with the reintroduction of tennis to the games.

And yet, competitors will arrive from smaller countries and take part in the lower profile sports as they might have done sixty years ago.

One thing is for sure, competitors cannot and will not be paid for their appearance in the Olympic Games.

And make no mistake, nothing in sport can rank as high as winning an Olympic Gold medal. That at least never changes.

THE SPORTS

There are twenty-three in all – two more than the 1984 games in Los Angeles. These are table-tennis, introduced to the Olympic programme for the first time, and tennis, which is making a return after a gap of sixty-four years.

In addition Taekwondo, Baseball and Women's Judo will be demonstration sports while Badminton and Bowling will be exhibited as well.

Detailed chapters of the twenty-three main sports follow.

ARCHERY

The sport was part of the Olympic programme from 1900 to 1920 (except in 1912) when basically it was told to go away and get its act together. In 1931 a world governing body was formed (FITA) The Federation Internationale de Tir de l'Arc, but it was not until 1972 that the sport returned to the Games, when the FITA system of scoring was used.

The 1904 games were dominated by Americans. Not really surprising as they were the only competitors.

Eighty years on, despite rather more fierce competition, the Americans were dominant again in the men's event.

But the South Koreans took gold and bronze medals in the women's event in Los Angeles which augured well for the Seoul Games.

THE COMPETITION

In the men's competition, the archers shoot a maximum of two FITA rounds. One FITA round consists of 144 arrows, 36 arrows shot at targets placed at 90, 70, 50, and 30 metres. For women, the distances are 70, 60, 50 and 30 metres.

The target itself is divided into ten rings in which the archer scores ten points for a bullseye, moving outwards to just one point for hitting the outer ring.

Thus, a perfect score for one round would be 1440 points. All competitors shoot one round and in previous games, they then all shot a second round. For the Seoul Olympics, however, there will be an elimination process after each 36 arrows of the second round and only the top eight archers will shoot the final 36 arrows, making 288 in all. For them, the possible maximum score would be 2880 points.

Archers compete in groups and shoot arrows in threes called an 'end'. There is a 2½ minute time limit for each 'end'.

For the first time there are team events for both men and women as well as the individual categories.

The top twelve countries for each will be decided after the first FITA round. They will remain in the competition.

EQUIPMENT

During the last twenty years, the march on technology has revolutionized archery equipment. Back in 1908 bows were made of yew, as they were in Robin Hood's day. They became stressed after constant use.

Today's bows contain laminated wood and fibre-glass, with stabilizers (those weird objects you see sticking out of them) to steady the vibrations. The bowsight is highly sophisticated and the string is now a synthetic fibre (Kevlon – used in bulletproof vests).

THE BRITISH

There have been no British medal winners since the reintroduction of archery to the Olympics in 1972. However at the 1908 Games in London, competition was on a totally different basis, William Dodd was a gold medallist and his sister, Lottie, the outstanding sportswoman of the era was a silver medallist. The same Lottie had

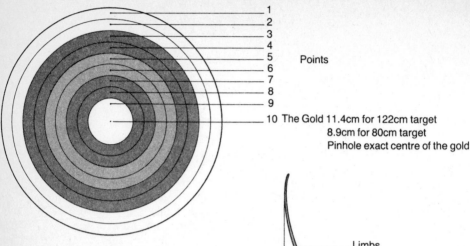

Points

10 The Gold 11.4cm for 122cm target
8.9cm for 80cm target
Pinhole exact centre of the gold

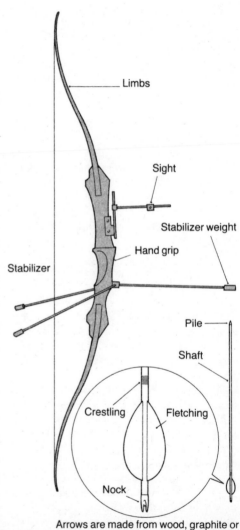

Limbs

Sight

Stabilizer weight

Hand grip

Stabilizer

Pile

Shaft

Crestling

Fletching

Nock

Arrows are made from wood, graphite or
aluminium tubing

already won five Wimbledon singles' tennis titles, the British Women's Golf Championship, and had played hockey for England.

She could have qualified for three different sports, were she alive for the 1988 Games.

THE STARS

The Americans have the best track record in the Games since 1972. Indeed, Darrell Pace won the men's title twice, in 1976 and '84. He and Richard McKinney (the silver medallist in Los Angeles) have dominated recent world championships as well. However, the current (1987) world champion is Vladimir Yesheyev of the Soviet Union. Expect the Americans and the Soviets (who did not, of course, compete in 1984) to contest the medals.

In the women's event, the South Koreans will have high hopes of taking the major prize, with the Chinese and Soviet archers their likely main rivals.

For the first time there are team events for both men and women. Surprisingly, the West Germans are very strong on a team basis in the men's competition, while the Soviets should be favourites for the women's team gold medals.

Not a lot of people know that

• At the 1900 Games, one of the archery events was 'Shooting the Live Pigeon'.
• A person who is an archery devotee is called a 'Taxophilite'.
• Bows may be as long as you like, but there is a limit on the 'draw' weight, i.e. strength of the bow. For men it is 45 lbs at full draw and for women 28 lbs.

VENUE

Hwarang Archery Field 18 km from Olympic Village. 1500 seats.

RESULTS

Double FITA round, Individual/*Men*

OR: 2616 pts Darrell Pace (USA) 1984

	Gold	Silver	Bronze
1972	John Williams (USA) 2528 pts	Gunnar Jarvil (SWE) 2481 pts	Kyösti Laasonen (FIN) 2467 pts
1976	Darrell Pace (USA) 2571 pts	Hiroshi Michinaga (JPN) 2502 pts	Giancarlo Ferrari (ITA) 2495 pts
1980	Tomi Poikolainen (FIN) 2455 pts	Boris Isachenko (URS) 2452 pts	Giancarlo Ferrari (ITA) 2449 pts
1984	Darrell Pace (USA) 2616 pts	Richard McKinney (USA) 2564 pts	Hiroshi Yamamoto (JPN) 2563 pts
1988	Result: 30 September		

Men's Team (new event for 1988)

1988   Result: 1 October

Double FITA round, Individual/*Women*

OR: 2568 pts Hyang-Soon Seo (KOR) 1984

	Gold	Silver	Bronze
1972	Doreen Wilber (USA) 2424 pts	Irena Szydlowska (POL) 2407 pts	Emma Gapchenko (URS) 2403 pts
1976	Luann Ryon (USA) 2499 pts	Valentina Kovpan (URS) 2460 pts	Zebeniso Rustamova (URS) 2407 pts
1980	Keto Losaberidze (URS) 2491 pts	Natalya Butuzova (URS) 2477 pts	Päivi Meriluoto (FIN) 2449 pts
1984	Hyang-Soon Seo (KOR) 2568 pts	Ling Juan Li (CHN) 2559 pts	Jin-Ho Kim (KOR) 2555 pts
1988	Result: 30 September		

Women's Team (new event for 1988)

1988   Result: 1 October

ATHLETICS

The centrepiece of the games. An Olympic gold medal is the highest accolade for any track and field star (although the World Championships inaugurated in 1983 now rival its importance).

It is fair to say that the outstanding performances on the track down the years are remembered more than achievements in any other Olympic sport. Although the Americans, East Germans and Soviets will dominate, medallists can come from anywhere in the world. African nations almost had a clean sweep of men's track titles from 800 metres up in the 1987 Rome World Championships and should do well again.

TRACK EVENTS

THE SPRINTS

Men and women each compete over:

100 metres
Men
WR: 9.83 (Ben Johnson CAN, 1987)
OR: 9.95 (Jim Hines USA, 1968)

Women
WR: 10.76 (Evelyn Ashford USA, 1984)
OR: 10.97 (Evelyn Ashford USA, 1984)

200 Metres
Men
WR: 19.72 (Pietro Mennea ITA, 1979)
OR: 19.80 (Carl Lewis USA, 1984)

Women
WR: 21.71 (Marita Koch GDR, 1979 twice),
(Heike Drechsler GDR, 1986 twice)
OR: 21.81 (Valerie Brisco-Hooks USA, 1984)

400 Metres
Men
WR: 43.86 (Lee Evans USA, 1968)
OR: 43.86 (Lee Evans USA, 1968)

Women
WR: 47.60 (Marita Koch GDR, 1985)
OR: 48.83 (Valerie Brisco-Hooks USA, 1984)

In these events, competitors will almost certainly have to run four times to gain a medal. If they are 'doubling up' events and also competing in relays, the schedule is highly demanding. The start is all-important in these events. Blocks are compulsory because they are wired up to detect a false start. Two false starts by an athlete means disqualification.

HURDLES

The high hurdles distance for men is 110 metres; for women it is 100 metres.

Both men and women compete at 400 metres hurdles.

110 metres
WR: 12.93 (Renaldo Nehemiah USA, 1981)
OR: 13.20 (Roger Kingdom USA, 1984)

100 metres
WR: 12.25 (Ginka Zagorcheva BUL, 1987)
OR: 12.56 (Vera Komissova URS, 1980)

400 metres
Men
WR: 47.02 (Ed Moses USA, 1983)
OR: 47.64 (Ed Moses USA, 1984)

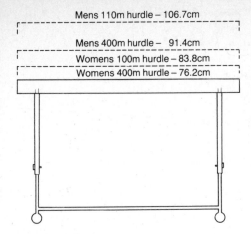

Mens 110m hurdle – 106.7cm
Mens 400m hurdle – 91.4cm
Womens 100m hurdle – 83.8cm
Womens 400m hurdle – 76.2cm

Women
WR: 52.94 (Marina Stepanova URS, 1986)
OR: 54.61 (Nawal El Moutawakel MAR, 1984)

An indication of the changing attitude to women's athletics can be gauged from the fact that the 400 metres hurdles which was always considered the 'man-killer' of the track events was added to the Olympic programme for women in 1984. All hurdles races involve ten barriers (the height varies – see diagram). Athletes can knock over as many of them as they like without disqualification, since hitting the hurdle slows the runner down as well as upsetting his rhythm. The hurdles are designed to fall in the direction in which the runner is moving.

If an athlete trails his leg 'around' a hurdle, he may be disqualified.

MIDDLE DISTANCE

These are over 800 metres and 1500 metres for both men and women.

800 metres
Men
WR: 1:41.73 (Sebastian Coe GBR, 1981)
OR: 1:43.00 (Joaquim Cruz BRA, 1984)
Women
WR: 1:53.28 (Jarmila Kratochvilova TCH, 1983)

OR: 1:53.43 (Nadyezda Olizarenko URS, 1980)

Two laps of the track, the race is run in lanes round the first bend, then athletes can break to the inside of the track. A potential medallist will have to run three races.

1500 metres
Men
WR: 3:29.46 (Said Aouita MAR, 1985)
OR: 3:32.53 (Sebastian Coe GBR, 1984)
Women
WR: 3:52.47 (Tatanya Kazankina URS, 1980)
OR: 3:56.56 (Tatanya Kazankina URS, 1980)

The metric mile, just short of four laps and the 'blue riband' event on the track. Athletes start from the top of the back straight and complete that lap and three others. This is the shortest race that does not begin in lanes.

DISTANCE

For men, these are over 3000 metres steeplechase, 5000 metres and 10,000 metres. For women they are over 3000 metres and 10,000 metres. The 10,000 metres which has been familiar in other major games for some time is introduced into Olympic competition for women for the first time in 1988.

Steeplechase
WR: 8:05.4 (Henry Rono KEN, 1978)
OR: 8:08.02 (Anders Garderud SWE, 1976)

So far there is no women's race in steeplechase. Athletes cover just over seven laps of the track and must clear thirty-five obstacles (four hurdles and a water jump on each lap). The barriers are 0.914 metres high. The race begins in the middle of the back straight and no obstacles are jumped until that 'half lap' has been completed. On the remaining seven laps, the obstacles are placed 77.7 metres apart and the water jump is cleared after the third hurdle. The athlete can clear the hurdle any way he likes. Most world-class steeplechasers jump the hurdles clear

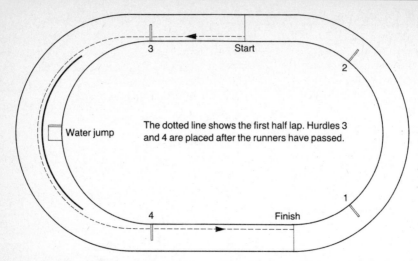

3 Start 2 Water jump 4 Finish 1

The dotted line shows the first half lap. Hurdles 3 and 4 are placed after the runners have passed.

but use a 'one-foot and push-off' method for the water jump. The water is 69.8 cm deep, getting progressively shallower, and is 3.66 metres long. It is a highly technical event and one of the most demanding.

3000 metres
WR: 8:22.62 (Tatanya Kazankina URS, 1984)

OR: 8:35.96 (Maricica Puica ROM, 1984)

So as you will have noticed, the women take longer to run 3000 metres flat than the men do to steeplechase the same distance. This women's event is the one that produced the famous Mary Decker/Zola Budd crash in the 1984 games.

5000 metres
WR: 12:58.39 (Said Aouita MAR, 1987)
OR: 13:05.59 (Said Aouita MAR, 1984)

Women do not race this distance in the Olympics. It is 12.5 laps of the track.

10,000 metres
Men
WR: 27:13.81 (Fernando Mamede POR, 1984)
OR: 27:38.35 (Lasse Viren FIN, 1972)
Women
WR: 30:13.74 (Ingrid Kristiansen NOR, 1986)
OR: Not held before

This is a new Olympic event for women, but has been a feature of World, Commonwealth and European Championships before. It is twenty-five laps of the track.

RELAYS

There are four relay races, the sprint relay (4 × 100 metres) and the one-lap relay (4 × 400 metres) for both men and women.

4 × 100
Men
WR: 37.83 (USA, 1984)
OR: 37.83 (USA, 1984)

Women
WR: 41.37 (East Germany, 1985)
OR: 41.60 (East Germany, 1980)

4 × 400
Men
WR: 2:56.16 (USA, 1968)
OR: 2:56.16 (USA, 1968)

Women
WR: 3:15.92 (East Germany, 1984)
OR: 3:18.29 (USA, 1984)

The relays traditionally bring the track and field programme to a close at major games. Passing the baton smoothly and accurately is, of course, vitally important.

In the sprint relay, there is a 10-metre zone where the athlete about to receive the baton begins his sprint. The baton must be handed over in the next 20-metre zone. If the takeover does not happen in that zone, disqualification is immediate. At each takeover, a judge will indicate whether or not it has been conducted successfully.

In the 4 × 400 metres relay, chaos sometimes reigns. The first leg is run in lanes as is the second leg as far as the back straight. Then it's a free-for-all at the subsequent changeovers (20-metre zones). The athletes about to receive the baton can move as near as they like to the inside curve. Tired 400-metre runners searching through a haze of exhaustion for colleagues can lead to all sorts of disasters.

The baton itself is light and hollow.

THE MARATHON

There is no world record for this event because courses vary. There is, however, an Olympic record. Women will compete in Marathon for the second Olympics running.

Men
WB: 2:06.50 (Belaine Dinsamo ETH, 1988)
OR: 2:09.21 (Carlos Lopes POR, 1984)

Women
WB: 2:21.06 (Ingrid Kristiansen NOR, 1985)
OR: 2:24.52 (Joan Benoit USA, 1984)

Run over the classic 26 miles 385 yards (42.19 km), this event conjures up more theatre and unpredictability than any other event. Most of the physical problems for competitors occur after the 17-mile mark. Athletes themselves talk about the 'lactic acid' problem. To you and me that means they are up against a fatigue barrier, commonly known as 'the wall'.

Standards are amazing. If the men's marathon winner records a time of 2 hours 8 minutes, he will have averaged each of the twenty-six miles in a fraction over 4 mins 52 seconds. Five minute miles would bring an athlete home in 2 hours 11 minutes and 9 seconds.

THE WALKS

There are two events – 20 km and 50 km, both for men. Women do not compete in walking events at the Olympics.

20 km
WB: 1:19.12 (Axel Noack GDR, 1987)
OR: 1:23.12 (Ernesto Canto MEX, 1984)
50 km
WB: 3:38.17 (Ronald Wiegel GDR, 1986)
OR: 3:47.76 (Raul Gonzalez MEX, 1984)

As in the marathon, there are no world records for these events because courses vary so much. There are world best times, however, as above.

To judge whether an athlete is walking or running is by far the most difficult job in athletics. The rule itself is simple: 'a walker must have part of one foot in contact with the ground at all times'. Judging whether that occurs is extremely difficult. The offence is called 'lifting', but the leg speed of the top walkers makes the dividing line between correct and unlawful techniques almost impossible to decipher with the naked eye.

FIELD EVENTS

JAVELIN

Men
WR: 87.66 (Jan Zelezny TCH, 1987)
OR: 94.58 (Miklos Nemeth HUN, 1976)
Note: this was with the 'old' javelin. See below.

Women
WR: 78.90 (Petre Falke GDR, 1987)
OR: 69.56 (Tessa Sanderson GBR, 1984)

From April 1986 the men's javelin was altered in design. The weight remained as before – 800 grams – but the centre of gravity was redesigned. The reason – with the old javelin top performers were getting close to throwing it out of stadiums. The world record was longer than the average football pitch. Safety had become a major problem. The new men's javelin will not fly so far.

The women's javelin, weighing 600 grams, has remained unaltered. In the Olympics, competitors have just three throws to qualify for the finals where they will have six more throws. Only distances thrown in the final count for medal positions.

DISCUS

Men
WR: 74.08 (Jurgen Schult GDR, 1986)
OR: 68.28 (Mac Wilkins USA, 1976)
Women
WR: 74.56 (Zdenka Silhara TCH, 1984)
OR: 69.96 (Evelin Jahl GDR, 1980)

A discipline of strength, speed and mobility like the javelin.

Competitors have three qualifying throws. Those that qualify for the finals then have six throws. Again, only throws in the final count for placings.

The great problem for discus-throwers is 'fouling the circle'. There is a small board at the end of the releasing arc, and any throw where the foot is placed on top of the board or beyond is disqualified.

The discus, now usually made of fibreglass, weighs 2 kg for men and 1 kg for women.

HAMMER

This is the only throwing event not contested by women. This can be the most dangerous throwing implement of all. Despite stringent safety rules a 7.26 kg weight, given added momentum by being swung on a chain some 1.19 metres long, and hurled the length of a soccer pitch can, if only released slightly off-balance, cause athletes, officials and spectators to take considerable evasive action. The hammer fouling rules are the same as those for the discus, though they are not thrown from the same circle. Throwers compete from inside a safety cage and sights of off-balance throwers failing to project the hammer out of the cage are commonplace.

The same qualifying and final rounds as in other throwing competitions apply. Throwers are allowed to wear a protective glove but fingers must be exposed.

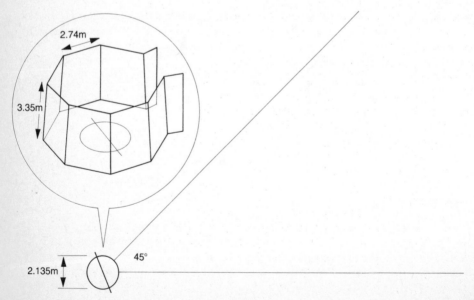

2.74m
3.35m
45°
2.135m

WR: 86.74 (Yuriy Sedykh URS, 1986)
OR: 81.80 (Yuriy Sedykh URS, 1980)

SHOT

Men

WR: 22.64 (Udo Beyer GDR, 1984)
OR: 21.35 (Vladimir Kiselyev URS, 1980)

Women

WR: 22.63 (Natalya Lisovskaya URS, 1987)
OR: 22.41 (Ilona Slupianek GDR, 1980)

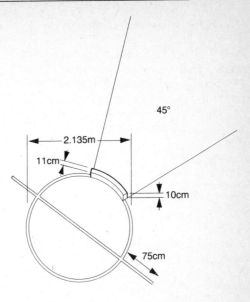

The men's shot weighs 7.25 kg and the women's 4 kg. A raised board some 12 cm high at the edge of the throwing circle acts as a brake when the putter releases the shot. Qualifying and final throws as in events above.

HIGH JUMP

Men

WR: 2.42 (Patrick Sjoberg SWE, 1987)
OR: 2.36 (Gerd Wessig GDR, 1980)

Women

WR: 2.09 (Stefka Kostadinova BUL, 1987)
OR: 2.02 (Ulrike Meyfarth FRG, 1984)

This event saw one of the great sporting innovations in the sixties when Dick Fosbury, the 1968 Olympic champion, revolutionized the technique. Whereas other athletes ran towards the bar and threw their leading leg up, twisting over in the style of the straddle jump, Fosbury, after a normal run-up, swung his right leg back and approached the bar head first and backwards! All leading jumpers now use this method. Take-off must be from one foot. Gymnastic and circus-type leaps are not permitted. In competition an athlete can pass at any height. Three successive failures result in elimination.

In the event of a tie, the following applies:
(a) the competitor with the fewest failures at the previous height wins;
(b) if there is still a tie, the competitor with the fewest total failures wins;

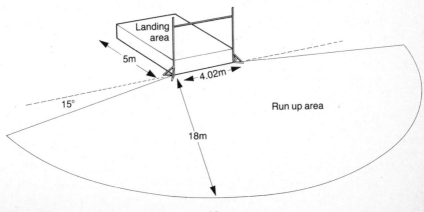

23

(c) if there is still a tie, the competitor with the fewest attempts wins;

(d) if that hasn't done it, the tie stands, except when first place is at stake. Those sharing first place have one extra jump at the winning height.

The uprights are set 4.02 metres apart. The bar weighs 2 kg.

LONG JUMP

Men
WR: 8.90 (Bob Beamon USA, 1968)
OR: 8.90 (Bob Beamon USA, 1968)
Women
WR: 7.45 (Heike Drechsler GDR, 1986), (Jackie Joyner USA, 1987)
OR: 7.06 (Tatyana Kolpakova URS, 1980)

A valid jump must be taken from, or just behind, the 20 cm take-off board. Plasticine pads placed just beyond the take-off board record no-jumps if they are not obvious. A following wind speed of over two metres per second invalidates a jump for record purposes.

A qualifying round is held, where the results are *not* carried forward.

The final group has three jumps, then the leading eight competitors three more.

TRIPLE JUMP

WR: 17.97 (Willie Banks USA, 1985)
OR: 17.39 (Victor Saneyev URS, 1968)

There is no women's event. It used to be known as the Hop, Step and Jump which is precisely what it is. The athlete hops on to the same foot from which he takes off, takes a step with the other foot and, hopefully with momentum maintained, completes the jump phase. The jump phase is nearly always the longest, then the hop, with the step shortest. The breakdown of Willie Banks' 1985 world record of 17.97 metres is: hop 6.2, step 5.3, and jump 6.5 metres.

It is a specialist event, putting severe pressure on an athlete's heels and Achilles'

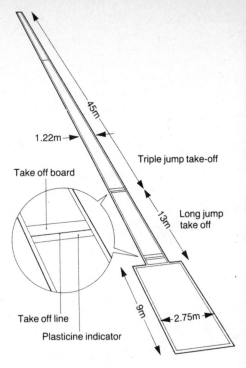

1.22m — Take off board — 45m — Triple jump take-off — 13m — Long jump take off — Take off line — Plasticine indicator — 9m — 2.75m

tendons. The long-jump pit is used with the take-off several metres back.

POLE VAULT

WR: 6.03 (Sergey Bubka URS, 1987)
OR: 5.78 (Wladislaw Kozakiewicz POL, 1980)

This is another event undertaken by men only.

In early modern Olympics, poles were made of bamboo or hickory. Later, metal poles were employed. Now, fibre-glass poles are used and unlike other field events, the competitor can use his own equipment. The event is highly technical and requires a good deal of physical courage.

Landing has been made considerably easier for vaulters since air-filled landing mats have replaced the old sandpits.

As in high jump, vaulters may pass on heights. Three successive failures means elimination.

The bar is 4.47 metres wide.

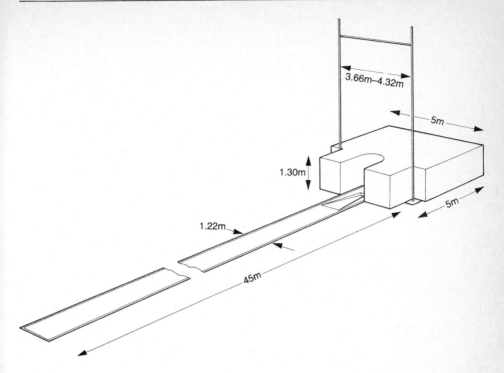

3.66m–4.32m

5m

1.30m

1.22m

5m

45m

DECATHLON

WR: 8847 (Daley Thompson GBR, 1984)
OR: 8797 (Daley Thompson GBR, 1984)

Note: points tables have since been revised.

Another men-only event.

The ten events are held over two days and provide a daunting test of skill, stamina, and technique. The decathlon combines sprinting with middle-distance running, throwing events with jumping and vaulting. It is held in the following order:

Day 1 100 metres, long jump, shot put, high jump, 400 metres.
Day 2 110 metres hurdles, discus, pole vault, javelin, 1500 metres.

There is a rest period of thirty minutes between each discipline.

The tables of points allocation per discipline were devised in 1962, and amended in 1971, 1977, and 1986.

The table on the next page show the times and distances that earn 1000 points alongside Daley Thompson's current world record performance.

In Olympic competition, athletes compete in 'pools' with the potential medallists usually competing in the same one.

HEPTATHLON

WR: 7158 (Jackie Joyner USA, 1986)
OR: 6390 (Glynis Nunn AUS, 1984)

This is the women's multi-discipline event and it replaced the pentathlon in 1980.

The seven disciplines are held over two days as follows:

Day 1 100 metres hurdles, high jump, shot put, 200 metres.
Day 2 Long jump, javelin, 800 metres.

The rules are similar to decathlon.

The table on the next page show the times and distances that earn 1000 points alongside Jackie Joyner's current world record performances.

DALEY THOMPSON (GBR) DECATHALON WORLD RECORD 1984

		points	1000 points
100 metres	10.44	989	10.39 = 1001 points (10.40 = 999 points)
Long Jump	8.01 m	1063	7.76 m
Shot	15.72 m	834	18.40 m
High Jump	2.03 m	831	2.21 m
400 metres	46.97	960	46.17
110 metres Hurdles	14.33	932	13.80
Discus	46.56 m	799	56.64 m
Pole Vault	5.00 m	910	5.29 m
Javelin	65.24 m	817	77.20 m
1500 metres	4:35.00	712	3:53.79
		8847	10,000

JACKIE JOYNER (USA) HEPTATHLON WORLD RECORD 1986

		points	1000 points
100 metres Hurdles	13.18	1097	13.85
High Jump	1.88 m	1080	1.82 m
Shot	15.20 m	874	17.07 m
200 metres	22.85	1094	23.80
Long Jump	7.03 m	1182	6.48 m
Javelin	50.12 m	862	57.18 m
800 metres	2:09.69	969	2:07.63
		7158	10,000

THE COMPETITION

East Germany will almost certainly pick up the most track and field medals. The United States and the Soviet Union will be vying for second place while the Chinese, who are making great strides in the sport, could pick up some medals.

For Britain, there have been signs that in sprinting and sprint hurdling, the gap at the top is narrowing. There will be a good medal chance for Britain's 4 × 400 men's relay squad as usual, but British domination of the men's middle-distance may be at an end if the 1987 World Championships are an accurate guideline.

Place your bets on Daley Thompson and Fatima Whitbread as Britain's two best gold medal hopes.

THE STARS

MEN

If Jesse Owens (USA) was the pre-war 'sprinter-supreme', that mantle surely falls to Carl Lewis (USA) in the postwar period. In 1984 he won four gold medals (100 metres, 200 metres, long jump, and relay). He will be favourite to retain three of those titles in Seoul, but Ben Johnson (CAN) should beat him over 100 metres.

Lee Evans (USA) was one of the athletes who benefited from the high altitude of Mexico City in 1968. He would have been great in any era, but his 400 metres winning time of 43.86 stands as the longest lasting individual men's track world record.

While three men have retained the Olympic title over 800 metres, Peter Snell (NZ)

26

was the last to do it – winner in 1960 and 1964, only Seb Coe (GBR) has managed the feat at 1500 metres since 1906. He will be going for the hat-trick in Seoul. Impossible? Do not discount it.

Lasse Viren (FIN) completed the 'double' in 1972, winning gold medals over 5000 metres and 10,000 metres. Amazingly, he retained both titles at the Montreal Games in 1976. But even Viren could not do what Emil Zatopek (TCH) achieved in 1952 (even though he tried – he finished 5th in the Marathon) and win 5000, 10,000 and the Marathon.

Two men have won the Marathon in successive Olympics – the great Abebe Bikila (ETH) in 1960 and 1964 and Waldemar Cierpinski (GDR) in 1976 and 1980.

Kip Keino (KEN) won the 1500 metres in 1968 and came second at 5000 metres. At the following games he took the silver medal at 1500 metres and gold in the steeplechase.

Another athlete attempting the feat of winning his event for the third Olympics running is Daley Thompson (GBR) in the decathlon. His first victory came in 1980 and he retained his title in 1984. But a man who was surely deprived of winning three titles running is Ed Moses (USA) 400 metres hurdles champion in 1976. The American boycott prevented him from competing in 1980. He won again in 1984 and will be going for gold once more in Seoul.

No one, however, is likely to surpass the exploits of Al Oerter (USA). Gold medallist in discus at four Olympics running between 1956 and 1968 or Viktor Sanayev (URS) – three gold and one silver in triple jump between 1968 and 1980.

WOMEN

Fanny Blankers-Koen (HOL) won a record four gold medals at the 1948 games (100 metres, 200 metres, 80 metres hurdles, and relay).

Irena Szewinska (POL) won seven medals between 1964 and 1976 (sprints and long jump) as did Shirley Strickland (AUS) (*née* de la Hunty) between 1948 and 1956.

Barbara Wockel (formerly Eckert) (GDR) won four gold medals between 1976 and 1980 (200 m and relays) as did Betty Cuthbert (AUS) between 1956 and 1964.

Tatanya Kazankina (URS) has equalled Seb Coe's record by retaining a 1500 m title (winner in 1976 and 1980). She also won the 800 m in 1976.

But what about this for a winning span? Ulrike Meyfarth (FRG) won the women's high jump at the Munich 1972 Games at the age of 16 years and 123 days. Twelve years later she won the gold in Los Angeles thus becoming the youngest and oldest gold medallist in the event.

BRITISH

MEN

Only two men have won a 100-metre gold medal for Britain – Harold Abrahams in 1924 (his story was told in the film *Chariots of Fire*), and Allan Wells in 1980. Wells was only hundredths of a second from completing the sprint 'double'. He was silver medallist over 200 metres.

Eric Liddell (the other subject of *Chariots of Fire*) was 400-metres gold medallist in 1924 and also won bronze at 200 metres.

Britain made a habit of winning the 800 metres before the Second World War, but since then the only gold medal has been won by Steve Ovett in 1980. Seb Coe was second, as he was in 1984.

Coe became the first British athlete in sixty years to take the 1500 metres title in 1980 and the only Olympian to defend it successfully for seventy-eight years, in 1984.

At 5000 metres, Gordon Pirie and Derek Ibbotson won silver and bronze behind Vladimir Kuts (URS) in 1956. Since then, Ian Stewert won bronze in 1972.

At 10,000 metres, Britain's only recent medal winners have been Brendan Foster (bronze, 1976) and Mike McLeod (silver, 1984). No British athlete has ever won a marathon gold medal. The last medallist was Charlie Spedding (bronze, 1984).

Chris Brasher, who now masterminds the London marathon, was gold medallist in steeplechase in 1956 after at first being disqualified for 'elbowing'. The two runners he was supposed to have 'elbowed' gave evidence on his behalf and he was reinstated. Since then, Maurice Herriott has won silver in 1964.

Britain's last medals in high hurdles were won by Don Finlay (bronze, 1932, silver, 1936). Two gold medals can be claimed at 400-metres hurdles – Lord Burghley (another *Chariots of Fire* man) in 1928 and David Hemery in 1968. John Sherwood won the bronze medal behind him. Hemery was a medallist again in 1972 (bronze).

The last sprint relay medal was won in 1960 (bronze) while silver medals have been won in 4 × 400 relay on three recent occasions (1964, 1972, and 1984).

The latest medals won in walking were Don Thompson (gold, 50 km, 1960), Ken Matthews (gold, 20 km, 1964) and Paul Nihill (silver, 50 km, 1964).

Daley Thompson has been the king of Olympic decathlon since 1980. He will be going for the hat trick in Seoul.

Medals in other field events have been few and far between. Only one gold has been won since the First World War – Lynn Davies (long jump, 1964).

WOMEN

Four gold medals have been won over the years. Ann Packer (800 metres, 1964). She also won silver at 400. Mary Rand (long jump, 1964). She also won silver in pentathlon. Mary Peters (pentathlon, 1972), and Tessa Sanderson (javelin, 1984).

Not a lot of people know that

• Women first took part in track and field events in 1928.
• The women's 3000 metres was not introduced until 1984 and the 10,000 metres will be a new event in 1988.
• Long jump and high jump were once 'standing start' events.

• The host nation for the 1988 Games has never won a track and field medal; however the 1936 Marathon was won by a Korean forced to compete under the Japanese flag, as was the bronze medallist. They were even forced to change their names.
• The USA have won the most gold medals, but in second place for men so far is Finland. USSR are second overall.
• On the same day that Emile Zatopek won the 5000 metres in 1952 – his wife Dana, who was born on the same day, won the javelin gold medal.
• Lasse Viren won the 1972 10,000 metres despite falling during the race.
• Olmeus Charles of Haiti took over 42 minutes to complete his heat of the men's 10,000 metres in the 1976 Olympics, thus ruining the world's TV schedules.
• Fred Lorz (USA) was about to be hailed winner of the 1904 Marathon when he admitted he had hitched a lift for 11 miles, as a joke.
• Jesse Owens (USA) came very close to being eliminated in the long jump qualifying rounds in 1936. Luz Long of Germany who was also competing advised Owens, who had already recorded two no jumps, to take off from behind the board for his final qualifying jump. Owens did this and went on to win one of his four gold medals. Long won the silver medal and was the first to congratulate Owens in full view of Adolf Hitler, whose hatred of black people was well known. Long and Owens remained friends until the German was killed in action in 1943. Owens continued to correspond with Long's family.
• In 1968, similar friendly advice to Bob Beamon kept him in the long-jump competition when he had looked like going out. It came that time though from a fellow-American, Ralph Boston who won the bronze medal.
• One of Fanny Blankers-Koen's neighbours gave her a bicycle as a present after the 1948 Olympics 'so that she

wouldn't have to run so much'.
● Wilma Rudolph, 100-metres gold medallist in 1960 was the 20th born of 22 children. She suffered from polio and had to wear a leg-brace until she was eleven.
● Elvira Ozolina (URS), the javelin champion of 1964, shaved her head in disgust at finishing only fifth in the 1968 Games.

VENUE

Olympic Stadium. Capacity 100,000.

RESULTS

100 metres/*Men*

WR: 9.83 Ben Johnson (CAN) 1987
OR: 9.95 James Hines (USA) 1968

	Gold	*Silver*	*Bronze*
1896	Thomas Burke (USA) 12.0	Fritz Hofmann (GER) 12.2	Alajos Szokolyi (HUN) 12.6
1900	Frank Jarvis (USA) 11.0	Walter Tewksbury (USA) 11.1	Stanley Rowley (AUS) 11.2
1904	Archie Hahn (USA) 11.0	Nathaniel Cartmell (USA) 11.2	William Hogenson (USA) 11.2
1906	Archie Hahn (USA) 11.2	Fay Moulton (USA) 11.3	Nigel Barker (AUS) 11.3
1908	Reginald Walker (SAF) 10.8 OR	James Rector (USA) 10.9	Robert Kerr (CAN) 11.0
1912	Ralph Craig (USA) 10.8	Alvah Meyer (USA) 10.9	Donald Lippincott (USA) 10.9
1920	Charles Paddock (USA) 10.8	Morris Kirksey (USA) 10.8	Harry Edward (GBR) 11.0
1924	Harold Abrahams (GBR) 10.6 OR	Jackson Scholz (USA) 10.7	Arthur Porritt (NZL) 10.8
1928	Percy Williams (CAN) 10.8	Jack London (GBR) 10.9	Georg Lammers (GER) 10.9
1932	Eddie Tolan (USA) 10.3 OR	Ralph Metcalfe (USA) 10.3	Arthur Jonath (GER) 10.4
1936	Jesse Owens (USA) 10.3 (w)	Ralph Metcalfe (USA) 10.4	Martinus Osendarp (HOL) 10.5
1948	Harrison Dillard (USA) 10.3 = OR	Norwood Ewell (USA) 10.4	Lloyd LaBeach (PAN) 10.4
1952	Lindy Remingino (USA) 10.4	Herb McKenley (JAM) 10.4	Emmanuel McD. Bailey (GBR) 10.4
1956	Bobby-Joe Morrow (USA) 10.5	Thane Baker (USA) 10.5	Hector Hogan (USA) 10.6
1960	Armin Hary (GER) 10.2 OR	David Sime (USA) 10.2	Peter Radford (GBR) 10.3
1964	Bob Hayes (USA) 10.0 = WR	Enrique Figuerola (CUB) 10.2	Harry Jerome (CAN) 10.2
1968	James Hines (USA) 9.9 WR	Lennox Miller (JAM) 10.0	Charles Greene (USA) 10.0
1972	Valeriy Borzov (URS) 10.14	Robert Taylor (USA) 10.24	Lennox Miller (JAM) 10.33
1976	Hasely Crawford (TRI) 10.06	Don Quarrie (JAM) 10.08	Valeriy Borzov (URS) 10.14
1980	Allan Wells (GBR) 10.25	Silvio Leonard (CUB) 10.25	Petar Petrov (BUL) 10.39
1984	Carl Lewis (USA) 9.99	Sam Graddy (USA) 10.19	Ben Johnson (CAN) 10.22

4. Ron Brown (USA) 5. Mike McFarlane (GBR) 6. Ray Stewart (JAM) 7. Donovan Reid (GBR) 8. Tony Sharpe (CAN)

1988 Semi-finals and final on 24 September

200 metres/*Men*

WR: 19.72 Pietro Mennea (ITA) 1979
OR: 19.80 Carl Lewis (USA) 1984

	Gold	Silver	Bronze
1900	Walter Tewksbury (USA) 22.2	Norman Pritchard (IND) 22.8	Stanley Rowley (AUS) 22.9
1904	Archie Hahn (USA) 21.6 OR★	Nathaniel Cartmell (USA) 21.9	William Hogenson (USA) d.n.a.
1908	Robert Kerr (CAN) 22.6	Robert Cloughen (USA) 22.6	Nathaniel Cartmell (USA) 22.7
1912	Ralph Craig (USA) 21.7	Donald Lippincott (USA) 21.8	Willie Applegarth (GBR) 22.0
1920	Allen Woodring (USA) 22.0	Charles Paddock (USA) 22.1	Harry Edward (GBR) 22.2
1924	Jackson Scholz (USA) 21.6	Charles Paddock (USA) 21.7	Eric Liddell (GBR) 21.9
1928	Percy Williams (CAN) 21.8	Walter Rangeley (GBR) 21.9	Helmut Kornig (GER) 21.9†
1932	Eddie Tolan (USA) 21.2 OR	George Simpson (USA) 21.4	Ralph Metcalfe (USA) 21.5★★
1936	Jesse Owens (USA) 20.7 OR	Mack Robinson (USA) 21.1	Martinus Osendarp (HOL) 21.3
1948	Mel Patton (USA) 21.1	Norwood Ewell (USA) 21.1	Lloyd LaBeach (PAN) 21.2
1952	Andrew Stanfield (USA) 20.7	Thane Baker (USA) 20.8	James Gathers (USA) 20.8
1956	Bobby-Joe Morrow (USA) 20.6 OR	Andrew Stanfield (USA) 20.7	Thane Baker (USA) 20.9
1960	Livio Berutti (ITA) 20.5 = WR	Lester Carney (USA) 20.6	Abdoulaye Seye (FRA) 20.7
1964	Henry Carr (USA) 20.3 OR	Paul Drayton (USA) 20.5	Edwin Roberts (TRI) 20.6
1968	Tommie Smith (USA) 19.8 WR	Peter Norman (AUS) 20.0	John Carlos (USA) 20.0
1972	Valeriy Borzov (URS) 20.00	Larry Black (USA) 20.19	Pietro Mennea (ITA) 20.30
1976	Don Quarrie (JAM) 20.23	Millard Hampton (USA) 20.29	Dwayne Evans (USA) 20.43
1980	Pietro Mennea (ITA) 20.19	Allan Wells (GBR) 20.21	Don Quarrie (JAM) 20.29
1984	Carl Lewis (USA) 19.80 OR	Kirk Baptiste (USA) 19.96	Thomas Jefferson (USA) 20.26

4. Joao Batista Silva (BRA) 5. Ralf Luebke (FRG) 6. Jean-Jacques Boussemart (FRA)
7. Pietro Mennea (ITA) 8. Ade Mafe (GBR)

1988 Semi-finals and final on 28 September

★ Run over straight course. Hahn's three opponents all given two yard handicaps for false starting.
† Kornig awarded bronze after a dead heat with Scholz, who then refused to rerun.
★★ It was later discovered that the lane in which Metcalfe was running was 1.5 metres too long.

400 metres/*Men*

WR: 43.86 Lee Evans (USA) 1968
OR: 43.86 Lee Evans (USA) 1968

	Gold	Silver	Bronze
1896	Thomas Burke (USA) 54.2	Herbert Jamison (USA) 55.2	Fritz Hofmann (GER) 55.6
1900	Maxwell Long (USA) 49.4 OR	William Holland (USA) 49.6	Ernst Schultz (DEN) 15 m.
1904	Harry Hillman (USA) 49.2 OR	Frank Waller (USA) 49.9	Hermann Groman (USA) 50.0
1906	Paul Pilgrim (USA) 53.2	Wyndham Halswelle (GBR) 53.8	Nigel Barker (AUS) 54.1
1908*	Wyndham Halswelle (GBR) 50.0	–	–
1912	Charles Reidpath (USA) 48.2 OR	Hanns Braun (GER) 48.3	Edward Lindberg (USA) 48.4
1920	Bevil Rudd (SAF) 49.6	Guy Butler (GBR) 49.9	Nils Engdahl (SWE) 50.0
1924	Eric Liddell (GBR) 47.6 OR	Horatio Fitch (USA) 48.4	Guy Butler (GBR) 48.6
1928	Ray Barbuti (USA) 47.8	James Ball (CAN) 48.0	Joachim Büchner (GER) 48.2
1932	William Carr (USA) 46.2 WR	Ben Eastman (USA) 46.4	Alexander Wilson (CAN) 47.4
1936	Archie Williams (USA) 46.5	Godfrey Brown (GBR) 46.7	James LuValle (USA) 46.8
1948	Arthur Wint (JAM) 46.2	Herb McKenley (JAM) 46.4	Mal Whitfield (USA) 46.9
1952	George Rhoden (JAM) 45.9 OR	Herb McKenley (JAM) 45.9 OR	Ollie Matson (USA) 46.8
1956	Charles Jenkins (USA) 46.7	Karl-Friedrich Haas (GER) 46.8	Voitto Hellsten (FIN) 47.0 Ardalion Ignatyev (URS) 47.0
1960	Otis Davis (USA) 44.9 WR	Carl Kaufmann (GER) 44.9 WR	Mal Spence (SAF) 45.5
1964	Mike Larrabee (USA) 45.1	Wendell Mottley (TRI) 45.2	Andrzej Badenski (POL) 45.6
1968	Lee Evans (USA) 43.8 WR	Larry James (USA) 43.9	Ron Freeman (USA) 44.4
1972	Vince Matthews (USA) 44.66	Wayne Collett (USA) 44.80	Julius Sang (KEN) 44.92
1976	Alberto Juantorena (CUB) 44.26	Fred Newhouse (USA) 44.40	Herman Frazier (USA) 44.95
1980	Viktor Markin (URS) 44.60	Rick Mitchell (USA) 44.84	Frank Schaffer (GDR) 44.87
1984	Alonzo Babers (USA) 44.27·	Gabriel Tiacoh (CIV) 44.54	Antonio McKay (USA) 44.71

4. Darren Clark (AUS) 5. Sunder Nix (USA) 6. Sunday Uti (NGR)
7. Innocent Egbunike (NGR) Bert Cameron (JAM) did not start

1988 Semi-finals on 26 September and final on 28 September

*Re-run necessary after a disqualification, but only Halswelle turned up so walked over.

800 Metres/*Men*

WR: 1:41.73 Sebastian Coe (GBR) 1981
OR: 1:43.00 Joachim Cruz (BRA) 1984

	Gold	*Silver*	*Bronze*
1896	Edwin Flack (AUS) 2:11.0	Nǎndor Dáni (HUN) 2:11.8	Dimitrios Golemis (GRE) 2:28.0
1900	Alfred Tysoe (GBR) 2:01.2	John Cregan (USA) 2:03.0	David Hall (USA) d.n.a.
1904	James Lightbody (USA) 1:56.0 OR	Howard Valentine (USA) 1:56.3	Emil Breitkreutz (USA) 1:56.4
1906	Paul Pilgrim (USA) 2:01.5	James Lightbody (USA) 2:01.6	Wyndham Halswelle (GBR) 2:03.0
1908	Mel Sheppard (USA) 1:52.8 WR	Emilio Lunghi (ITA) 1:54.2	Hanns Braun (GER) 1:55.2
1912	James Meredith (USA) 1:51.9 WR	Mel Sheppard (USA) 1:52.0	Ira Davenport (USA) 1:52.0
1920	Albert Hill (GBR) 1:53.4	Earl Eby (USA) 1:53.6	Bevil Rudd (SAF) 1:54.0
1924	Douglas Lowe (GBR) 1:52.4	Paul Martin (SUI) 1:52.6	Schuyler Enck (USA) 1:53.0
1928	Douglas Lowe (GBR) 1:51.8 OR	Erik Bylehn (SWE) 1:52.8	Hermann Englehardt (GER) 1:53.2
1932	Thomas Hampson (GBR) 1:49.7 WR	Alexander Wilson (CAN) 1:49.9	Phil Edwards (CAN) 1:51.5
1936	John Woodruff (USA) 1:52.9	Mario Lanzi (ITA) 1:53.3	Phil Edwards (CAN) 1:53.6
1948	Mal Whitfield (USA) 1:49.2 OR	Arthur Wint (JAM) 1:49.5	Marcel Hansenne (FRA) 1:49.8
1952	Mal Whitfield (USA) 1:49.2 = OR	Arthur Wint (JAM) 1:49.4	Heinz Ulzheimer (GER) 1:49.7
1956	Tom Courtney (USA) 1:47.7 OR	Derek Johnson (GBR) 1:47.8	Audun Boysen (NOR) 1:48.1
1960	Peter Snell (NZL) 1:46.3 OR	Roger Moens (BEL) 1:46.5	George Kerr (BWI) 1:47.1
1964	Peter Snell (NZL) 1:45.1 OR	Bill Crothers (CAN) 1:45.6	Wilson Kiprugut (KEN) 1:45.9
1968	Ralph Doubell (AUS) 1:44.3 = WR	Wilson Kiprugut (KEN) 1:44.5	Tom Farrell (USA) 1:45.4
1972	Dave Wottle (USA) 1:45.9	Yevgeniy Arzhanov (URS) 1:45.9	Mike Boit (KEN) 1:46.0
1976	Alberto Juantorena (CUB) 1:43.5 WR	Ivo Van Damme (BEL) 1:43.9	Richard Wohlhuter (USA) 1:44.1
1980	Steve Ovett (GBR) 1:45.4	Sebastian Coe (GBR) 1:45.9	Nikolai Kirov (URS) 1:46.0
1984	Joaquim Cruz (BRA) 1:43.0 OR	Sebastian Coe (GBR) 1:43.64	Earl Jones (USA) 1:43.83

4. Billy Konchellah (KEN) 5. Donato Sabia (ITA) 6. Edwin Koech (KEN)
7. Johnny Gray (USA) 8. Steve Ovett (GBR)

1988	Semi-finals on 25 September and final on 26 September

1500 metres/*Men*

WR: 3:29.46 Said Aouita (MAR) 1985
OR: 3:32.53 Sebastian Coe (GBR) 1984

	Gold	*Silver*	*Bronze*
1896	Edwin Flack (AUS) 4:33.2	Arthur Blake (USA) 4:34.0	Albin Lermusiaux (FRA) 4:36.0
1900	Charles Bennett (GBR) 4:06.2	Henri Deloge (FRA) 4:06.6	John Bray (USA) 4:07.2
1904	James Lightbody (USA) 4:05.4 WR	William Verner (USA) 4:06.8	Lacey Hearn (USA) d.n.a.
1906	James Lightbody (USA) 4:12.0	John McGough (GBR) 4:12.6	Kristian Hellström (SWE) 4:13.4
1908	Mel Sheppard (USA) 4:03.4 OR	Harold Wilson (GBR) 4:03.6	Norman Hallows (GBR) 4:04.0
1912	Arnold Jackson (GBR) 3:56.8 OR	Abel Kiviat (USA) 3:56.9	Norman Taber (USA) 3:56.9
1920	Albert Hill (GBR) 4:01.8	Philip Baker (GBR) 4:02.4	Lawrence Sheilds (USA) 4:03.1
1924	Paavo Nurmi (FIN) 3:53.6 OR	Willy Schärer (SUI) 3:55.0	Henry Stallard (GBR) 3:55.6
1928	Harri Larva (FIN) 3:53.2 OR	Jules Ladoumégue (FRA) 3:53.8	Eino Purje (FIN) 3:56.4
1932	Luigi Beccali (ITA) 3:51.2 OR	John Cornes (GBR) 3:52.6	Phil Edwards (CAN) 3:52.8
1936	Jack Lovelock (NZL) 3:47.8 WR	Glenn Cunningham (USA) 3:48.4	Luigi Beccali (ITA) 3:49.2
1948	Henry Eriksson (SWE) 3:49.8	Lennart Strand (SWE) 3:50.4	Willem Slijkhuis (HOL) 3:50.4
1952	Josef Barthel (LUX) 3:45.1 OR	Bob McMillen (USA) 3:45.2	Werner Lueg (GER) 3:45.4
1956	Ron Delany (IRL) 3:41.2 OR	Klaus Richtzenhaim (GER) 3:42.0	John Landy (AUS) 3:42.0
1960	Herb Elliot (AUS) 3:35.6 WR	Michel Jazy (FRA) 3:38.4	István Rózsavölgyi (HUN) 3:39.2
1964	Peter Snell (NZL) 3:38.1	Josef Odlozil (TCH) 3:39.6	John Davies (NZL) 3:39.6
1968	Kipchoge Keino (KEN) 3:34.9 OR	Jim Ryun (USA) 3:37.8	Bodo Tümmler (FRG) 3:39.0
1972	Pekka Vasala (FIN) 3:36.3	Kipchoge Keino (KEN) 3:36.8	Rod Dixon (NZL) 3:37.5
1976	John Walker (NZL) 3:39.2	Ivo Van Damme (BEL) 3:39.3	Paul-Heinz Wellman (FRG) 3:39.3
1980	Sebastian Coe (GBR) 3:38.4	Jürgen Straub (GDR) 3:38.8	Steve Ovett (GBR) 3:39.0
1984	Sebastian Coe (GBR) 3:32.53 OR	Steve Cram (GBR) 3:33.4	Jose Abascal (ESP) 3:34.3

4. Joseph Chesire (KEN) 5. Jim Spivey (USA) 6. Peter Wirz (SUI) 7. Andres Vera (ESP)
8. Khalifa Omar (SUD) 9. Anthony Rogers (NZL) 10. Steve Scott (USA)
11. Riccardo Materazzi (ITA) Steve Ovett (GBR) did not finish

1988	Semi-finals on 30 September and final on 1 October

5000 metres/*Men*

WR: 12:58.39 Said Aouita (MAR) 1987
OR: 13:05.59 Said Aouita (MAR) 1984

	Gold	*Silver*	*Bronze*
1912	Hannes Kolehmainen (FIN) 14:36.6 WR	Jean Bouin (FRA) 14:36.7	George Hutson (GBR) 15:07.6
1920	Joseph Guillemot (FRA) 14:55.6	Paavo Nurmi (FIN) 15:00.0	Erik Backman (SWE) 15:13.0
1924	Paavo Nurmi (FIN) 14:31.2 OR	Ville Ritola (FIN) 14:31.4	Edvin Wide (SWE) 15:01.8
1928	Ville Ritola (FIN) 14:38.0	Paavo Nurmi (FIN) 14.40.0	Edvin Wide (SWE) 14:41.2
1932	Lauri Lehtinen (FIN) 14:30.0 OR	Ralph Hill (USA) 14.30.0 OR	Lauri Virtanen (FIN) 14:44.0
1936	Gunnar Höckert (FIN) 14:22.2 OR	Lauri Lehtinen (FIN) 14:25.8	Henry Jonsson (SWE) 14:29.0
1948	Gaston Rieff (BEL) 14:17.6 OR	Emil Zatopek (TCH) 14:17.8	Willem Slijkhuis (HOL) 14:26.8
1952	Emil Zatopek (TCH) 14:06.6 OR	Alain Mimoun (FRA) 14:07.4	Herbert Schade (GER) 14:08.6
1956	Vladimir Kuts (URS) 13:39.6 OR	Gordon Pirie (GBR) 13:50.6	Derek Ibbotson (GBR) 13:54.4
1960	Murray Halberg (NZL) 13:43.4	Hans Grodotzki (GER) 13:44.6	Kazimierz Zimny (POL) 13:44.8
1964	Bob Schul (USA) 13:48.8	Harald Norpoth (GER) 13:49.6	Bill Dellinger (USA) 13:49.8
1968	Mohamed Gammoudi (TUN) 14:05.0	Kipchoge Keino (KEN) 14:05.2	Naftali Temu (KEN) 14:06.4
1972	Lasse Viren (FIN) 13:26.4 OR	Mohamed Gammoudi (TUN) 13:27.4	Ian Stewart (GBR) 13:27.6
1976	Lasse Viren (FIN) 13:24.8	Dick Quax (NZL) 13:25.2	Klaus-Peter Hildenbrand (FRG) 13:25.4
1980	Miruts Yifter (ETH) 13:21.0	Suleiman Nyambui (TAN) 13:21.6	Kaarlo Maaninka (FIN) 13:22.0
1984	Said Aouita (MAR) 13:05.59 OR	Markus Ryffel (SUI) 13:07.54	Antonio Leitao (POR) 13:09.20

4. Tim Hutchings (GBR) 5. Paul Kipkoech (KEN) 6. Charles Cheruiyot (KEN)
7. Doug Padilla (USA) 8. John Walker (NZL) 9. Ezequiel Canario (POR)
10. Wilson Waigwa (KEN) 11. Ray Flynn (IRL) 12. Mats Erixon (SWE)
13. Eamonn Martin (GBR) 14. David Moorcroft (GBR) Martti Vainio (FIN) didn't start

1988 Semi-finals on 29 September and final on 1 October

10,000 metres/*Men*

WR: 27:13.81 Fernando Mamede (POR) 1984
OR: 27:38.4 Lasse Viren (FIN) 1972

Gold	*Silver*	*Bronze*
1906★ Henry Hawtrey (GBR) 26:11.8	John Svanberg (SWE) 26.19.4	Edward Dahl (SWE) 26:26.2
1908★ Emil Voigt (GBR) 25:11.2	Edward Owen (GBR) 25:24.0	John Svanberg (SWE) 25:37.2
1912 Hannes Kolehmainen (FIN) 31:20.8	Louis Tewanima (USA) 32:06.6	Albin Stenroos (FIN) 32:21.8
1920 Paavo Nurmi (FIN) 31:45.8	Joseph Guillemot (FRA) 31:47.2	James Wilson (GBR) 31:50.8
1924 Ville Ritola (FIN) 30:23.2 WR	Edvin Wide (SWE) 30:55.2	Eero Berg (FIN) 31:43.0
1928 Paavo Nurmi (FIN) 30:18.8 OR	Ville Ritola (FIN) 30:19.4	Edvin Wide (SWE) 31:00.8
1932 Janusz Kusocinski (POL) 30:11.4 OR	Volmari Iso-Hollo (FIN) 30:12.6	Lauri Virtanen (FIN) 30:35.0
1936 Ilmari Salminen (FIN) 30:15.4	Arvo Askola (FIN) 30:15.6	Volmari Iso-Hollo (FIN) 30:20.2
1948 Emil Zatopek (TCH) 29:59.6 OR	Alain Mimoun (FRA) 30:47.4	Bertil Albertsson (SWE) 30:53.6
1952 Emil Zatopek (TCH) 29:17.0 OR	Alain Mimoun (FRA) 29:32.8	Aleksandr Aunfriyev (URS) 29:48.2
1956 Vladimir Kuts (URS) 28:45.6 OR	József Kovács (HUN) 28:52.4	Allan Lawrence (AUS) 28:53.6
1960 Pyotr Bolotnikov (URS) 28:32.2 OR	Hans Grodotzki (GER) 28:37.0	David Power (AUS) 28:38.2
1964 Billy Mills (USA) 28:24.4 OR	Mohamed Gammoudi (TUN) 28:24.8	Ron Clarke (AUS) 28:25.8
1968 Naftali Temu (KEN) 29:27.4	Mamo Walde (ETH) 29:28.0	Mohamed Gammoudi (TUN) 29:34.2
1972 Lasse Viren (FIN) 27:38.4 WR	Emiel Puttemans (BEL) 27:39.6	Miruts Yifter (ETH) 27:41.0
1976 Lasse Viren (FIN) 27:40.4	Carlos Lopes (POR) 27:45.2	Brendan Foster (GBR) 27:54.9
1980 Miruts Yifter (ETH) 27:42.7	Kaarlo Maaninka (FIN) 27:44.3	Mohammed Kedir (ETH) 27:44.7
1984 Alberto Cova (ITA) 27:47.54	Martti Vainio (FIN) 27:51.10	Mike McLeod (GBR) 28:06.22

4. Mike Musyoki (KEN) 5. Salvatore Antibo (ITA) 6. Christoph Herle (FRG)
7. Sosthenes Bitok (KEN) 8. Yutaka Kanai (JPN) 9. Steve Jones (GBR)
10. John Treacy (IRL) Nick Rose (GBR) was 13th

1988 Final on 26 September

★ Held over 5 miles (8046 m).

Marathon/*Men*

Distance fixed at 26 miles 385 yds (42,195 m) since 1924

WB: 2h 06.50 Belaine Dinsamo (ETH) 1988
OB: 2h 09:21 Carlos Lopes (POR) 1984

	Gold	*Silver*	*Bronze*
1896	Spyridon Louis (GRE) 2h 58:50	Charilaos Vasilakos (GRE) 3h 06:03	Gyula Kellner (HUN) 3h 06:35
1900	Michel Theato (FRA) 2h 59:45	Emile Champion (FRA) 3h 04:17	Ernst Fast (SWE) 3h 37:14
1904	Thomas Hicks (USA) 3h 28:35	Albert Corey (FRA) 3h 34:52	Arthur Newton (USA) 3h 47:33
1906	William Sherring (CAN) 2h 51:23.6	John Svanberg (SWE) 2h 58:20.8	William Frank (USA) 3h 00:46.8
1908*	John Hayes (USA) 2h 55:18.4 OB	Charles Hefferon (SAF) 2h 56:06.0	Joseph Forshaw (USA) 2h 57:10.4
1912	Kenneth McArthur (SAF) 2h 36:54.8	Christian Gitsham (SAF) 2h 37:52.0	Gaston Strobino (USA) 2h 38:42.4
1920	Hannes Kolehmainen (FIN) 2h 32:35.8 WB	Jüri Lossman (EST) 2h 32:48.6	Valerio Arri (ITA) 2h 36:32.8
1924	Albin Stenroos (FIN) 2h 41:22.6	Romeo Bertini (ITA) 2h 47:19.6	Clarence DeMar (USA) 2h 48:14.0
1928	Mohamed El Ouafi (FRA) 2h 32:57	Miguel Plaza (CHI) 2h 33:23	Martti Marttelin (FIN) 2h 35:02
1932	Juan Carlos Zabala (ARG) 2h 31:36 OB	Sam Ferris (GBR) 2h 31:55	Armas Toivonen (FIN) 2h 32:12
1936	Kitei Son (JPN) 2h 29:19.2 OB	Ernest Harper (GBR) 2h 31:23.2	Shoryu Nan (JPN) 2h 31:42.0
1948	Delfo Cabrera (ARG) 2h 34:51.6	Tom Richards (GBR) 2h 35:07.6	Etienne Gailly (BEL) 2h 35:33.6
1952	Emil Zatopek (TCH) 2h 23:03.2 OB	Reinaldo Gorno (ARG) 2h 25:35.0	Gustaf Jansson (SWE) 2h 26:07.0
1956	Alain Mimoun (FRA) 2h 25:0	Franjo Mihalic (YUG) 2h 26:32	Veikko Karvonen (FIN) 2h 27:47
1960	Abebe Bikila (ETH) 2h 15:16.2 WB	Rhadi Ben Abdesselem (MAR) 2h 15:41.6	Barry Magee (NZL) 2h 17:18.2
1964	Abebe Bikila (ETH) 2h 12:11.2 WB	Basil Heatley (GBR) 2h 16:19.2	Kokichi Tsuburaya (JPN) 2h 16:22.8
1968	Mamo Wolde (ETH) 2h 20:26.4	Kenji Kimihara (JPN) 2h 23:31.0	Michael Ryan (NZL) 2h 23:45.0
1972	Frank Shorter (USA) 2h 12:19.8	Karel Lismont (BEL) 2h 14:31.8	Mamo Wolde (ETH) 2h 15:08.4
1976	Waldemar Cierpinski (GDR) 2h 09:55.0 OB	Frank Shorter (USA) 2h 10:45.8	Karel Lismont (BEL) 2h 11:12.6
1980	Waldemar Cierpinski (GDR) 2h 11:03	Gerard Nijboer (HOL) 2h 11:20	Setymkul Dzhumanazarov (URS) 2h 11:35

*Dorando Pietri of Italy finished first but had received assistance from the officials after entering the stadium, as he was on the point of collapse. He was tragically disqualified.

1984	Carlos Lopes (POR) 2h 09:21 OB	John Treacy (IRL) 2h 09:56	Charles Spedding (GBR) 2h 09:58

4. Takeshi So (JPN) 5. Robert DeCastella (AUS) 6. Juma Ikangaa (TAN)
7. Joseph Nzau (KEN) 8. Djama Robleh (DJI) 9. Jerry Kiernan (IRL)
10. Rodney Dixon (NZL) 11. Peter Pfitzinge (USA) 12. Hugh Jones (GBR)

1988   On 2 October

3000 metres steeplechase/*Men*

WR: 8:05.4 Henry Rono (KEN) 1978
OR: 8:08.2 Anders Garderud (SWE) 1976
(Distance standardized in 1920)

Gold	*Silver*	*Bronze*
1900* George Orton (CAN) 7:34.4	Sidney Robinson (GBR) 7:38.0	Jacques Chastanié (FRA) d.n.a.
1900* John Rimmer (GBR) 12:58.4	Charles Bennett (GBR) 12:58.6	Sidney Robinson (GBR) 12:58.8
1904 James Lightbody (USA) 7:39.6	John Daly (GBR) 7:40.6	Arthur Newton (USA) 25 m
1908 Arthur Russell (GBR) 10:47.8	Archie Robertson (GBR) 10:48.4	John Eisele (USA) 20 m
1920 Percy Hodge (GBR) 10:00.4 OR	Patrick Flynn (USA) 100 m	Ernesto Amrosini (ITA) 30 m
1924 Ville Ritola (FIN) 9:33.6 =WR	Elias Katz (FIN) 9:44.0	Paul Bontemps (FRA) 9:45.2
1928 Toivo Loukola (FIN) 9:21.8 WR	Paavo Nurmi (FIN) 9:31.2	Ove Andersen (FIN) 9:35.6
1932† Volmari Iso-Hollo (FIN) 10:33.4	Tom Evenson (GBR) 10:46.0	Joseph McCluskey (USA) 10:46.2
1936 Volmari Iso-Hollo (FIN) 9:03.8 WR	Kaarlo Tuominen (FIN) 9:06.8	Alfred Dompert (GER) 9:07.2
1948 Tore Sjöstrand (SWE) 9:04.6	Erik Elmsäter (SWE) 9:08.2	Göte Hagström (SWE) 9:11.8
1952 Horace Ashenfelter (USA) 8:45.4 WR	Vladimir Kazantsev (URS) 8:51.6	John Disley (GBR) 8:51.8
1956 Chris Brasher (GBR) 8:41.2 OR	Sándor Rozsnyói (HUN) 8:43.6	Ernst Larsen (NOR) 8:44.0
1960 Zdzislaw Krzyszkowiak (POL) 8:34.2 OR	Nikolai Sokolov (URS) 8:36.4	Semyon Rzhishchin (URS) 8:42.2
1964 Gaston Roelants (BEL) 8:30.8 OR	Maurice Herriott (GBR) 8:32.4	Ivan Belyayev (URS) 8:33.8
1968 Amos Biwott (KEN) 8:51.0	Benjamin Kogo (KEN) 8:51.6	George Young (USA) 8:51.8
1972 Kipchoge Keino (KEN) 8:23.6 OR	Benjamin Kogo (KEN) 8:24.6	Tapio Kantanen (FIN) 8:24.8
1976 Anders Garderud (SWE) 8:08.2 WR	Bronislaw Malinowski (POL) 8:09.11	Frank Baumgartl (GDR) 8:10.4
1980 Bronislaw Malinowski (POL) 8:09.7	Filbert Bayi (TAN) 8:12.5	Eshetu Tura (ETH) 8:13.6

*Two races held, one over 2500 m and the other over 4000 m.
† They ran 3460 m because of a mistake in the lap scoring.

1984   Julius Korir (KEN) 8:11.80   Joseph Mahmoud (FRA)   Brian Diemer (USA) 8:14.06
                                       8:13.31

   4. Henry Marsh (USA) 5. Colin Reitz (GBR) 6. Domingo Ramon (ESP)
   7. Julius Kariuki (KEN) 8. Pascal Debacker (FRA) 9. Tommy Ekblom (FIN)
   10. Roger Hackney (GBR)

1988   Semi-finals on 28 September and the final on 30 September

110 metres hurdles/*Men*

WR: 12.93 Renaldo Nehemiah (USA) 1981
OR: 13.20 Roger Kingdom (USA) 1984

	Gold	*Silver*	*Bronze*
1896	Thomas Curtis (USA) 17.6	Grantley Goulding (GBR) 17.7	
1900	Alvin Kraenzlein (USA) 15.4 OR	John McLean (USA) 15.5	Fred Moloney (USA) 15.6
1904	Frederick Schule (USA) 16.0	Thaddeus Shideler (USA) 16.3	Lesley Ashburner (USA) 16.4
1906	Robert Leavitt (USA) 16.2	Alfred Healey (GBR) 16.2	Vincent Duncker (SAF) 16.3
1908	Forrest Smithson (USA) 15.0 WR	John Garrels (USA) 15.7	Arthur Shaw (USA) 15.8
1912	Frederick Kelly (USA) 15.1	James Wendell (USA) 15.2	Martin Hawkins (USA) 15.3
1920	Earl Thomson (CAN) 14.8 WR	Harold Barron (USA) 15.1	Frederick Murray (USA) 15.2
1924	Daniel Kinsey (USA) 15.0	Sydney Atkinson (SAF) 15.0	Sten Pettersson (SWE) 15.4
1928	Sydney Atkinson (SAF) 14.8	Stephen Anderson (USA) 14.8	John Collier (USA) 14.9
1932	George Saling (USA) 14.6	Percy Beard (USA) 14.7	Don Finlay (GBR) 14.8
1936	Forrest Towns (USA) 14.2	Don Finlay (GBR) 14.4	Fred Pollard (USA) 14.4
1948	William Porter (USA) 13.9 OR	Clyde Scott (USA) 14.1	Craig Dixon (USA) 14.1
1952	Harrison Dillard (USA) 13.7 OR	Jack Davis (USA) 13.7	Art Barnard (USA) 14.1
1956	Lee Calhoun (USA) 13.5 OR	Jack Davis (USA) 13.5	Joel Shankle (USA) 14.1
1960	Lee Calhoun (USA) 13.8	Willie May (USA) 13.8	Hayes Jones (USA) 14.0
1964	Hayes Jones (USA) 13.6	Blaine Lindgren (USA) 13.7	Anatoliy Mikhailov (URS) 13.7
1968	Willie Davenport (USA) 13.3 =WR	Ervin Hall (USA) 13.4	Eddy Ottoz (ITA) 13.4
1972	Rod Milburn (USA) 13.24 =WR	Guy Drut (FRA) 13.34	Tom Hill (USA) 13.48
1976	Guy Drut (FRA) 13.30	Alejandro Casanas (CUB) 13.33	Willie Davenport (USA) 13.38
1980	Thomas Munkelt (GDR) 13.39	Alejandro Casanas (CUB) 13.40	Aleksandr Puchkov (URS) 13.44
1984	Roger Kingdom (USA) 13.20 OR	Greg Foster (USA) 13.23	Arto Bryggare (FIN) 13.40

4. Mark McKoy (CAN) 5. Anthony Campbell (USA) 6. Stephane Caristan (FRA)
   7. Carlos Sala (ESP) 8. Jeff Glass (CAN)

1988   Semi-finals and final on 26 September

400 metres hurdles/*Men*

WR: 47.02 Edwin Moses (USA) 1983
OR: 47.64 Edwin Moses (USA) 1976

	Gold	*Silver*	*Bronze*
1900	Walter Tewksbury (USA) 57.6	Henri Tauzin (FRA) 58.3	George Orton (CAN) d.n.a.
1904	Harry Hillman (USA) 53.0*	Frank Waller (USA) 53.2	George Poage (USA) 30 metres
1908	Charles Bacon (USA) 55.0 WR	Harry Hillman (USA) 55.3	Leonard Tremeer (GBR) 57.0
1920	Frank Loomis (USA) 54.0 WR	John Norton (USA) 54.3	August Desch (USA) 54.5
1924	Morgan Taylor (USA) 52.6*	Erik Vilen (FIN) 53.8 OR	Ivan Riley (USA) 54.2
1928	Lord Burghley (GBR) 53.4 OR	Frank Cuhel (USA) 53.6	Morgan Taylor (USA) 53.6
1932	Bob Tisdall (IRL) 51.7*	Glenn Hardin (USA) 51.9 WR	Morgan Taylor (USA) 52.0
1936	Glenn Hardin (USA) 52.4	John Loaring (CAN) 52.7	Miguel White (PHI) 52.8
1948	Roy Cochran (USA) 51.1 OR	Duncan White (SRI) 51.8	Rune Larsson (SWE) 52.2
1952	Charlie Moore (USA) 50.8 OR	Yuriy Lituyev (URS) 51.3	John Holland (NZL) 52.2
1956	Glenn Davis (USA) 50.1 OR	Eddie Southern (USA) 50.8	Josh Culbreath (USA) 51.6
1960	Glenn Davis (USA) 49.3 OR	Cliff Cushman (USA) 49.6	Dick Howard (USA) 49.7
1964	Rex Cawley (USA) 49.6	John Cooper (GBR) 50.1	Salvadore Morale (ITA) 50.1
1968	David Hemery (GBR) 48.12 WR	Gerhard Hennige (FRG) 49.0	John Sherwood (GBR) 49.0
1972	John Akii-Bua (UGA) 47.82 WR	Ralph Mann (USA) 48.51	David Hemery (GBR) 48.52
1976	Edwin Moses (USA) 47.64 WR	Mike Shine (USA) 48.69	Yevgeniy Gavrilenko (URS) 49.45
1980	Volker Beck (GDR) 48.70	Vasiliy Arkhipenko (URS) 48.86	Gary Oakes (GBR) 49.11
1984	Edwin Moses (USA) 47.75	Danny Harris (USA) 48.13	Harald Schmid (FRG) 48.19

4. Sven Nylander (SWE) 5. Amadou Diaba (SEN) 6. Tranel Hawkins (USA)
7. Michel Zimmerman (BEL) 8. Henry Amike (NGR)

1988   Semi-finals on 24 September and final on 25 September

*Record not allowed as they hit a hurdle which was then not allowed for record purposes.

4 × 100 metres relay/*Men*

WR: 37.83 USA (Sam Graddy, Ron Brown, Calvin Smith, Carl Lewis) 1984
OR: 37.83 USA (Sam Graddy, Ron Brown, Calvin Smith, Carl Lewis) 1984

	Gold	*Silver*	*Bronze*
1912*	GREAT BRITAIN 42.4 OR	SWEDEN 42.6	—
1920	UNITED STATES 42.2 WR	FRANCE 42.6	SWEDEN 42.9
1924	UNITED STATES 41.0 =WR	GREAT BRITAIN 41.2	NETHERLANDS 41.8
1928	UNITED STATES 41.0 =WR	GERMANY 41.2	GREAT BRITAIN 41.8
1932	UNITED STATES 40.0 WR	GERMANY 40.9	ITALY 41.2
1936	UNITED STATES 39.8 WR	ITALY 41.1	GERMANY 41.2
1948	UNITED STATES 40.6	GREAT BRITAIN 41.3	ITALY 41.5
1952	UNITED STATES 40.1	USSR 40.3	HUNGARY 40.5
1956	UNITED STATES 39.5 WR	USSR 39.8	GERMANY 40.3
1960	GERMANY 39.5 =WR	USSR 40.1	GREAT BRITAIN 40.2
1964	UNITED STATES 39.0 WR	POLAND 39.3	FRANCE 39.3
1968	UNITED STATES 38.2 WR	CUBA 38.3	FRANCE 38.4
1972	UNITED STATES 38.19 =WR	USSR 38.50	WEST GERMANY 38.79
1976	UNITED STATES 38.33	EAST GERMANY 38.66	USSR 38.78
1980	USSR 38.26	POLAND 38.33	FRANCE 38.53
1984	UNITED STATES 37.83 WR	JAMAICA 38.62	CANADA 38.70
	Sam Graddy	Albert Lawrence	Ben Johnson
	Ron Brown	Gregory Meghoo	Tony Sharpe
	Calvin Smith	Don Quarrie	Desai Williams
	Carl Lewis	Ray Stewart	Sterling Hinds

4. Italy 5. West Germany 6. France 7. Great Britain 8. Brazil

1988   Semi-finals and final on 1 October

*German team finished 2nd but were disqualified.

4 × 400 metres relay/*Men*

WR: 2:56.16 USA 1968
OR: 2:56.16 USA 1968

	Gold	*Silver*	*Bronze*
1908	UNITED STATES 3:29.4	GERMANY 3:32.4	HUNGARY 3:32.5
1912	UNITED STATES 3:16.6 WR	FRANCE 3:20.7	GREAT BRITAIN 3:23.2
1920	GREAT BRITAIN 3:22.2	SOUTH AFRICA 3:24.2	FRANCE 3:24.8
1924	UNITED STATES 3:16.0 WR	SWEDEN 3:17.0	GREAT BRITAIN 3:17.4
1928	UNITED STATES 3:14.2 WR	GERMANY 3:14.8	CANADA 3:15.4

1932	UNITED STATES 3:08.2 WR	GREAT BRITAIN 3:11.2	CANADA 3:12.8
1936	GREAT BRITAIN 3:09.0	UNITED STATES 3:11.0	GERMANY 3:11.8
1948	UNITED STATES 3:10.4	FRANCE 3:14.8	SWEDEN 3:16.3
1952	JAMAICA 3:03.9 WR	UNITED STATES 3:04.0	GERMANY 3:06.6
1956	UNITED STATES 3:04.8	AUSTRALIA 3:06.2	GREAT BRITAIN 3:07.2
1960	UNITED STATES 3:02.2 WR	GERMANY 3:02.7	BRITISH WEST INDIES 3:04.0
1964	UNITED STATES 3:00.7 WR	GREAT BRITAIN 3:01.6	TRINIDAD 3:01.7
1968	UNITED STATES 2:56.1 WR	KENYA 2:59.6	WEST GERMANY 3:00.5
1972	KENYA 2:59.83	GREAT BRITAIN 3:00.46	FRANCE 3:00.65
1976	UNITED STATES 2:58.65	POLAND 3:01.43	WEST GERMANY 3:01.98
1980	USSR 3:01.08	EAST GERMANY 3:01.26	ITALY 3:04.3
1984	UNITED STATES 2:57.91	GREAT BRITAIN 2:59.13	NIGERIA 2:59.32
	Sunder Nix	Kriss Akabusi	Sunday Uti
	Ray Armstead	Garry Cook	Moses Ugbusien
	Alonzo Babers	Todd Bennett	Rotimi Peters
	Antonio McKay	Philip Brown	Innocent Egbunike

4. Australia 5. Italy 6. Barbados 7. Uganda 8. Canada

1988 Semi-finals on 30 September and final on 1 October

20,000 metres road walk/*Men*

WB: 1:19.12 Axel Noack (GDR) 1987
OB: 1:23.13 Ernesto Canto (MEX) 1984

	Gold	*Silver*	*Bronze*
1956	Leonid Spirin (URS) 1h 31:27.4 OB	Antonas Mikenas (URS) 1h 32:03.0	Bruno Junk (URS) 1h 32:12.0
1960	Vladimir Golubnichiy (URS) 1h 34:07.2	Noel Freeman (AUS) 1h 34:16.4	Stan Vickers (GBR) 1h 34:56.4
1964	Ken Matthews (GBR) 1h 29:34.0 OB	Dieter Lindner (GER) 1h 31:13.2	Vladimir Golubnichiy (URS) 1h 31:59.4
1968	Vladimir Golubnichiy (URS) 1h 33:58.4	José Pedraza (MEX) 1h 34:00.0	Nikolai Smaga (URS) 1h 34:03.4
1972	Peter Frenkel (GDR) 1h 26:42.4 OB	Vladimir Golubnichiy (URS) 1h 26:55.2	Hans Reimann (GDR) 1h 27:16.6
1976	Daniel Bautista (MEX) 1h 24:40.6 OB	Hans Reimann (GDR) 1h 25:13.8	Peter Frenkel (GDR) 1h 25:29.4
1980	Maurizio Damilano (ITA) 1h 23:35.5 OB	Pyotr Pochenchuk (URS) 1h 24:45.4	Roland Wieser (GDR) 1h 25:58.2
1984	Ernesto Canto (MEX) 1h 23:13 OB	Raul Gonzalez (MEX) 1h 23:20	Maurizio Damilano (ITA) 1h 23.26

4. Guillaume Leblanc (CAN) 5. Carlo Mattioli (ITA) 6. Jose Marin (ESP)
7. Marco Evoniuk (USA) 8. Erling Andersen (NOR)

1988 On 23 September

50,000 metres road walk/*Men*

WB: 3:38.17 Ronald Wiegel (GDR) 1986
OB: 3:47.26 Raul Gonzalez (MEX) 1984

	Gold	*Silver*	*Bronze*
1932	Thomas Green (GBR) 4h 50:10	Janis Dalinsh (LAT) 4h 57:20	Ugo Frigerio (ITA) 4h 59.06
1936	Harold Whitlock (GBR) 4h 30:41.1 OB	Arthur Schwab (SUI) 4h 32:09.2	Adalberts Bubenko (LAT) 4h 32:42.2
1948	John Ljunggren (SWE) 4h 41:52	Gaston Godel (SUI) 4h 48:17	Tebbs Lloyd Johnson (GBR) 4h 48:31
1952	Giuseppe Dordoni (ITA) 4h 28:07.8 OR	Josef Dolezal (TCH) 4h 30:17.8	Antal Róka (HUN) 4h 31:27.2
1956	Norman Read (NZL) 4h 30:42.8	Yevgeniy Maskinskov (URS) 4h 32:57.0	John Ljunggren (SWE) 4h 35:02.0
1960	Don Thompson (GBR) 4h 25:30.0 OB	John Ljunggren (SWE) 4h 25:47.0	Abdon Pamich (ITA) 4h 27:55.4
1964	Abdon Pamich (ITA) 4h 11:12.4 OB	Paul Nihill (GBR) 4h 11:31.2	Ingvar Pettersson (SWE) 4h 14:17.4
1968	Christopher Höhne (GDR) 4h 20:13.6	Antal Kiss (HUN) 4h 30:17.0	Larry Young (USA) 4h 31:55.4
1972	Bernd Kannenberg (FRG) 3h 56:11.6 OB	Venjamin Soldatenko (URS) 3h 58:24.0	Larry Young (USA) 4h 00:46.0
1980	Hartwig Gauder (GDR) 3h 49:24 OB	Jorge Llopart (ESP) 3h 51:25	Yeveniy Ivchenko (URS) 3h 56:32
1984	Raul Gonzalez (MEX) 3h 47:26 OB	Bo Gustafsson (SWE) 3h 53:19	Sandro Bellucci (ITA) 3h 53:45

4. Reima Salonen (FIN) 5. Raffaello Ducceschi (ITA) 6. Carl Schueler (USA)
7. Jorge Llopart (ESP) 8. Jose Pinto (POR)

1988   On 30 September

High jump/*Men*

WR: 2.42 m Patrik Sjöberg (SWE) 1987
OR: 2.36 m Gerd Weissig (GDR) 1980

	Gold	*Silver*	*Bronze*
1896	Ellery Clark (USA) 1.81 m	James Connolly (USA) 1.65 m Robert Garrett (USA) 1.65 m	—
1900	Irving Baxter (USA) 1.90 m OR	Patrick Leahy (GBR) 1.78 m	Lajos Gönczy (HUN) 1.75 m
1904	Samuel Jones (USA) 1.80 m	Garrett Serviss (USA) 1.77 m	Paul Weinstein (GER) 1.77 m
1906	Con Leahy (GBR) 1.77 m	Lajos Gönczy (HUN) 1.75 m	Herbert Kerrigan (USA) 1.72 m Themistoklis Diakidis (GRE) 1.72 m
1908	Harry Porter (USA) 1.905 m OR	Con Leahy (GBR) 1.88 m István Somodi (HUN) 1.88 m Georges André (FRA) 1.88 m	—

1912	Alma Richards (USA) 1.93 m OR	Hans Liesche (GER) 1.91 m	George Horine (USA) 1.89 m
1920	Richmond Landon (USA) 1.94 m OR	Harold Muller (USA) 1.90 m	Bo Ekelund (SWE) 1.90 m
1924	Harold Osborn (USA) 1.98 m OR	Leroy Brown (USA) 1.95 m	Pierre Lewden (FRA) 1.92 m
1928	Robert King (USA) 1.94 m	Ben Hedges (USA) 1.91 m	Claude Ménard (FRA) 1.91 m
1932	Duncan McNaughton (CAN) 1.97 m	Robert Van Osdel (USA) 1.97 m	Simeon Toribio (PHI) 1.97 m
1936	Cornelius Johnson (USA) 2.03 m OR	David Albritton (USA) 2.00 m	Delos Thurber (USA) 2.00 m
1948	John Winter (AUS) 1.98 m	Björn Paulsen (NOR) 1.95 m	George Stanich (USA) 1.95 m
1952	Walt Davis (USA) 2.04 m OR	Ken Wiesner (USA) 2.01 m	Jose Telles da Conceicao (BRA) 1.98 m
1956	Charlie Dumas (USA) 2.12 m OR	Chilla Porter (AUS) 2.10 m	Igor Kashkarov (URS) 2.08 m
1960	Robert Shavlakadze (URS) 2.16 m OR	Valeriy Brumel (URS) 2.16 m OR	John Thomas (USA) 2.14 m
1964	Valeriy Brumel (URS) 2.18 m OR	John Thomas (USA) 2.18 m OR	John Rambo (USA) 2.16 m
1968	Dick Fosbury (USA) 2.24 m OR	Ed Caruthers (USA) 2.22 m	Valentin Gavrilov (URS) 2.20 m
1972	Yuriy Tarmak (URS) 2.23 m	Stefan Junge (GDR) 2.21 m	Dwight Stones (USA) 2.21 m
1976	Jacek Wszola (POL) 2.25 m OR	Greg Joy (CAN) 2.23 m	Dwight Stones (USA) 2.21 m
1980	Gerd Weissig (GDR) 2.36 m WR	Jacek Wszola (POL) 2.31 m	Jörg Freimuth (GDR) 2.31 m
1984	Dietmar Mögenburg (FRG) 2.35 m	Patrik Sjöberg (SWE) 2.33 m	Zhu Jianhua (CHN) 2.31 m

4. Dwight Stones (USA) 5. Doug Nordquist (USA) 6. Milt Ottey (CAN)
7. Yunpeng Liu (CHN) 8. Shu Cai (CHN)

1988 Final on 25 September

Pole Vault/*Men*

WR: 6.03 m Sergey Bubka (URS) 1987
OR: 5.78 m Wladislaw Kozakiewicz (POL) 1980

	Gold	*Silver*	*Bronze*
1896	William Hoyt (USA) 3.30 m OR	Albert Tyler (USA) 3.25 m	Evangelos Damaskos (GRE) 2.85 m
1900	Irving Baxter (USA) 3.30 m =OR	Michael Colkett (USA) 3.25 m	Carl-Albert Andersen (NOR) 3.20 m
1904	Charles Dvorak (USA) 3.50 m OR	LeRoy Samse (USA) 3.43 m	Louis Wilkins (USA) 3.43 m
1906	Fernand Gonder (FRA) 3.50 m	Bruno Söderström (SWE) 3.40 m	Ernest Glover (USA) 3.35 m

1908	Edward Cooke (USA) 3.71 m Alfred Gilbert (USA) 3.71 m	—	Edward Archibald (CAN) 3.58 m Charles Jacobs (USA) 3.58 m Bruno Söderström (SWE) 3.58 m
1912	Harry Babcock (USA) 3.95 m OR	Frank Nelson (USA) 3.85 m Marcus Wright (USA) 3.85 m	—
1920	Frank Foss (USA) 4.09 m WR	Henry Petersen (DEN) 3.70 m	Edwin Meyers (USA) 3.60 m
1924	Lee Barnes (USA) 3.95 m	Glenn Graham (USA) 3.95 m	James Brooker (USA) 3.90 m
1928	Sabin Carr (USA) 4.20 m OR	William Droegemuller (USA) 4.10 m	Charles McGinnis (USA) 3.95 m
1932	William Miller (USA) 4.31 m OR	Shuhei Nishida (JPN) 4.30 m	George Jefferson (USA) 4.20 m
1936	Earle Meadows (USA) 4.35 m OR	Shuhei Nishida (JPN) 4.25 m	Sueo Oe (JPN) 4.25 m
1948	Guinn Smith (USA) 4.30 m	Erkki Kataja (FIN) 4.20 m	Bob Richards (USA) 4.20 m
1952	Bob Richards (USA) 4.55 m OR	Don Laz (USA) 4.50 m	Ragnar Lundberg (SWE) 4.40 m
1956	Bob Richards (USA) 4.56 m OR	Bob Gutowski (USA) 4.53 m	Georgios Roubanis (GRE) 4.50 m
1960	Don Bragg (USA) 4.70 m OR	Ron Morris (USA) 4.60 m	Eeles Landström (FIN) 4.55 m
1964	Fred Hansen (USA) 5.10 m OR	Wolfgang Reinhardt (GER) 5.05 m	Klaus Lehnertz (GER) 5.00 m
1968	Bob Seagren (USA) 5.40 m OR	Claus Schiprowski (FRG) 5.40 m OR	Wolfgang Nordwig (GDR) 5.40 m OR
1972	Wolfgang Nordwig (GDR) 5.50 m OR	Bob Seagren (USA) 5.40 m	Jan Johnson (USA) 5.35 m
1976	Tadeusz Slusarski (POL) 5.50 m = OR	Antti Kalliomaki (FIN) 5.50 m = OR	David Roberts (USA) 5.50 m = OR
1980	Wladislaw Kozakiewicz (POL) 5.78 m WR	Tadeusz Slusarski (POL) 5.65 m Konstantin Volkov (URS) 5.65 m	—
1984	Pierre Quinon (FRA) 5.75 m	Mike Tully (USA) 5.65 m	Earl Bell (USA) 5.60 m Thierry Vigneron (FRA) 5.60 m

5. Kimmo Pallonen (FIN) 6. Doug Lytle (USA)
7. Felix Boehni (SUI) & Mauro Barella (ITA)

1988   Final on 28 September

Triple jump/*Men*

WR: 17.97 m Willie Banks (USA) 1985
OR: 17.39 m Viktor Saneyev (URS) 1968

	Gold	*Silver*	*Bronze*
1896	James Connolly (USA) 13.71 m OR	Alexandre Tuffere (FRA) 12.70 m	Ioannis Persakis (GRE) 12.52 m
1900	Myer Prinstein (USA) 14.47 m OR	James Connolly (USA) 13.97 m	Lewis Sheldon (USA) 13.64 m
1904	Myer Prinstein (USA) 14.35 m	Frederick Englehardt (USA) 13.90 m	Robert Stangland (USA) 13.36 m
1906	Peter O'Connor (GBR) 14.07 m	Con Leahy (GBR) 13.98 m	Thomas Cronan (USA) 13.70 m
1908	Tim Ahearne (GBR) 14.91 m OR	Garfield MacDonald (CAN) 14.76 m	Edvard Larsen (NOR) 14.39 m
1912	Gustaf Lindblom (SWE) 14.76 m	Georg Aberg (SWE) 14.51 m	Erik Almlöf (SWE) 14.17 m
1920	Vilho Tuulos (FIN) 14.50 m	Folke Jansson (SWE) 14.48 m	Erik Almlöf (SWE) 14.27 m
1924	Anthony Winter (AUS) 15.52 m WR	Luis Brunetto (ARG) 15.42 m	Vilho Tuulos (FIN) 15.37 m
1928	Mikio Oda (JPN) 15.21 m	Levi Casey (USA) 15.17 m	Vilho Tuulos (FIN) 15.11 m
1932	Chuhei Nambu (JPN) 15.72 m WR	Erik Svensson (SWE) 15.32 m	Kenkichi Oshima (JPN) 15.12 m
1936	Naoto Tajima (JPN) 16.00 m WR	Masao Harada (JPN) 15.66 m	John Metcalfe (AUS) 15.50 m
1948	Arne Ahman (SWE) 15.40 m	George Avery (AUS) 15.36 m	Ruhi Sarialp (TUR) 15.02 m
1952	Adhemar Ferreira da Silva (BRA) 16.22 m WR	Leonid Shcherbakov (URS) 15.98 m	Arnoldo Devonish (VEN) 15.52 m
1956	Adhemar Ferreira da Silva (BRA) 16.35 m OR	Vilhjalmur Einarsson (ISL) 16.26 m	Vitold Kreyer (URS) 16.02 m
1960	Jozef Schmidt (POL) 16.81 m OR	Vladimir Goryayev (URS) 16.63 m	Vitold Kreyer (URS) 16.43 m
1964	Jozef Schmidt (POL) 16.85 m OR	Oleg Fedoseyev (URS) 16.58 m	Viktor Kravchenko (URS) 16.57 m
1968	Viktor Saneyev (URS) 17.39 m WR	Nelson Prudencio (BRA) 17.27 m	Giuseppe Gentile (ITA) 17.22 m
1972	Viktor Saneyev (URS) 17.35 m	Jörg Drehmel (GDR) 17.31 m	Nelson Prudencio (BRA) 17.05 m
1976	Viktor Saneyev (URS) 17.29 m	James Butts (USA) 17.18 m	Joao de Oliveira (BRA) 16.90 m
1980	Jaak Uudmäe (URS) 17.35 m	Viktor Saneyev (URS) 17.24 m	Joao de Oliveira (BRA) 17.22 m
1984	Al Joyner (USA) 17.26 m	Mike Conley (USA) 17.18 m	Keith Connor (GBR) 16.87 m

4. Zhenxian Zou (CHN) 5. Peter Bouschen (FRG) 6. Willie Banks (USA)
7. Ajayi Agbebaku (NGR) 8. Eric McCalla (GBR) 9. Joseph Taiwo (NGR)
10. John Herbert (GBR)

1988 Final on 24 September

Long jump/*Men*

WR: 8.90 m Bob Beamon (USA) 1968
OR: 8.90 m Bob Beamon (USA) 1968

	Gold	*Silver*	*Bronze*
1896	Ellery Clark (USA) 6.35 m OR	Robert Garrett (USA) 6.18 m	James Connolly (USA) 6.11 m
1900	Alvin Kraenzlein (USA) 7.18 m OR	Myer Prinstein (USA) 7.17 m	Patrick Leahy (GBR) 6.95 m
1904	Myer Prinstein (USA) 7.34 m OR	Daniel Frank (USA) 6.89 m	Robert Strangland (USA) 6.88 m
1906	Myer Prinstein (USA) 7.20 m	Peter O'Connor (GBR) 7.02 m	Hugo Friend (USA) 6.96 m
1908	Francis Irons (USA) 7.48 m OR	Daniel Kelly (USA) 7.09 m	Calvin Bricker (CAN) 7.08 m
1912	Albert Gutterson (USA) 7.60 m OR	Calvin Bricker (CAN) 7.21 m	Georg Aberg (SWE) 7.18 m
1920	William Petterssen (SWE) 7.15 m	Carl Johnson (USA) 7.09 m	Erik Abrahamsson (SWE) 7.08 m
1924	William DeHart Hubbard (USA) 7.44 m	Ed Gourdin (USA) 7.27 m	Sverre Hansen (NOR) 7.26 m
1928	Edward Hamm (USA) 7.73 m OR	Silvio Cator (HAI) 7.58 m	Alfred Bates (USA) 7.40 m
1932	Ed Gordon (USA) 7.64 m	Lambert Redd (USA) 7.60 m	Chuhei Nambu (JPN) 7.45 m
1936	Jesse Owens (USA) 8.06 m OR	Luz Long (GER) 7.87 m	Naoto Tajima (JPN) 7.74 m
1948	Willie Steele (USA) 7.82 m	Thomas Bruce (AUS) 7.55 m	Herbert Douglas (USA) 7.54 m
1952	Jerome Biffle (USA) 7.57 m	Meredith Gourdine (USA) 7.53 m	Odön Földessy (HUN) 7.30 m
1956	Greg Bell (USA) 7.83 m	John Bennett (USA) 7.68 m	Jorma Valkama (FIN) 7.48 m
1960	Ralph Boston (USA) 8.12 m OR	Irvin Robertson (USA) 8.11 m	Igor Ter-Ovanesyan (URS) 8.04 m
1964	Lynn Davies (GBR) 8.07 m	Ralph Boston (USA) 8.03 m	Igor Ter-Ovanesyan (URS) 7.99 m
1968	Bob Beamon (USA) 8.90 m WR	Kalus Beer (GDR) 8.19 m	Ralph Boston (USA) 8.16 m
1972	Randy Williams (USA) 8.24 m	Hans Baumgartner (FRG) 8.18 m	Arnie Robinson (USA) 8.03 m
1976	Arnie Robinson (USA) 8.35 m	Randy Williams (USA) 8.11 m	Frank Wartenberg (GDR) 8.02 m
1980	Lutz Dombrowski (GDR) 8.45 m	Frank Paschek (GDR) 8.21 m	Valeriy Podluzhny (URS) 8.18 m
1984	Carl Lewis (USA) 8.54 m	Gary Honey (AUS) 8.24 m	Giovanni Evangelisti (ITA) 8.24 m

4. Larry Myricks (USA) 5. Yuhuang Liu (CHN) 6. Joey Wells (BAH)
7. Junichi Usui (JPN) 8. Jong-Il Kim (KOR)

1988	Final on 26 September

Shot put/*Men*

WR: 22.64 m Udo Beyer (GDR) 1984
OR: 21.35 m Vlademir Kiselyev (URS) 1980

	Gold	*Silver*	*Bronze*
1896	Robert Garrett (USA) 11.22 m OR	Miltiades Gouskos (GRE) 11.20 m	Georgios Papasideris (GRE) 10.36 m
1900	Richard Sheldon (USA) 14.10 m OR	Josiah McCracken (USA) 12.85 m	Robert Garrett (USA) 12.37 m
1904	Ralph Rose (USA) 14.81 m WR	Wesley Coe (USA) 14.40 m	Leon Feuerbach (USA) 13.37 m
1906	Martin Sheridan (USA) 12.32 m	Maihály Dávid (HUN) 11.83 m	Erik Lemming (SWE) 11.26 m
1908	Ralph Rose (USA) 14.21 m	Dennis Horgan (GBR) 13.62 m	John Garrels (USA) 13.18 m
1912	Patrick McDonald (USA) 15.34 m OR	Ralph Rose (USA) 15.25 m	Lawrence Whitney (USA) 13.93 m
1920	Ville Pörhölä (FIN) 14.81 m	Elmer Niklander (FIN) 14.155 m	Harry Liversedge (USA) 14.15 m
1924	Clarence Houser (USA) 14.99 m	Glenn Hartranft (USA) 14.895 m	Ralph Hills (USA) 14.64 m
1928	John Kuck (USA) 15.87 m WR	Herman Brix (USA) 15.75 m	Emil Hirschfeld (GER) 15.72 m
1932	Leo Sexton (USA) 16.00 m OR	Harlow Rothert (USA) 15.67 m	Frantisek Douda (TCH) 15.61 m
1936	Hans Woellke (GER) 16.20 m OR	Sulo Bärlund (FIN) 16.12 m	Gerhard Stöck (GER) 15.66 m
1948	Wilbur Thompson (USA) 17.12 m OR	Jim Delaney (USA) 16.68 m	Jim Fuchs (USA) 16.42 m
1952	Parry O'Brien (USA) 17.41 m OR	Darrow Hooper (USA) 17.39 m	Jim Fuchs (USA) 17.06 m
1956	Parry O'Brien (USA) 18.57 m OR	Bill Nieder (USA) 18.18 m	Jiri Skobla (TCH) 17.65 m
1960	Bill Nieder (USA) 19.68 m OR	Parry O'Brien (USA) 19.11 m	Dallas Long (USA) 19.01 m
1964	Dallas Long (USA) 20.33 m OR	Randy Matson (USA) 20.20 m	Vilmos Varju (HUN) 19.39 m
1968	Randy Matson (USA) 20.54 m	George Woods (USA) 20.12 m	Eduard Gushchin (URS) 20.09 m
1972	Wladyslaw Komar (POL) 21.18 m OR	George Woods (USA) 21.17 m	Hartmut Briesenick (GDR) 21.14 m
1976	Udo Beyer (GDR) 21.05 m	Yevgeniy Mironov (URS) 21.03 m	Aleksandr Baryshnikov (URS) 21.00 m
1980	Vladimir Kiselyev (URS) 21.35 m OR	Aleksandr Baryshnikov (URS) 21.08 m	Udo Beyer (GDR) 21.06 m
1984	Alessandro Andrei (ITA) 21.26 m	Michael Carter (USA) 21.09 m	Dave Laut (USA) 20.97 m

4. Augie Wolf (USA) 5. Werner Guenthoer (SUI) 6. Marco Montelatici (ITA)
7. Soeren Tallhem (SWE) 8. Erik De Bruin (HOL)

1988 Final on 23 September

Discus/*Men*

WR: 74.08 m Jurgen Schult (GDR) 1986
OR: 68.28 m Mac Wilkins (USA) 1976 (in qualifying round)

	Gold	*Silver*	*Bronze*
1896	Robert Garrett (USA) 29.15 m OR	Panagotis Paraskevopoulos (GRE) 28.95 m	Sotirios Versis (GRE) 28.78 m
1900	Rudolf Bauer (HUN) 36.04 m OR	Frantisek Janda-Suk (BOH) 35.25 m	Richard Sheldon (USA) 34.60 m
1904	Martin Sheridan (USA) 39.28 m OR	Ralph Rose (USA) 39.28 m OR	Nicolaos Georgantas (GRE) 37.68 m
1906	Martin Sheridan (USA) 41.46 m OR	Nicolaos Georgantas (GRE) 38.06 m	Werner Järvinen (FIN) 36.82 m
1908	Martin Sheridan (USA) 40.89 m	Merritt Giffin (USA) 40.70 m	Marquis Horr (USA) 39.44 m
1912	Armas Taipale (FIN) 45.21 m OR	Richard Byrd (USA) 42.32 m	James Duncan (USA) 42.28 m
1920	Elmer Niklander (FIN) 44.68 m	Armas Taipale (FIN) 44.19 m	Augustus Pope (USA) 42.13 m
1924	Clarence Houser (USA) 46.15 m OR	Vilho Niittymaa (FIN) 44.95 m	Thomas Lieb (USA) 44.83 m
1928	Clarence Houser (USA) 47.32 m OR	Antero Kivi (FIN) 47.23 m	James Corson (USA) 47.10 m
1932	John Anderson (USA) 49.49 m OR	Henri Laborde (USA) 48.47 m	Paul Winter (FRA) 47.85 m
1936	Ken Carpenter (USA) 50.48 m OR	Gordon Dunn (USA) 49.36 m	Giorgio Oberweger (ITA) 49.23 m
1948	Adolfo Consolini (ITA) 52.78 m OR	Giuseppe Tosi (ITA) 51.78 m	Fortune Gordien (USA) 50.77 m
1952	Sim Iness (USA) 55.03 m OR	Adolfo Consolini (ITA) 53.78 m	James Dillon (USA) 53.28 m
1956	Al Oerter (USA) 56.36 m OR	Fortune Gordien (USA) 54.81 m	Des Koch (USA) 54.40 m
1960	Al Oerter (USA) 59.18 m OR	Rink Babka (USA) 58.02 m	Dick Cochran (USA) 57.16 m
1964	Al Oerter (USA) 61.00 m OR	Ludvik Danek (TCH) 60.52 m	Dave Weill (USA) 59.49 m
1968	Al Oerter (USA) 64.78 m OR	Lothar Milde (GDR) 63.08 m	Ludvik Danek (TCH) 62.92 m
1972	Ludvik Danek (TCH) 64.40 m	Jay Silvester (USA) 63.50 m	Ricky Bruch (SWE) 63.40 m
1976	Mac Wilkins (USA) 67.50 m OR	Wolfgang Schmidt (GDR) 66.22 m	John Powell (USA) 65.70 m
1980	Viktor Rashchupkin (URS) 66.64 m	Imrich Bugár (TCH) 66.38 m	Luis Delis (CUB) 66.32 m
1984	Rolf Danneberg (FRG) 66.60 m	Mac Wilkins (USA) 66.30 m	John Powell (USA) 65.46 m

4. Knut Hjeltnes (NOR) 5. Art Burns (USA) 6. Alwin Wagner (FRG)
7. Luciano Zerbini (ITA) 8. Stefan Fernholm (SWE)

1988 Final on 1 October

Hammer

WR: 86.74 m Yuriy Sedykh (URS) 1986
OR: 81.80 m Yuriy Sedykh (URS) 1980

	Gold	*Silver*	*Bronze*
1900	John Flanagan (USA) 49.73 m	Truxton Hare (USA) 49.13 m	Josiah McCracken (USA) 42.46 m
1904	John Flanagan (USA) 51.23 m OR	John DeWitt (USA) 50.26 m	Ralph Rose (USA) 45.73 m
1908	John Flanagan (USA) 51.92 m OR	Matt McGrath (USA) 51.18 m	Con Walsh (CAN) 48.50 m
1912	Matt McGrath (USA) 54.74 m OR	Duncan Gillis (CAN) 48.39 m	Clarence Childs (USA) 48.17 m
1920	Patrick Ryan (USA) 52.87 m	Carl Lind (SWE) 48.43 m	Basil Bennett (USA) 48.25 m
1924	Fred Tootell (USA) 53.29 m	Matt McGrath (USA) 50.84 m	Malcolm Nokes (GBR) 48.87 m
1928	Patrick O'Callaghan (IRL) 51.39 m	Ossian Skiöld (SWE) 51.29 m	Edmund Black (USA) 49.03 m
1932	Patrick O'Callaghan (IRL) 53.92 m	Ville Pörhölä (FIN) 52.27 m	Peter Zaremba (USA) 50.33 m
1936	Karl Hein (GER) 56.49 m OR	Erwin Blask (GER) 55.04 m	Fred Warngard (SWE) 54.83 m
1948	Imre Németh (HUN) 56.07 m	Ivan Gubijan (YUG) 54.27 m	Bob Bennett (USA) 53.73 m
1952	József Csermák (HUN) 60.34 m WR	Karl Storch (GER) 58.86 m	Imre Németh (HUN) 57.74 m
1956	Harold Connolly (USA) 63.19 m OR	Mikhail Krivonosov (URS) 63.03 m	Anatoliy Samotsvetov (URS) 62.56 m
1960	Vasily Rudenkov (URS) 67.10 m OR	Gyula Zsivótzky (HUN) 65.79 m	Tadeusz Rut (POL) 65.64 m
1964	Romuald Klim (URS) 69.74 m OR	Gyula Zsivótzky (HUN) 69.09 m	Uwe Beyer (GER) 68.09 m
1968	Gyula Zsivótzky (HUN) 73.36 m OR	Romuald Klim (URS) 73.28 m	Lázár Lovász (HUN) 69.78 m
1972	Anatoliy Bondarchuk (URS) 75.50 m OR	Jochen Sachse (GDR) 74.96 m	Vasiliy Khmelevski (URS) 74.04 m
1976	Yuriy Sedykh (URS) 77.52 m OR	Aleksey Spiridinov (URS) 76.08 m	Anatoliy Bondarchuk (URS) 75.48 m
1980	Yuriy Sedykh (URS) 81.80 m WR	Sergey Litvinov (URS) 80.64 m	Yuriy Tamm (URS) 78.96 m
1984	Juha Tiainen (FIN) 78.08 m	Karl-Hans Riehm (FRG) 77.98 m	Klaus Ploghaus (FRG) 76.68 m

4. Giampaolo Urlando (ITA) 5. Orlando Bianchini (ITA) 6. Bill Green (USA)
7. Harri Huhtala (FIN) 8. Walter Ciofani (FRA) 9. Bob Weir (GBR)
10. Martin Girvan (GBR) 11. = Matt Mileham (GBR) & Christoph Sahner (FRG)

| 1988 | Final on 26 September |

Javelin/*Men*

WR: 87.66 m Jan Zelezny (TCH) 1987
OR: 94.58 m Miklos Németh (HUN) 1976

	Gold	*Silver*	*Bronze*
1906	Erik Lemming (SWE) 53.90 m WR	Knut Lindberg (SWE) 45.17 m	Brüno Soderström (SWE) 44.92 m
1908	Erik Lemming (SWE) 54.82 m WR	Arne Halse (NOR) 50.57 m	Otto Nilsson (SWE) 47.10 m
1912	Erik Lemming (SWE) 60.64 m WR	Juho Saaristo (FIN) 58.66 m	Mór Kóczán (HUN) 55.50 m
1920	Jonni Myyrä (FIN) 65.78 m OR	Urho Peltonen (FIN) 63.50 m	Pekka Johansson (FIN) 63.09 m
1924	Jonni Myyrä (FIN) 62.96 m	Gunnar Lindström (SWE) 60.92 m	Eugene Oberst (USA) 58.35 m
1928	Erik Lundkvist (SWE) 66.60 m OR	Béla Szepes (HUN) 65.26 m	Olav Sunde (NOR) 63.97 m
1932	Matti Järvinen (FIN) 72.71 m OR	Matti Sippala (FIN) 69.80 m	Eino Penttila (FIN) 68.70 m
1936	Gerhard Stöck (GER) 71.84 m	Yrjö Nikkanen (FIN) 70.77 m	Kalervo Toivonen (FIN) 70.72 m
1948	Tapio Rautavaara (FIN) 69.77 m	Steve Seymour (USA) 67.56 m	József Várszegi (HUN) 67.03 m
1952	Cyrus Young (USA) 73.78 m OR	Bill Miller (USA) 72.46 m	Toivo Hyytiainen (FIN) 71.89 m
1956	Egil Danielsen (NOR) 85.71 m WR	Janusz Sidlo (POL) 79.98 m	Viktor Tsibulenko (URS) 79.50 m
1960	Viktor Tsibulenko (URS) 84.64 m	Walter Krüger (GER) 79.36 m	Gergely Kulcsár (HUN) 78.57 m
1964	Pauli Nevala (FIN) 82.66 m	Gergely Kulcsár (HUN) 82.32 m	Janis Lusis (URS) 80.57 m
1968	Janis Lusis (URS) 90.10 m OR	Jorma Kinnunen (FIN) 88.58 m	Gergeley Kulcsár (HUN) 87.06 m
1972	Klaus Wolfermann (FRG) 90.48 m OR	Janis Lusis (URS) 90.46 m	Bill Schmidt (USA) 84.42 m
1976	Miklos Németh (HUN) 94.58 m WR	Hannu Siitonen (FIN) 87.92 m	Gheorghe Megelea (ROM) 87.16 m
1980	Dainis Kula (URS) 91.20 m	Aleksandr Makarov (URS) 89.64 m	Wolfgang Hanisch (GDR) 86.72 m
1984	Arto Härkönen (FIN) 86.76 m	David Ottley (GBR) 85.74 m	Kenth Eldebrink (SWE) 83.72 m

4. Wolfram Gambke (FRG) 5. Masami Yoshida (JPN) 6. Einar Vilhjalmsson (ISL)
7. Roald Bradstock (GBR) 8. Laslo Babits (CAN)

1988 Final on 25 September

Decathlon/*Men*

WR: 8847 pts Daley Thompson (GBR) 1984
(adjusted by 1986 tables – set in Los Angeles)
OR: 8797 pts Daley Thompson (GBR) 1984
The scoring system has varied over the years but the scores given have all been calculated on the 1962 tables which are currently in use.

	Gold	*Silver*	*Bronze*
1904	Thomas Kiely (GBR) 6036 pts	Adam Gunn (USA) 5907 pts	Truxton Hare (USA) 5813 pts
1912*	Hugo Wieslander (SWE) 6161 pts	Charles Lomberg (SWE) 5943 pts	Gösta Holmer (SWE) 5956 pts
1920	Helge Lövland (NOR) 5970 pts	Brutus Hamilton (USA) 5940 pts	Bertil Ohlsson (SWE) 5825 pts
1924	Harold Osborn (USA) 6668 pts WR	Emerson Norton (USA) 6340 pts	Aleksandr Klumberg (EST) 6260 pts
1928	Paavo Yrjölä (FIN) 6774 pts WR	Akilles Järvinen (FIN) 6815 pts	Ken Doherty (USA) 6593 pts
1932	Jim Bausch (USA) 6986 pts WR	Akilles Järvinen (FIN) 7038 pts	Wolrad Eberle (GER) 6830 pts
1936	Glenn Morris (USA) 7421 pts WR	Robert Clark (USA) 7226 pts	Jack Parker (USA) 6918 pts
1948	Bob Mathias (USA) 6826 pts	Ignace Heinrich (FRA) 6740 pts	Floyd Simmons (USA) 6711 pts
1952	Bob Mathias (USA) 7731 pts WR	Milt Campbell (USA) 7132 pts	Floyd Simmons (USA) 7069 pts
1956	Milt Campbell (USA) 7708 pts OR	Rafer Johnson (USA) 7568 pts	Vasiliy Kuznetsov (URS) 7461 pts
1960	Rafer Johnson (USA) 8001 pts OR	Chuan-Kwang Yang (TAI) 7930 pts	Vasiliy Kuznetsov (URS) 7624 pts
1964	Willi Holdorf (GER) 7887 pts	Rein Aun (URS) 7842 pts	Hans-Joachim Walde (GER) 7809 pts
1968	Bill Toomey (USA) 8193 pts OR	Hans-Joachim Walde (FRG) 8111 pts	Kurt Bendlin (FRG) 8064 pts
1972	Nikolai Avilov (URS) 8454 pts WR	Leonid Litvinenko (URS) 8035 pts	Ryszard Katus (POL) 7984 pts
1976	Bruce Jenner (USA) 8617 pts WR	Guido Kratschmer (FRG) 8411 pts	Nikolai Avilov (URS) 8369 pts
1980	Daley Thompson (GBR) 8495 pts	Yuriy Kutsenko (URS) 8331 pts	Sergey Zhelanov (URS) 8135 pts
1984	Daley Thompson (GBR) 8797 pts OR	Jurgen Hingsen (FRG) 8673 pts	Siegfried Wentz (FRG) 8412 pts

4. Guido Kratschmer (FRG) 5. William Motti (FRA) 6. John Crist (USA)
7. Jim Wooding (USA) 8. Dave Steen (CAN)

1988   On 28 and 29 September

*Jim Thorpe (USA) was disqualified having finished first but in 1982 was reinstated as joint first. He scored 6845 points.

100 metres/*Women*

WR: 10.76 Evelyn Ashford (USA) 1984
OR: 10.97 Evelyn Ashford (USA) 1984

	Gold	*Silver*	*Bronze*
1928	Elizabeth Robinson (USA) 12.2 =WR	Fanny Rosenfeld (CAN) 12.3	Ethel Smith (CAN) 12.3
1932	Stanislawa Walasiewicz (POL) 11.9 =WR	Hilda Strike (CAN) 11.9 =WR	Wilhelmina von Bremen (USA) 12.0
1936	Helen Stephens (USA) 11.4 (w)	Stanislawa Walasiewicz (POL) 11.7	Kathe Krauss (GER) 11.9
1948	Fanny Blankers-Koen (HOL) 11.9	Dorothy Manley (GBR) 12.2	Shirley Strickland (AUS) 12.2
1952	Marjorie Jackson (AUS) 11.5 =WR	Daphne Hasenjager (SAF) 11.8	Shirley Strickland (AUS) 11.9
1956	Betty Cuthbert (AUS) 11.5 (w)	Christa Stubnick (GER) 11.7	Marlene Matthews (AUS) 11.7
1960	Wilma Rudolph (USA) 11.0 (w)	Dorothy Hyman (GBR) 11.3	Giuseppina Leone (ITA) 11.3
1964	Wyomia Tyus (USA) 11.4	Edith Maguire (USA) 11.6	Ewa Klobukowska (POL) 11.6
1968	Wyomia Tyus (USA) 11.0 WR	Barbara Ferrell (USA) 11.1	Irena Szewinska (POL) (née Kirszenstein) 11.1
1972	Renate Stecher (GDR) 11.07	Raelene Boyle (AUS) 11.23	Silvia Chivas (CUB) 11.24
1976	Annegret Richter (FRG) 11.08	Renate Stecher (GDR) 11.13	Inge Helten (FRG) 11.17
1980	Ludmila Kondratyeva (URS) 11.06	Marlies Göhr (GDR) 11.07	Ingred Auerswald (GDR) 11.14
1984	Evelyn Ashford (USA) 10.97 OR	Alice Brown (USA) 11.13	Merlene Ottey-Page (JAM) 11.16

4. Jeanette Bolden (USA) 5. Grace Jackson (JAM) 6. Angela Bailey (CAN) 7. Heather Oakes (GBR) 8. Angela Taylor (CAN)

1988 Semi-finals and final on 25 September

200 metres/*Women*

WR: 21.71 Marita Koch (GDR) 1979 (twice)
　　　 Heike Drechsler (GDR) 1986 (twice)
OR: 21.81 Valerie Brisco-Hooks (USA) 1984

	Gold	*Silver*	*Bronze*
1948	Fanny Blankers-Koen (HOL) 24.4	Audrey Williamson (GBR) 25.1	Audrey Patterson (USA) 25.2
1952	Marjorie Jackson (AUS) 23.7	Bertha Brouwer (HOL) 24.2	Nadyezda Khnykina (URS) 24.2
1956	Betty Cuthbert (AUS) 23.4 = OR	Christa Stubnick (GER) 23.7	Marlene Matthews (AUS) 23.8
1960	Wilma Rudolph (USA) 24.0	Jutta Heine (GER) 24.4	Dorothy Hyman (GBR) 24.7

	Gold	Silver	Bronze
1964	Edith Maguire (USA) 23.0 OR	Irena Kirszenstein (POL) 23.1	Marilyn Black (AUS) 23.1
1968	Irena Szewinska (née Kirszenstein) (POL) 22.5 WR	Raelene Boyle (AUS) 22.7	Jennifer Lamy (AUS) 22.8
1972	Renate Stecher (GDR) 22.40 =OR	Raelene Boyle (AUS) 22.45	Irena Szewinska (née Kirszenstein) (POL) 22.74
1976	Bärbel Eckert (GDR) 22.37 OR	Annegret Richter (FRG) 22.39	Renate Stecher (GDR) 22.47
1980	Bärbel Wöckel (née Eckert) 22.03 OR	Natalya Bochina (URS) 22.19	Merlene Ottey (JAM) 22.20
1984	Valerie Brisco-Hooks (USA) 21.81 OR	Florence Griffiths (USA) 22.04	Merlene Ottey-Page (JAM) 22.09

4. Kathryn Cook (GBR) 5. Grace Jackson (JAM) 6. Randy Givens (USA)
7. Rose Aimée Bacoul (FRA) 8. Liliane Gaschet (FRA)

1988 Semi-finals and final on 29 September

400 metres/*Women*

WR: 47.60 Marita Koch (GDR) 1985
OR: 48.83 Valerie Brisco-Hooks (USA) 1984

	Gold	*Silver*	*Bronze*
1964	Betty Cuthbert (AUS) 52.0 OR	Ann Packer (GBR) 52.2	Judith Amoore (AUS) 53.4
1968	Colette Besson (FRA) 52.0 =OR	Lillian Board (GBR) 52.1	Natalya Pechenkina (URS) 52.2
1972	Monika Zehrt (GDR) 51.08 OR	Rita Wilden (FRG) 51.21	Kathy Hammond (USA) 51.64
1976	Irena Szewinska (née Kirszenstein) (POL) 49.29 WR	Christina Brehmer (GDR) 50.51	Ellen Streidt (GDR) 50.55
1980	Marita Koch (GDR) 48.88 OR	Jarmila Kratochvilova (TCH) 49.46	Christina Lathan (née Brehmer) (GDR) 49.66
1984	Valerie Brisco-Hooks (USA) 48.83 OR	Chandra Cheeseborough (USA) 49.05	Kathryn Cook (GBR) 49.42

4. Marita Payne (CAN) 5. Lillie Leatherwood (USA) 6. Ute Thimm (FRG)
7. Charmaine Crooks (CAN) 8. Ruth Waithera (KEN)

1988 Semi-finals on 25 and final on 26 September

800 metres/*Women*

WR: 1:53.28 Jarmila Kratochvilova (TCH) 1983
OR: 1:53.43 Nadyezda Olizarenko (URS) 1980

	Gold	Silver	Bronze
1928	Lina Radke (GER) 2:16.8 WR	Kinuye Hitomi (JPN) 2:17.6	Inga Gentzel (SWE) 2:17.8
1960	Ludmila Shevtsova (URS) 2:04.3 =WR	Brenda Jones (AUS) 2:04.4	Ursula Donath (GER) 2:05.6
1964	Ann Packer (GBR) 2:01.1 OR	Maryvonne Durpureur (FRA) 2:01.9	Marise Chamberlain (NZL) 2:02.8
1968	Madeline Manning (USA) 2:00.9 OR	Ilona Sila (ROM) 2:02.5	Maria Gommers (HOL) 2:02.6
1972	Hildegard Falck (FRG) 1:58.6 OR	Niole Sabaite (URS) 1:58.7	Gunhild Hoffmeister (GDR) 1:59.2
1976	Tatanya Kazankina (URS) 1:54.9 WR	Nikolina Shtereva (BUL) 1:55.4	Elfi Zinn (GDR) 1:55.6
1980	Nadyezda Olizarenko (URS) 1:53.5 WR	Olga Mineyeva (URS) 1:54.9	Tatyana Providokhina (URS) 1:55.5
1984	Doina Melinte (ROM) 1:57.60	Kim Gallagher (USA) 1:58.63	Fita Lovin (ROM) 1:58.83

4. Gabriella Dorio (ITA) 5. Lorraine Baker (GBR) 6. Ruth Wysocki (USA)
7. Margrit Klinger (FRG) 8. Caroline O'Shea (IRL)

1988 Semi-finals on 25 and final on 26 September

1500 metres/*Women*

WR: 3:52.47 Tatanya Kazankina (URS) 1980
OR: 3:56.6 Tatanya Kazankina (URS) 1980

	Gold	Silver	Bronze
1972	Ludmila Bragina (URS) 4:01.4 WR	Gunhild Hoffmeister (GDR) 4:02.8	Paola Cacch-Pigni (ITA) 4:02.9
1976	Tatanya Kazankina (URS) 4:05.5	Gunhild Hoffmeister (GDR) 4:06.0	Ulrike Klapezynski (GDR) 4:06.1
1980	Tatanya Kazankina (URS) 3:56.6 OR	Christiane Wartenberg (GDR) 3:57.8	Nadyezda Olizarenko (URS) 3:59.6
1984	Gabriella Dorio (ITA) 4:03.25	Doina Melinte (ROM) 4:03.76	Maricica Puica (ROM) 4:04.15

4. Roswitha Gerdes (FRG) 5. Christine Benning (GBR) 6. Christina Boxer (GBR)
7. Brit McRoberts (CAN) 8. Ruth Wysocki (USA) 9. Fita Lovin (ROM)
10. Debbie Scott (CAN) 11. Lynne MacDougall (GBR) 12. Elly Van Hulst (HOL)

1988 Semi-finals on 29 September and final on 1 October

3000 metres/*Women*

WR: 8:22.62 Tatanya Kazankina (URS) 1984
OR: 8:35.96 Maricica Puica (ROM) 1984

	Gold	*Silver*	*Bronze*
1984	Maricica Puica (ROM) 8:35.96 OR	Wendy Sly (GBR) 8:39.47	Lynn Williams (CAN) 8:42.14

4. Cindy Bremser (USA) 5. Cornelia Buerki (SUI) 6. Aurora Cunha (POR)
7. Zola Budd (GBR) 8. Joan Hansen (USA) 9. Dianne Rodger (NZL)
10. Angese Possamai (ITA)

1988 Final on 25 September

10,000 metres/*Women*

WR: 30:13.74 Ingrid Kristiansen (NOR) 1986
OR: Not held before

1988 On 30 September

Marathon/*Women*

WB: 2:21.06 Ingrid Kristiansen (NOR) 1985
OB: 2:24.52 Joan Benoit (USA) 1984

	Gold	*Silver*	*Bronze*
1984	Joan Benoit (USA) 2h 24.52	Grete Waitz (NOR) 2h 26.18	Rosa Mota (POR) 2h 26.57

4. Ingrid Kristiansen (NOR) 5. Lorraine Moller (NZL) 6. Priscilla Welch (GBR)
7. Lisa Martin (AUS) 8. Sylvie Ruegger (CAN)

1988 On 2 October

100 metres hurdles/*Women*

WR: 12.25 Ginka Zagorcheva (BUL) 1987
OR: 12.56 Vera Komisova (URS) 1980

	Gold	*Silver*	*Bronze*
1932	Mildred Didriksen (USA) 11.7 WR	Evelyne Hall (USA) 11.7	Marjorie Clark (SAF) 11.8
1936	Trebisonda Valla (ITA) 11.7	Anny Steuer (GER) 11.7	Elizabeth Taylor (CAN) 11.7
1948	Fanny Blankers-Koen (HOL) 11.2 OR	Maureen Gardner (GBR) 11.2	Shirley Strickland (AUS) 11.4
1952	Shirley de la Hunty (née Strickland) (AUS) 10.9 WR	Maria Golubnichaya (URS) 11.1	Maria Sander (GER) 11.1
1956	Shirley de la Hunty (née Strickland) (AUS) 10.7 OR	Gisela Köhler (GER) 10.9	Norma Thrower (AUS) 11.0
1960	Irina Press (URS) 10.8	Carol Quinton (GBR) 10.9	Gisela Birkemeyer (née Köhler) (GER) 11.0

1964	Karin Balzer (GER) 10.5	Tereza Ciepla (POL) 10.5	Pam Kilborn (AUS) 10.5
1968	Maureen Caird (AUS) 10.3 OR	Pam Kilborn (AUS) 10.4	Chi Cheng (TAI) 10.4
1972	Annelie Ehrhardt (GDR) 12.59 WR	Valeria Bufanu (ROM) 12.84	Karin Balzer (GDR) 12.90
1976	Johanna Schaller (GDR) 12.77	Tatyana Anisimova (URS) 12.78	Natalya Lebedeva (URS) 12.80
1980	Vera Komisova (URS) 12.56 OR	Johanna Klier (née Schaller) (GDR) 12.63	Lucyna Langer (POL) 12.65
1984	Benita Fitzgerald-Brown (USA) 12.84	Shirley Strong (GBR) 12.88	Kim Turner (USA) 13.06 Michelle Chardonnet (FRA) 13.06*

5. Glynis Nunn (AUS) 6. Marie Noelle Savigny (FRA) 7. Ulrike Denk (FRG)
8. Pamela Page (USA)

1988 Semi-finals and final on 30 September

*Relegated to 4th in Los Angeles but later credited with joint-third.

400 metres hurdles/*Women*

WR: 52.94 Marina Stepanove (URS) 1986
OR: 54.61 Nawal El Moutawakel (MAR) 1984

	Gold	*Silver*	*Bronze*
1984	Nawal El Moutawakel (MAR) 54.61 OR	Judi Brown (USA) 55.20	Christina Cojocaru (ROM) 55.41

4. P. T. Usha (IND) 5. Ann Louise Skoglund (SWE) 6. Debbie Flintoff (AUS)
7. Tuija Helander (FIN) 8. Sandra Farmer (JAM)

1988 Semi-finals on 26 and final on 28 September

4 × 100 metres relay/*Women*

WR: 41.37 East Germany 1985
OR: 41.60 East Germany 1980

	Gold	*Silver*	*Bronze*
1928	CANADA 48.4 WR	UNITED STATES 48.8	GERMANY 49.0
1932	UNITED STATES 47.0	CANADA 47.0	GREAT BRITAIN 47.6
1936	UNITED STATES 46.9	GREAT BRITAIN 47.6	CANADA 47.8
1948	NETHERLANDS 47.5	AUSTRALIA 47.6	CANADA 47.8
1952	UNITED STATES 45.9 WR	GERMANY 45.9 WR	GREAT BRITAIN 46.2
1956	AUSTRALIA 44.5 WR	GREAT BRITAIN 44.7	UNITED STATES 44.9
1960	UNITED STATES 44.5	GERMANY 44.8	POLAND 45.0
1964	POLAND 43.6 WR	UNITED STATES 43.9	GREAT BRITAIN 44.0
1968	UNITED STATES 42.8 WR	CUBA 43.3	USSR 43.4
1972	WEST GERMANY 42.81 =WR	EAST GERMANY 42.95	CUBA 43.36

1976 EAST GERMANY 42.55 OR	WEST GERMANY 42.59	USSR 43.09
1980 EAST GERMANY 41.60 WR	USSR 42.10	GREAT BRITAIN 42.43
1984 UNITED STATES 41.65	CANADA 42.77	GREAT BRITAIN 43.11
Alice Brown	Angela Bailey	Simone Jacobs
Jeanette Bolden	Marita Payne	Kathryn Cook
Chandra Cheeseborough	Angella Taylor	Beverley Callender
Evelyn Ashford	France Gareau	Heather Oakes

4. France 5. West Germany 6. Bahamas 7. Trinidad 8. Jamaica

1988 Semi-finals and final on 1 October

4 × 400 metres relay/*Women*

WR: 3:15.92 East Germany 1984
OR: 3:18.29 United States 1984

	Gold	*Silver*	*Bronze*
1972	EAST GERMANY 3:22.95 WR	UNITED STATES 3:25.15	WEST GERMANY 3:26.51
1976	EAST GERMANY 3:19.23 WR	UNITED STATES 3:22.81	USSR 3:24.24
1980	USSR 3:20.2	EAST GERMANY 3:20.35	GREAT BRITAIN 3:27.5
1984	UNITED STATES 3:18.29 OR	CANADA 3:21.21	WEST GERMANY 3:22.98
	Lillie Leatherwood	Charmaine Crooks	Heike Schulte-Mattler
	Sherri Howard	Jullian Richardson	Ute Thimm
	Valerie Brisco-Hooks	Molly Killingbeck	Heide Gaugel
	Chandra Cheeseborough	Marita Payne	Gaby Bussmann

4. Great Britain (Michelle Scutt, Helen Barnett, Gladys Taylor, Jocelyn Hoyte-Smith)
5. Jamaica 6. Italy 7. India (Puerto Rico did not start)

1988 Semi-finals on 30 September and final on 1 October

High jump/*Women*

WR: 2.09 m Stefka Kostadinova (BUL) 1987
OR: 2.02 m Ulrike Meyfarth (FRG) 1984

	Gold	*Silver*	*Bronze*
1928	Ethel Catherwood (CAN) 1.59 m OR	Carolina Gisolf (HOL) 1.56 m	Mildred Wiley (USA) 1.56 m
1932	Jean Shiley (USA) 1.65 m WR	Mildred Didriksen (USA) 1.65 m WR	Eva Dawes (CAN) 1.60 m
1936	Ibolya Csák (HUN) 1.60 m	Dorothy Odam (GBR) 1.60 m	Elfriede Kaun (GER) 1.60 m
1948	Alice Coachman (USA) 1.68 m OR	Dorothy Tyler (née Odam) (GBR) 1.68 m OR	Micheline Ostermeyer (FRA) 1.61 m
1952	Esther Brand (SAF) 1.67 m	Sheila Lerwill (GBR) 1.65 m	Aleksandra Chudina (URS) 1.63 m

1956	Mildred McDaniel (USA) 1.76 m WR	Thelma Hopkins (GBR) 1.67 m Maria Pissaryeva (URS) 1.67 m	—
1960	Iolanda Balas (ROM) 1.85 m OR	Jaroslawa Jozwiakowska (POL) 1.71 m Dorothy Shirley (GBR) 1.71 m	—
1964	Iolanda Balas (ROM) 1.90 m OR	Michelle Brown (AUS) 1.80 m	Taisia Chenchik (URS) 1.78 m
1968	Miloslava Rezkova (TCH) 1.82 m	Antonina Okorokova (URS) 1.80 m	Valentina Kozyr (URS) 1.80 m
1972	Ulrike Meyfarth (FRG) 1.92 m =WR	Yordanka Blagoyeva (BUL) 1.88 m	Ilona Gusenbauer (AUT) 1.88 m
1976	Rosemarie Ackermann (GDR) 1.93 m OR	Sara Simeoni (ITA) 1.91 m	Yordanka Blagoyeva (BUL) 1.91 m
1980	Sara Simeoni (ITA) 1.97 m OR	Urszula Kielan (POL) 1.94 m	Jutta Kirst (GDR) 1.94 m
1984	Ulrike Meyfarth (FRG) 2.02 m OR	Sara Simeoni (ITA) 2.00 m	Joni Huntley (USA) 1.97 m

4. Maryse Ewanje-Epee (FRA) 5. Debbie Brill (CAN) 6. Vanessa Browne (AUS)
7. Zheng Dazhen (CHN) 8. Louise Ritter (USA) 9. = Diana Elliott (GBR) &
Wenqin Yang (CHN)

1988   Final on 30 September

Long jump/*Women*

WR: 7.45 m Heike Dreschler (GDR) 1986
         Jackie Joyner (USA) 1987
OR: 7.06 m Tatyana Kolpakova (URS) 1980

	Gold	*Silver*	*Bronze*
1948	Olga Gyarmati (HUN) 5.69 m OR	Noemi Simonetto de Portela (ARG) 5.60 m	Ann-Britt Leyman (SWE) 5.57 m
1952	Yvette Williams (NZL) 6.24 m OR	Aleksandra Chudina (URS) 6.14 m	Shirley Cawley (GBR) 5.92 m
1956	Elzbieta Krzesinska (POL) 6.35 m =WR	Willye White (USA) 6.09 m	Nadyezda Dvalishvili (née Khnykina) (URS) 6.07 m
1960	Vera Krepkina (URS) 6.37 m OR	Elzbieta Krzesinska (POL) 6.27 m	Hildrun Claus (GER) 6.21 m
1964	Mary Rand (née Bignal) (GBR) 6.76 m WR	Irena Kirszenstein (POL) 6.60 m	Tatyana Schelkanova (URS) 6.42 m
1968	Viorica Viscopoleanu (ROM) 6.82 m WR	Sheila Sherwood (GBR) 6.68 m	Tatyana Talysheva (URS) 6.66 m
1972	Heidemarie Rosendahl (FRG) 6.78 m	Diana Yorgova (BUL) 6.77 m	Eva Suranova (TCH) 6.67 m
1976	Angela Voigt (GDR) 6.72 m	Kathy McMillan (USA) 6.66 m	Lidia Alfeyeva (URS) 6.60 m
1980	Tatyana Kolpakova (URS) 7.06 m OR	Brigitte Wujak (GDR) 7.04 m	Tatyana Skatchko (URS) 7.01 m

| 1984 | Anisoara Stanciu (ROM) 6.96 m | Vali Ionescu (ROM) 6.81 m | Susan Hearnshaw (GBR) 6.80 m |

4. Angela Thacker (USA) 5. Jackie Joyner (USA) 6. Robyn Lorraway (AUS)
7. Glynis Nunn (AUS) 8. Shonel Ferguson (BAH)

1988 Final on 29 September

Shot put/*Women*

WR: 22.63 m Natalya Lisovskaya (URS) 1987
OR: 22.41 m Ilona Slupianek (GDR) 1980

	Gold	*Silver*	*Bronze*
1948	Micheline Ostermeyer (FRA) 13.75 m OR	Amelia Piccinini (ITA) 13.09 m	Ina Schäffer (AUT) 13.08 m
1952	Galina Zybina (URS) 15.28 m WR	Marianne Werner (GER) 14.57 m	Klaudia Tochenova (URS) 14.50 m
1956	Tamara Tyshkevich (URS) 16.59 m OR	Galina Zybina (URS) 16.53 m	Marianne Werner (GER) 15.61 m
1960	Tamara Press (URS) 17.32 m OR	Johanna Lüttge (GER) 16.61 m	Earlene Brown (USA) 16.42 m
1964	Tamara Press (URS) 18.14 m OR	Renate Garisch (GDR) 17.61 m	Galina Zybina (URS) 17.45 m
1968	Margitta Gummel (GDR) 19.61 m WR	Marita Lange (GDR) 18.78 m	Nadyezda Chizhova (URS) 18.19 m
1972	Nadyezda Chizhova (URS) 21.03 m WR	Margitta Gummel (GDR) 20.22 m	Ivanka Khristova (BUL) 19.35 m
1976	Ivanka Khristova (BUL) 21.16 m OR	Nadyezda Chizhova (URS) 20.96 m	Helena Fibingerova (TCH) 20.67 m
1980	Ilona Slupianek (GDR) 22.41 m OR	Svetlana Krachevskaya (URS) 21.42 m	Margitta Pufe (GDR) 21.20 m
1984	Claudia Losch (FRG) 20.48 m	Mihaela Loghin (ROM) 20.47 m	Gael Martin (AUS) 19.19 m

4. Judy Oakes (GBR) 5. Li Meisu (CHN) 6. Venissa Head (GBR) 7. Carol Cady (USA)
8. Florenta Craciunescu (ROM)

1988 Final on 1 October

Discus/*Women*

WR: 74.56 m Zdenka Silhava (TCH) 1984
OR: 69.96 m Evelin Jahl (née Schlaak) (GDR) 1980

	Gold	*Silver*	*Bronze*
1928	Halina Konopacka (POL) 39.62 m WR	Lillian Copeland (USA) 37.08 m	Ruth Svedberg (SWE) 35.92 m
1932	Lillian Copeland (USA) 40.58 m OR	Ruth Osburn (USA) 40.12 m	Jadwiga Wajsówna (POL) 38.74 m
1936	Gisela Mauermayer (GER) 47.63 m OR	Jadwiga Wajsówna (POL) 46.22 m	Paula Mollenhauer (GER) 39.80 m

1948	Micheline Ostermeyer (FRA) 41.92 m	Edera Gentile (ITA) 41.17 m	Jacqueline Mazeas (FRA) 40.47 m
1952	Nina Romashkova (URS) 51.42 m OR	Elizaveta Bagriantseva (URS) 47.08 m	Nina Dumbadze (URS) 46.29 m
1956	Olga Fikotova (TCH) 53.69 m OR	Irina Beglyakova (URS) 52.54 m	Nina Ponomaryeva (née Romashkova) (URS) 52.02 m
1960	Nina Ponomaryeva (née Romashkova) (URS) 55.10 m OR	Tamara Press (URS) 52.59 m	Lia Manoliu (ROM) 52.36 m
1964	Tamara Press (URS) 57.27 m OR	Ingrid Lotz (GER) 57.21 m	Lia Manoliu (ROM) 56.97 m
1968	Lia Manoliu (ROM) 58.28 m OR	Liesel Westermann (FRG) 57.76 m	Jolán Kleiber (HUN) 54.90 m
1972	Faina Melnik (URS) 66.62 m OR	Argentina Menis (ROM) 65.06 m	Vasilka Stoyeva (BUL) 64.34 m
1976	Evelin Schlaak (GDR) 69.00 m OR	Maria Vergova (BUL) 67.30 m	Gabriele Hinzmann (GDR) 66.84 m
1980	Evelin Jahl (née Schlaak) (GDR) 69.96 m OR	Maria Petkova (née Vergova) (BUL) 67.90 m	Tatyana Lesovaya (URS) 67.40 m
1984	Ria Stalman (HOL) 65.36 m	Leslie Deniz (USA) 64.86 m	Florenta Craciunescu (ROM) 63.64 m

4. Ulla Lundholm (FIN) 5. Meg Ritchie (GBR) 6. Ingra Manecke (FRG)
7. Venissa Head (GBR) 8. Gael Martin (AUS)

1988   Final on 29 September

Javelin/*Women*

WR: 78.90 m Petra Felke (GDR) 1987
OR: 69.56 m Tessa Sanderson (GBR) 1984

	Gold	*Silver*	*Bronze*
1932	Mildred Didriksen (USA) 43.68 m OR	Ellen Braumüller (GER) 43.49 m	Tilly Fleischer (GER) 43.00 m
1936	Tilly Fleischer (GER) 45.18 m OR	Luise Krüger (GER) 43.29 m	Marja Kwasniewska (POL) 41.80 m
1948	Herma Bauma (AUT) 45.57 m OR	Kaisa Parviainen (FIN) 43.79 m	Lily Carlstedt (DEN) 42.08 m
1952	Dana Zatopková (TCH) 50.47 m OR	Aleksandra Chudina (URS) 50.01 m	Yelena Gorchakova (URS) 49.76 m
1956	Ines Jaunzeme (URS) 53.86 m OR	Marlene Ahrens (CHI) 50.38 m	Nadyezda Konyayeva (URS) 50.28 m
1960	Elvira Ozolina (URS) 55.98 m OR	Dana Zatopková (TCH) 53.78 m	Birute Kalediene (URS) 53.45 m
1964	Mihaela Penes (ROM) 60.54 m	Márta Rudas (HUN) 58.27 m	Yelena Gorchakova (URS) 57.06 m
1968	Angela Németh (HUN) 60.36 m	Mihaela Penes (ROM) 59.92 m	Eva Janko (AUT) 58.04 m

1972	Ruth Fuchs (GDR) 63.88 m OR	Jacqueline Todten (GDR) 62.54 m	Kathy Schmidt (USA) 59.94 m
1976	Ruth Fuchs (GDR) 65.94 m OR	Marion Becker (FRG) 64.70 m	Kathy Schmidt (USA) 63.96 m
1980	Maria Colon (CUB) 68.40 m OR	Saida Gunba (URS) 67.76 m	Ute Hommola (GDR) 66.56 m
1984	Tessa Sanderson (GBR) 69.56 m OR	Tiina Lillak (FIN) 69.00 m	Fatima Whitbread (GBR) 67.14 m

4. Tuula Laaksalo (FIN) 5. Trine Solberg (NOR) 6. Ingrid Thyssen (FRG)
7. Beate Peters (FRG) 8. Karin Smith (USA) 9. Sharon Gibson (GBR)

1988   Final on 26 September

Heptathlon/*Women*

WR: 7158 pts Jackie Joyner (USA) 1986
OR: 6390 pts Glynis Nunn (AUS) 1984
Note: Until 1984 women competed in the Pentathlon – 5 events on one day.
The heptathlon consists of seven events over two days – day 1: 100 m hurdles, high jump, shot and 200 m and on day 2: long jump, javelin and 800 m.
The Pentathlon results up to 1980 are listed here under Heptathlon.

	Gold	*Silver*	*Bronze*
PENTATHLON			
1964	Irina Press (URS) 5246 pts WR	Mary Rand (née Bignal) (GBR) 5035 pts	Galina Bystrova (URS) 4956 pts
1968	Ingrid Becker (FRG) 5098 pts	Liese Prokop (AUT) 4966 pts	Annamaria Tóth (HUN) 4959 pts
1972*	Mary Peters (GBR) 4801 pts WR	Heidemarie Rosendahl (FRG) 4791 pts	Burglinde Pollak (GDR) 4768 pts
1976*	Siegrun Siegl (GDR) 4745 pts	Christine Laser (GDR) 4745 pts	Burglinde Pollak (GDR) 4740 pts
1980	Nadyezda Tkachenko (URS) 5083 pts WR	Olga Rukavishnikova (URS) 4937 pts	Olga Kuragina (URS) 4875 pts
HEPTATHLON			
1984	Glynis Nunn (AUS) 6390 pts OR	Jackie Joyner (USA) 6385 pts	Sabine Everts (FRG) 6363 pts

4. Cindy Greiner (USA) 5. Judy Simpson (GBR) 6. Sabine Braun (FRG)
7. Tineke Hidding (HOL) 8. Kim Hagger (GBR)

1988   On 23 and 24 September

*New tables used for scoring.
†Siegl won the gold by virtue of the fact that she finished ahead of Laser in three events.

BASKETBALL

Although there were ancient games similar in concept, modern basketball was the invention of an American, Dr James Naismith, at Springfield College (Massachusetts) in 1891. It was thought up as a recreation for young men at a Christian Association School.

Having been invented by an American, the Americans fittingly dominated the sport at Olympic Games from its first inclusion in 1936 until the return of the games to Germany in 1972.

The first basketball competition was played in Berlin on outdoor courts, often in the foulest weather. Since then, however, it has become an indoor sport at this highest level.

The American men have failed to win the gold medal on only two occasions, in 1972 when they lost to the Soviet Union by a single point in a highly controversial final, and in 1980 when they did not take part. Yugoslavia won on that occasion.

The 1972 final will always rankle with the Americans. They had been struggling against the Soviets, but were within just one point of them with seconds to go. The American player Doug Collins was sent flying by two Soviet players. When he recovered, he scored both free throws to put the Americans into a one point lead. Play was restarted with one second to go. The Soviets failed to score – everyone thought the Americans had won, but the referee ordered the one second to be played again. Once more the buzzer sounded, the Americans rejoiced again. But then, Dr William Jones, the British Secretary-General of the Games' governing body, dictated that not one but three extra seconds should have been allowed for play. After much delay, play began again. The Soviets scored – the victory was theirs. USA 50–USSR 51. The American protests were long and loud but to no avail. However their silver medals remain in a Munich bank vault. They refused to collect them.

The reigning champions are once more the United States. But remember, the Soviet bloc did not take part in 1984.

The women's game was included for the first time at Montreal in 1976, but again the United States won in 1984.

THE COMPETITION

The men play on a group basis. Twelve countries qualify and play in two groups of six. They play on a round-robin basis with each group eliminating two teams each. They then play on a knockout basis with the leading qualifiers from Group A playing the fourth qualifiers from Group B, and so on (which produces its own kind of seeding).

The women play on a round-robin basis with all six qualifying countries playing each other. The top two then play again in the final. The next two meet again for the bronze. The Americans and the Soviets will be the favourites for both the men's and women's competitions. Yugoslavia are very strong in men's basketball, with Spain and Italy close contenders.

In the women's game, look out also for Bulgaria and the host nation, South Korea.

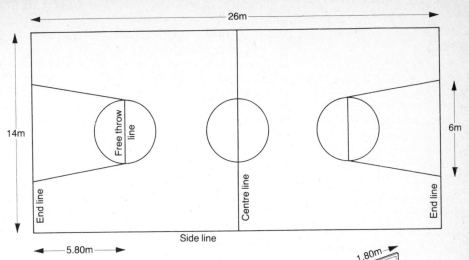

26m

14m

Free throw line

End line

Centre line

6m

End line

Side line

5.80m

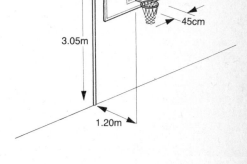

1.80m

45cm

3.05m

1.20m

THE GAME

The team can consist of twelve players but with only five allowed on court. The idea is simple – to put the ball in the opponent's basket. Doing so gains two points from open play and one point from a free throw.

Games last 40 minutes – two halves of 20 minutes. Teams can call 'time-outs' of one minute twice in each half for tactical reasons, to regroup or recover.

A player may take only two steps while holding the ball but any number while 'dribbling', i.e. bouncing the ball with one hand. Players may pass, throw, roll or bat the ball but not carry it or kick it. A team must shoot within thirty seconds of possession. This prevents a team from playing for time and they must move the ball from their back court to front court within ten seconds. Again this rule makes for a fast attacking game rather than a slow cautious one.

cipation in either the men's or women's competition in Seoul.

Entry is restricted to twelve men's and eight women's teams. All, except the gold medal winners in 1984 and the host nation, must qualify. The British standard falls well short of Olympic standard.

Britain's men have played only once, in the 1948 Games, when they were the host nation. They finished twentieth out of twenty-three, losing all their matches.

BRITISH RECORD

Britain has never won an Olympic medal in the sport and there will be no British parti-

THE STARS

There are many who support the notion that the United States' squad which included

Jerry West, Jerry Lucas, Oscar Robertson, Walt Bellamy, Terry Dischinger, and John Havlicek at the Rome Olympics in 1960 was the best ever assembled.

Sergey Belov of the Soviet Union won a gold and three bronze medals between 1968 and 1980. He was a member of the Soviet team that had the controversial one point victory over the Americans in 1972. He also had the honour of carrying the Soviet flag at the Moscow Olympics of 1980.

Iuliana Semenova of the Soviet Union, standing 7 ft 2 ins, dominated the women's competition at the 1976 and 1980 Games.

Not a lot of people know that

● The game might well have become 'Boxball'. Dr Naismith, the game's inventor, had asked the janitor at Springfield College to hang two boxes in order to play the game. The janitor, a Mr Stebbins, could not find any boxes but came up with two peach baskets instead. Hence the name.

● Until their defeat in 1972, the United States' men had never lost an Olympic match. They had a run of 63 consecutive victories producing seven Olympic titles.

● Several American Olympic high jumpers have become pro basketball players. Bill Russell, a member of the 1956 Olympic basketball team was, in the same year, ranked eleventh best high jumper in the world.

VENUE

Chamsil Gymnasium in Seoul Sports Complex. Capacity 20,000.

RESULTS

Men

	Gold	Silver	Bronze
1936	UNITED STATES	CANADA	MEXICO
1948	UNITED STATES	FRANCE	BRAZIL
1952	UNITED STATES	USSR	URUGUAY
1956	UNITED STATES	USSR	URUGUAY
1960	UNITED STATES	USSR	BRAZIL
1964	UNITED STATES	USSR	BRAZIL
1968	UNITED STATES	YUGOSLAVIA	USSR
1972	USSR	UNITED STATES	CUBA
1976	UNITED STATES	YUGOSLAVIA	USSR
1980	YUGOSLAVIA	ITALY	USSR
1984	UNITED STATES	SPAIN	YUGOSLAVIA

1988   Result on 30 September

Women

	Gold	Silver	Bronze
1976	USSR	UNITED STATES	BULGARIA
1980	USSR	BULGARIA	YUGOSLAVIA
1984	UNITED STATES	KOREA	CHINA

1988   Result on 29 September

Country placing in first eight/*Men*

	1936	1948	1952	1956	1960	1964	1968	1972	1976	1980	1984
ARGENTINA	–	–	4								
AUSTRALIA									8	8	7
BRAZIL		3	6	6	3	3	4	7	–	5	
BULGARIA	–	–	7	5							
CANADA	2								4		4
CHILE	–	6	5	8							
CUBA								3	7	6	
CZECHOSLOVAKIA	–	7	–	–	5	–	–	8	6	–	–
FRANCE	–	2	8	4							
ITALY	7	–	–	–	4	5	8	4	5	2	5
KOREA	–	8									
MEXICO	3	4					5				
PERU	8	–	–								
PHILIPPINES	5	–	–	7	–	–					
POLAND	4				7	6	6			7	
PUERTO RICO						4	–	6			
SPAIN								7		4	2
USA	1	1	1	1	1	1	1	2	1	–	1
URUGUAY	6	5	3	3	8	8	–	–	–	–	6
USSR	–	–	2	2	2	2	3	1	3	3	–
YUGOSLAVIA	–	–	–	–	6	7	2	5	2	1	3
WEST GERMANY	–	–	–	–	–	–	–	–	–	–	8

BOXING

Boxing is one of the truly international sports. Nearly every country in the world has active participants. The competition will make great viewing. The stars will come from the Soviet Union and the USA but medals will be won by countries all around the globe. Sadly, the Cubans, with the world's best squad of amateur boxers, have withdrawn from the Games.

Boxing was included in the ancient Olympics. Competitors wore leather thongs around their hands and as the games began to fall into disrepute, metal studs were added in order to inflict further injuries for the delight of a bloodthirsty audience.

The sport was not part of the first two modern games but was included for the first time in 1904 and has been part of every celebration since.

Nowadays, every care is taken to see that contestants take no undue risks with their health. Medical supervision is of paramount importance, as is good refereeing.

However, the sport is a direct contact one, and so attracts criticism, often based, however, on statistics gained from the sport's professional counterpart.

THE COMPETITION

Because of the American withdrawal in 1980 and the non-participation of the Eastern bloc and Cuba in 1984, you have to go back to the Montreal Games in 1976 for the last truly competitive Olympic boxing programme. (Even then many of the Africans were missing.) That was the Games that produced

Ray Leonard, and Michael and Leon Spinks.

In Los Angeles four years ago, the Americans won nine of the 12 available gold medals, but the Cubans in particular would have made vast inroads into that total had they been present.

The Cubans would have been favourites to gain most of the medals, had they not decided to boycott the Games.

The Americans have a knack of timing their preparations and team selections to perfection and will be a strength. The Soviets and East Germans will lead the way for Eastern Europe, while Italy, although losing so many stars to the professional ranks could be the most successful nation from Western Europe.

Britain suffers even more from talented amateurs turning professional, but under the excellent guidance of long-time coach Kevin Hickey will be as capable as ever of picking up a medal or two.

The African nations continue to improve but the South Koreans themselves have big ambitions in this sport. They produced the middleweight champion (Joon-Sup Shin) in Los Angeles and also claimed silver and bronze medals there. They have had victories over visiting USA teams in preparation and, in front of a home crowd, should improve on last time's medal tally.

WEIGHT DIVISIONS

There are twelve in all with the limits as follows:

	kg	lbs
Light-flyweight	48	106
Flyweight	51	112
Bantamweight	54	119
Featherweight	57	126
Lightweight	60	132
Light-welterweight	63.5	140
Welterweight	67	148
Light-middleweight	71	156
Middleweight	75	165
Light-heavyweight	81	178
Heavyweight	91	201
Super-heavyweight	91+	201+

BOUTS

These are over three rounds, three minutes each round with a one minute break between them.

A referee controls the bout, but has no say in the judging if the bout goes the distance. He has the authority to stop a bout if a contestant is being hurt badly or outclassed, or if a boxer persistently breaks the rules.

A boxer will be disqualified if he receives three public warnings (each warning is brought to the attention of the five ringside judges).

The warnings could be for hitting other than on the target area, not hitting with the knuckle part of the glove, or transgressing the rules in some other way.

The target area

This is the torso above the waist and the front and side of the head (but not the top or back of the head).

The knuckle part of the glove

Scoring punches must be delivered with this part (it is coloured white on the gloves used in Olympic competition). Punches delivered with an open glove are against the rules, do not score and are subject to warnings.

JUDGING

This has often proved to be a contentious issue at Olympic Games. There have been many accusations of bias or 'political' allegiances during past Games, but, in general terms, the vast majority of decisions are clear cut and obvious.

There are five ringside judges for each bout who sit well apart and have no communication during the bout. Each of the officials will be from a different country and differ from the nationality of the two contestants.

Each judge awards the boxer he considers to have won the round twenty points. His opponent will get proportionately fewer. A close round might therefore be scored 20–19 in favour of the better boxer. If the judge decides the same boxer has won all three rounds narrowly, that judge's final score will be 60–57. So if all five judges saw the bout identically, the score for the contest would read 60–57, 60–57, 60–57, 60–57, 60–57, producing a unanimous 5–0 win.

If a boxer wins a round more convincingly, a judge might score it 20–18 in his favour. A totally one-sided round would be scored 20–17. The loser of a round would not realistically score fewer points because if he was being that outclassed, the bout would surely be stopped.

Points are awarded for punches landed on the target area with the knuckle part of the glove. Punches which merely connect without weight of body or shoulder behind them do not score. Thus a very light hitter who may just be 'posing' would not catch the judge's eye even though he may technically be making contact with the target area of a harder-hitting opponent.

When it comes down to it, rounds are scored on an impression of which boxer has been the most dominant. Hence there is sometimes a disparity in the scoring (as there is in any sport where judging is involved). Bouts in major games are often won on a 3–2 majority verdict of the judges. Consider this

67

scoring which happened at a previous Olympics) 60–58, 60–57, 59–59*, 59–60, 59–60. Here the winner, on a majority decision, has actually scored fewer points, but the judge who scored it even at 59–59 gave preference (*) to that boxer. (A judge who scores the contest even must make that choice. There can be no draw in amateur boxing.) But you will agree that the defeated boxer here can consider himself very unlucky indeed, and an observer could come away wondering if all five officials had been watching the same bout.

Bear in mind that the outcome of the vast majority of bouts is clear cut and although it is the 'opinion' of the judges that counts, the experience on which those opinions are formed is usually very extensive and subject to continual review and scrutiny.

At the Los Angeles Olympics some of the judges' verdicts were altered by a review committee where they were thought to be incorrect. But, of course, who's to say the 'reviewers' are always right?

KNOCKDOWNS

Referees are more protective towards boxers in the amateur code than in the professional ring. When a boxer is knocked down, a mandatory 'eight' count is given, even though he may be back on his feet at the count of two. After the 'eight' count is reached, the referee will check on the welfare of the boxer before ordering the contest to continue. If the referee thinks the boxer is still groggy or unable to defend himself, then he will continue the count to ten and the bout will be over.

The referee can also, at his discretion, award a standing 'eight' count against a boxer if he is under severe pressure or has taken hard head punches without being knocked down.

If there is a knockdown in the last few seconds of a round, the count continues after the bell. It means a boxer cannot be 'saved'

by the bell. The exception to this is the last round of the final bout to decide gold and silver medals. At that stage any knockout must take place before the contest is into the last ten seconds. Later than that and the judges could decide that the man flat on his back has still won the gold medal. He may have dominated the bout before walking on to a late 'haymaker'.

Note: In amateur boxing no extra points are awarded for knockdowns. This sometimes confuses the uninformed onlooker who wonders how a boxer who has been on the canvas can possibly win the round.

EQUIPMENT

Gloves

Boxers up to the welterweight category (67 kg) use 227 g (8 oz) gloves. Boxers at light-middleweight (71 kg) and up use 284 g (10 oz) gloves.

Headguards

These are now mandatory at Olympic Games. You may recall that at the 1986 Commonwealth Games, boxers could choose whether or not to use them.

Vests

These help identification and reduce perspiration. They are obligatory.

Gumshields

These also *must* be used. If the gumshieid drops out during a bout, the contest will be stopped until it is washed and replaced.

Foul protector

Again, obligatory and consummate good sense. A low blow would otherwise end a bout on a foul and could be most damaging to a very sensitive area.

Bandages

Hand bandages of a length up to 2.5 m can be used as protection. Only one strip of adhesive maximum length of 7.6 cm may be used.

Substances

A mixture of 1/1000th adrenalin may be used to control bleeding. Grease and other substances are strictly forbidden.

CORNER-MEN

Two corner-men are allowed to assist each boxer. Only one may enter the ring between rounds. Coaching from ringside *during* the rounds is not allowed and sometimes results in a corner-man being removed.

THE DRAW

This is made after the boxers undergo medicals and weigh-in. It is always an anxious time for boxers and coaches. The 'draw' is all important. A contestant will hope to avoid a tough opponent in his first bout.

There is no seeding so the two favourites for the gold medal could meet straight away. It has happened in major games that a potential medallist has lost narrowly to his main rival for honours, who has then gone on through a relatively easy draw all the way to win gold.

Once the number of contestants in each weight division is known, the draw is completed and bouts allocated to each session. The twelve finals are held on the same night starting with the light-flyweights through to the super-heavyweights.

Weigh-ins

Boxers must weigh-in on the day of each bout. It is not sufficient simply to make the weight before the competition begins. Boxers therefore have to take care with their diet, except for the super-heavyweights of course, although they, too, wish to stay around their best 'fighting' weight.

BRITISH SUCCESSES

Britain's most successful games since the Second World War, were the Melbourne Olympics of 1956. Terry Spinks won the gold medal at flyweight (51 kg) and Dick McTaggart won the lightweight gold (60 kg). McTaggart of Scotland went on to gain a bronze medal at the following Olympics in Rome in 1960. He never turned professional. Spinks did and became British featherweight champion from 1960 to 1961.

Britain's last gold-medal winner was Chris Finnegan who won the middleweight (75 kg) title in Mexico in 1968. He went on to become a very popular British and European champion at light-heavyweight in the professional ring and also made a valiant challenge for the world title, only to lose to one of the all-time 'greats', Bob Foster of the United States.

The 1972 Games in Munich produced three British medals, all bronze. Ralph Evans at light-flyweight (48 kg), George Turpin at bantamweight (54 kg) and Alan Minter at light-middleweight (71 kg). Minter was on the receiving end of some dreadful judging in his semi-final, when the verdict went to the West German Dieter Kottysch on a 3–2 majority. All impartial observers felt Minter had won clearly. So, incidentally, did Kottysch and the two boxers have kept up a friendship ever since. Ironically, Minter is half-German. Of course, he went on to be undisputed middleweight champion of the world as a professional.

In each of the last three Olympic Games, Britain has claimed just one bronze medal on each occasion. Pat Cowdell at bantamweight (54 kg) in 1976, Tony Willis at light-welter (63.5 kg) in 1980 and superheavy (91 kg+) Bobby Wells in 1984. Wells earned his medal with just one victory. The entry for the super-heavyweights is always small, whereas competition in the lighter weights is far more fierce.

THE STARS

Teofilo Stevenson of Cuba has won three titles at heavyweight and would have been favourite again in Los Angeles had the Cubans taken part. Lásló Papp, a Hungarian, won the middleweight title in 1948 and the light-middleweight division in 1952 and '56. He went on to become the first professional champion from the Eastern bloc, at over 30 years of age, and has since been an integral part of Hungarian Olympic boxing.

The first man to retain an Olympic boxing title was British – middleweight Harry Mallin won in 1920 and 1924.

Six professional world heavyweight champions were previously Olympic gold medallists. The greatest of them all, Muhammad Ali, won the light-heavyweight title as the 18-year-old Cassius Clay in 1960. In 1952, the 17-year-old Floyd Patterson had been a mere middleweight while Joe Frazier in 1964 and George Forman in 1968 were heavyweight gold medallists.

The 1976 Olympics in Montreal produced the fantastic Spinks brothers. Michael at middleweight and Leon at light-heavy. Both won their divisions in brilliant style and both became professional champions; Michael at light-heavyweight and heavyweight and Leon at heavyweight.

Sugar Ray Leonard (without Sugar in those days) won the light-welterweight gold in 1976 and went on to be the most famous professional boxer outside the heavyweight division, winning world titles at welterweight, light-middleweight and in 1987 at middleweight when he returned to the ring after retirement to defeat the outstanding Marvin Hagler.

Ingemar Johansson of Sweden, another professional heavyweight champion, was runner-up in the Olympic heavyweight division in 1952. His silver medal was not awarded at the time for 'inactivity in the ring'. He did, however, receive it some thirty years later.

Not a lot of people know that

- John Douglas, who won the middleweight title for Britain in 1908, went on to captain England at cricket.
- The Val Barker Cup has been awarded to the best boxer at each Olympics since 1936. Cassius Clay was not the recipient in 1960 – that honour fell to the Italian welterweight Nino Benvenuti who went on to become a professional world champion. Ray Leonard failed to win it in 1976, it went then to another of the American team, lightweight Howard Davis, who subsequently failed in his bid to take the professional world title from Scotland's Jim Watt. Dick McTaggart, Britain's lightweight gold medallist of the 1956 Games received the award for that year – the only British boxer ever to do so.

In 1984, the winner was Paul Gonzales (USA) in the light-flyweight category (48 kg).
- The Korean, Dong-Kih Choh, unable to accept disqualification from a quarter-final flyweight bout at the 1964 Games, created a one-man sit-down strike in the middle of the ring. It lasted fifty-one minutes before he was persuaded to leave.
- At the 1948 Games, bantamweight Arnaldo Pares of Argentina had trouble making the weight. His seconds cut off his hair, gave him fierce rub downs, scraped the soles of his feet and eventually reduced him to tears. Tough on Señor Pares – the scales were found to be inaccurate.

VENUE

Chamsil Students' Gymnasium in Seoul. Seating capacity 8100.

RESULTS

Light flyweight (weight up to 48 kg 105.8 lb 7 st 7½ lb)

	Gold	Silver	Bronze
1968	Francisco Rodriguez (VEN) Dec 3–2	Yong-ju Jee (KOR)	Harlan Marbley (USA) Hubert Skrzypczak (POL)
1972	György Gedo (HUN) Dec 5–0	U Gil Kim (PRK)	Ralph Evans (GBR) Enrique Rodriguez (ESP)
1976	Jorge Hernandez (CUB) Dec 4–1	Byong Uk Li (PRK)	Orlando Maldonado (PUR) Payao Pooltarat (THA)
1980	Shamil Sabirov (URS) Dec 3–2	Hipolito Ramos (CUB)	Byong Uk Li (PRK) Ismail Moustafov (BUL)
1984	Paul Gonzales (USA) W/O	Salvatore Todisco (ITA)	Jose Bolivar (VEN) Keith Mwila (ZAM)
1988	First rounds on 17 September with final on 1 October		

Flyweight (weight up to 51 kg 112½ lb 8 st 0½ lb)

	Gold	Silver	Bronze
1904	George Finnegan (USA) RSC 1	Miles Burke (USA)	—
1920	Frank De Genaro (USA) Dec	Anders Petersen (DEN)	William Cuthbertson (GBR)
1924	Fidel LaBarba (USA) Dec	James McKenzie (GBR)	Raymond Fee (USA)
1928	Antal Kocsis (HUN) Dec	Armand Appel (FRA)	Carlo Cavagnoli (ITA)
1932	István Énekes (HUN) Dec	Francisco Cabanas (MEX)	Louis Salica (USA)
1936	Willi Kaiser (GER) Dec	Gavino Matta (ITA)	Louis Laurie (USA)
1948	Pascual Perez (ARG) Dec	Spartaco Bandinelli (ITA)	Soo-Ann Han (KOR)
1952	Nathan Brooks (USA) Dec 3–0	Edgar Basel (GER)	Anatoliy Bulakov (URS) William Toweel (SAF)
1956	Terence Spinks (GBR) Dec	Mircea Dobrescu (ROM)	John Caldwell (IRL) René Libeer (FRA)
1960	Gyula Török (HUN) Dec 3–2	Sergey Sivko (URS)	Abdelmoneim Elguindi (EGY) Kiyoshi Tanabe (JPN)
1964	Fernando Atzori (ITA) Dec 4–1	Arthur Olech (POL)	Robert Carmody (USA) Stanislav Sorokin (URS)
1968	Ricardo Delgado (MEX) Dec 5–0	Artur Olech (POL)	Servilio Oliveira (BRA) Leo Rwabwogo (UGA)
1972	Gheorghi Kostadinov (BUL) Dec 5–0	Leo Rwabwogo (UGA)	Leszek Blazynski (POL) Douglas Rodriguez (CUB)
1976	Leo Randolph (USA) Dec 3–2	Ramon Duvalon (CUB)	Leszek Blazynski (POL) David Torosyan (URS)
1980	Peter Lessov (BUL) RSC 2	Viktor Miroshnichenko (URS)	Hugh Russell (IRL) Janos Varadi (HUN)
1984	Steven McCrory (USA) Dec 4–1	Redzep Redzepovski (YUG)	Ibrahim Bilali (KEN) Eyup Can (TUR)
1988	First rounds on 17 September with final on 1 October		

Bantamweight (weight up to 54 kg 119 lb 8 st 7 lb)

	Gold	Silver	Bronze
1904	Oliver Kirk (USA) RSC 3	George Finnegan (USA)	—
1908	Henry Thomas (GBR) Dec	John Condon (GBR)	William Webb (GBR)
1920	Clarence Walker (SAF) Dec	Christopher Graham (CAN)	James McKenzie (GBR)
1924	William Smith (SAF) Dec	Salvatore Tripoli (USA)	Jean Ces (FRA)
1928	Vittorio Tamagnini (ITA) Dec	John Daley (USA)	Harry Isaacs (SAF)
1932	Horace Gwynne (CAN)	Hans Ziglarski (GER)	José Villanueva (PHI)
1936	Ulderico Sergo (ITA) Dec	Jack Wilson (USA)	Fidel Ortiz (MEX)
1948	Tibor Csik (HUN) Dec	Giovanni Zuddas (ITA)	Juan Venegas (PUR)
1952	Pentti Hämäläinen (FIN) Dec 2–1	John McNally (IRL)	Gennadiy Garbuzov (URS) Joon-Ho Kang (KOR)
1956	Wolfgang Behrendt (GER) Dec	Soon-Chun Song (KOR)	Claudio Barrientos (CHI) Frederick Gilroy (IRL)
1960	Oleg Grigoryev (URS) Dec	Primo Zamparini (ITA)	Brunoh Bendig (POL) Oliver Taylor (AUS)
1964	Takao Sakurai (JPN) RSC 2	Shin Cho Chung (KOR)	Juan Fabila Mendoza (MEX) Washington Rodriguez (URU)
1968	Valeriy Sokolov (URS) RSC 2	Eridadi Mukwanga (UGA)	Kyou-Chull Chang (KOR) Eiji Morioka (JPN)
1972	Orlando Martinez (CUB) Dec 5–0	Alfonso Zamora (MEX)	Ricardo Carreras (USA) George Turpin (GBR)
1976	Yong Jo Gu (PRK) Dec 5–0	Charles Mooney (USA)	Patrick Cowdell (GBR) Chulsoon Hwang (KOR)
1980	Juan Hernandez (CUB) Dec 5–0	Bernardo Pinango (VEN)	Dumitru Cipere (ROM) Michael Anthony (GUY)
1984	Maurizio Stecca (ITA) Dec 4–1	Hector Lopez (MEX)	Pedro Nolasco (DOM) Dale Walters (CAN)
1988	First rounds on 17 September with the finals on 1 October		

Featherweight (weight up to 57 kg 126 lb 9 st 0 lb)

	Gold	Silver	Bronze
1904	Oliver Kirk (USA) Dec	Frank Haller (USA)	Fred Gilmore (USA)
1908	Richard Gunn (GBR) Dec	C. W. Morris (GBR)	Hugh Roddin (GBR)
1920	Paul Fritsch (FRA) Dec	Jean Gachet (FRA)	Eduardo Garzena (ITA)
1924	John Fields (USA) Dec	Joseph Salas (USA)	Pedro Quartucci (ARG)
1928	Lambertus van Klaveren (HOL) Dec	Victor Peralta (ARG)	Harold Devine (USA)
1932	Carmelo Robledo (ARG) Dec	Josef Schleinkofer (GER)	Carl Carlsson (SWE)
1936	Oscar Casanovas (ARG) Dec	Charles Catterall (SAF)	Josef Miner (GER)
1948	Ernesto Formenti (ITA) Dec	Denis Shepherd (SAF)	Aleksey Antkiewicz (POL)
1952	Jan Zachara (TCH) Dec 2–1	Sergio Caprari (ITA)	Leonard Leisching (SAF) Joseph Ventaja (FRA)
1956	Vladimir Safronov (URS) Dec	Thomas Nicholls (GBR)	Pentti Hämäläinen (FIN) Henryk Niedzwiedzki (POL)

1960	Francesco Musso (ITA) Dec 4–1	Jerzy Adamski (POL)	Jorma Limmonen (FIN) William Meyers (SAF)
1964	Stanislav Stepashkin (URS) Dec 3–2	Antony Villaneuva (PHI)	Charles Brown (USA) Heinz Schultz (GER)
1968	Antonio Roldan (MEX) Disq 2	Albert Robinson (USA)	Ivan Michailov (BUL) Philip Waruinge (KEN)
1972	Boris Kuznetsov (URS) Dec 3–2	Philip Waruinge (KEN)	András Botos (HUN) Clemente Rojas (COL)
1976	Angel Herrera (CUB) KO 2	Richard Nowakowski (GDR)	Leszek Kosedowski (POL) Juan Paredes (MEX)
1980	Rudi Fink (GDR) Dec 4–1	Adolfo Horta (CUB)	Krzysztof Kosedowski (POL) Viktor Rybakov (URS)
1984	Meldrick Taylor (USA) Dec 5–0	Peter Konyegwachie (NGR)	Turgut Aykac (TUR) Omar Catari Peraza (VEN)
1988	First round on 17 September with the final on 1 October		

Lightweight (weight up to 60 kg 132 lb 9 st 6 lb)

	Gold	*Silver*	*Bronze*
1904	Harry Spanger (USA) Dec	James Eagan (USA)	Russell Van Horn (USA)
1908	Frederick Grace (GBR) Dec	Frederick Spiller (GBR)	H. H. Johnson (GBR)
1920	Samuel Mosberg (USA) Dec	Gotfred Johansen (DEN)	Clarence Newton (CAN)
1924	Hans Nielsen (DEN) Dec	Alfredo Coppello (ARG)	Frederick Boylstein (USA)
1928	Carl Orlandi (ITA) Dec	Stephen Halaiko (USA)	Gunnar Berggren (SWE)
1932	Lawrence Stevens (SAF) Dec	Thure Ahlqvist (SWE)	Nathan Bor (USA)
1936	Imre Harangi (HUN) Dec	Nikolai Stepulov (EST)	Erik Agren (SWE)
1948	Gerald Dreyer (SAF) Dec	Joseph Vissers (BEL)	Svend Wad (DEN)
1952	Aureliano Bolognesi (ITA) Dec 2–1	Aleksey Antkiewicz (POL)	Gheorghe Fiat (ROM) Erkki Pakkanen (FIN)
1956	Richard McTaggart (GBR) Dec	Harry Kurschat (GER)	Anthony Byrne (IRL) Anatoliy Lagetko (URS)
1960	Kazimierz Pazdzior (POL) Dec 4–1	Sandro Lopopoli (ITA)	Abel Laudonio (ARG) Richard McTaggart (GBR)
1964	Józef Grudzien (POL) Dec	Vellikton Barannikov (URS)	Ronald Harris (USA) James McCourt (IRL)
1968	Ronald Harris (USA) Dec 5–0	Józef Grudzien (POL)	Calistrat Cutov (ROM) Zvonimir Vujin (YUG)
1972	Jan Szczepanski (POL) Dec 5–0	László Orban (HUN)	Samuel Mbugua (KEN) Alfonso Perez (COL)
1976	Howard Davis (USA) Dec 5–0	Simion Cutov (ROM)	Ace Rusevski (YUG) Vasiliy Solomin (URS)
1980	Angel Herrera (CUB) RSC 3	Viktor Demianenko (URS)	Kazimierz Adach (POL) Richard Nowakowski (GDR)
1984	Pernell Whitaker (USA) Ret 2	Luis Ortiz (PUR)	Chil-Sung Chun (KOR) Martin Ebanga (CMR)
1988	First round on 17 September with final on 1 October		

Light-welterweight (weight up to 63.5 kg 140 lb 10 st)

	Gold	Silver	Bronze
1952	Charles Adkins (USA) Dec 2–1	Viktor Mednov (URS)	Erkki Mallenius (FIN) Bruno Visintin (ITA)
1956	Vladimir Yengibaryan (URS) Dec	Franco Nenci (ITA)	Constantin Dumitrescu (ROM) Henry Loubscher (SAF)
1960	Bohumil Nemecek (TCH) Dec 5–0	Clement Quartey (GHA)	Quincy Daniels (USA) Marian Kasprzyk (POL)
1964	Jerzy Kulej (POL) Dec 5–0	Yvgeniy Frolov (URS)	Eddie Blay (GHA) Habib Galhia (TUN)
1968	Jerzy Kulej (POL) Dec 3–2	Enrique Regueiferos (CUB)	Arto Nilsson (FIN) James Wallington (USA)
1972	Ray Seales (USA) Dec 3–2	Anghel Anghelov (BUL)	Issaka Daborg (NIG) Zvonimir Vujin (YUG)
1976	Ray Leonard (USA) Dec 5–0	Andres Aldama (CUB)	Vladimir Kolev (BUL) Kazimierz Szczerba (POL)
1980	Patrizio Oliva (ITA) Dec 4–1	Serik Konakbayev (URS)	Jose Aguilar (CUB) Anthony Willis (GBR)
1984	Jerry Page (USA) Dec 5–0	Dhawee Umponmaha (THA)	Mircea Fulger (ROM) Mirko Puzovic (YUG)

1988   First round on 17 September with the final on 1 October

Welterweight (weight up to 67 kg 148 lb or 10 st 8 lb)

	Gold	Silver	Bronze
1904	Albert Young (USA) Dec	Harry Spanger (USA)	James Eagan (USA) Joseph Lydon (USA)
1920	Albert Schneider (CAN) Dec	Alexander Ireland (GBR)	Frederick Colberg (USA)
1924	Jean Delarge (BEL) Dec	Héctor Mendez (ARG)	Douglas Lewis (CAN)
1928	Edward Morgan (NZL) Dec	Raul Landini (ARG)	Raymond Smillie (CAN)
1932	Edward Flynn (USA) Dec	Erich Campe (GER)	Bruno Ahlberg (FIN)
1936	Sten Suvio (FIN) Dec	Michael Murach (GER)	Gerhard Petersen (DEN)
1948	Julius Torma (TCH) Dec	Horace Herring (USA)	Alessandro D'Ottavio (ITA)
1952	Zygmunt Chychla (POL) Dec 3–0	Sergey Schtscherbakov (URS)	Gunther Heidemann (GER) Victor Jörgensen (DEN)
1956	Nicholae Linca (ROM) Dec 3–2	Frederick Tiedt (IRL)	Nicholas Gargano (GBR) Kevin Hogarth (AUS)
1960	Giovanni Benvenuti (ITA) Dec 4–1	Yuriy Radonyak (URS)	Leszek Drogosz (POL) James Lloyd (GBR)
1964	Marian Kasprzyk (POL) Dec 4–1	Ritschardas Tamulis (URS)	Silvano Bertini (ITA) Pertti Purhonen (FIN)
1968	Manfred Wolke (GDR) Dec 4–1	Joseph Bessala (CMR)	Mario Guilloti (ARG) Vladimir Mussalimov (URS)
1972	Emilio Correa (CUB) Dec 5–0	Janos Kajdi (HUN)	Dick Murunga (KEN) Jesse Valdez (USA)
1976	Jochen Bachfeld (GDR) Dec 3–2	Pedro Gamarro (VEN)	Reinhard Skricek (FRG) Victor Zilberman (ROM)

1980	Andres Aldama (CUB) Dec 4–1	John Mugabi (UGA)	Karl-Heinz Kruger (GDR) Kazimierz Szczerba (POL)
1984	Mark Breland (USA) Dec 5–0	Young-Su An (KOR)	Luciano Bruno (ITA) Joni Nyman (FIN)

1988   First round on 17 September with the final on 1 October

Light-middleweight (weight up to 71 kg, 157 lb or 11 st 3 lb)

	Gold	*Silver*	*Bronze*
1952	László Papp (HUN) Dec 3–0	Theunis van Schalkwyk (SAF)	Eladio Herrera (ARG) Boris Tishin (URS)
1956	László Papp (HUN) Dec	José Torres (USA)	John McCormack (GBR) Zbigniew Pietrzykowski (POL)
1960	Wilbert McClure (USA) Dec 4–1	Carmelo Bossi (ITA)	William Fisher (GBR) Boris Lagutin (URS)
1964	Boris Lagutin (URS) Dec 4–1	Josef Gonzales (FRA)	Jozef Grzesiak (POL) Nojim Maiyegun (NGR)
1968	Boris Lagutin (URS) Dec 5–0	Rolando Garbey (CUB)	John Baldwin (USA) Günther Meier (FRG)
1972	Dieter Kottysch (FRG) Dec 3–2	Wieslaw Rudkowski (POL)	Alan Minter (GBR) Peter Tiepold (GDR)
1976	Jerzy Rybicki (POL) Dec 5–0	Tadija Kacar (YUG)	Rolando Garbey (CUB) Viktor Savchenko (URS)
1980	Armando Martinez (CUB) Dec 4–1	Aleksandr Koshkin (URS)	Jan Franek (TCH) Detlef Kastner (GDR)
1984	Frank Tate (USA) Dec 5–0	Shawn O'Sullivan (CAN)	Christophe Tiozzo (FRA) Manfred Zielonka (FRG)

1988   First round on 17 September with the final on 1 October

Middleweight (weight up to 75 kg, 165 lb or 11 st 11 lb)

	Gold	*Silver*	*Bronze*
1904	Charles Mayer (USA) RSC 3	Benjamin Spradley (USA)	—
1908	John Douglas (GBR) Dec	Reginald Baker (AUS/NZL)	W. Philo (GBR)
1920	Harry Mallin (GBR) Dec	Georges Prud'homme (CAN)	Moe Herscovitch (CAN)
1924	Harry Mallin (GBR) Dec	John Elliott (GBR)	Joseph Beecken (BEL)
1928	Piero Toscani (ITA) Dec	Jan Hermánek (TCH)	Léonard Steyaert (BEL)
1932	Carmen Barth (USA) Dec	Amado Azar (ARG)	Ernest Pierce (SAF)
1936	Jean Despeaux (FRA) Dec	Henry Tiller (NOR)	Raúl Villareal (ARG)
1948	László Papp (HUN) Dec	John Wright (GBR)	Ivano Fontana (ITA)
1952	Floyd Patterson (USA) KO 1	Vasile Tito (ROM)	Boris Nikolov (BUL) Stig Sjolin (SWE)
1956	Gennadiy Schatkov (URS) KO 1	Ramón Tapia (CHI)	Gilbert Chapron (FRA) Victor Zalazar (ARG)
1960	Edward Crook (USA) Dec 3–2	Tadeusz Walasek (POL)	Evgeniy Feofanov (URS) Ion Monea (ROM)

1964	Valeriy Popentschenko (URS) RSC 1	Emil Schultz (GER)	Franco Valle (ITA) Tadeusz Walasek (POL)
1968	Christopher Finnegan (GBR) Dec 3–2	Aleksey Kisselyov (URS)	Alfred Jones (USA) Agustin Zaragoza (MEX)
1972	Vyatcheslav Lemechev (URS) KO 1	Reima Virtanen (FIN)	Prince Amartey (GHA) Marvin Johnson (USA)
1976	Michael Spinks (USA) RSC 3	Rufat Riskiev (URS)	Luis Martinez (CUB) Alec Nastac (ROM)
1980	Jose Gomez (CUB) Dec 4–1	Viktor Savchenko (URS)	Jerzy Rybicki (POL) Valentin Silaghi (ROM)
1984	Joon-Sup Shin (KOR) Dec 3–2	Virgil Hill (USA)	Aristides Gonzalez (PUR) Mohamed Zaoui (ALG)
1988	First round on 17 September with the final on 1 October		

Light-heavyweight (weight up to 81 kg, 178½ lb or 12 st 10½ lb)

	Gold	*Silver*	*Bronze*
1920	Edward Eagan (USA) Dec	Sverre Sörsdal (NOR)	H. Franks (GBR)
1924	Harry Mitchell (GBR) Dec	Thyge Petersen (DEN)	Sverre Sörsdal (NOR)
1928	Victor Avendano (ARG) Dec	Ernst Pistulla (GER)	Karel Miljon (HOL)
1932	David Carstens (SAF) Dec	Gino Rossi (ITA)	Peter Jörgensen (DEN)
1936	Roger Michelot (FRA) Dec	Richard Vogt (GER)	Francisco Risiglione (ARG)
1948	George Hunter (SAF) Dec	Donald Scott (GBR)	Maurio Cia (ARG)
1952	Norvel Lee (USA) Dec 3–0	Antonio Pacenza (ARG)	Anotiliy Perov (URS) Harri Siljander (FIN)
1956	James Boyd (USA) Dec	Gheorghe Negrea (ROM)	Carlos Lucas (CHI) Romualdas Murauskas (URS)
1960	Cassius Clay (USA) Dec 5–0	Zbigniew Pietrzykowski (POL)	Anthony Madigan (AUS) Giulio Saraudi (ITA)
1964	Cosimo Pinto (ITA) Dec 3–2	Aleksey Kisselyov (URS)	Aleksandr Nikolov (BUL) Zbigniew Pietrzykowski (POL)
1968	Dan Poznyak (URS) Def	Ion Monea (ROM)	Stanislav Dragan (POL) Georgy Stankov (BUL)
1972	Mate Parlov (YUG) RSC 2	Gilberto Carrillo (CUB)	Janusz Gortat (POL) Isaac Ikhouria (NGR)
1976	Leon Spinks (USA) RSC 3	Sixto Soria (CUB)	Costica Danifoiu (ROM) Janusz Gortat (POL)
1980	Slobodan Kacar (YUG) Dec 4–1	Pavel Skrzecz (POL)	Herbert Bauch (GDR) Ricardo Rojas (CUB)
1984	Anton Josipovic (YUG) WO	Kevin Barry (NZL)	Evander Holyfield (USA) Mustapha Moussa (ALG)
1988	First round on 17 September with the final on 1 October		

Heavyweight (weight up to 91 kg, 200½ lb or 14 st 4½ lb)

Note that from 1952 until 1980 the weight for this division was over 81 kg and there was no Super-heavyweight division

	Gold	*Silver*	*Bronze*
1904	Samuel Berger (USA) Dec	Charles Mayer (USA)	William Michaels (USA)
1908	Albert Oldham (GBR) KO 1	S. C. H. Evans (GBR)	Frederick Parks (GBR)
1920	Ronald Rawson (GBR) Dec	Sören Petersen (DEN)	Xavier Eluère (FRA)
1924	Otto von Porat (NOR) Dec	Sören Petersen (DEN)	Alfredo Porzio (ARG)
1928	Arturo Rodriguez Jurado (ARG) RSC 1	Nils Ramm (SWE)	Jacob Michaelsen (DEN)
1932	Santiago Lovell (ARG) Dec	Luigi Rovati (ITA)	Frederick Feary (USA)
1936	Herbert Runge (GER) Dec	Guillermo Lovell (ARG)	Erling Nilsen (NOR)
1948	Rafael Iglesias (ARG) KO 2	Gunnar Nilsson (SWE)	John Arthur (SAF)
1952	Hayes Edward Sanders (USA) Disq 2	Ingemar Johansson (SWE)★	Ilkka Koski (FIN) Andries Nieman (SAF)
1956	Peter Rademacher (USA) RSC 1	Lev Mukhin (URS)	Daniel Bekker (SAF) Giacomo Bozzano (ITA)
1960	Franco de Piccoli (ITA) KO 1	Daniel Bekker (SAF)	Josef Nemec (TCH) Günter Siegmund (GER)
1964	Joe Frazier (USA) Dec 3–2	Hans Huber (GER)	Guiseppe Ros (ITA) Vadim Yemelyanov (URS)
1968	George Foreman (USA) RSC 2	Ionas Tschepulis (URS)	Giorgio Bambini (ITA) Joaquin Rocha (MEX)
1972	Teofilo Stevenson (CUB) Def	Ion Alexe (ROM)	Peter Hussing (FRG) Hasse Thomsen (SWE)
1976	Teofilio Stevenson (CUB) KO 3	Mircea Simon (ROM)	Clarence Hill (BER) Johnny Tate (USA)
1980	Teofilio Stevenson (CUB) Dec 4–1	Pyotr Zayev (URS)	Jurgen Fanghanel (GDR) Istvan Levai (HUN)
1984	Henry Tillman (USA) Dec 5–0	Willie Dewit (CAN)	Angelo Musone (ITA) Arnold Vanderlijde (HOL)

1988 First round on 17 September with the final on 1 October

★ Originally Johansson was disqualified and not awarded his silver medal for 'not giving of his best', but he was reinstated in 1982.

Super-heavyweight (weight over 91 kg, 200½ lb or 14 st 4½ lb)

	Gold	*Silver*	*Bronze*
1984	Tyrell Biggs (USA) Dec 4–1	Francesco Damiani (ITA)	Salihu Azis (YUG) Robert Wells (GBR)

1988 First round on 17 September with the final on 1 October

CANOEING

This sport was introduced to the Olympic Games in Berlin in 1936 for men, and women took part for the first time in London in 1948.

The craft are derived from the hunting kayak of the Eskimo and the canoe of the North American Indians.

Rules for racing go back to 1880 in the United States. The first international body dates from 1924.

THE EVENTS

Two types of canoe are raced:

Kayaks: These are the craft, familiar in Britain, where the canoeist paddles from a sitting position. He uses a double-bladed paddle.

Canadian: These are propelled from a kneeling position and a single-bladed paddle is used.

Thus races are designated either K for kayak races or C for Canadian Canoe races.

So K1 is a kayak event for a single canoeist, K2 for two canoeists, and K4 for four in the boat. Similarly for Canadian Canoe, the designations are C1 and C2 (there are no four-men Canadian Canoes in Olympic competition).

The races then are as follows with nine Olympic titles in the men's competition in Seoul and three for women.

Men

K1	500 metres
K2	500 metres
K1	1000 metres
K2	1000 metres
K4	1000 metres
C1	500 metres
C2	500 metres
C1	1000 metres
C2	1000 metres

Women

K1	500 metres
K2	500 metres
K4	500 metres

You will have noticed, therefore, that women do not compete in the Canadian Canoe and, further, do not compete at a distance over 500 metres.

RULES

As in rowing, heats take place with qualification for further progression depending on overall number of entries. Losers in heats will have another chance to qualify through the repechage system.

Canoes have a maximum length, plus a maximum and minimum width.

There must be a minimum of one hour between rounds.

All types of construction are permitted provided that the canoes conform to size and shape limitations.

Any competitor or crew making two false starts is disqualified.

COMPETITION

Eastern Europe has dominated in recent years with the exception of the Los Angeles games when of course (apart from Rumania) they did not compete.

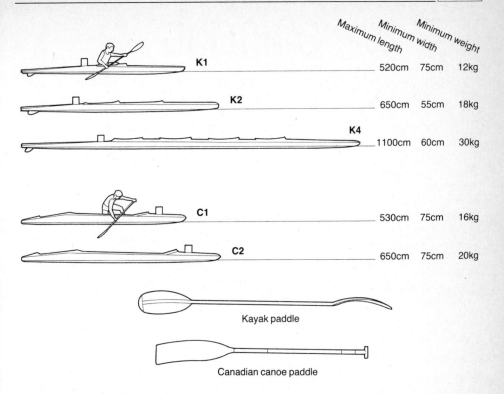

	Maximum length	Minimum width	Minimum weight
K1	520cm	75cm	12kg
K2	650cm	55cm	18kg
K4	1100cm	60cm	30kg
C1	530cm	75cm	16kg
C2	650cm	75cm	20kg

Kayak paddle

Canadian canoe paddle

On that occasion New Zealand took the opportunity to win four of the nine available gold medals in the men's events. The Swedes took two of the three available gold medals in the women's events.

With the Eastern Bloc back in business in Seoul, expect most of the medals to go once again in that direction, with the Soviets and East Germans strongest.

THE STARS

Ian Ferguson of New Zealand won three gold medals in Los Angeles to equal the record of Vladimir Parfenovich of the Soviet Union in 1980.

The most successful of all time is Gert Fredriksson of Sweden who won six golds, one silver and one bronze between 1948 and 1960.

Best performance among the women is by Ludmila Pinayeva (Khvedosyuk) who won three gold medals and one bronze between 1964 and 1972.

THE BRITISH

Not much to report. Unlike their rowing colleagues, British canoeists have never won any kind of Olympic medal. Best placing to date is fifth. Do not anticipate any improvement.

Not a lot of people know that

● At the 1972 Games in Munich 'wild-water slalom' events were included for the only time. Britain failed to gain any success. However, if wild-water events had been included for the Seoul Games, Britain would have had a good chance of medals. Liz Sharman is the reigning women's world slalom champion. Richard Fox was men's world champion three times in the eighties.

- Steering rudders are permitted on kayaks, but not on Canadian canoes.
- Coxes play no part in this sport, unlike rowing.
- Gert Fredriksson of Sweden, the leading medal winner in the sport was over 40 when he won his last gold in 1960.
- Surprisingly, Canada has only ever won three gold medals in the sports. They have never won a medal in Canadian canoeing.
- There used to be an event called 'folding' kayak singles and pairs. Competitors were obliged to get out of their craft, fold it up and carry it for a while before returning to the water.
- While races are now over 500 or 1000 metres, until 1956 there was also a marathon event over 10,000 metres, for both K2 and C2.
- A good K4 squad would give an ordinary rowing eight a very close race over 1000 metres.

VENUE

Han River Regatta Course. 10 km from Olympic Village. Capacity 25,000 spectators.

RESULTS

500 metres kayak singles (K1)/*Men*

	Gold	Silver	Bronze
1976	Vasile Diba (ROM) 1:46.41	Zoltan Szytanity (HUN) 1:46.95	Rüdiger Helm (GDR) 1:48.30
1980	Vladimir Parfenovich (URS) 1:43.43	John Sumegi (AUS) 1:44.12	Vasile Diba (ROM) 1:44.90
1984	Ian Ferguson (NZL) 1:47.84	Lars-Erik Moberg (SWE) 1:48.18	Bernard Bregeon (FRA) 1:48.41

4. Vasile Diba (ROM) 5. David Upson (GBR) 6. Daniele Scarpa (ITA)
7. Guillermo DelRiego (ESP) 8. Reiner Scholl (FRG)

1988	Final on 30 September		

1000 metres kayak singles (K1)/*Men*

	Gold	Silver	Bronze
1936	Gregor Hradetzky (AUT) 4:22.9	Helmut Cämmerer (GER) 4:25.6	Jacob Kraaier (HOL) 4:35.1
1948	Gert Fredriksson (SWE) 4:33.2	Johan Kobberup (DEN) 4:39.9	Henri Eberhardt (FRA) 4:41.4
1952	Gert Fredriksson (SWE) 4:07.9	Thorvald Strömberg (FIN) 4:09.7	Louis Gantois (FRA) 4:20.1
1956	Gert Fredriksson (SWE) 4:12.8	Igor Pissaryev (URS) 4:15.3	Lajos Kiss (HUN) 4:16.2
1960	Erik Hansen (DEN) 3:53.00	Imre Szöllösi (HUN) 3:54.02	Gert Fredriksson (SWE) 3:55.89
1964	Rolf Peterson (SWE) 3:57.13	Mihály Hesz (HUN) 3:57.28	Aurel Vernescu (ROM) 4:00.77
1968	Mihály Hesz (HUN) 4:02.63	Aleksandr Shaparenko (URS) 4:03.58	Erik Hansen (DEN) 4:04.39

1972	Aleksandr Shaparenko (URS) 3:48.06	Rolf Peterson (SWE) 3:48.35	Geza Csapo (HUN) 3:49.38
1976	Rüdiger Helm (GDR) 3:48.20	Geza Csapo (HUN) 3:48.84	Vasile Diba (ROM) 3:49.65
1980	Rüdiger Helm (GDR) 3:48.77	Alain Lebas (FRA) 3:50.20	Ion Birladeanu (ROM) 3:50.49
1984	Alan Thompson (NZL) 3:45.73	Milan Janic (YUG) 3:46.88	Greg Barton (USA) 3:47.38

4. Kalle Sundqvist (SWE) 5. Peter Genders (AUS) 6. Philippe Boccara (FRA)
7. Vasile Diba (ROM) 8. Stephen Jackson (GBR) 9. Pedro Alegre (ESP)

1988 Final on 1 October

500 metres kayak pairs (K2)/*Men*

	Gold	*Silver*	*Bronze*
1976	EAST GERMANY 1:35.87 Joachim Mattern Bernd Olbricht	USSR 1:36.81 Sergey Nagorny Vladimir Romanovski	ROMANIA 1:37.43 Larion Serghei Policarp Malihin
1980	USSR 1:32.38 Vladimir Parfenovich Sergey Chukhrai	SPAIN 1:33.65 Herminio Menendez Guillermo Del Reigo	EAST GERMANY 1:34.00 Bernd Olbricht Rüdiger Helm
1984	NEW ZEALAND 1:34.21 Ian Ferguson Paul MacDonald	SWEDEN 1:35.26 Per-Inge Bengtsson Lars-Erik Moberg	CANADA 1:35.41 Hugh Fisher Alwyn Morris

4. Italy 5. Romania 6. France 7. West Germany 8. Great Britain
9. Austria

1988 Final on 30 September

1000 metres kayak pairs (K2)/*Men*

	Gold	*Silver*	*Bronze*
1936	AUSTRIA 4:03.8 Adolf Kainz Alfons Dorfner	GERMANY 4:08.9 Ewald Tilker Fritz Bondroit	NETHERLANDS 4:12.2 Nicolaas Tates Willem van der Kroft
1948	SWEDEN 4:07.3 Hans Berglund Lennart Klingström	DENMARK 4:07.5 Ejvind Hansen Bernhard Jensen	FINLAND 4:08.7 Thor Axelsson Nils Björklöf
1952	FINLAND 3:51.1 Kurt Wires Yrjö Hietanen	SWEDEN 3:51.1 Lars Glassér Ingemar Hedberg	AUSTRIA 3:51.4 Max Raub Herbert Wiedermann
1956	GERMANY 3:49.6 Michel Scheuer Meinrad Miltenberger	USSR 3:51.4 Mikhail Kaaleste Anatoliy Demitkov	AUSTRIA 3:55.8 Max Raub Herbert Wiedermann
1960	SWEDEN 3:34.73 Gert Fredriksson Sven-Olov Sjödelius	HUNGARY 3:34.91 András Szente György Mészáros	POLAND 3:37.34 Stefan Kaplaniak Wladyslaw Zielinski
1964	SWEDEN 3:38.54 Sven-Olov Sjödelius Nils Utterberg	NETHERLANDS 3:39.30 Antonius Geurts Paul Hoekstra	GERMANY 3:40.69 Heinz Buker Holger Zander

1968	USSR 3:37.54	HUNGARY 3:38.44	AUSTRIA 3:40.71
	Aleksandr Shaparenko	Csaba Giczi	Gerhard Seibold
	Vladimir Morozov	István Timár	Gunther Pfaff
1972	USSR 3:31.23	HUNGARY 3:32.00	POLAND 3:33.83
	Nikolai Gorbachev	Jozsef Deme	Wladyslaw Szuszkiewicz
	Viktor Kratassyuk	Janos Ratkai	Rafal Piszcz
1976	USSR 3:29.01	EAST GERMANY 3:29.33	HUNGARY 3:30.36
	Sergey Nagorny	Joachim Mattern	Zoltan Bako
	Vladimir Romanovski	Bernd Olbricht	István Szabó
1980	USSR 3:26.72	HUNGARY 3:28.49	SPAIN 3:28.66
	Vladimir Parfenovich	István Szabó	Luis Ramos-Misione
	Sergey Chukhrai	István Joós	Herminio Menendez
1984	CANADA 3:24.22	FRANCE 3:25.97	AUSTRALIA 3:26.80
	Hugh Fisher	Bernard Bregeon	Barry Kelly
	Alwyn Morris	Patrick Lefoulon	Grant Kenny

4. United States 5. West Germany 6. Italy 7. Spain 8. Sweden 9. Belgium

1988   Final on 1 October

1000 metres kayak fours (K4)/*Men*

	Gold	*Silver*	*Bronze*
1964	USSR 3:14.67	GERMANY 3:15.39	ROMANIA 3:15.51
1968	NORWAY 3:14.38	ROMANIA 3:14.81	HUNGARY 3:15.10
1972	USSR 3:14.02	ROMANIA 3:15.07	NORWAY 3:15.27
1976	USSR 3:08.69	SPAIN 3:08.95	EAST GERMANY 3:10.76
1980	EAST GERMANY 3:13.76	ROMANIA 3:15.35	BULGARIA 3:15.46
1984	NEW ZEALAND 3:02.28	SWEDEN 3:02.81	FRANCE 3:03.94
	Ian Ferguson	Per-Inge Bengtsson	François Barouh
	Grant Bramwell	Tommy Karls	Philippe Boccara
	Paul MacDonald	Lars-Erik Moberg	Pascal Boucherit
	Alan Thompson	Thomas Ohlsson	Didier Vavasseur

4. Romania 5. Great Britain 6. Spain 7. Australia 8. West Germany
9. Canada

1988   Final on 1 October

500 metres Canadian singles (C1)/*Men*

	Gold	*Silver*	*Bronze*
1976	Aleksandr Rogov (URS) 1:59.23	John Wood (CAN) 1:59.58	Martija Ljubek (YUG) 1:59.60
1980	Sergey Postrekhin (URS) 1:53.37	Lubomir Lubenov (BUL) 1:53.49	Olaf Heukrodt (GDR) 1:54.38
1984	Larry Cain (USA) 1:57.01	Henning Jakobsen (DEN) 1:58.45	Costica Olaru (ROM) 1:59.86

4. Philippe Renaud (FRA) 5. Timo Gronlund (FIN) 6. Kiyoto Inoue (JPN)
7. Hartmut Faust (FRG) 8. Robert Rozsnski (NOR) 9. Francisco Lopez (ESP)

1988   Final on 30 September

1000 metres Canadian singles (C1)/*Men*

	Gold	*Silver*	*Bronze*
1936	Francis Amyot (CAN) 5:32.1	Bohuslav Karlik (TCH) 5:36.9	Erich Koschik (GER) 5:39.0
1948	Josef Holeček (TCH) 5:42.0	Douglas Bennett (CAN) 5:53.3	Robert Boutigny (FRA) 5:55.9
1952	Josef Holeček (TCH) 4:56.3	János Parti (HUN) 5:03.6	Olavi Ojanperä (FIN) 5:08.5
1956	Leon Rotman (ROM) 5:05.3	István Hernek (HUN) 5:06.2	Gennadiy Bukharin (URS) 5:12.7
1960	János Parti (HUN) 4:33.93	Aleksandr Silayev (URS) 4:34.41	Leon Rotman (ROM) 4:35.87
1964	Jürgen Eschert (GER) 4:35.14	Andrei Igorov (ROM) 4:37.89	Yevgeny Penyayev (URS) 4:38.31
1968	Tibor Tatai (HUN) 4:36.14	Detlef Lewe (FRG) 4:38.31	Vitaly Galkov (URS) 4:40.42
1972	Ivan Patzaichin (ROM) 4:08.94	Tamas Wichmann (HUN) 4:12.42	Detlef Lewe (FRG) 4:13.63
1976	Matija Ljubek (YUG) 4:09.51	Vasiliy Urchenko (URS) 4:12.57	Tamas Wichmann (HUN) 4:14.11
1980	Lubomir Lubenov (BUL) 4:12.38	Sergey Postrekhin (URS) 4:13.53	Eckhard Leue (GDR) 4:15.02
1984	Ulrich Eicke (FRG) 4:06.32	Larry Cain (CAN) 4:08.67	Henning Jakobsen (DEN) 4:09.51

4. Timo Gronlund (FIN) 5. Costica Olaru (ROM) 6. Stephen Train (GBR)
7. Bruce Merritt (USA) 8. Kiyoto Inoue (JPN) 9. Francisco Lopez (ESP)

1988 Final on 1 October

500 metres Canadian pairs (C2)/*Men*

	Gold	*Silver*	*Bronze*
1976	USSR 1:45.81 Sergey Petrenko Aleksandr Vinogradov	POLAND 1:47.77 Jerzy Opara Andrzej Gronowicz	HUNGARY 1:48.35 Tamas Buday Oszkar Frey
1980	HUNGARY 1:43.39 Lászlo Foltán István Vaskuti	ROMANIA 1:44.12 Ivan Patzaichin Petre Capusta	BULGARIA 1:44.83 Borislaw Ananiev Nikolai Ilkov
1984	YUGOSLAVIA 1:43.67 Matija Ljubek Mirko Nisovic	ROMANIA 1:45.68 Ivan Patzaichin Toma Simionov	SPAIN 1:47.71 Enrique Miguez Narciso Suarez

4. France 5. Canada 6. West Germany 7. Great Britain 8. Japan
9. United States

1988 Final on 30 September

1000 metres Canadian pairs (C2)/*Men*

	Gold	*Silver*	*Bronze*
1936	CZECHOSLOVAKIA 4:50.1 Vladimir Syrovátka Jan-Felix Brzák	AUSTRIA 4:53.8 Rupert Weinstabl Karl Proisl	CANADA 4:56.7 Frank Saker Harvey Charters
1948	CZECHOSLOVAKIA 5:07.1 Jan-Felix Brzák Bohumil Kudrna	UNITED STATES 5:08.2 Stephen Lysak Stephan Macknowski	FRANCE 5:15.2 Georges Dransart Georges Gandil
1952	DENMARK 4:38.3 Bent Peder Rasch Finn Haunstoft	CZECHOSLOVAKIA 4:42.9 Jan-Felix Brzák Bohumil Kudrna	GERMANY 4:48.3 Egon Drews Wilfried Soltau
1956	ROMANIA 4:47.4 Alexe Dumitru Simion Ismailciuc	USSR 4:48.6 Pavel Kharin Gratsian Botev	HUNGARY 4:54.3 Károly Wieland Ferenc Mohácsi
1960	USSR 4:17.94 Leonid Geyshtor Sergey Makarenko	ITALY 4:20.77 Aldo Dezi Francesco La Macchia	HUNGARY 4:20.89 Imre Farkas András Törö
1964	USSR 4:04.64 Andrey Khimich Stepan Oschepkov	FRANCE 4:06.52 Jean Boudehen Michel Chapuis	DENMARK 4:07.48 Peer N. Nielsen John Sorenson
1968	ROMANIA 4:07.18 Ivan Patzaichin Sergei Covaliov	HUNGARY 4:08.77 Tamas Wichmann Gyula Petrikovics	USSR 4:11.30 Naum Prokupets Mikhail Zamotin
1972	USSR 3:52.60 Vlados Chessyunas Yuri Lobanov	ROMANIA 3:52.63 Ivan Patzaichin Serghei Covaliov	BULGARIA 3:58.10 Fedia Damianov Ivan Bourtchine
1976	USSR 3:52.76 Sergey Petrenko Aleksandr Vinogradov	ROMANIA 3:54.28 Gheorghe Danielov Gheorghe Simionov	HUNGARY 3:55.66 Tamás Buday Oszkar Frey
1980	ROMANIA 3:47.65 Ivan Patzaichin Toma Simionov	EAST GERMANY 3:49.93 Olaf Heukrodt Uwe Madeja	USSR 3:51.28 Vasiliy Yurchenko Yuriy Lobanov
1984	ROMANIA 3:40.60 Ivan Patzaichin Toma Simionov	YUGOSLAVIA 3:41.56 Matija Ljubek Mirko Nisovic	FRANCE 3:48.01 Didier Hoyer Eric Renaud

4. West Germany 5. United States 6. Spain 7. Canada 8. Mexico 9. Great Britain

1988 Final on 1 October

500 metres kayak singles (K1)/*Women*

	Gold	*Silver*	*Bronze*
1948	Karen Hoff (DEN) 2:31.9	Alide Van de Anker-Doedans (HOL) 2:32.8	Fritzi Schwingl (AUT) 2:32.9
1952	Sylvi Saimo (FIN) 2:18.4	Gertrude Liebhart (AUT) 2:18.8	Nina Savina (URS) 2:21.6
1956	Elisaveta Dementyeva (URS) 2:18.9	Therese Zenz (GER) 2:19.6	Tove Söby (DEN) 2:22.3
1960	Antonina Seredina (URS) 2:08.08	Therese Zenz (GER) 2:08.22	Daniela Walkowiak (POL) 2:10.46

1964	Ludmila Khvedosyuk (URS) 2:12.87	Hilde Lauer (ROM) 2:15.35	Marcia Jones (USA) 2:15.68
1968	Ludmila Pinayeva (née Khvedosyak) (URS) 2:11.09	Renate Breuer (FRG) 2:12.71	Viorica Dumitru (ROM) 2:13.22
1972	Yulia Ryabchinskaya (URS) 2:03.17	Mieke Jaapies (HOL) 2:04.03	Anna Pfeffer (HUN) 2:05.50
1976	Carola Zirzow (GDR) 2:01.05	Tatyana Korshunova (URS) 2:03.07	Klara Rajnai (HUN) 2:05.01
1980	Birgit Fischer (GDR) 1:57.96	Vanya Ghecheva (BUL) 1:59.48	Antonina Melnikova (URS) 1:59.66
1984	Agneta Andersson (SWE) 1:58.72	Barbara Schuttpelz (FRG) 1:59.93	Annemiek Derckx (HOL) 2:00.11

4. Tecla Marinescu (ROM) 5. Beatrice Basson (FRA) 6. Sheila Conover (USA)
7. Lucie Guay (CAN) 8. Elizabeth Blencowe (AUS) 9. Lesley Smither (GBR)

1988   Final on 30 September

500 metres kayak pairs (K2)/*Women*

	Gold	*Silver*	*Bronze*
1960	USSR 1:54.76 Maria Zhubina Antonina Seredina	GERMANY 1:56.66 Therese Zenz Ingrid Hartmann	HUNGARY 1:58.22 Vilma Egresi Klára Fried-Bánfalvi
1964	GERMANY 1:56.95 Roswitha Esser Annemarie Zimmermann	UNITED STATES 1:59.16 Francine Fox Gloriane Perrier	ROMANIA 2:00.25 Hilde Lauer Cornelia Sideri
1968	WEST GERMANY 1:56.44 Roswitha Esser Annemarie Zimmermann	HUNGARY 1:58.60 Anna Pfeffer Katalin Rosznyói	USSR 1:58.61 Ludmila Pinayeva (née Khvedosyuk) Antonina Seredina
1972	USSR 1:53.50 Ludmila Pinayeva (Née Khvedosyuk) Ekaterina Kuryshko	EAST GERMANY 1:54.30 Ilse Kaschube Petra Grabowsky	ROMANIA 1:55.01 Maria Nichiforov Viorica Dumitru
1976	USSR 1:51.15 Nina Gopova Galina Kreft	HUNGARY 1:51.69 Anna Pfeffer Klára Rajnai	EAST GERMANY 1:51.81 Barbel Koster Carola Zirzow
1980	EAST GERMANY 1:43.88 Carsta Genäuss Martina Bischof	USSR 1:46.91 Galina Alexeyava Nina Trofimova	HUNGARY 1:47.95 Éva Rakusz Mária Zakariás
1984	SWEDEN 1:45.25 Agneta Andersson Anna Olsson	CANADA 1:47.13 Alexandra Barre Sue Holloway	WEST GERMANY 1:47.32 Josefa Idem Barbara Schuttpelz

4. Romania 5. United States 6. France 7. Norway 8. Great Britain 9. Belgium

1988   Final on 30 September

500 metres kayak fours (K4)/*Women*

Gold	*Silver*	*Bronze*
1984 ROMANIA 1:38.34	SWEDEN 1:38.87	CANADA 1:39.40
Agafia Constantin	Agneta Andersson	Alexandra Barre
Nastasia Ionescu	Anna Olsson	Lucie Guay
Tecia Marinescu	Eva Karlsson	Sue Holloway
Maria Stefan	Suzanne Wiberg	Barb Olmsted

4. United States 5. West Germany 6. Norway 7. Great Britain

1988   Final on 1 October

CYCLING

With world championships taking place in 1893 and 1894, the sport was well placed for inclusion in the first modern Games and has remained a vital part of every Olympics since.

A women's road race was included for the first time only in 1984. In Seoul this will be repeated plus a new women's event – 1000 metres sprint.

THE EVENTS

MEN'S TRACK

1000 metres individual time trial

The rider on his own racing around the track to clock the fastest time – three circuits of the velodrome. Cyclists will keep as close as possible to the sprint line marker so that no time is lost and the shortest possible course is taken.

1000 metres sprint

The 'Blue Riband' event of the track and the most exciting to watch. Two cyclists compete over three races against each other, three laps of the velodrome each race. Competitors play cat and mouse for the first couple of laps, slowing the race often to a dead stop. The art is to make one's opponent take the lead. He will then have to make a long sprint for home, but having been man-oeuvred to the front will suffer from being a target for the other rider.

Competition is on a knockout basis, however there is a repechage system where beaten riders can try again. Having raced individually over 200 m against the clock a seeding system applies so that the best riders do not meet early in the competition.

4000 metres individual pursuit

Two riders involved at a time. They start at either side of the track. If a rider is caught by the other, he is eliminated. Otherwise the best time counts. The distance is 1000 metres shorter than in professional competition where they ride over 5000 metres.

4000 metres team pursuit

As in the individual race, but teams of four riders compete as a unit. One man can be dropped, and the time is taken as the *third* rider crosses the line. Watch how the teams rotate position, taking it in turns to act as pacemaker. Sometimes a team will sacrifice one man to do most of the pacemaking, keeping the remaining three fresh for a final push.

Individual points race

This was a new event at the 1984 Games and is a 50 km track race. Riders compete for points at stages of the race (à la Tour de France). These consist of a series of hard sprints, usually every five laps. Points available are doubled at the half-way stage and finish.

It is a severe test of sprinting ability under the stress of distance riding. Undoubtedly the most difficult category for spectators (and some commentators) to understand.

MEN'S ROAD RACING

100 km team time trial

Each country fields a team of four riders – three must finish the course in order to be classified. Teams set off at two-minute intervals. Third man's time counts.

Road race

A 'mini' Tour de France – just one stage. The distance is approximately 190 kilometres. It is always a spectacular race with riders forming groups to defend or challenge the lead. Despite the distance mere seconds or even parts of a second can decide the winner. Maximum of three riders per nation.

WOMEN'S TRACK

1000 metres sprint

This is the first track event for women ever to be included in the Games. Conducted exactly the same as the men's, watch for the cat-and-mouse tactics as the riders jockey for position until the finish approaches.

WOMEN'S ROAD RACING

This is included in the Olympics for only the second time. The distance raced is shorter than for the men – 80 kilometres.

As in the men's race – each nation is limited to three riders.

THE BIKES

Track

These are fixed-wheel machines without gears or brakes. The 1984 Games saw the introduction of new 'low profile' machines with solid graphite-sheeted disc wheels to produce better drag coefficient (cut down air resistance). They were said to have cost the Americans millions of dollars in research. They are now widely used. Riders often wear aerodynamic headgear, too. Speeds of over 40 miles per hour can be reached.

Road

Here the machines are more traditional in design. Spoked wheels are still used and the machines have brakes and gears. The motto in design is 'strong as possible – but light as possible'.

THE COMPETITION

Down the years, those outstanding cycling nations France and Italy have been the most prolific medal winners. However, as in most Olympic sports, the Eastern Europeans now compete very strongly.

In their absence in 1984, the Americans were a revelation, especially in the track events where they used their new aerodynamic machines to telling effect. They also won the men's and women's road race titles – Connie Carpenter-Phinney thus becoming the first woman to win an Olympic cycling gold medal.

Back in 1980, the Soviet Union and East Germany were highly successful with only Robert Dill-Bundi of Switzerland able to deprive one or other of them of a gold medal. He won the 4000 metres individual pursuit.

In Seoul, the East Germans and Soviets will be likely to gain the best medal haul again, but the sport is booming worldwide and medallists can come from anywhere in Europe, North America or Australasia. China, who have a few hundred million cyclists, have not really got into the sport yet. When they do – watch out!

THE STARS

Daniel Morelon (FRA) is the finest sprinter of modern times. He won two gold, a silver and a bronze in the sport's premier event. He also won the tandem race with Pierre Trentin in 1968 (discontinued event).

Eddy Merckx (BEL) and Jacques Anquetil (FRA), both of whom won the famous Tour de France five times, had previously competed in Olympic Games but were not medal winners.

In Seoul, Jennie Longo (FRA) is favourite for the women's road race.

THE BRITISH

Reg Harris remains the outstanding name in British cycling although his major exploits in the Games were 40 years ago. At those London Games of 1948 he won two silver medals – in the sprint and the tandem race. Many years later, Harris came out of retirement and was still good enough to win a British professional title at over 50 years of age.

Britain gained no medals in 1984, the last successes coming in the 1972 and 1976 Games when bronze medals were won in team pursuit.

Best medal hopes for 1988 could be Paul Curran in the Men's Road Race and 19-year-old Colin Sturgess who won a silver medal in individual pursuit in pre-Olympic competition.

Not a lot of people know that

● Bicycles made for two were last seen at the 1972 Games. There have been no tandem races since then.
● Cycling is becoming the new 'cult' sport, overtaking jogging in popularity due to the fact that less stress is put on ageing joints of keep-fit enthusiasts
● In 1976, the Czech team got off to a bad start. All their bicycle wheels and spare tyres were inadvertently collected by the rubbish men and fed into a refuse compactor. However, on substitute equipment Anton Tkac still beat the favourite Daniel Morelon (FRA) for the sprint gold medal.
● The 1956 road race was delayed for 15 minutes when it was found there were two extra Irish cyclists. They turned out to be a butcher and a carpenter, who when removed started handing out Irish nationalist literature.
● In road racing, officials have the right to pull out any cyclist who drops too far behind the pace.
● In the same event, if there is a dead heat for first place, the riders involved will ride again over 1000 metres to decide the gold medal.

VENUE

Track events at Olympic Velodrome in Olympic Park. Capacity 6000. Road races at Tongil-Ro.

RESULTS

1000 metres time-trial/Men

	Gold	Silver	Bronze
1896	Paul Masson (FRA) 24.0	Stamatios Nikolopoulos (GRE) 25.4	Adolf Schmal (AUT) 26.6
1906	Francesco Verri (ITA) 22.8	H. Crowther (GBR) 22.8	Menjou (FRA) 23.2
1928	Willy Falck-Hansen 1:14.4	Gerard Bosch van Drakestein (HOL) 1:15.2	Edgar Gray (AUS) 1:15.6
1932	Edgar Gray (AUS) 1:13.0	Jacobus van Egmond (HOL) 1:13.3	Charles Rampelberg (FRA) 1:13.4
1936	Arie van Vliet (HOL) 1:12.0	Pierre Georget (FRA) 1:12.8	Rudolf Karsch (GER) 1:13.2
1948	Jacques Dupont (FRA) 1:13.5	Pierre Nihant (BEL) 1:14.5	Thomas Godwin (GBR) 1:15.0
1952	Russell Mockridge (AUS) 1:11.1	Marino Morettini (ITA) 1:12.7	Raymond Robinson (SAF) 1:13.0

1956	Leandro Faggin (ITA) 1:09.8	Ladislav Foucek (TCH) 1:11.4	J. Alfred Swift (SAF) 1:11.6
1960	Sante Gaiardoni (ITA) 1:07.27	Dieter Gieseler (GER) 1:08.75	Rotislav Vargashkin (URS) 1:08.86
1964	Patrick Sercu (BEL) 1:09.59	Giovanni Pettenella (ITA) 1:10.09	Pierre Trentin (FRA) 1:10.42
1968	Pierre Trentin (FRA) 1:03.91	Niels-Christian Fredborg (DEN) 1:04.61	Janusz Kierzkowski (POL) 1:04.63
1972	Niels-Christian Fredborg (DEN) 1:06.44	Daniel Clark (AUS) 1:06.87	Jurgen Schuetze (GDR) 1:07.02
1976	Klaus-Jürgen Grunke (GDR) 1:05.93	Michel Vaarten (BEL) 1:07.52	Niels-Christian Fredborg (DEN) 1:07.62
1980	Lothar Thoms (GDR) 1:02.955 OR	Aleksandr Panfilov (URS) 1:04.845	David Weller (JAM) 1:05.241
1984	Fredy Schmidtke (FRG) 1:06.10	Curtis Harnett (CAN) 1:06.44	Fabrice Colas (FRA) 1:06.65
1988	Final on 20 September		

1000 metres sprint/*Men*

(Since 1924 only times for the last 200 m have been recorded)

	Gold	*Silver*	*Bronze*
1896*	Paul Masson (FRA) 4:56.0	Stamatios Nikolopoulos (GRE) 5:00.2	Léon Flameng (FRA)
1900*	Georges Taillandier (FRA) 2:52.0	Fernand Sanz (FRA)	John Henry Lake (USA)
1906	Francesco Verri (ITA) 1:42.2	H. C. Bouffler (GBR)	Eugène Debougnie (BEL)
1920	Maurice Peeters (HOL) 1:38.3	H. Thomas Johnson (GBR)	Harry Ryan (GBR)
1924	Lucien Michard (FRA) 12.8	Jacob Meijer (HOL)	Jean Cugnot (FRA)
1928	René Beaufrand (FRA) 13.2	Antoine Mazairac (HOL)	Willy Falck-Hansen (DEN)
1932	Jacobus van Egmond (HOL) 12.6	Louis Chaillot (FRA)	Bruno Pellizzari (ITA)
1936	Toni Merkens (GER) 11.8	Arie van Vliet (HOL)	Louis Chaillot (FRA)
1948	Mario Ghella (ITA) 12.0	Reginald Harris (GBR)	Axel Schandorff (DEN)
1952	Enzo Sacchi (ITA) 12.0	Lionel Cox (AUS)	Werner Potzernheim (GER)
1956	Michel Rousseau (FRA) 11.1	Guglielmo Pesenti (ITA)	Richard Ploog (AUS)
1960	Sante Gaiardoni (ITA) 11.1	Leo Sterckx (BEL)	Valentino Gasparella (ITA)
1964	Giovanni Pettenella (ITA) 13.69	Sergio Bianchetto (ITA)	Daniel Morelon (FRA)
1968	Daniel Morelon (FRA) 10.68	Giordano Turrini (ITA)	Pierre Trentin (FRA)
1972	Daniel Morelon (FRA) 11.25	John Nicholson (AUS)	Omari Phakadze (URS)
1976	Anton Tkac (TCH) 10.78	Daniel Morelon (FRA)	Hans-Jurgen Geschke (GDR)
1980	Lutz Hesslich (GDR) 11.40	Yave Cahard (FRA)	Sergey Kopylov (URS)
1984	Mark Gorski (USA) 10.49	Nelson Vails (USA)	Tsutomu Sakamoto (JPN)
1988	Final on 24 September		

* Distance 2000 m.

4000 metres individual pursuit/*Men*

	Gold	Silver	Bronze
1964	Jiři Daler (TCH) 5:04.75	Giorgio Ursi (ITA) 5:05.96	Preben Isaksson (DEN) 5:01.90
1968	Daniel Rebillard (FRA) 4:41.71	Mogens Frey Jensen (DEN) 4:42.43	Xaver Kurmann (SUI) 4:39.42
1972	Knut Knudsen (NOR) 4:45.74	Xaver Kurmann (SUI) 4:51.96	Hans Lutz (FRG) 4:50.80
1976	Gregor Braun (FRG) 4:47.61	Herman Ponsteen (HOL) 4:49.72	Thomas Huschke (GDR) 4:52.71
1980	Robert Dill-Bundi (SUI) 4:35.66	Alain Bondue (FRA) 4:42.96	Hans-Henrik Örsted (DEN) 4:36.54
1984	Steve Hegg (USA) 4:39.35	Rolf Golz (FRG) 4:43.82	Leonard Nitz (USA) 4:44.03
1988	Final on 22 September		

4000 metres team pursuit/*Men*

	Gold	Silver	Bronze
1908*	GREAT BRITAIN 2:18.6	GERMANY 2:28.6	CANADA 2:29.6
1920	ITALY 5:20.0	GREAT BRITAIN n.t.a.	SOUTH AFRICA n.t.a.
1924	ITALY 5:15.0	POLAND n.t.a.	BELGIUM n.t.a.
1928	ITALY 5:01.8	NETHERLANDS 5:06.2	GREAT BRITAIN n.t.a.
1932	ITALY 4:53.0	FRANCE 4:55.7	GREAT BRITAIN 4:56.0
1936	FRANCE 4:45.0	ITALY 4:51.0	GREAT BRITAIN 4:53.6
1948	FRANCE 4:57.8	ITALY 5:36.7	GREAT BRITAIN 4:55.8
1952	ITALY 4:46.1	SOUTH AFRICA 4:53.6	GREAT BRITAIN 4:51.5
1956	ITALY 4:37.4	FRANCE 4:39.4	GREAT BRITAIN 4:42.2
1960	ITALY 4:30.90	GERMANY 4:35.78	USSR 4:34.05
1964	GERMANY 4:35.67	ITALY 4:35.74	NETHERLANDS 4:38.99
1968	DENMARK 4:22.44†	WEST GERMANY 4:18.94	ITALY 4:18.35
1972	WEST GERMANY 4:22.14	EAST GERMANY 4:25.25	GREAT BRITAIN 4:23.78
1976	WEST GERMANY 4:21.06	USSR 4:27.15	GREAT BRITAIN 4:22.41
1980	USSR 4:15.70	EAST GERMANY 4:19.67	CZECHOSLOVAKIA**
1984	AUSTRALIA 4:25.99 Michael Grenda Kevin Nichols Michael Turtur Dean Woods	UNITED STATES 4:29.85 David Grylls Steve Hegg Patrick McDonough Leonard Nitz	WEST GERMANY 4:25.60 Reinhard Alber Rolf Golz Roland Gunther Michael Marx
1988	Final on 24 September		

*Distance 1810.5 metres.
†West Germany finished first but were disqualified. After the games they were awarded the silver medal.
**Italy were overtaken in 3rd place race.

100 km team time-trial/*Men*

	Gold	Silver	Bronze
1960	ITALY 2h 14:33.53	GERMANY 2h 16:56.31	USSR 2h 18:41.67
1964	NETHERLANDS 2h 26:31.19	ITALY 2h 26:55.39	SWEDEN 2h 27:11.52
1968	NETHERLANDS 2h 07:49.06	SWEDEN 2h 09:26.60	ITALY 2h 10:18.74
1972	USSR 2h 11:17.8	POLAND 2h 11:47.5	★
1976	USSR 2h 08:53.0	POLAND 2h 09:13.0	DENMARK 2h 12:20.0
1980	USSR 2h 01:21.7	EAST GERMANY 2h 02:53.2	CZECHOSLOVAKIA 2h 02:53.9
1984	ITALY 1h 58.28 Marcello Bartalini Marco Giovannetti Eros Poli Claudio Vandelli	SWITZERLAND 2h 02.38 Alfred Acherman Richard Trinkler Laurent Vial Benno Wiss	UNITED STATES 2h 02.46 Ronald Kiefel Roy Knickman David Phinney Andrew Weaver

4. Netherlands 5. Sweden 6. France 7. Denmark 8. Great Britain

1988	On 18 September

*Netherlands had their bronze medal withdrawn following a dope test.

Individual points race/*Men*

	Gold	Silver	Bronze
1984	Roger Ilegems (BEL)	Uwe Messerschmidt (FRG)	Jose Youshimatz (MEX)

4. Joerg Mueller (SUI) 5. Juan Curuchet (ARG) 6. Glenn Clarke (AUS)
7. Brian Fowler (NZL) 8. Derk VanEgmond (HOL)

1988	On 24 September

Individual road race/*Men*

	Gold	Silver	Bronze
1896	Aristidis Konstantinidis (GRE) 3h 22:31.0	August Goedrich (GER) 3h 42.18.0	F. Battel (GBR) d.n.a.
1906	Fernand Vast (FRA) 2h 41:28.0	Maurice Bardonneau (FRA) 2h 41:28.4	Edmond Luget (FRA) 2h 41:28.6
1912	Rudolf Lewis (SAF) 10h 42:39.0	Frederick Grubb (GBR) 10h 51:24.2	Carl Schutte (USA) 10h 52:38.8
1920	Harry Stenqvist (SWE) 4h 40:01.8	Henry Kaltenbrun (SAF) 4 h 41:26.6	Fernand Canteloube (FRA) 4h 42:54.4
1924	Armand Blanchonnet (FRA) 6h 20:48.0	Henry Hoevenaers (BEL) 6h 30:27.0	René Hamel (FRA) 6h 30:51.6
1928	Henry Hansen (DEN) 4h 47:18.0	Frank Southall (GBR) 4h 55:06.0	Gösta Carlsson (SWE) 5h 00:17.0
1932	Attilio Pavesi (ITA) 2h 28:05.6	Guglielmo Segato (ITA) 2h 29:21.4	Bernhard Britz (SWE) 2h 29:45.2

	Gold	Silver	Bronze
1937	Robert Charpentier (FRA) 2h 33:05.0	Guy Lapébie (FRA) 2h 33:05.2	Ernst Nievergelt (SUI) 2h 3:05.8
1948	José Beyaert (FRA) 5h 18:12.6	Gerardus Voorting (HOL) 5h 18:16.2	Lode Wouters (BEL) 5h 18:16.2
1952	André Noyelle (BEL) 5h 06:03.4	Robert Grondelaers (BEL) 5h 06:51.2	Edi Ziegler (GER) 5h 07:47.5
1956	Ercole Baldini (ITA) 5h 21:17.0	Arnaud Geyre (FRA) 5h 23:16.0	Alan Jackson (GBR) 5h 23:16.0
1960	Viktor Kapitonov (URS) 4h 20:37.0	Livio Trapé (ITA) 4h 20:37.0	Willy van den Berghen (BEL) 4h 20:57.0
1964	Mario Zanin (ITA) 4h 39:51.63	Kjell Rodian (DEN) 4h 39:51.65	Walter Godefroot (BEL) 4h 39:51.74
1968	Pierfranco Vianelli (ITA) 4h 41:25.24	Leif Mortensen (DEN) 4h 42:49.71	Gösta Pettersson (SWE) 4h 43:15.24
1972	Hennie Kuiper (HOL) 4h 14:37.0	Kevin Sefton (AUS) 4h 15:04.0	*
1976	Bernt Johansson (SWE) 4h 46:52.0	Giuseppe Martinelli (ITA) 4h 47:23.0	Mieczyslaw Nowicki (POL) 4h 47:23.0
1980	Sergey Sukhoruchenkov (URS) 4h 48:28.9	Czeslaw Lang (POL) 4h 51:26.9	Yuriy Barinov (URS) 4h 51:26.9
1984	Alexi Grewal (USA) 4h 59:57.0	Steve Bauer (CAN) 4h 59:57.0	Dag Otto Lauritzen (NOR) 5h 00:18.0

4. Morten Saether (NOR) 5. David Phinney (USA) 6. Thurlow Rogers (USA)
7. Bojan Ropert (YUG) 8. Nestor Mora (COL)

1988   On 26 September

* Jaime Huelamo (ESP) finished third but failed a drug test.

Individual road race/*Women*

	Gold	Silver	Bronze
1984	Connie Carpenter-Phinney (USA) 2h 11:14.0	Rebecca Twigg (USA) 2h 11:14.0	Sandra Schumacher (FRG) 2h 11:14.0

4. Unni Larsen (NOR) 5. Maria Canins (ITA) 6. Jeannie Longo (FRA)
7. Helle Soerensen (DEN) 8. Ute Enzenauer (FRG)

1988   On 25 September

1000 metres sprint/*Women*

Gold	Silver	Bronze

1988   Final on 24 September

(This is the first time this has been held)

EQUESTRIANISM

Equestrianism in some form has been included in all the modern games since 1900. Women have competed only since 1952. Indeed, until that year, only commissioned officers were allowed to take part in the dressage competition.

Medal winners come mostly from Europe and North America.

This is the only Olympic sport in which men and women compete in the same competition on equal terms throughout. (As do horses, male, female or neuter.)

THE COMPETITIONS

There are three distinct competitions – Grand Prix (dressage), Grand Prix (jumping) and Three-Day Event. We will refer to them as dressage, show-jumping and eventing. Two of the three disciplines within eventing are show-jumping and dressage, but these are quite separate from the Grand Prix competitions.

DRESSAGE

This is a sort of ballet for horses requiring the highest degree of co-ordination between horse and rider. It tests their ability in patterns of movement. It is the direct outcome of the exercises taught in the early French and Italian riding academies. Riders must take their horses through all the tests without apparent effort, as though the horse was in control of all movements and entirely self-disciplined.

Tests include walking, trotting, cantering, and the 'counter-canter' in which the horse leads with the foreleg which usually follows (the outside). A variety of paces, figures, etc. (there are 39 recognized movements in all) are required and marks given for each. Top mark is ten from each of five judges.

There are individual and team events. Each country may select four riders, the top three scores count. The top 12 individual scorers go on to compete over more tests for the individual medals.

SHOW-JUMPING

This is divided into individual and team competitions. The procedure is simple and very familiar. The object of the exercise is to avoid knocking down the obstacles. 'Refusals' also gain penalty points and if there is a jump-off against the clock, so will time faults.

In the team event, a country may enter four riders, the best three will score. The best 12 teams qualify for the second round. Scores from the first round and second round are added together.

In the individual competition, the top 20 riders qualify for a second round with the best scoring rider from round one, going last.

There are four faults for a fence knocked down, three for a refusal, plus faults for going slower than the allotted time. The course can range from 700 to 900 metres and have between 12 and 15 obstacles. The obstacles will be either 'verticals' or 'spreads' and range in height from 1.4 to 1.7 metres, and up to 2.0 metres in width. The water jump can be as wide as 4.75 metres.

EVENTING

Although commonly known as the three-day event, competition is actually over four days because the dressage section takes up the first two days. Horses competing are 'all-rounders' able to cope with both of the above disciplines plus the rigorous speed and endurance section (this is commonly known as cross-country – but includes tests over roads and tracks, steeplechase, *and* cross-country). Thus the standard of dressage will not compare with that of the separate dressage (Grand Prix), where horses are especially trained with only that in mind.

The cross-country stage is the most demanding. The courses are long, and the obstacles imaginative and fixed. A fall can be traumatic for horse and rider. Competitors set off at five-minute intervals. There are jumping and time faults.

The third stage is the show-jumping (known strictly in the sport as 'Stadium Jumping' – not that they jump over stadiums, merely in them).

There are 10 to 15 fences to negotiate. Maximum height here is 1.2 metres – less demanding than the separate show-jumping (Grand Prix) competition, but bear in mind what horse and rider will have already gone through. Each fence down costs five penalty points and, although in this competition a refusal receives no faults, it will certainly cost precious seconds as this is also a timed discipline.

The individual and team competition run together, with the team event being merely the best three total scores achieved for each country. The fewer points accumulated, the better.

There is no minimum weight for the dressage section, but for the show-jumping and eventing, a minimum of 75 kg must be carried.

BRITISH SUCCESSES

There has never been a British medal winner in dressage. However, in 1972, Lorna John-stone competed for Britain at the age of 70, thus becoming the oldest Olympic competitor in any sport in the modern Games. She finished in 12th place.

No British competitor has ever won the individual gold medal in show-jumping. Marian Coakes and Ann Moore won silver medals in 1968 and '72 respectively. David Broome won a bronze medal in both 1960 and '68 and Peter Robeson won a bronze in 1964.

Britain did win the team gold medal in Helsinki in 1952, the team silver in Los Angeles in 1984, and the team bronze medals in 1948 and 1956.

In eventing, Richard Meade won the individual gold in 1972 plus a team gold medal in that year and in 1968.

The most recent individual medal was won by Virginia Leng (Holgate), a bronze in 1984.

Britain also won the team silver medals in the Los Angeles Games.

Princess Anne, now the Princess Royal, competed for Britain in the 1976 Games in Montreal. Her horse was Goodwill.

THE STARS

In dressage, Henry St Cyr (Sweden) won the individual gold medals in 1952 and '56. He also won team gold medals in those years and would have already won his first in 1948, had not the Swedish team been disqualified after finishing in first place after it was discovered that one of them was not a fully commissioned officer (see above).

Reiner Klimke (FDR) the individual gold medal winner in 1984 also won team gold medals in 1964, '68 and '76. He also has two bronze medals in his tally.

The first woman to win a medal in dressage was Lisa Hartel of Denmark – bronze (1952). She suffered from the effects of polio and always had to be helped on and off her horse. At the Helsinki Games, when women were competing for the first time, Henry St

Cyr, the gold medallist helped her on to the victory rostrum.

In show-jumping, Hans Gunter Winkler (FDR) has won a total of five gold, one silver and one bronze medals.

Pierre Jonquères d'Oriola (France) won the indivdual title twice in 1952 and 1964.

Raimondo D'Inzeo (Italy) competed in a record eight Games from 1948 to '76, winning a gold, two silvers and three bronze medals.

Richard Meade has a tally of three gold medals in eventing (see above). The only man to retain the individual eventing title has been Charles Pahud de Mortanges (Holland), winner in 1928 and '32.

The USA has won the team title on four occasions, Great Britain on three.

Not a lot of people know that

• In the eventing competition in 1936, no fewer than three horses were killed.
• In that same year, Captain Richard Fanshawe of Great Britain had a bad fall in the speed and endurance tests, breaking his arm in the process.

However, he knew he had to finish to keep the team in the medal hunt. He not only finished but had to run to catch his horse which had bolted in order to do so. The good captain helped Britain to the bronze team medal.

• Again in 1936 (a momentous year, at the Berlin Olympics), Lieutenant Otomar Bures of Czechoslovakia took 2 hours 46 minutes and 36 seconds to complete the cross-country course. The time allotted was 17 minutes and 46 seconds. He accumulated 18,130.7 penalty points. The individual winner a mere 37.7.

• In the 1900 Games there were medals awarded for equestrian long jump and high jump.

VENUE

Seoul Equestrian Park Kwachon for dressage and show-jumping plus those sections of the three-day event.
Wondong Ranch for the cross-country section of the three-day event.
Olympic Stadium for final of show-jumping (Grand Prix).

RESULTS

Grand Prix jumping

	Gold	Silver	Bronze
1900	Aimé Haegeman (BEL) *Benton II*	Georges van de Poele (BEL) *Windsor Squire*	M. de Champsavin (FRA) *Terpsichore*
1912*	Jean Cariou (FRA) *Mignon* 186 pts	Rabod von Kröcher (GER) *Dohna* 186 pts	Emanuel de Blomaert de Soye (BEL) *Clonmore* 185 pts
1920	Tommaso Lequio (ITA) *Trebecco* 2 faults	Alessandro Valerio (ITA) *Cento* 3 faults	Gustaf Lewenhaupt (SWE) *Mon Coeur* 4 faults
1924	Àlphonse Gemuseus (SUI) *Lucette* 6 faults	Tommaso Lequio (ITA) *Trebecco* 8.75 faults	Adam Krolikiewicz (POL) *Picador* 10 faults
1928†	Frantisek Ventura (TCH) *Eliot* 0 faults	Pierre Bertrand de Balanda (FRA) *Papillon* 2 faults	Charles Kuhn (SUI) *Pepita* 4 faults
1932	Takeichi Nishi (JPN) *Uranus* 8 pts	Harry Chamberlin (USA) *Show Girl* 12 pts	Clarence von Rosen Jr (SWE) *Empire* 16 pts
1936*	Kurt Hasse (GER) *Tora* 4 faults	Henri Rang (ROM) *Delfis* 4 faults	Jozsef von Platthy (HUN) *Sellö* 8 faults
1948	Humberto Mariles Cortés (MEX) *Arete* 6.25 faults	Rubén Uriza (MEX) *Harvey* 8 faults	Jean d'Orgeix (FRA) *Sucre de Pomme* 8 faults

1952*	Pierre Jonquères d'Oriola (FRA) *Ali Baba* 0 faults	Oscar Cristi (CHI) *Bambi* 4 faults	Fritz Thiedemann (GER) *Meteor* 8 faults
1956	Hans Günter Winkler (GER) *Halla* 4 faults	Raimondo d'Inzeo (ITA) *Merano* 8 faults	Piero d'Inzeo (ITA) *Uruguay* 11 faults
1960	Raimondo d'Inzeo (ITA) *Posillippo* 12 faults	Piero d'Inzeo (ITA) *The Rock* 16 faults	David Broome (GBR) *Sunsalve* 23 faults
1964	Pierre Jonquères d'Oriola (FRA) *Lutteur* 9 faults	Hermann Schridde (GER) *Dozent* 13.75 faults	Peter Robeson (GBR) *Firecrest* 16 faults
1968	William Steinkraus (USA) *Snowbound* 4 faults	Marian Coakes (GBR) *Stroller* 8 faults	David Broome (GBR) *Mister Softee* 12 faults
1972*	Graziano Mancinelli (ITA) *Ambassador* 0 faults	Ann Moore (GBR) *Psalm* 3 faults	Neal Shapiro (USA) *Sloopy* 8 faults
1976	Alwin Schockemöhle (FRG) *Warwick Rex* 0 faults	Michael Vaillancourt (CAN) *Branch County* 4 faults	François Mathy (BEL) *Gai Luron* 8 faults
1980	Jan Kowalczyk (POL) *Artemor* 8 faults	Nikolai Korolkov (URS) *Espadron* 9.5 faults	Joaquin Perez Heras (MEX) *Alymony* 12 faults
1984	Joe Fargis (USA) *Touch of Class* 4 faults	Conrad Homfeld (USA) *Abdullah* 4 faults	Heidi Robbiani (SUI) *Jessica V* 8 faults
1988	Final round on 2 October		

* After one jump-off.
† After two jump-offs.

Grand Prix jumping team

	Gold	Silver	Bronze
1912	SWEDEN 545 pts	FRANCE 538 pts	GERMANY 530 pts
1920	SWEDEN 14 faults	BELGIUM 16.25 faults	ITALY 18.75 faults
1924	SWEDEN 12.25 pts	SWITZERLAND 50 pts	PORGUTAL 53 pts
1928	SPAIN 4 faults	POLAND 8 faults	SWEDEN 10 faults
1932*	—	—	—
1936	GERMANY 44 faults	NETHERLANDS 51.5 faults	PORTUGAL 56 faults
1948	MEXICO 34.25 faults	SPAIN 56.50 faults	GREAT BRITAIN 67 faults
1952	GREAT BRITAIN 40.75 faults	CHILE 45.75 faults	UNITED STATES 52.25 faults
1956	GERMANY 40 faults	ITALY 66 faults	GREAT BRITAIN 69 faults
1960	GERMANY 46.50 faults	UNITED STATES 66 faults	ITALY 80.50 faults
1964	GERMAN 68.50 faults	FRANCE 77.75 faults	ITALY 88.50 faults
1968	CANADA 102.75 faults	FRANCE 110.50 faults	WEST GERMANY 117.25 faults
1972	WEST GERMANY 32 faults	UNITED STATES 32.25 faults	ITALY 48 faults
1976	FRANCE 40 faults	WEST GERMANY 44 faults	BELGIUM 63 faults
1980	USSR 16 faults	POLAND 32 faults	MEXICO 39.25 faults

* No country had three riders complete the course.

1984	UNITED STATES 12 faults	GREAT BRITAIN	WEST GERMANY
	Joe Fargis *Touch of Class*	36.75 faults	39.25 faults
	Conrad Homfeld *Abdullah*	Michael Whitaker *Overton*	Paul Schockemöhle *Deister*
	Leslie Burr *Albany*	*Amanda*	Peter Luther *Livius*
	Melanie Smith *Calypso*	John Whitaker *Ryan's Son*	Franke Sloothaak *Farmer*
		Steven Smith *Shining Example*	Fritz Ligges *Ramzes*
		Timothy Grubb *Linky*	

4. Canada 5. Switzerland 6. France 7. Spain 8. Italy

1988   On 27 September

Grand Prix dressage

	Gold	Silver	Bronze
1912	Carl Bonde (SWE) *Emperor* 15 pts	Gustaf-Adolf Boltenstern Sr (SWE) *Neptun* 21 pts	Hans von Blixen-Finecke (SWE) *Maggie* 32 pts
1920	Janne Lundblad (SWE) *Uno* 27,937 pts	Bertil Sandström (SWE) *Sabel* 26,312 pts	Hans von Rosen (SWE) *Running Sister* 25,125 pts
1924	Ernst Linder (SWE) *Piccolomini* 276.4 pts	Bertil Sandström (SWE) *Sabel* 275.8 pts	Xavier Lesage (FRA) *Plumard* 265.8 pts
1928	Carl von Langen (GER) *Draüfgänger* 237.42 pts	Charles Marion (FRA) *Linon* 231.00 pts	Ragnar Olsson (SWE) *Günstling* 229.78 pts
1932	Xavier Lesage (FRA) *Taine* 343.75 pts	Charles Marion (FRA) *Linon* 305.42 pts	Hiram Tuttle (USA) *Olympic* 300.50 pts
1936	Heinz Pollay (GER) *Kronos* 1760 pts	Friedrich Gerhard (GER) *Absinth* 1745.5 pts	Alois Podhajsky (AUT) *Nero* 1721.5 pts
1948	Hans Moser (SUI) *Hummer* 492.5 pts	André Jousseaume (FRA) *Harpagon* 480.0 pts	Gustaf-Adolf Boltenstern Jr (SWE) *Trumpf* 477.5 pts
1952	Henri St Cyr (SWE) *Master Rufus* 561 pts	Lis Hartel (DEN) *Jubilee* 541.5 pts	André Jousseaume (FRA) *Harpagon* 541 pts
1956	Henri St Cyr (SWE) *Juli* 860 pts	Lis Hartel (DEN) *Jubilee* 850 pts	Liselott Linsenhoff (GER) *Adular* 832 pts
1960	Sergey Filatov (URS) *Absent* 2144 pts	Gustav Fischer (SUI) *Wald* 2087 pts	Josef Neckermann (GER) *Asbach* 2082 pts
1964	Henri Chammartin (SUI) *Woermann* 1504 pts	Harry Boldt (GER) *Remus* 1503 pts	Sergey Filatov (URS) *Absent* 1486 pts
1968	Ivan Kizimov (URS) *Ichor* 1572 pts	Josef Neckermann (FRG) *Mariano* 1546 pts	Reiner Klimke (FRG) *Dux* 1537 pts
1972	Liselott Linsenhoff (FRG) *Piaff* 1229 pts	Elena Petuchkova (URS) *Pepel* 1185 pts	Josef Neckermann (FRG) *Venetia* 1177 pts
1976	Christine Stückelberger (SUI) *Granat* 1486 pts	Harry Boldt (FRG) *Woycek* 1435 pts	Reiner Klimke (FRG) *Mehmed* 1395 pts
1980	Elisabeth Theurer (AUT) *Mon Cherie* 1370 pts	Yuriy Kovshov (URS) *Igrok* 1300 pts	Viktor Ugryumov (URS) *Shkval* 1234 pts
1984	Reiner Klimke (FRG) *Ahlerich* 1504 pts	Anne Grethe Jensen (DEN) *Marzog* 1442 pts	Otto Hofer (SUI) *Limandus* 1364 pts

1988   Final on 28 September

Grand Prix dressage team

Gold	Silver	Bronze
1928 GERMANY 669.72 pts	SWEDEN 650.86 pts	NETHERLANDS 642.96 pts
1932 FRANCE 2818.75 pts	SWEDEN 2678 pts	UNITED STATES 2576.75 pts
1936 GERMANY 5074 pts	FRANCE 4846 pts	SWEDEN 4660.5 pts
1948* FRANCE 1269 pts	UNITED STATES 1256 pts	PORTUGAL 1182 pts
1952 SWEDEN 1597.5 pts	SWITZERLAND 1579 pts	GERMANY 1501 pts
1956 SWEDEN 2475 pts	GERMANY 2346 pts	SWITZERLAND 2346 pts
1964 GERMANY 2558 pts	SWITZERLAND 2526 pts	USSR 2311 pts
1968 WEST GERMANY 2699 pts	USSR 2657 pts	SWITZERLAND 2547 pts
1972 USSR 5095 pts	WEST GERMANY 5083 pts	SWEDEN 4849 pts
1976 WEST GERMANY 5155 pts	SWITZERLAND 4684 pts	UNITED STATES 4647 pts
1980 USSR 4383 pts	BULGARIA 3580 pts	ROMANIA 3346 pts
1984 WEST GERMANY 4955 pts Reiner Klimke *Ahlerich* Uwe Sauer *Montevideo* Herbert Krug *Muscadeur*	SWITZERLAND 4673 pts Otto Hofer *Limandus* Christine Stückelberger *Tansanit* Amy De Bary *Aintree*	SWEDEN 4630 pts Ulla Hakanson *Flamingo* Ingamay Bylund *Aleks* Louise Nathhorst *Inferno*

1988   25 and 26 September

* Sweden came first but were disqualified a year later.

Three day event

Gold	Silver	Bronze
1912 Axel Nordlander (SWE) *Lady Artist* 46.59 pts	Friedrich von Rochow (GER) *Idealist* 46.42 pts	Jean Cariou (FRA) *Cocotte* 46.32 pts
1920 Helmer Mörner (SWE) *Germania* 1775 pts	Age Lundström (SWE) *Yrsa* 1738.75 pts	Ettore Caffaratti (ITA) *Traditore* 1733.75 pts
1924 Adolph van der Voort van Zijp (HOL) *Silver Piece* 1976 pts	Fröde Kirkebjerg (DEN) *Meteor* 1853.5 pts	Sloan Doak (USA) *Pathfinder* 1845.5 pts
1928 Charles Pahud de Mortanges (HOL) *Marcroix* 1969.82 pts	Gerard de Kruyff (HOL) *Va-t-en* 1967.26 pts	Bruno Neumann (GER) *Ilja* 1944.42 pts
1932 Charles Pahud de Mortanges (HOL) *Marcroix* 1813.83 pts	Earl Thompson (USA) *Jenny Camp* 1811 pts	Clarence von Rosen Jr (SWE) *Sunnyside Maid* 1809.42 pts
1936 Ludwig Stubbendorff (GER) *Nurmi* 37.7 pts	Earl Thompson (USA) *Jenny Camp* 99.9 pts	Hans Mathiesen-Lunding (DEN) *Jason* 102.2 pts
1948 Bernard Chevallier (FRA) *Aiglonne* +4 pts	Frank Henry (USA) *Swing Low* −21 pts	Robert Selfelt (SWE) *Claque* −25 pts
1952 Hans von Blixen-Finecke Jr (SWE) *Jubal* 28.33 pts	Guy Lefrant (FRA) *Verdun* 54.50 pts	Wilhelm Büsing (GER) *Hubertus* 55.50 pts
1956 Petrus Kastenman (SWE) *Iluster* 66.53 pts	August Lütke-Westhues (GER) *Trux von Kamax* 84.87 pts	Frank Weldon (GBR) *Kilbarry* 85.48 pts
1960 Lawrence Morgan (AUS) *Salad Days* +7.15 pts	Neale Lavis (AUS) *Mirrabooka* −16.50 pts	Anton Bühler (SUI) *Gay Spark* −51.21 pts

1964	Mauro Checcoli (ITA) *Surbean* 64.40 pts	Carlos Moratorio (ARG) *Chalan* 56.40 pts	Fritz Ligges (GER) *Donkosak* 49.20 pts
1968	Jean-Jacques Guyon (FRA) *Pitou* 38.86 pts	Derek Allhusen (GBR) *Lochinvar* 41.61 pts	Michael Page (USA) *Faster* 52.31 pts
1972	Richard Meade (GBR) *Laurieston* 57.73 pts	Alessandro Argenton (ITA) *Woodland* 43.33 pts	Jan Jonsson (SWE) *Sarajevo* 39.67 pts
1976	Edmund Coffin (USA) *Bally-Cor* 114.99 pts	John Plumb (USA) *Better & Better* 125.85 pts	Karl Schultz (FRG) *Madrigal* 129.45 pts
1980	Frederico Roman (ITA) *Rossinan* 108.60 pts	Aleksandr Blinov (URS) *Galzun* 120.80 pts	Yuriy Salnikov (URS) *Pintset* 151.60 pts
1984	Mark Todd (NZL) *Charisma* 51.60 pts	Karen Stives (USA) *Ben Arthur* 54.20 pts	Virginia Holgate (GBR) *Priceless* 56.80 pts

1988   19 until 22 September

Three day event team

	Gold	Silver	Bronze
1912	SWEDEN 139.06 pts	GERMANY 138.48 pts	UNITED STATES 137.33 pts
1920	SWEDEN 5057.5 pts	ITALY 4735 pts	BELGIUM 4560 pts
1924	NETHERLANDS 5297.5 pts	SWEDEN 4743.5 pts	ITALY 4512.5 pts
1928	NETHERLANDS 5865.68 pts	NORWAY 5395.68 pts	POLAND 5067.92 pts
1932	UNITED STATES 5038.08 pts	NETHERLANDS 4689.08 pts	—*
1936	GERMANY 676.75 pts	POLAND 991.70 pts	GREAT BRITAIN 9195.50 pts
1948	UNITED STATES 161.50 pts	SWEDEN 165.00 pts	MEXICO 305.25 pts
1952	SWEDEN 221.94 pts	GERMANY 235.49 pts	UNITED STATES 587.16 pts
1956	GREAT BRITAIN 355.48 pts	GERMANY 475.91 pts	CANADA 572.72 pts
1960	AUSTRALIA 128.18 pts	SWITZERLAND 386.02 pts	FRANCE 515.71 pts
1964	ITALY 85.80 pts	UNITED STATES 65.86 pts	GERMANY 56.73 pts
1968	GREAT BRITAIN 175.93 pts	UNITED STATES 245.87 pts	AUSTRALIA 331.26 pts
1972	GREAT BRITAIN 95.53 pts	UNITED STATES 10.81 pts	WEST GERMANY −18.00 pts
1976	UNITED STATES 441.0 pts	WEST GERMANY 584.60 pts	AUSTRALIA 599.54 pts
1980	USSR 457.00 pts	ITALY 656.20 pts	MEXICO 1172.85 pts
1984	UNITED STATES 186.00 pts Michael Plumb *Blue Stone* Karen Stives *Ben Arthur* Torrance Fleischmann *Finvarra* Bruce Davidson *J. J. Babu*	GREAT BRITAIN 189.20 pts Virginia Holgate *Priceless* Ian Stark *Oxford Blue* Diana Clapham *Windjammer* Lucinda Green *Regal Realm*	WEST GERMANY 234.00 pts Dietmar Hogrefe *Foliant* Bettina Overesch *Peacetime* Burkhard Tesdorpf *Freedom* Claus Erhoen *Fair Lady*

1988   From 19 to 22 September

*No other teams finished.

FENCING

The sport has been part of every Olympic Games of the modern era for men. Women have taken part since the Games of 1924. It is the only sport in which amateurs *and* professionals were allowed to compete before those distinctions became rather blurred. In the Games of 1900, there were special events for fencing masters (the professionals).

For years, the Italians and French dominated the sport but from the sixties, the Eastern Europeans took over. However, in their absence, Italy and France won five of the eight gold medals available in the 1984 Games.

The gold medal in the women's individual foil, however, went to Jujie Luan of China, their first ever Olympic medal in the sport.

THE COMPETITION

There are individual and team competitions in each of three weapons for men – foil, épée, and sabre. Women compete in foil only at individual and team level.

WEAPONS

The foil and épée are similar and are thrusting weapons. Hits are scored with the point only.

The sabre is both a cutting and thrusting weapon and hits may be made with the cutting edge as well as the point.

The foil

This is the most popular weapon and usually the first learnt by a fencer. A competitor may not score a hit directly. There is a 'phrase' which has to be followed – attack, riposte, counter-riposte, before a hit is valid.

The épée

For this weapon there is no priority system. A hit may be scored directly. This is the sword used by competitors in the Modern Pentathlon. The épée is the same length as the foil but is somewhat stiffer and heavier.

The sabre

A cut and thrust weapon which has a flattened V-shape blade.

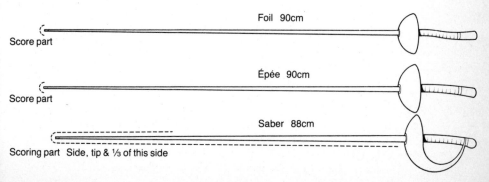

Foil 90cm
Score part

Épée 90cm
Score part

Saber 88cm
Scoring part Side, tip & ⅓ of this side

101

THE RULES

Individual competitions are run on a pool system with everyone fencing everyone else. The top 40 go forward to a second round, run the same way, and the top 24 from there, again competition is on a pool system which produces a final 16. Here there is an element of repechages (heats), but eventually the competition is whittled down to the top eight who compete on a straight knockout basis. As you can imagine, the competition lasts a very long time.

The team event is also run on a pool system firstly and then a knockout basis.

Bouts last for 10 minutes for men and eight minutes for women. The fencer scoring the most hits in that time is the winner or the fencer who first scores either five hits for men or four for women, should that happen within the time limit.

The target areas for each weapon are different – as illustrated.

Electronic apparatus has been used to register hits since the 1936 Games for the épée and since the 1956 Games for the foil. A system has not yet been perfected for the sabre. It is possible to register a double hit, i.e. both fencers registering a hit within 1/125 of a second in the épée, but not in foil where the 'phrase' or build up to the hit has to be analysed by the jury before being awarded.

DRESS

Clothing and equipment must give freedom of movement combined with maximum protection. Accidents have been known to happen, sometimes fatal.

Clothing must be white. Jackets and collars must be fastened up. The jacket sleeve on the sword arm must be lined so that there is a double thickness of material.

For épée, a jacket covering the whole of the front of the trunk of the body must be worn. For foil and sabre a shorter jacket may be worn. All fencers wear a protective

Mask usually stainless steel mesh with 2.1mm spacing

undergarment called a plastron. Women wear rigid breast protectors.

A glove of gauntlet type must be worn on the fencing arm and most important of all is the mask usually made of wire-mesh stainless steel.

BRITISH SUCCESSES

In men's fencing, Britain's best results were achieved by Allan Jay and Bill Hoskyns who won individual silver medals in épée in 1960 and '64 respectively. Hoskyns competed in six consecutive Games.

In women's competition, Gladys Davis, Muriel Freeman, and Heather Guiness won

Foil score area   Épée score area   Saber score area

silver medals in 1924, '28 and '32. Remember, women compete in foil only.

Britain's only gold medal winner in the history of the Games is Gillian Sheen, champion in Melbourne in 1956.

THE STARS

Edoardo Mangiarotti of Italy won 13 medals, six of them gold in foil and épée between 1936 and 1960. He was a natural right-hander but was forced by his father, a fencing master, to become a left-handed fencer which is thought by some to be a distinct advantage. It certainly worked for Edoardo.

Aladar Gerevich of Hungary won seven gold medals in the sabre between 1932 and 1960. He was never out of the medals at six consecutive Games.

Ramon Fonst of Cuba won three individual medals in the épée in 1900 and the foil and épée in 1904.

Elena Novikova won four gold medals between 1968 and 1976 (one individual, three team).

Ildiko Sagi-Retjo of Hungary picked up seven medals, two of them gold over five Games from 1960. She was born deaf.

Not a lot of people know that

● Ivan Osiier of Denmark first appeared in the Games of 1908 and was still competing at the 1948 Olympics in London. In all that time he won just one silver medal.

● There have been occasions when arguments over judging have led to real life duels. In 1924, the Italian-born coach of the Hungarian team, 60-year-old Italo Santelli challenged the Italian captain Adolfo Contronei, who had accused him of lying.

They met in a small town near the Hungarian border and fought with heavy sabres. Santelli slashed Contronei deeply on the side of the head and drew blood. Doctors halted the duel.

● In the same year a judge called Kovacs accused the Italians of throwing matches so that one of their team, Puliti, would win the gold medal. Kovacs told Puliti he could not understand the furious fencer's protests as he did not speak Italian. At this point, Puliti hit Kovacs in the face and said he might understand that.

Four months later a duel took place on the Yugoslav/Hungarian border. After slashing away at each other for an hour, they were eventually separated by spectators concerned by the wounds that both men had received. Honour restored, the combatants shook hands and made up.

VENUE

Fencing Gymansium, Olympic Park. Capacity 7000.

RESULTS

Foil individual/*Men*

	Gold	*Silver*	*Bronze*
1896	Emile Gravelotte (FRA) 4 wins	Henri Callot (FRA) 3 wins	Perikles Mavromichalis-Pierrakos (GRE) 2 wins
1900	Emile Coste (FRA) 6 wins	Henri Masson (FRA) 5 wins	Jacques Boulenger (FRA) 4 wins
1904	Ramón Fonst (CUB) 3 wins	Albertson Van Zo Post (CUB) 2 wins	Charles Tatham (CUB) 1 win
1906	Georges Dillon-Kavanagh (FRA) d.n.a.	Gustav Casmir (GER) d.n.a.	Pierre d'Hugues (FRA) d.n.a.

1912	Nedo Nadi (ITA) 7 wins	Pietro Speciale (ITA) 5 wins	Richard Verderber (AUT) 4 wins
1920	Nedo Nadi (ITA) 10 wins	Philippe Cattiau (FRA) 9 wins	Roger Ducret (FRA) 9 wins
1924	Roger Ducret (FRA) 6 wins	Philippe Cattiau (FRA) 5 wins	Maurice van Damme (BEL) 4 wins
1928	Lucien Gaudin (FRA) 9 wins	Erwin Casmir (GER) 9 wins	Giulio Gaudini (ITA) 9 wins
1932	Gustavo Marzi (ITA) 9 wins	Joseph Levis (USA) 6 wins	Giulio Gaudini (ITA) 5 wins
1936	Giulio Gaudini (ITA) 7 wins	Edouard Gardère (FRA) 6 wins	Giorgio Bocchino (ITA) 4 wins
1948	Jean Buhan (FRA) 7 wins	Christian d'Oriola (FRA) 5 wins	Lajos Maszlay (HUN) 4 wins
1952	Christian d'Oriola (FRA) 8 wins	Edoardo Mangiarotti (ITA) 6 wins	Manlio di Rosa (ITA) 5 wins
1956	Christian d'Oriola (FRA) 6 wins	Giancarlo Bergamini (ITA) 5 wins	Antonio Spallino (ITA) 5 wins
1960	Viktor Zhdanovich (URS) 7 wins	Yuriy Sissikin (URS) 4 wins	Albert Axelrod (USA) 3 wins
1964	Egon Franke (POL) 3 wins	Jean-Claude Magnan (FRA) 2 wins	Daniel Revenu (FRA) 1 win
1968	Ion Drimba (ROM) 4 wins	Jenö Kamuti (HUN) 3 wins	Daniel Revenu (FRA) 3 wins
1972	Witold Woyda (POL) 5 wins	Jenö Kamuti (HUN) 4 wins	Christian Nöel (FRA) 2 wins
1976	Fabio Dal Zotto (ITA) 4 wins	Aleksandr Romankov (URS) 4 wins	Bernard Talvard (FRA) 3 wins
1980	Vladimir Smirnov (URS) 5 wins	Paskal Jolyot (FRA) 5 wins	Aleksandr Romankov (URS) 5 wins
1984	Mauro Numa (ITA) 5 wins	Matthias Behr (FRG) 4 wins	Stefano Cerioni (ITA) 4 wins
1988	Final on 21 September		

Men's foil team/*Men*

	Gold	*Silver*	*Bronze*
1904	CUBA 7 wins	UNITED STATES 2 wins	—
1920	ITALY 4 wins	FRANCE 3 wins	UNITED STATES 2 wins
1924	FRANCE 3 wins	BELGIUM 2 wins	HUNGARY 1 win
1928	ITALY 3 wins	FRANCE 2 wins	ARGENTINA 1 win
1932	FRANCE 4 wins	ITALY 3 wins	UNITED STATES 2 wins
1936	ITALY 3 wins	FRANCE 2 wins	GERMANY 1 win
1948	FRANCE 3 wins	ITALY 2 wins	BELGIUM 1 win
1952	FRANCE 3 wins	ITALY 2 wins	HUNGARY 1 win
1956	ITALY 3 wins	FRANCE 2 wins	HUNGARY 1 win
1960	USSR 9 wins	ITALY 4 wins	GERMANY
1964	USSR 9 wins	POLAND 7 wins	FRANCE
1968	FRANCE 9 wins	USSR 6 wins	POLAND
1972	POLAND 9 wins	USSR 5 wins	FRANCE
1976	WEST GERMANY 9 wins	ITALY 6 wins	FRANCE

1980	FRANCE 8 wins	USSR 8 wins	POLAND
1984	ITALY	WEST GERMANY	FRANCE

1980	FRANCE 8 wins	USSR 8 wins	POLAND
1984	ITALY	WEST GERMANY	FRANCE
	Maurio Numa	Matthias Behr	Philippe Omnes
	Andrea Borella	Mathias Gey	Patrick Groc
	Stefan Cerioni	Harald Hein	Frederick Pietruszka
	Angelo Scuri	Frank Beck	Pascal Jolyot
	Andrea Cipressa	Klaus Reichert	Marc Cerboni

1988   Final on 27 September

Épée individual/*Men*

	Gold	*Silver*	*Bronze*
1900	Ramón Fonst (CUB)	Louis Perrée (FRA)	Léon Sée (FRA)
1904	Ramón Fonst (CUB) 3 wins	Charles Tatham (CUB) 2 wins	Albertson Van Zo Post (CUB) 1 win
1906	Georges de la Falaise (FRA) d.n.a.	Georges Dillon-Kavanagh (FRA) d.n.a.	Alexander van Blijenburgh (HOL) d.n.a.
1908	Gaston Alibert (FRA) 5 wins	Alexandre Lippmann (FRA) 4 wins	Eugène Olivier (FRA) 4 wins
1912	Paul Anspach (BEL) 6 wins	Ivan Osiier (DEN) 5 wins	Philippe Le Hardy de Beaulieu (BEL) 4 wins
1920	Armand Massard (FRA) 9 wins	Alexandre Lippmann (FRA) 7 wins	Gustave Buchard (FRA) 6 wins
1924	Charles Delporte (BEL) 8 wins	Roger Ducret (FRA) 7 wins	Nils Hellsten (SWE) 7 wins
1928	Lucien Gaudin (FRA) 8 wins	Georges Buchard (FRA) 7 wins	George Calnan (USA) 6 wins
1932	Giancarlo Cornaggia-Medici (ITA) 8 wins	Georges Buchard (FRA) 8 wins	Carlo Agostini (ITA) 7 wins
1936	Franco Riccardi (ITA) 5 wins	Saverio Ragno (ITA) 6 wins	Giancarlo Cornaggia-Medici (ITA) 6 wins
1948	Luigi Cantone (ITA) 7 wins	Oswald Zappelli (SUI) 5 wins	Edoardo Mangiarotti (ITA) 5 wins
1952	Edoardo Mangiarotti (ITA) 7 wins	Dario Mangiarotti (ITA) 6 wins	Oswald Zappelli (SUI) 6 wins
1956	Carlo Pavesi (ITA) 5 wins	Giuseppe Delfino (ITA) 5 wins	Edoardo Mangiarotti (ITA) 5 wins
1960	Giuseppe Delfino (ITA) 5 wins	Allan Jay (GBR) 5 wins	Bruno Khabarov (URS) 4 wins
1964	Grigoriy Kriss (URS) 2 wins	William Hoskyns (GBR) 2 wins	Guram Kostava (URS) 1 win
1968	Gyözö Kulcsár (HUN) 4 wins	Grigoriy Kriss (URS) 4 wins	Gianluigi Saccaro (ITA) 4 wins
1972	Csaba Fenyvesi (HUN) 4 wins	Jacques la Degaillerie (FRA) 3 wins	Gyözö Kulcsár (HUN) 3 wins
1976	Alexander Pusch (FRG) 3 wins	Jürgen Hehn (FRG) 3 wins	Gyözö Kulcsár (HUN) 3 wins

1980	Johan Harmenberg (SWE) 4 wins	Ernö Kolczonay (HUN) 3 wins	Philippe Riboud (FRA) 3 wins
1984	Philippe Boisse (FRA)	Bjorne Vaggo (SWE)	Philippe Riboud (FRA)
1988	Final on 24 September		

Épée team

	Gold	*Silver*	*Bronze*
1906	FRANCE 9 wins	GREAT BRITAIN 6 wins	BELGIUM
1908	FRANCE 9 wins	GREAT BRITAIN 7 wins	BELGIUM
1912	BELGIUM 3 wins	GREAT BRITAIN 1 win	NETHERLANDS 1 win
1920	ITALY 5 wins	BELGIUM 4 wins	FRANCE 3 wins
1924	FRANCE 3 wins	BELGIUM 2 wins	ITALY 1 win
1928	ITALY 3 wins	FRANCE 2 wins	PORTUGAL 1 win
1932	FRANCE 3 wins	ITALY 2 wins	UNITED STATES 1 win
1936	ITALY 3 wins	SWEDEN 2 wins	FRANCE 1 win
1948	FRANCE 3 wins	ITALY 2 wins	SWEDEN 1 win
1952	ITALY 3 wins	SWEDEN 2 wins	SWITZERLAND 1 win
1956	ITALY 3 wins	HUNGARY 2 wins	FRANCE 1 win
1960	ITALY 9 wins	GREAT BRITAIN 5 wins	USSR
1964	HUNGARY 8 wins	ITALY 3 wins	FRANCE
1968	HUNGARY 7 wins	USSR 4 wins	POLAND
1972	HUNGARY 8 wins	SWITZERLAND 4 wins	USSR
1976	SWEDEN 8 wins	WEST GERMANY 5 wins	SWITZERLAND
1980	FRANCE 8 wins	POLAND 4 wins	USSR
1984	WEST GERMANY Elmar Boorman Volker Fischer Gerhard Heer Rafael Nickel Alexander Pusch	FRANCE Philippe Boisse Jean Michel Henry Olivier Lenglet Philippe Riboud Michel Salesse	ITALY Stefano Bellone Sandro Cuomo Cosimo Ferro Roberto Manzi Angelo Mazzoni
1988	Final on 30 September		

Sabre individual/*Men*

	Gold	*Silver*	*Bronze*
1896	Jean Georgiadis (GRE) 4 wins	Telemachos Karakalos (GRE) 3 wins	Holger Nielsen (DEN) 2 wins
1900	Georges de la Falaise (FRA) d.n.a.	Léon Thiébaut (FRA) d.n.a.	Siegfried Flesch (AUT) d.n.a.
1904	Manuel Diaz (CUB) 3 wins	William Grebe (USA) 2 wins	Albertson Van Zo Post (CUB) 2 wins
1906	Jean Georgiadis (GRE) d.n.a.	Gustav Casmir (GER) d.n.a.	Federico Cesarano (ITA) d.n.a.
1908	Jenö Fuchs (HUN) 6 wins	Béla Zulavsky (HUN) 6 wins	Vilem Goppold von Lobsdorf (BOH) 4 wins

1912	Jenö Fuchs (HUN) 6 wins	Béla Békéssy (HUN) 5 wins	Ervin Mészáros (HUN) 5 wins
1920	Nedo Nadi (ITA) 11 wins	Aldo Nadi (ITA) 9 wins	Adrianus E. W. de Jong (HOL) 7 wins
1924	Sándor Posta (HUN) 5 wins	Roger Ducret (FRA) 5 wins	János Garai (HUN) 5 wins
1928	Ödön Tersztyánszky (HUN) 9 wins	Attila Petschauer (HUN) 9 wins	Bino Bini (ITA) 8 wins
1932	György Piller (HUN) 8 wins	Giulio Gaudini (ITA) 7 wins	Endre Kabos (HUN) 5 wins
1936	Endre Kabos (HUN) 7 wins	Gustavo Marzi (ITA) 6 wins	Aladár Gerevich (HUN) 6 wins
1948	Aldár Gerevich (HUN) 7 wins	Vincenzo Pinton (ITA) 5 wins	Pál Kovács (HUN) 5 wins
1952	Pál Kovács (HUN) 8 wins	Aladár Gerevich (HUN) 7 wins	Tibor Berczelly (HUN) 5 wins
1956	Rudolf Kárpáti (HUN) 6 wins	Jerzy Pawlowski (POL) 5 wins	Lev Kuznyetsov (URS) 4 wins
1960	Rudolf Kárpáti (HUN) 5 wins	Zoltán Horvath (HUN) 4 wins	Wladimiro Calarese (ITA) 4 wins
1964	Tibor Pézsa (HUN) 2 wins	Claude Arabo (FRA) 2 wins	Umar Mavlikhanov (URS) 1 win
1968	Jerzy Pawlowski (POL) 4 wins	Mark Rakita (URS) 4 wins	Tibor Pézsa (HUN) 3 wins
1972	Viktor Sidiak (URS) 4 wins	Peter Maroth (HUN) 3 wins	Vladimir Nazlimov (URS) 3 wins
1976	Victor Krovopouskov (URS) 5 wins	Vladimir Nazlimov (URS) 4 wins	Viktor Sidiak (URS) 3 wins
1980	Viktor Krovopouskov (URS) 4 wins	Mikhail Burtsev (URS) 4 wins	Imre Gedovari (HUN) 3 wins
1984	Jean François Lamour (FRA)	Marco Marin (ITA)	Peter Westbrook (USA)
1988	Final on 23 September		

Sabre team/*Men*

	Gold	*Silver*	*Bronze*
1906	GERMANY	GREECE	NETHERLANDS
1908	HUNGARY	ITALY	BOHEMIA
1912	HUNGARY	AUSTRIA	NETHERLANDS
1920	ITALY 6 wins	FRANCE 5 wins	NETHERLANDS 4 wins
1924	ITALY 3 wins	HUNGARY 2 wins	NETHERLANDS 1 win
1928	HUNGARY 2 wins	ITALY 1 win	POLAND 1 win
1932	HUNGARY 3 wins	ITALY 2 wins	POLAND 1 win
1936	HUNGARY 3 wins	ITALY 2 wins	GERMANY 1 win
1948	HUNGARY 3 wins	ITALY 2 wins	UNITED STATES 1 win
1952	HUNGARY 3 wins	ITALY 2 wins	FRANCE 1 win
1956	HUNGARY 3 wins	POLAND 2 wins	USSR 1 win
1960	HUNGARY 9 wins	POLAND 7 wins	ITALY
1964	USSR 9 wins	ITALY 6 wins	POLAND
1968	USSR 9 wins	ITALY 7 wins	HUNGARY
1972	ITALY 9 wins	USSR 5 wins	HUNGARY
1976	USSR 9 wins	ITALY 4 wins	ROMANIA

1980	USSR 9 wins	ITALY 2 wins	HUNGARY
1984	ITALY	FRANCE	ROMANIA
	Marco Marin	Jean-François Lamour	Marin Mustata
	Gianfranco Dalla Barba	Pierre Guichot	Ion Pop
	Giovanni Scalzo	Herve Granger-Veyron	Alexandru Chiculita
	Ferdinando Meglio	Philippe Delrieu	Corneliu Marin
	Angelo Arcidiacono	Franck Ducheix	
1988	Final on 29 September		

Foil individual/*Women*

	Gold	*Silver*	*Bronze*
1924	Ellen Osiier (DEN) 5 wins	Gladys Davis (GBR) 4 wins	Grete Heckscher (DEN)
1928	Helène Mayer (GER) 7 wins	Muriel Freeman (GBR) 6 wins	Olga Oelkers (GER) 4 wins
1932	Ellen Preis (AUT) 8 wins	Heather Guinness (GBR) 8 wins	Erna Bogen (HUN) 7 wins
1936	Ilona Elek (HUN) 6 wins	Helène Mayer (GER) 5 wins	Ellen Preis (AUT) 5 wins
1948	Ilona Elek (HUN) 6 wins	Karen Lachmann (DEN) 5 wins	Ellen Müller-Preis (AUT) 5 wins
1952	Irene Camber (ITA) 5 wins	Ilona Elek (HUN) 5 wins	Karen Lachmann (DEN) 4 wins
1956	Gillian Sheen (GBR) 6 wins	Olga Orban (ROM) 6 wins	Renée Garilhe (FRA) 5 wins
1960	Heidi Schmid (GER) 6 wins	Valentina Rastvorova (URS) 5 wins	Maria Vicol (ROM) 4 wins
1964	Ildikó Ujlaki-Rejtö (HUN) 2 wins	Helga Mees (GER) 2 wins	Antonella Ragno (ITA) 2 wins
1968	Elena Novikova (URS) 4 wins	Pilar Roldan (MEX) 3 wins	Ildikó Ujlaki-Rejtö (HUN) 3 wins
1972	Antonella Ragno-Lonzi (ITA) 4 wins	Ildikó Bóbis (HUN) 3 wins	Galina Gorokhova (URS) 3 wins
1976	Ildikó Schwarczenberger (HUN) 4 wins	Maria Collino (ITA) 4 wins	Elena Novikova-Belova (URS) 3 wins
1980	Pascale Trinquet (FRA) 4 wins	Magda Maros (HUN) 3 wins	Barbara Wysoczanwka (POL) 3 wins
1984	Jujie Luan (CHN)	Cornelia Hanisch (FRG)	Dorina Vaccaroni (ITA)
1988	Final on 22 September		

Team foil/*Women*

	Gold	*Silver*	*Bronze*
1960	USSR 9 wins	HUNGARY 3 wins	ITALY
1964	HUNGARY 9 wins	USSR 7 wins	GERMANY
1968	USSR 9 wins	HUNGARY 3 wins	ROMANIA
1972	USSR 9 wins	HUNGARY 5 wins	ROMANIA
1976	USSR 9 wins	FRANCE 2 wins	HUNGARY
1980	FRANCE 9 wins	USSR 6 wins	HUNGARY
1984	WEST GERMANY	ROMANIA	FRANCE
	Christiane Weber	Aurora Dan	Laurence Modaine
	Cornelia Hanisch	Koszto Veber	Pascale Trinquet-Hachin
	Sabine Bischoff	Rozalia Oros	Brigitte Gaudin
	Zita Funkenhauser	Marcela Zsak	Véronique Brouquier
	Ute Wessel	Elizabeta Guzanu	Anne Meygret
1988	Final on 28 September		

FOOTBALL

The sport appeared in the second modern Games in 1900, although only three countries took part. In the early days it was common for a single club to represent a country, e.g., Upton Park represented Great Britain in 1900 and won the gold.

With the barriers between amateur and professional sketchy, to say the least, in many countries, qualification for eligibility for the Games has become something of a farce. In simple terms, the only players disbarred are those who have played in any world cup tournament (preliminaries or finals). This means that most of the professional players in world football can be involved.

In Los Angeles in 1984, the sport attracted the biggest crowds of all, 101,799 watching the final in which France beat Brazil. The first round matches were watched by some 800,000 people. This in a country where soccer plays only a minor role.

Quite often, the Olympic stars of today will be the stars of the World Cup finals two years hence.

Largely because football in the UK is organized by four different bodies, (the Football Association, the Scottish Football Association, the Welsh Football Association and the Irish Football Association), there has not been a Great Britain entry in the Olympics in recent years.

Unlike hockey, for example, there is no separate women's Olympic football competition.

THE COMPETITION

Sixteen countries will qualify from the various worldwide qualifying groups. France, the holders, did not have automatic qualification and have been eliminated and therefore unable to defend their Olympic title.

The teams will play in groups of four and will be split (as far as possible) by seeding and geographical location. Group games will be on a league basis. The top two from each group will progress to the quarterfinals. Winners of groups will play runners-up from groups, and competition will then proceed on a knockout basis.

Matches will be over the normal ninety minutes, but from the knockout stage, extra time will be played if required and then penalty shoot outs.

The Eastern Europeans are likely to be strong, but now that the Western Europeans can call on players from the Bundesliga and the Italian and Spanish first divisions, things will be more even.

BRITISH SUCCESSES

Britain has won the Olympic title three times, but not since before the First World War.

THE STARS

The Uruguayans won the gold medal in 1924 and defended the title successfully in 1928.

Nine of that victorious team were in the side that won the 1930 World Cup.

The Hungarian team that won in 1952 included Puskas, Hideguti and Boszik who, the following year, came to Wembley and inflicted England's first ever home defeat by a foreign country.

In 1972 in Munich, Poland paraded the team which 12 months later, almost to a man, knocked England out of the World Cup.

And as ever, the South Americans will be potential medallists.

Not a lot of people know that

• If Great Britain entered a team, it could look something like this: Woods (Rangers), Parker (QPR), Bruce (Manchester United), Adams (Arsenal), Pearce (Nott'm Forest), Davis (Arsenal), Rocastle (Arsenal), Webb (Nott'm Forest), Johnstone (Liverpool), Regis (Coventry), and Clough (Nott'm Forest).

There could be many such concoctions and, indeed, Britain could probably find a half dozen 'elevens' who could compete with the best. However, the above players would lose eligibility if they played a World Cup qualifying match between now and the start of the Games on 17 September 1988.

• Denmark beat Poland 2–0 in a qualifying match but because their Anderlecht forward, Per Frimann, had played in three World Cup matches in 1986, the result was reversed by FIFA.
• The Nordahl family of Sweden achieved a remarkable distinction in 1948. Bertil (centre half), Knut (right back) and Gunnar (centre forward) all won gold medals in the same competition at the same Games.
• The most goals scored in one tournament is 12 by Ferenc Bene (Hungary) in 1964.

VENUES

Pusan Stadium. 480 km from Olympic Village. Capacity 25,000.
Tongdaeum Stadium. 13 km from Olympic Village. Capacity 30,000.
Taejon Stadium. 200 km from Olympic Village. Capacity 30,000.
Kwangju Stadium. 325 km from Olympic Village. Capacity 24,000.
Taegu Stadium. 290 km from Olympic Village. Capacity 30,000.
Quarterfinals at all except Taejon.
Semifinals, Pusan and Olympic.
Final, Olympic Stadium.

RESULTS

	Gold	Silver	Bronze
1900	GREAT BRITAIN	FRANCE	BELGIUM
1904	CANADA	UNITED STATES	UNITED STATES
1906	DENMARK	SMYRNA (Greece)	THESSALONIKA (Greece)
1908	GREAT BRITAIN	DENMARK	NETHERLANDS
1912	GREAT BRITAIN	DENMARK	NETHERLANDS
1920	BELGIUM	SPAIN	NETHERLANDS
1924	URUGUAY	SWITZERLAND	SWEDEN
1928	URUGUAY	ARGENTINA	ITALY
1936	ITALY	AUSTRIA	NORWAY

1948	SWEDEN	YUGOSLAVIA	DENMARK
1952	HUNGARY	YUGOSLAVIA	SWEDEN
1956	USSR	YUGOSLAVIA	BULGARIA
1960	YUGOSLAVIA	DENMARK	HUNGARY
1964	HUNGARY	CZECHOSLOVAKIA	GERMANY
1968	HUNGARY	BULGARIA	JAPAN
1972	POLAND	HUNGARY	EAST GERMANY*
1976	EAST GERMANY	POLAND	USSR
1980	CZECHOSLOVAKIA	EAST GERMANY	USSR
1984	FRANCE	BRAZIL	YUGOSLAVIA

1988   Final on 1 October (3rd and 4th place match on 30 September)

*Tie declared after extra time played.

GYMNASTICS

The sport has been part of the Olympics since the first Games of the modern era in 1896. Women's individual competition was introduced in 1952 with the Soviet Union making an immediate impact.

There is no disputing that television has made the sport highly popular. In 1972 Olga Korbut became world famous and four years later the tiny Rumanian Nadia Comeneci, also just 4 ft 11 ins tall, dominated the sport.

Indeed, the women gymnasts have become far more famous than the men. Their grace, coupled with sheer courage, make them compulsively attractive to watch and again in Seoul the eyes of the world will be upon them.

MEN'S EVENTS

There are eight Olympic titles available. One for the team championship, one for the individual overall championship, and then separate titles for the best in each individual discipline.

The disciplines

Horizontal bar
Parallel bars
Long horse vault
Side horse (pommel horse)
Rings
Floor exercises

Each country enters a maximum of six gymnasts who compete in all six disciplines. Each performs a compulsory and voluntary exercise on each. Total scores decide the team competition.

The best thirty-six competitors go forward to the individual overall competition. They carry with them the average of their compulsory and optional marks already gained in team competition. They then perform further optional exercises in all six disciplines. Marks are added to that previous average.

After this, the best eight from the original team competition in each discipline (with a maximum of two per country) go forward to perform a further optional exercise in that discipline. Marks here are added to the average mark produced in the original team competition in the said discipline.

In short, the team competition becomes a qualifying round for the overall and separate discipline titles. There is no way back for a competitor not finishing in the top thirty-six places there.

WOMEN'S EVENTS

There are seven Olympic titles available. As in the men's there is a team championship and an overall individual title, and then separate titles for the best in each individual discipline.

The disciplines

Side horse vault
Asymmetrical bars
Balance beam
Floor exercises

There is now a further category in women's gymnastics, which was first introduced in 1984, rhythmic gymnastics.

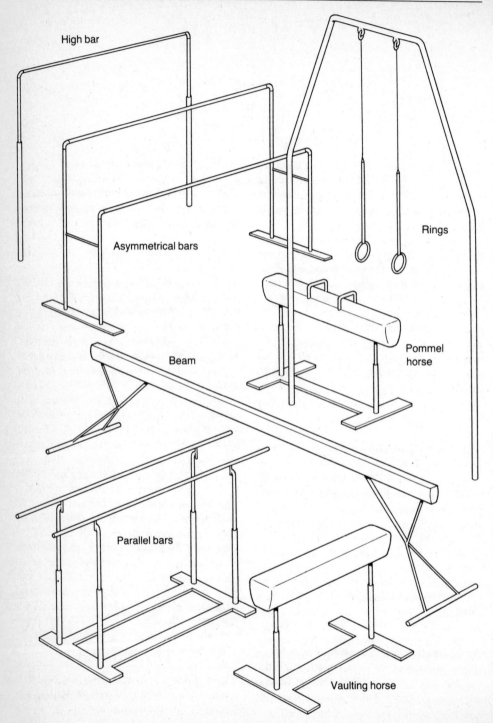

High bar

Asymmetrical bars

Rings

Pommel
horse

Beam

Parallel bars

Vaulting horse

114

Rope   Clubs   Ribbon   Ball   Hoop

The women's competition is run on much the same lines as the men's, except that rhythmic gymnastics is a separate event where hoops and ribbons, ropes and clubs are used. It is the gymnast's equivalent of synchronized swimming.

JUDGING

Four judges award marks out of ten. The highest and lowest are discarded, and the remaining two marks are averaged. The application of awarding marks is, as in similar sports, highly complicated and often contentious.

COMPETITION

The men's competition will be a direct fight between the Soviet Union and Japan with China next best. The Soviets have the current overall world champion in Dimitri Belozerchev. He had been world champion in 1983 and would have been favourite for several gold medals in the 1984 Olympics had the Soviets taken part. His feat in regaining the world championship in 1987 was remarkable. He had to recover from a horrific car crash in which he broke 40 bones.

The women's competition will see the Soviets and Rumanians having their usual dog fight but the Chinese are improving rapidly and the Americans who did so well on home territory have the know-how and coaching to produce some more medallists.

The Bulgarians will fancy their chances in rhythmic gymnastics.

THE STARS

Dimitri Belozerchev, of the Soviet Union, is the present outstanding male gymnast. The Soviets have produced many stars down the years. Boris Shakhlin and Nikolai Andrianov both won six gold medals. Alexsandr Ditiatin won a medal in all eight categories in the 1980 Games: two gold, four silver and two bronze.

In terms of world fame, the women have outshone the men. In the sixties there was Vera Caslavska (TCH), winner of a record seven individual gold medals. Olga Korbut was the darling of the Munich Olympics. There was Ludmila Tourischeva and Nellie Kim, while Nadia Comeneci (ROM), usually unsmiling, scored the first perfect 10 in 1976. She went on to score seven 10s – all at the age of fourteen.

In the Los Angeles Games, an American girl, Mary Lou Retton, won the overall gold, plus two silvers and two bronze medals, but even more successful was Ecaterina Szabo (ROM) with four golds and one silver medal.

THE BRITISH

The standard of British gymnastics is well below Olympic medal potential. Britain has managed a silver and bronze in men's

115

events, but nothing since 1912. Britain's women managed bronze medals in the team event in 1928.

Not a lot of people know that

• Larissa Latynina (URS) won a total of eighteen medals between 1956 and 1964, the first of them when almost twenty-two and the last when nearly thirty. By modern standards she would be a veteran.
• Most women gymnasts today are retired by the age of twenty.
• When competitors first scored perfect 10s in 1976, the scoreboard was not capable of showing it and put the score up as 1.00.

• The closest margin in marks awarded is 0.05.
• George Eyser (USA) won a total of five medals at the 1904 Games. Not that incredible except that George had a wooden leg.
• Some of the great manoeuvres in the sport are now described by the name of the gymnast who first perfected them. Male gymnasts in Seoul will be attempting 'Tsukahara's' and 'Yamashita's'.

VENUE

Gymnastics Hall in Olympic Park. Capacity 15,000.

RESULTS

Team competition/*Men*

	Gold	*Silver*	*Bronze*
1904	UNITED STATES 374.43 pts	UNITED STATES 356.37 pts	UNITED STATES 349.69 pts
1906	NORWAY 19.00 pts	DENMARK 18.00 pts	ITALY 16.71 pts
1908	SWEDEN 438 pts	NORWAY 425 pts	FINLAND 405 pts
1912	ITALY 265.75 pts	HUNGARY 227.25 pts	GREAT BRITAIN 184.50 pts
1920	ITALY 359.855 pts	BELGIUM 346.785 pts	FRANCE 340.100 pts
1924	ITALY 839.058 pts	FRANCE 820.528 pts	SWITZERLAND 816.661 pts
1928	SWITZERLAND 1718.625 pts	CZECHOSLOVAKIA 1712.250 pts	YUGOSLAVIA 1648.750 pts
1932	ITALY 541.850 pts	UNITED STATES 522.275 pts	FINLAND 509.995 pts
1936	GERMANY 657.430 pts	SWITZERLAND 654.802 pts	FINLAND 638.468 pts
1948	FINLAND 1358.3 pts	SWITZERLAND 1356.7 pts	HUNGARY 1330.85 pts
1952	USSR 575.4 pts	SWITZERLAND 567.5 pts	FINLAND 564.2 pts
1956	USSR 568.25 pts	JAPAN 566.40 pts	FINLAND 555.95 pts
1960	JAPAN 575.20 pts	USSR 572.70 pts	ITALY 559.05 pts
1964	JAPAN 577.95 pts	USSR 575.45 pts	GERMANY 565.10 pts
1968	JAPAN 575.90 pts	USSR 571.10 pts	EAST GERMANY 557.15 pts
1972	JAPAN 571.25 pts	USSR 564.05 pts	EAST GERMANY 559.70 pts
1976	JAPAN 576.85 pts	USSR 576.45 pts	EAST GERMANY 564.65 pts
1980	USSR 589.60 pts	EAST GERMANY 581.15 pts	HUNGARY 575.00 pts

1984	USA 591.40 pts	CHINA 590.80 pts	JAPAN 586.70 pts
	Timothy Daggett	Yun Lou	Shinji Morisue
	Scott Johnson	Yuejiu Li	Noritoshi Hirata
	Mitchell Gaylord	Xu Zhiqiang	Koji Sotomura
	James Hartung	Fei Tong	Nobuyuki Kajitani
	Peter Vidmar	Ning Li	Kyoji Yamawaki
	Bart Conner	Xiaoping Li	Koji Gushiken

1988   18 and 20 September

Individual combined exercises/*Men*

	Gold	*Silver*	*Bronze*
1900	Gustave Sandras (FRA) 302	Noël Bas (FRA) 295	Lucien Démanet (FRA) 293
1904	Julius Lenhart (AUT) 69.80	Wilhelm Weber (GER) 69.10	Adolf Spinnler (SUI) 67.99
1906*	Pierre Payssé (FRA) 97	Alberto Braglia (ITA) 95	Georges Charmoille (FRA) 94
1906	Pierre Payssé (FRA) 116	Alberto Braglia (ITA) 115	Georges Charmoille (FRA) 113
1908	Alberto Braglia (ITA) 317.0	S. W. Tysal (GBR) 312.0	Louis Ségura (FRA) 297.0
1912	Alberto Braglia (ITA) 135.0	Louis Ségura (FRA) 132.5	Adolfo Tunesi (ITA) 131.5
1920	Giorgio Zampori (ITA) 88.35	Marco Torrés (FRA) 87.62	Jean Gounot (FRA) 87.45
1924	Leon Stukelj (YUG) 110.340	Robert Prazák (TCH) 110.323	Bedrich Supcik (TCH) 106.930
1928	Georges Miez (SUI) 247.500	Hermann Hänggi (SUI) 246.625	Leon Stukelj (YUG) 244.875
1932	Romeo Neri (ITA) 140.625	Istvan Pelle (HUN) 134.925	Heikki Savolainen (FIN) 134.575
1936	Alfred Schwarzmann (GER) 113.100	Eugen Mack (SUI) 112.334	Konrad Frey (GER) 111.532
1948	Veikko Huhtanen (FIN) 229.7	Walter Lehmann (SUI) 229.0	Paavo Aaltonen (FIN) 228.8
1952	Viktor Chukarin (URS) 115.70	Grant Shaginyan (URS) 114.95	Josef Stalder (SUI) 114.75
1956	Viktor Chukarin (URS) 114.25	Takashi Ono (JPN) 114.20	Yuriy Titov (URS) 113.80
1960	Boris Shakhlin (URS) 115.95	Takashi Ono (JPN) 115.90	Yuriy Titov (URS) 115.60
1964	Yukio Endo (JPN) 115.95	Shuji Tsurumi (JPN) 115.40 Boris Shakhlin (URS) 115.40 Viktor Lisitsky (URS) 115.40	—
1968	Sawao Kato (JPN) 115.90	Mikhail Voronin (URS) 115.85	Akinori Nakayama (JPN) 115.65
1972	Sawao Kato (JPN) 114.650	Eizo Kenmotsu (JPN) 114.575	Akinori Nakayama (JPN) 114.325
1976	Nikolai Andrianov (URS) 116.650	Sawao Kato (JPN) 115.650	Mitsuo Tsukahara (JPN) 115.575
1980	Aleksandr Ditiatin (URS) 118.650	Nikolai Andrianov (URS) 118.225	Stoyan Deltchev (BUL) 118.000
1984	Koji Gushiken (JPN) 118.700	Peter Vidmar (USA) 118.675	Ning Li (CHN) 118.575

1988   Final on 22 September

* Two competitions, one on five apparati, the other on six.

Floor exercises/*Men*

Gold	Silver	Bronze
1932 István Pelle (HUN) 9.60	Georges Miez (SUI) 9.47	Mario Lertora (ITA) 9.23
1936 Georges Miez (SUI) 18.666	Josef Walter (SUI) 18.500	Konrad Frey (GER) 18.466 Eugen Mack (SUI) 18.466
1948 Ferenc Pataki (HUN) 38.7	János Mogyorósi-Klencs (HUN) 38.4	Zdenek Ružička (TCH) 38.1
1952 William Thoresson (SWE) 19.25	Tadao Uesako (JPN) 19.15 Jerzy Jokiel (POL) 19.15	—
1956 Valentin Muratov (URS) 19.20	Nobuyuki Aihara (JPN) 19.10 Viktor Chukarin (URS) 19.10 William Thoresson (SWE) 19.10	—
1960 Nobuyuki Aihara (JPN) 19.450	Yuriy Titov (URS) 19.325	Franco Menichelli (ITA) 19.275
1964 Franco Menichelli (ITA) 19.45	Viktor Lisitsky (URS) 19.35 Yukio Endo (JPN) 19.35	—
1968 Sawao Kato (JPN) 19.475	Akinori Nakayama (JPN) 19.400	Takeshi Kato (JPN) 19.275
1972 Nikolai Andrianov (URS) 19.175	Akinori Nakayama (JPN) 19.125	Shigeru Kasamatsu (JPN) 19.025
1976 Nikolai Andrianov (URS) 19.450	Vladimir Marchenko (URS) 19.425	Peter Kormann (USA) 19.300
1980 Roland Brückner (GDR) 19.750	Nikolai Andrianov (URS) 19.725	Aleksandr Ditiatin (URS) 19.700
1984 Ning Li (CHN) 19.925	Yun Lou (CHN) 19.775	Koji Sotomura (JPN) 19.700 Philippe Vatuone (FRA) 19.700

1988 Final on 24 September

Parallel bars/*Men*

Gold	Silver	Bronze
1896 Alfred Flatow (GER) d.n.a.	Jules Zutter (SUI)	Hermann Weingärtner (GER)
1904 George Eyser (USA) 44	Anton Heida (USA) 43	John Duha (USA) 40
1924 August Güttinger (SUI) 21.63	Robert Pražák (TCH) 21.61	Giorgio Zampori (ITA) 21.45
1928 Ladislav Vácha (TCH) 18.83	Josip Primožič (YUG) 18.50	Hermann Hànggi (SUI) 18.08
1932 Romeo Neri (ITA) 18.97	István Pelle (HUN) 18.60	Heikki Savolainen (FIN) 18.27
1936 Konrad Frey (GER) 19.067	Michael Reusch (SUI) 19.034	Alfred Schwarzmann (GER) 18.967
1948 Michael Reusch (SUI) 39.5	Veikkö Huhtanen (FIN) 39.3	Christian Kipfer (SUI) 39.1 Josef Stalder (SUI) 39.1
1952 Hans Eugster (SUI) 19.65	Viktor Chukarin (URS) 19.60	Josef Stalder (SUI) 19.50
1956 Viktor Chukarin (URS) 19.20	Masami Kubota (JPN) 19.15	Takashi Ono (JPN) 19.10 Masao Takemoto (JPN) 19.10

1960	Boris Shakhlin (URS) 19.400	Giovanni Carminucci (ITA) 19.375	Takashi Ono (JPN) 19.350
1964	Yukio Endo (JPN) 19.675	Shuji Tsurumi (JPN) 19.450	Franco Menichelli (ITA) 19.350
1968	Akinori Nakayama (JPN) 19.475	Mikhail Voronin (URS) 19.425	Vladimir Klimenko (URS) 19.225
1972	Sawao Kato (JPN) 19.475	Shigeru Kasamatsu (JPN) 19.375	Eizo Kenmotsu (JPN) 19.250
1976	Sawao Kato (JPN) 19.675	Nikolai Andrianov (URS) 19.500	Mitsuo Tsukahara (JPN) 19.475
1980	Aleksandr Tkachyov (URS) 19.775	Aleksandr Ditiatin (URS) 19.750	Roland Brückner (GDR) 19.650
1984	Bart Conner (USA) 19.950	Nobuyuki Kajitani (JPN) 19.925	Mitchell Gaylord (USA) 19.850
1988	Final on 24 September		

Pommel horse/*Men*

	Gold	*Silver*	*Bronze*
1896	Jules Zutter (SUI) d.n.a.	Hermann Weingartner (GER)	—
1904	Anton Heida (USA) 42	George Eyser (USA) 33	William Merz (USA) 29
1924	Josef Wilhelm (SUI) 21.23	Jean Gutweiniger (SUI) 21.13	Antoine Rebetez (SUI) 20.73
1928	Hermann Hänggi (SUI) 19.75	Georges Miez (SUI) 19.25	Heikki Savolainen (FIN) 18.83
1932	István Pelle (HUN) 19.07	Omero Bonoli (ITA) 18.87	Frank Haubold (USA) 18.57
1936	Konrad Frey (GER) 19.333	Eugen Mack (SUI) 19.167	Albert Bachmann (SUI) 19.067
1948	Paavo Aaltonen (FIN) 38.7 Veikkö Huhtanen (FIN) 38.7 Heikki Savolainen (FIN) 38.7	Luigi Zanetti (ITA) 38.3	Guido Figone (ITA) 38.2
1952	Viktor Chukarin (URS) 19.50	Yevgeniy Korolkov (URS) 19.40 Grant Shaginyan (URS) 19.40	—
1956	Boris Shakhlin (URS) 19.25	Takashi Ono (JPN) 19.20	Viktor Chukarin (URS) 19.10
1960	Eugen Ekman (FIN) 19.375 Boris Shakhlin (URS) 19.375	—	Shuji Tsurumi (JPN) 19.150
1964	Miroslav Cerar (YUG) 19.525	Shuji Tsurumi (JPN) 19.325	Yuriy Tsapenko (URS) 19.200
1968	Miroslav Cerar (YUG) 19.325	Olli Laiho (FIN) 19.225	Mikhail Voronin (URS) 19.200
1972	Viktor Klimenko (URS) 19.125	Sawao Kato (JPN) 19.000	Eizo Kenmotsu (JPN) 18.950
1976	Zoltan Magyar (HUN) 19.700	Eizo Kenmotsu (JPN) 19.575	Nikolai Andrianov (URS) 19.525
1980	Zoltan Magyar (HUN) 19.925	Aleksandr Ditiatin (URS) 19.800	Michael Nikolay (GDR) 19.775
1984	Ning Li (CHN) 19.950 Peter Vidmar (USA) 19.950	—	Timothy Daggett (USA) 19.825
1988	Final on 24 September		

Rings/*Men*

	Gold	Silver	Bronze
1896	Ioannis Mitropoulos (GRE) d.n.a.	Hermann Weingärtner (GER)	Petros Persakis (GRE)
1904	Herman Glass (USA) 45	William Merz (USA) 35	Emil Voight (USA) 32
1924	Franco Martino (ITA) 21.553	Robert Pražák (TCH) 21.483	Ladislav Vácha (TCH) 21.430
1928	Leon Škutelj (YUG) 19.25	Ladislav Vácha (TCH) 19.17	Emanuel Löffler (TCH) 18.83
1932	George Gulack (USA) 18.97	William Denton (USA) 18.60	Giovanni Lattuada (ITA) 18.50
1936	Alois Hudec (TCH) 19.433	Leon Škutelj (YUG) 18.867	Matthias Valz (GER) 18.667
1948	Karl Frei (SUI) 39.60	Michael Reusch (SUI) 39.10	Zdenek Ružička (TCH) 38.302
1952	Grant Shaginyan (URS) 19.75	Viktor Chukarin (URS) 19.55	Hans Eugster (SUI) 19.40 Dimitriy Leonkin (URS) 19.40
1956	Albert Azaryan (URS) 19.35	Valentin Muratov (URS) 19.15	Masao Takemoto (JPN) 19.10 Masami Kubota (JPN) 19.10
1960	Albert Azaryan (URS) 19.725	Boris Shakhlin (URS) 19.500	Velik Kapsazov (BUL) 19.425 Takashi Ono (JPN) 19.425
1964	Takuji Hayata (JPN) 19.475	Franco Menichelli (ITA) 19.425	Boris Shakhlin (URS) 19.400
1968	Akinori Nakayama (JPN) 19.450	Mikhail Voronin (URS) 19.325	Sawao Kato (JPN) 19.225
1972	Akinori Nakayama (JPN) 19.350	Mikhail Voronin (URS) 19.275	Mitsuo Tsukahara (JPN) 19.225
1976	Nikolai Andrianov (URS) 19.650	Aleksandr Ditiatin (URS) 19.550	Danut Grecu (ROM) 19.500
1980	Aleksandr Ditiatin (URS) 19.875	Aleksandr Tkachyov (URS) 19.725	Jiri Tabak (TCH) 19.600
1984	Koji Gushiken (JPN) 19.850 Ning Li (CHN) 19.850	—	Mitchell Gaylord (USA) 19.825
1988	Final on 24 September		

Horizontal bar/*Men*

	Gold	Silver	Bronze
1896	Hermann Weingärtner (GER) d.n.a.	Alfred Flatow (GER)	—
1904	Anton Heida (USA) 40 Edward Hennig (USA) 40	—	George Eyser (USA) 39
1924	Leon Štukelj (YUG) 19.730	Jean Gutweniger (SUI) 19.236	André Higelin (FRA) 19.163
1928	Georges Miez (SUI) 19.17	Romeo Neri (ITA) 19.00	Eugen Mack (SUI) 18.92
1932	Dallas Bixler (USA) 18.33	Heikki Savolainen (FIN) 18.07	Einari Teräsvirta (FIN) 18.07*

*Conceded silver to Savolainen.

1936	Aleksanteri Saarvala (FIN) 19.367	Konrad Frey (GER) 19.267	Alfred Schwarzmann (GER) 19.233
1948	Josef Stalder (SUI) 39.7	Walter Lehmann (SUI) 39.4	Veikkö Huhtanen (FIN) 39.2
1952	Jack Günthard (SUI) 19.55	Josef Stalder (SUI) 19.50 Albert Schwarzmann (GER) 19.50	—
1956	Takashi Ono (JPN) 19.60	Yuriy Titov (URS) 19.40	Masao Takemoto (JPN) 19.30
1960	Takashi Ono (JPN) 19.60	Masao Takemoto (JPN) 19.525	Boris Shakhlin (URS) 19.475
1964	Boris Shakhlin (URS) 19.625	Yuriy Titov (URS) 19.55	Miroslav Cerar (YUG) 19.50
1968	Mikhail Voronin (URS) 19.550 Akinori Nakayama (JPN) 19.550	—	Eizo Kenmotsu (JPN) 19.375
1972	Mitsuo Tsukahara (JPN) 19.725	Sawao Kato (JPN) 19.525	Shigeru Kasamatsu (JPN) 19.450
1976	Mitsuo Tsukahara (JPN) 19.675	Eizo Kenmotsu (JPN) 19.500	Henry Boerio (FRA) 19.475 Eberhard Gienger (FRG) 19.475
1980	Stoyan Deltchev (BUL) 19.825	Aleksandr Ditiatin (URS) 19.750	Nikolai Andrianov (URS) 19.675
1984	Shinje Morisue (JPN) 20.000	Fei Tong (CHN) 19.975	Koji Gushiken (JPN) 19.950
1988	Final on 24 September		

Horse vault/*Men*

	Gold	*Silver*	*Bronze*
1896	Karl Schumann (GER) d.n.a.	Jules Zutter (SUI)	—
1904	Anton Heida (USA) 36 George Eyser (USA) 36	—	William Merz (USA) 31
1924	Frank Kriz (USA) 9.98	Jan Koutny (TCH) 9.97	Bohumil Mořkovsky (TCH) 9.93
1928	Eugen Mack (SUI) 9.58	Emanuel Löffler (TCH) 9.50	Stane Derganc (YUG) 9.46
1932	Savino Guglielmetti (ITA) 18.03	Alfred Jochim (GER) 17.77	Edward Carmichael (USA) 17.53
1936	Alfred Schwarzmann (GER) 19.200	Eugen Mack (SUI) 18.967	Matthias Volz (GER) 18.467
1948	Paavo Aaltonen (FIN) 39.10	Olvai Rove (FIN) 39.00	János Mogyorósi-Klencs (HUN) 38.50 Ferenc Pataki (HUN) 38.50 Leos Sotornik (TCH) 38.50
1952	Viktor Chukarin (URS) 19.20	Masao Takemoto (JPN) 19.15	Tadao Uesako (JPN) 19.10 Takashi Ono (JPN) 19.10
1956	Helmuth Bantz (GER) 18.85 Valentin Muratov (URS) 18.85	—	Yuriy Titov (URS) 18.75
1960	Takashi Ono (JPN) 19.350 Boris Shakhlin (URS) 19.350	—	Vladimir Portnoi (URS) 19.225

121

1964	Haruhiro Yamashita (JPN) 19.600	Viktor Lisitsky (URS) 19.325	Hannu Rantakari (FIN) 19.300
1968	Mikhail Voronin (URS) 19.000	Yukio Endo (JPN) 18.950	Sergey Diomidov (URS) 18.925
1972	Klaus Köste (GDR) 18.850	Viktor Klimenko (URS) 18.825	Nikolai Andrianov (URS) 18.800
1976	Nikolai Andrianov (URS) 19.450	Mitsuo Tsukahara (JPN) 19.375	Hiroshi Kajiyama (JPN) 19.275
1980	Nikolai Andrianov (URS) 19.825	Aleksandr Ditiatin (URS) 19.800	Roland Brückner (GDR) 19.775
1984	Yun Lou (CHN) 19.950	Ning Li (CHN) 19.825 Koji Gushiken (JPN) 19.825 Mitchell Gaylord (USA) 19.825 Shinje Morisue (JPN) 19.825	—

1988   Final on 24 September

Team competition/*Women*

	Gold	*Silver*	*Bronze*
1928	NETHERLANDS 316.75	ITALY 289.00	GREAT BRITAIN 258.25
1936	GERMANY 506.50	CZECHOSLOVAKIA 503.60	HUNGARY 499.00
1948	CZECHOSLOVAKIA 445.45	HUNGARY 440.55	UNITED STATES 422.63
1952	USSR 527.03	HUNGARY 520.96	CZECHOSLOVAKIA 503.32
1956	USSR 444.80	HUNGARY 443.50	ROMANIA 438.20
1960	USSR 382.320	CZECHOSLOVAKIA 373.323	ROMANIA 372.053
1964	USSR 380.890	CZECHOSLOVAKIA 379.989	JAPAN 377.889
1968	USSR 382.85	CZECHOSLOVAKIA 382.20	EAST GERMANY 379.10
1972	USSR 380.50	EAST GERMANY 376.55	HUNGARY 368.25
1976	USSR 390.35	ROMANIA 387.15	EAST GERMANY 385.10
1980	USSR 394.90	ROMANIA 393.50	EAST GERMANY 392.55
1984	ROMANIA 392.20 Simona Pauca Michaela Stanulet Cristina Grigoras Laura Cutina Lavinia Agache Ecaterina Szabo	UNITED STATES 391.20 Pamela Bileck Tracee Talavera Kathy Johnson Michelle Dusserre Mary Lou Retton Julianne McNamara	CHINA 388.60 Qun Huang Qiurui Zhou Yongyan Chen Yanhong Ma Jiani Wu Ping Zhou

1988   On 19 and 21 September

Individual combined exercises/*Women*

	Gold	*Silver*	*Bronze*
1952	Maria Gorokhovskaya (URS) 76.78	Nina Bocharova (URS) 75.94	Margit Korondi (HUN) 75.82
1956	Larissa Latynina (URS) 74.933	Ágnes Keleti (HUN) 74.633	Sofia Muratova (URS) 74.466
1960	Larissa Latynina (URS) 77.031	Sofia Muratova (URS) 76.696	Polina Astakhova (URS) 76.164
1964	Vera Čáslavská (TCH) 77.564	Larissa Latynina (URS) 76.998	Polina Astakhova (URS) 76.965
1968	Vera Čáslavská (TCH) 78.25	Zinaida Voronina (URS) 76.85	Natalya Kuchinskaya (URS) 76.75
1972	Ludmila Tourischeva (URS) 77.025	Karin Janz (GDR) 76.875	Tamara Lazakovitch (URS) 76.850
1976	Nadia Comaneci (ROM) 79.275	Nelli Kim (URS) 78.675	Ludmila Tourischeva (URS) 78.625
1980	Elena Davydova (URS) 79.150	Maxi Gnauck (GDR) 79.075 Nadia Comaneci (ROM) 79.075	—
1984	Mary Lou Retton (USA) 79.175	Ecaterina Szabo (ROM) 79.125	Simona Pauca (ROM) 78.675
1988	Final on 23 September		

Asymmetrical bars/*Women*

	Gold	*Silver*	*Bronze*
1952	Margit Korondi (HUN) 19.40	Maria Gorokhovskaya (URS) 19.26	Ágnes Keleti (HUN) 19.16
1956	Ágnes Keleti (HUN) 18.966	Larissa Latynina (URS) 18.833	Sofia Muratova (URS) 18.800
1960	Polina Astakhova (URS) 19.616	Larissa Latynina (URS) 19.416	Tamara Lyukhina (URS) 19.399
1964	Polina Astakhova (URS) 19.332	Katalin Makray (HUN) 19.216	Larissa Latynina (URS) 19.199
1968	Vera Čáslavská (TCH) 19.650	Karin Janz (GDR) 19.500	Zinaida Voronina (URS) 19.425
1972	Karin Janz (GDR) 19.675	Olga Korbut (URS) 19.450 Erika Zuchold (GDR) 19.450	—
1976	Nadia Comaneci (ROM) 20.000	Teodora Ungureanu (ROM) 19.800	Marta Egervari (HUN) 19.775
1980	Maxi Gnauck (GDR) 19.875	Emilia Eberle (ROM) 19.850	Maria Filatova (URS) 19.775 Steffi Kräker (GDR) 19.775 Melita Ruhn (ROM) 19.775
1984	Yanhong Ma (CHN) 19.950 Julianne McNamara (USA) 19.950	—	Mary Lou Retton (USA) 19.800
1988	Final on 25 September		

Individual balance beam/*Women*

	Gold	Silver	Bronze
1952	Nina Bocharova (URS) 19.22	Maria Gorokhovskaya (URS) 19.13	Margit Korondi (HUN) 19.02
1956	Ágnes Keleti (HUN) 18.80	Eva Bosáková (TCH) 18.63 Tamara Manina (URS) 18.63	—
1960	Eva Bosáková (TCH) 19.283	Larissa Latynina (URS) 19.233	Sofia Muratova (URS) 19.232
1964	Vera Čáslavská (TCH) 19.449	Tamara Manina (URS) 19.399	Larissa Latynina (URS) 19.382
1968	Natalya Kuchinskaya (URS) 19.650	Vera Čáslavská (TCH) 19.575	Larissa Petrik (URS) 19.250
1972	Olga Korbut (URS) 19.575	Tamara Lazakovitch (URS) 19.375	Karin Janz (GDR) 18.975
1976	Nadia Comaneci (ROM) 19.950	Olga Korbut (URS) 19.725	Teodora Ungureanu (ROM) 19.700
1980	Nadia Comaneci (ROM) 19.800	Elena Davydova (URS) 19.750	Natalya Shaposhnikova (URS) 19.725
1984	Simona Pauca (ROM) 19.800 Ecaterina Szabo (ROM) 19.800	—	Kathy Johnson (USA) 19.650
1988	Final on 25 September		

Floor exercises/*Women*

	Gold	Silver	Bronze
1952	Ágnes Keleti (HUN) 19.36	Maria Gorokhovskaya (URS) 19.20	Margit Korondi (HUN) 19.00
1956	Larissa Latynina (URS) 18.733 Agnes Keleti (HUN) 18.733	—	Elena Leustean (ROM) 18.70
1960	Larissa Latynina (URS) 19.583	Polina Astakhova (URS) 19.532	Tamara Lyukhina (URS) 19.449
1964	Larissa Latynina (URS) 19.599	Polina Astakhova (URS) 19.500	Anikó Jánosi (HUN) 19.300
1968	Larissa Petrik (URS) 19.675 Vera Čásavská (TCH) 19.675	—	Natalya Kuchinskaya (URS) 19.650
1972	Olga Korbut (URS) 19.575	Ludmila Tourischeva (URS) 19.550	Tamara Lazakovitch (URS) 19.450
1976	Nelli Kim (URS) 19.850	Ludmila Tourischeva (URS) 19.825	Nadia Comaneci (ROM) 19.750
1980	Nelli Kim (URS) 19.875 Nadia Comaneci (ROM) 19.875	—	Natalya Shaposhnikova (URS) 19.825 Maxi Gnauck (GDR) 19.825
1984	Ecaterina Szabo (ROM) 19.975	Julianne McNamara (USA) 19.950	Mary Lou Retton (USA) 19.775
1988	Final on 25 September		

Individual horse vault/*Women*

Gold	*Silver*	*Bronze*
1952 Yekaterina Kalinchuk (URS) 19.20	Maria Gorokhovskaya (URS) 19.19	Galina Minaitscheva (URS) 19.16
1956 Larissa Latynina (URS) 18.833	Tamara Manina (URS) 18.800	Ann-Sofi Colling (SWE) 18.733 Olga Tass (HUN) 18.733
1960 Margarita Nikolayeva (URS) 19.316	Sofia Muratova (URS) 19.049	Larissa Latynina (URS) 19.016
1964 Vera Čáslavská (TCH) 19.483	Larissa Latynina (URS) 19.283 Birgit Radochla (GER) 19.283	—
1968 Vera Čáslavská (TCH) 19.775	Erika Zuchold (GDR) 19.625	Zinaida Voronina (URS) 19.500
1972 Karin Janz (GDR) 19.525	Erika Zuchold (GDR) 19.275	Ludila Tourischeva (URS) 19.250
1976 Nelli Kim (URS) 19.800	Carola Dombeck (GDR) 19.650 Ludmila Tourischeva (URS) 19.650	—
1980 Natalya Shaposhnikova (URS) 19.725	Steffi Kräker (GDR) 19.675	Melita Ruhn (ROM) 19.650
1984 Ecaterina Szabo (ROM) 19.875	Mary Lou Retton (USA) 19.850	Lavinia Agache (ROM) 19.750

1988 Final on 25 September

Rhythmic all round/*Women*

Gold	*Silver*	*Bronze*
1984 Lori Fung (CAN) 57.950	Doina Staiculescu (ROM) 57.900	Regina Weber (FRG) 57.700

4. Alina Dragan (ROM) 5. Milena Reljin (YUG) 6. Marta Canton (ESP)
7. Giulia Staccioli (ITA) 8. Hiroko Yamasaki (JPN)

1988 From 28 to 30 September

HANDBALL

The first thing to get clear is that there are two sports called 'handball'.

One, played predominately in Ireland and the United States, is a game rather like squash in that it is played by two (or four in doubles) against a wall. Instead of using a racquet, the players simply use their hands, hence the name. That sport, which is popular and has a world championship, has nothing to do with Olympic handball.

Olympic handball is a game played between two teams of seven players, a sort of cross between football and basketball, where the players shoot into a soccer-like goal.

While basketball and volleyball began in the United States, the Germans are largely responsible for handball as played today. They introduced it as an Olympic sport in Berlin in 1936 and reintroduced it when the Games returned to that country, to Munich in 1972. The difference being that in 1936 competition was outdoors between teams of eleven players while from 1972 it was indoors between teams of seven. (Teams actually comprise twelve players, but only seven play at any one time.)

Women's handball appeared in the Olympics for the first time in 1976.

The first world governing body was formed in 1928.

THE GAME

Similar to basketball except that the ball is throw into a goal. The yielding of midfield possession to concentrate on defence is similar to basketball.

The court is 40 metres by 20 metres and the goal, defended by a goalkeeper, is two metres high and three metres wide.

Players may not use their bodies below the knees to control the ball. A maximum of three steps can be taken while holding the ball. The ball may be held for a maximum of three seconds. 'Dribbling' is allowed. Quick passing is the key. The ball is smaller than a basketball (54 cm compared to 75 cm approx. in circumference). Around each goal is a semicircle six metres in radius. Only the goalkeeper may stand in this area, and he alone may use his legs or feet to make a save. Basic defence entails the six outfielders blocking the opposition at the edge of the goal area. The attackers' task is to find a way around that wall.

Matches last one hour (two halves of 30 minutes).

THE COMPETITION

Yugoslavia won both the men's and women's gold medals in Los Angeles in 1984. Although the rest of Eastern Europe was absent (except Rumania), the Yugoslavs were worthy winners. They usually do well and their men have been Olympic champions before (1972).

With the Soviets, etc., back in the fold, competition will be much tougher. They, the East Germans and Yugoslavs will be the best bet for medals in both men's and women's competitions, but the South Koreans on home ground will get tremendous backing and could be a threat in the women's competition. They took silver in 1984.

THE EVENTS

MEN

Twelve countries will take part. They will play in two groups of six, with the top two from each group contesting the medals. Winners of Group A play runners-up of Group B in the semi-final and so on.

WOMEN

There will be eight countries. Two groups of four, with the top two in each contesting the medals as semi-finalists (see above).

THE STARS

Four Rumanians have each won three medals. Six of the Soviet women's team won gold medals in both 1976 and 1980.

THE BRITISH

The sport is played in Britain, but there are no players of Olympic standard and Britain has never qualified for the Games.

Not a lot of people know that

• Hans George Beyer of East Germany, a member of the gold-medal winning team of 1980 and who scored the winning goal against the Soviet Union, is the brother of the more famous Udo Beyer, the 1976 Shot gold medallist. Their sister Gisela finished fourth in the discus in 1980.

• Roswitha Kraus who played in the East German women's team and won the silver medal in 1980 had previously been a member of the 4 × 100 freestyle swimming team in 1968 when she also won a silver medal.

• The silver medal won by South Korea and the bronze won by China in the women's competition in 1984 were the only medals ever won by non-European countries in this sport.

• Barcelona, whilst having an excellent football team and basketball team, also won handball's European Cup for men three times in the eighties.

VENUE

Prelims: Suwon Gymnasium 40 km from Olympic Village. Capacity 5500.
Finals: Olympic Gymnastics Hall in Olympic Park. Capacity 15,000.

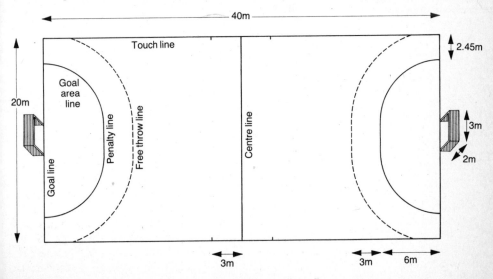

RESULTS

Men

	Gold	Silver	Bronze
1936	GERMANY	AUSTRIA	SWITZERLAND
1972	YUGOSLAVIA	CZECHOSLOVAKIA	ROMANIA
1976	USSR	ROMANIA	POLAND
1980	EAST GERMANY	USSR	ROMANIA
1984	YUGOSLAVIA	WEST GERMANY	ROMANIA

1988   Final on 1 October

Women

	Gold	Silver	Bronze
1976	USSR	EAST GERMANY	HUNGARY
1980	USSR	YUGOSLAVIA	EAST GERMANY
1984	YUGOSLAVIA	S. KOREA	CHINA

1988   Final round on 29 September

HOCKEY

The sport was first included for men in the 1908 Games in London, when England, Scotland, Ireland and Wales all entered separate teams. Only two other nations took part and all the four home countries won medals as, for the only time, both losing semifinalists were awarded a bronze. The Stockholm Games of 1912 did not include hockey, but it reappeared for the 1920 Games in Antwerp. Here Britain was represented by an England team and again won the gold medal.

However, the Hockey Association, which ruled the sport in England, withdrew from the British Olympic Association the following year, because 'they were opposed to competitions involving medals and prizes'. Now that is what I call amateurism.

It was not until 1948 that a Great Britain team took part in the Olympics again. On that occasion they won the silver medal, losing to India in the final. If Brazil are the great 'artists' of soccer, then that mantle surely falls to India in the sport of hockey. They have won the Olympic title on eight occasions and set the standard for skill, stick handling and goal scoring.

The women's game has only been part of the Olympic Games since 1980 when to much delight little Zimbabwe (population eight million) won the gold medal ahead of Czechoslovakia and the host country, the Soviet Union (population 230 million). Holland are the reigning champions.

THE COMPETITION

When Pakistan became a separate nation from India in 1947, they became great rivals in the sport and Pakistan are the current Olympic champions. In Seoul, expect both of them to be strong again, but Australia, who are the current World Cup holders, plus Great Britain, West Germany, Holland and the Soviet Union, whilst still sometimes falling short in terms of pure skill in comparison to players from the Indian subcontinent, can sometimes surpass them in terms of fitness and tactics.

Qualifying for the Olympics is based on world-ranking position. For Britain's men – no problem. They were second in the World Cup, third in the last Olympics and are ranked second in the world.

Britain's women were ranked eighth equal with the Soviet Union. The countries met in play-off matches in December 1987. Britain qualified by winning 4–1, 5–1 and drawing 1–1.

THE GAME

Teams are 11 a side (with two substitutes). Matches are played over 70 minutes (two halves of 35 minutes). Extra time can be added when the tournament gets to the knockout stage.

Rather like soccer, hockey teams no longer employ the '2-3-5' formation. The game has become highly mobile with forwards expected to show the same kind of 'work rate' as their soccer counterparts.

The rules are similar to soccer except that:
– Goals cannot be scored from outside the 'circle'
– Penalty corners (short corners) are awarded against defenders for:

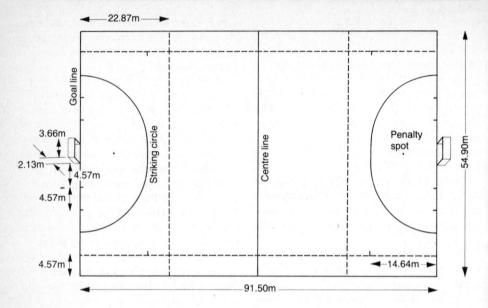

(a) Deliberately playing the ball over the goal line

(b) An offence within the circle (unless a full penalty is given, as per soccer for a *deliberate* foul within the circle)

(c) A deliberate foul within the 25-yard line

– For penalty corners, six defenders may stand behind their own goal line. The rest of the team must be beyond the centre line

– Attackers, apart obviously from the 'taker' of the penalty corner, must be outside the 'circle'. There can be no score direct from a penalty corner and the ball must be stopped before another player has a strike on goal

– Normal corners apply if a defender accidentally plays the ball over his own goal line

– Matches are controlled by two umpires

EQUIPMENT

Stick

Only the 'flat' side of the stick may be used for play and all are 'right-handed'. The rounded side of the stick may not be used to control the ball.

Ball

White leather over a cork and twine centre. It weighs 156 gms, is approximately cricket ball size, and is very hard.

Goalkeepers' kit

Goalkeepers, who are the only players allowed to use their bodies to control the ball, wear special hard-toe kicking shoes, leg guards, gloves, chest protectors, helmets, and face-masks.

BRITISH SUCCESSES

After early domination of Olympic men's hockey, Britain had a lean time from 1952 to 1984. In Los Angeles, the British team was included only after the withdrawal of the Soviet Union, but they took their opportunity magnificently to gain the first British Olympic medal in this sport in 32 years, a bronze.

THE STARS

Ian Taylor, the man behind the mask in Britain's goal in Los Angeles, has for some years been considered the number one goal-keeper in the world, while Sean Kerly has proved himself the 'Ian Rush' of the British team with a superb goal-scoring record in major championships.

Top British player in 1987 was the wing forward, Imran Sherwani.

Look out for two doctors in Seoul. Dr Rick Charlesworth, the Australian captain, is playing in his fifth Olympics. He once opened the batting for Western Australia and he is also an MP.

Dr Moira McLeod was Britain's heroine in the play-off matches against the Soviet Union. She scored four goals.

Dhyan Chand, the great centre-forward of India's all-conquering teams in the twenties and thirties, was one of the most prolific goal scorers of all time. He led India to three consecutive Olympic titles (1928 –36) when their goal scoring record was 102 for and six against.

Not a lot of people know that

● The Zimbabwe team that won the women's gold medal in 1980 were only called into the Games five weeks before they started. They replaced one of the countries who took part in President Carter's boycott.

In addition to their gold medals, each member of the team (who incidentally were all white) was awarded an ox by the Zimbabwean Minister of Sport.

● After West Germany beat Pakistan in the 1972 final, the Pakistan team were so incensed at the officiating that they stormed the judges' table and poured water over the President of the International Hockey Federation. At the medal ceremony, they refused to face the German flag during the playing of the national anthem.

All eleven Pakistani players were banned for life, but this penalty was subsequently modified.

● The highest score ever achieved in an Olympic hockey match was in Los Angeles in 1932 when India beat the United States 24–1. Despite that, the Americans took the bronze medal.

VENUE

Songnam Stadium. 10 km from Olympic Village. Capacity 27,000.

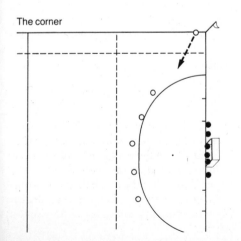

The corner

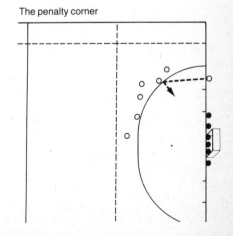

The penalty corner

RESULTS

Men

	Gold	Silver	Bronze
1908	ENGLAND	IRELAND	SCOTLAND WALES
1920	ENGLAND	DENMARK	BELGIUM
1928	INDIA	NETHERLANDS	GERMANY
1932	INDIA	JAPAN	UNITED STATES
1936	INDIA	GERMANY	NETHERLANDS
1948	INDIA	GREAT BRITAIN	NETHERLANDS
1952	INDIA	NETHERLANDS	GREAT BRITAIN
1956	INDIA	PAKISTAN	GERMANY
1960	PAKISTAN	INDIA	SPAIN
1964	INDIA	PAKISTAN	AUSTRALIA
1968	PAKISTAN	AUSTRALIA	INDIA
1972	WEST GERMANY	PAKISTAN	INDIA
1976	NEW ZEALAND	AUSTRALIA	PAKISTAN
1980	INDIA	SPAIN	USSR
1984	PAKISTAN	WEST GERMANY	GREAT BRITAIN

1988   Final on 1 October

Women

	Gold	Silver	Bronze
1980	ZIMBABWE	CZECHOSLOVAKIA	USSR
1984	NETHERLANDS	WEST GERMANY	UNITED STATES

1988   Final on 30 September

132

JUDO

The sport has evolved from a mixture of ancient Japanese fighting arts, the most important of which is ju-jitsu. Ju-jitsu was a system of unarmed combat perfected by early Japanese monks and used later by Samurai warriors when they were disarmed. Judo, meaning 'the easy way', is derived from ju-jitsu and is in simplistic terms a form of wrestling with very strict customs and complicated terminology.

The ground (or mat) rules were set up in the 1880s by the Japanese Jigoro Kano. Indeed, he approached the International Olympic Committee to have the sport included in the first modern Games of 1896. However, the sport at that time had not expanded out of Japan and it was not until the Games were first held in the Orient 68 years later, in 1964, that judo entered the Olympic programme. Women's judo is still not part of the Games, but will be a demonstration sport in Seoul with the prospect of being fully accepted for Barcelona in 1992.

The first judo club in Europe, the Budokwai, was founded in London in 1918. It still exists.

There is a system of grading in the sport, awarded for skill and experience. A beginner starts as a yellow belt (white in Japan) and progresses through various colours to black belt standard. Above this the grading is described as Dans (not Desperate Dans). Theoretically it is possible to reach 12th dan, but in practice this has never been awarded. Top international judo players are usually fourth or fifth dan.

THE 'GAME'

The object is to throw your opponent cleanly, hold him immobile on his back for 30 seconds, force him to submit through pressure of an armlock or other hold, or more usually be awarded a decision given by a referee and two judges.

A very formal sport, the players or 'judokas' bow to each other before the battle commences as the referee calls 'Haijime', meaning begin (not 'See You Jimmy').

If a 'judoka' fails to render his opponent immobile, the contest will be decided by the officials. However, this seemingly innocent aim of finding a winner and a loser can be highly complicated and certainly very confusing to the innocent onlooker. The problem is that the technicalities are referred to in the original Japanese.

Here is a list of terminology.

Scoring
Ippon Full point
Waza-ari Almost Ippon
Yuko Almost Waza-ari
Koka Almost Yuko

Penalties
Hansoku make (= *ippon*) Disqualification
Keikoku (= *Waza-ari*) Warning
Chui (= *Yuko*) Caution
Shido (= *Koka*) Note

Throws and holds
Harai-goshi Sweeping loin throw
Kami-shiho-gatame Upper four quarters hold

133

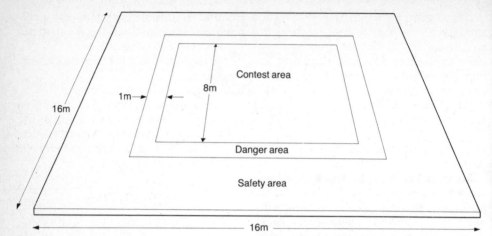

Contest area

8m

1m

16m

Danger area

Safety area

16m

Kesa-gatame Sash hold

Kuzure-kami-shiho-gatame Modified upper four quarters hold

O-soto-gari Major outside reaping throw (outside clip or kickback throw)

O-uchi-gari Manor inner reaping throw (inside clip or innercut throw)

Seoi-nage Over-the-shoulder throw

Tai-otoshi Body drop

Uchi-mata Inner thigh throw

Yoko-shiho-gatame Side four quarters hold

Other terms

Awasewaza Combination of two techniques

Katsu A system of resuscitation

Kinsa Slight superiority or close decision

Shime-waza Strangulation techniques

Yushi-gachi Win by superiority (referee's decision)

Basically, players are judged on holding and throwing techniques. Violations of the rules are also a determining factor. An 'Ippon'-point wins a contest immediately and is awarded for a throw of considerable force, lifting the opponent from mat to shoulder height, or making an effective stranglehold or lock last for 30 seconds. For reference, two 'waza-ari' equal an 'ippon' but to get more complicated than that would not be appropriate here. Suffice it to say that

the team of officials decide the winner. Their decisions are ideally unanimous, but sometimes on majority.

Contests normally last five minutes.

EQUIPMENT

Contests take place on a nine-metre square green mat around which there is a one metre wide red danger area. Surrounding this is a safety area of green matting to prevent injuries. The entire competition area measures 16 metres by 16 metres. The contest must be fought within the limits of the contest area.

The costumes (judogi) must be white or off-white and the jackets must cover the hips. Sleeves must be loose and cover half the forearm. Trousers must be loose and cover half the lower leg. The belt fastens the jacket at the waist and is long enough to go twice round the body.

COMPETITION

There are seven weight categories plus an 'open' category, thus there are eight gold medals available. These are as follows:

Up to 60 kg	86 kg
65 kg	95 kg
71 kg	Over 95 kg
78 kg	

134

As you might expect, the Japanese are the strongest nation. They won four of the eight gold medals in 1984, but as in almost every other sport, there will be more competition in Seoul with the complete Eastern European contingent taking part.

The Soviets will be strong, but Western Europeans hold their own in this sport.

Greatest improvement will almost certainly be by the host nation who won five medals in 1984, two of them gold.

Bouts are on straight knockout basis. However when the finalists are decided, any player who has lost to either of them will compete again. This is a kind of repechage round, again producing two finalists who will be awarded bronze medals. (As in boxing, two bronze medals are awarded.) Unlike boxing, there is seeding. The top four men are seeded in each weight category.

THE STARS

The Japanese continually produce a crop of outstanding performers and in 1964 they won every category except the open class, when their representative Akio Kaminaga was beaten by the giant Dutchman Antonius Geesink. There was disbelief throughout

Japan at the time that any European could beat their best man. Since then the sport has become even more international.

The individual who has become most international must be Angelo Parisi. Parisi was born in Italy, became a naturalized Briton, winning a bronze medal for Britain in 1972. However, he then married a French girl, went to live in that country and represented them in the 1980 Games when he won both gold and silver for France.

THE BRITISH

British competitors have done well in this sport but a gold medal has so far eluded them. Parisi would have done the trick, but for his changing nationalities.

Neil Adams has been closest, twice winning silver medals, in 1980 and 1984. It is hoped that after a brief retirement Adams will be available for Seoul. Adams was a world champion in 1981.

The first British judo medals were won in 1972 by David Starbrook (silver) and Brian Jacks (bronze).

Not a lot of people know that

• In 1964 Akio Kaminaga of Japan took only four seconds to throw Thomas Ong of the Philippines – an Olympic record. However, in the final he met that man Geesing of Holland and had to be content with the silver medal.
• Sumio Endo of Japan at 5 ft 6½ ins and 259 lbs beat the 7 ft 350 lbs Jong-Gil Pak of North Korea in 1976. Endo was world champion.
• Basic throws in the sport are divided into five categories but each has many variations. Over 40 holds or throws are listed.

VENUE

Changchung Gymnasium. 15 km from Olympic Village. Capacity 8000.

RESULTS

In 1980 the weight categories were altered. The results have been listed in the categories *closest* to those that exist at present

Extra-lightweight up to 60 kg (9 st 7 lb)

	Gold	*Silver*	*Bronze*
1980	Thierry Rey (FRA) Koka 7:00	Rafael Carbonell (CUB)	Aramby Emizh (URS) Tibor Kincses (HUN)
1984	Shinji Hosokawa (JPN) Yoko-shiho-gatame 1:09	Jae-Yup Kim (KOR)	Neil Eckersley (GBR) Edward Liddie (USA)
1988	Final on 25 September		

Half lightweight up to 65 kg (10 st 3 lb)

	Gold	*Silver*	*Bronze*
1964*	Takehide Nakatani (JPN) Awasewaza 1:15	Eric Hänni (SUI)	Aron Bogulubov (URS) Oleg Stepanov (URS)
1972*	Takao Kawaguchi (JPN) Kami-shiho-gatame 0:39	—†	Jean-Jacques Mounier (FRA) Yong Ik Kim (PRK)
1976*	Hector Rodriguez (CUB) Uchi-mata 10:00	Eunkyung Chang (KOR)	Felice Mariani (ITA) Jozsef Tuncsik (HUN)
1980	Nikolai Solodukhin (URS) Koka/shido 7:00	Tsendying Damdin (MGL)	Ilian Nedkov (BUL) Janusz Pawlowski (POL)
1984	Yoshiyuki Matsuoka (JPN) Seio-nage 7:00	Jung-Oh Hwang (KOR)	Marc Alexandre (FRA) Josef Reiter (AUT)
1988	Final on 26 September		

*Up to 63 kg.
† Bakhaavaa Buidaa (MGL) was disqualified after drugs test.

Lightweight up to 71 kg (11 st 2 lbs)

	Gold	**Silver**	**Bronze**
1980	Ezio Gamba (ITA) Yushi-gachi 7:00	Neil Adams (GBR)	Ravdan Davaadalai (MGL) Karl-Heinz Lehmann (GDR)
1984	Byeong-Keun Ahn (KOR) Seoi-nage 7:00	Ezio Gamba (ITA)	Kerrith Brown (GBR) Luis Onmura (BRA)
1988	Final on 27 September		

Half middleweight up to 78 kg (12 st 4 lb)

Gold	Silver	Bronze
1972* Toyokazu Nomura (JPN) Seoi-nage 0:27	Anton Zajkowski (POL)	Dietmar Hötger (GDR) Anatoliy Novikov (URS)
1976* Vladimir Nevzorov (URS) Tai-otoshi 10:00	Koji Kuramoto (JPN)	Marian Talaj (POL) Patrick Vial (FRA)
1980 Shota Khabaleri (URS) Yuko 7:00	Juan Ferrer La Hera (CUB)	Harald Heinke (GDR) Bernard Tchoullouyan (FRA)
1984 Frank Wieneke (FRG) Seio-nage 4:04	Neil Adams (GBR)	Mircea Fratica (ROM) Michel Nowak (FRA)

1988   Final on 28 September

*63 kg to 70 kg.

Middleweight up to 86 kg (13 st 8 lb)

Gold	Silver	Bronze
1964* Isao Okano (JPN) Yoko-shiho-gatame 1:36	Wolfgang Hofmann (GER)	James Bregman (USA) Eui Tae Kim (KOR)
1972* Shinobu Sekine (JPN) Yushi-gachi 10:00	Seung-Lip Oh (KOR)	Jean-Paul Coché (FRA) Brian Jacks (GBR)
1976* Isamu Sonoda (JPN) O-uchi-gari 10:00	Valeriy Dvoinikov (URS)	Slavko Obadov (YUG) Youngchul Park (KOR)
1980 Jürg Röthlisberger (SUI) Yuko 7:00	Isaac Azcuy Oliva (CUB)	Detlef Ultsch (GDR) Aleksandr Yatskevich (URS)
1984 Peter Seisenbacher (AUT) Uchi-mata 2:26	Robert Berland (USA)	Walter Carmona (BRA) Seiki Nose (JPN)

1988   Final on 29 September

*70 to 80 kg.

Half heavyweight up to 95 kg (14 st 15 lb)

Gold	Silver	Bronze
1972* Shota Chochoshvili (URS) Yushi-gachi 10:00	David Starbrook (GBR)	Paul Barth (FRG) Chiaki Ishii (BRA)
1976* Kazuhiro Ninomiya (JPN) Keikoku 10:00	Ramaz Harshiladze (URS)	Jürg Röthlisberger (SUI) David Starbrook (GBR)
1980 Robert Van de Walle (BEL) Koka 7:00	Tengiz Khubuluri (URS)	Dietmar Lorenz GDR) Henk Numan (HOL)
1984 Hyoung-Zoo Ha (KOR) Yusei-gachi 7:00	Douglas Vieira (BRA)	Bjarni Fridriksson (ISL) Gunther Neureuther (FRG)

1988   Final on 30 September

*80 to 93 kg.

Heavyweight over 95 kg (14 st 15 lb)

	Gold	*Silver*	*Bronze*
1964*	Isao Inokuma (JPN) Kinsa 15:00	Alfred Rogers (CAN)	Parnaoz Chikviladze (URS) Anzor Kiknadze (URS)
1972*	Wilhelm Ruska (HOL) Harai-goshi 1:43	Klaus Glahn (FRG)	Motoki Nishimura (JPN) Givi Onashvili (URS)
1976*	Sergey Novikov (URS) O-soto-gari 1:19	Gunther Neureuther (FRG)	Sumio Endo (JPN) Allen Coage (USA)
1980	Angelo Parisi (FRA) Ippon 6:14	Dimitar Zaprianov (BUL)	Vladimir Kocman (TCH) Radomir Kovacevic (YUG)
1984	Hitoshi Saito (JPN) Shido 7:00	Angelo Parisi (FRA)	Mark Berger (CAN) Yong-Chul Cho (KOR)
1988	Final on 1 October		

*Over 93 kg.

Open category (no weight limit)

	Gold	*Silver*	*Bronze*
1964	Antonius Geesink (HOL) Kesa-gatame 9:22	Akio Kaminaga (JPN)	Theodore Boronovskis (AUS) Klaus Glahn (GER)
1972	Wilhelm Ruska (HOL) Yoko-shiho-gatame 3:58	Vitaliy Kuznetsov (URS)	Jean-Claude Brondani (FRA) Angelo Parisi (GBR)
1976	Haruki Uemura (JPN) Kuzure-kami-shiho-gatame 7:28	Keith Remfry (GBR)	Shota Chochoshvili (URS) Jeaki Cho (KOR)
1980	Dietmar Lorenz (GDR) Yushi-gachi 7:00	Angelo Parisi (FRA)	Arthur Mapp (GBR) Andras Ozsvar (HUN)
1984	Yasuhiro Yamashita (JPN) Yoko-shiho-gatame 1:05	Mohamed Rashwan (EGY)	Mihai Cioc (ROM) Arthur Schnabel (FRG)
1988	Not being held		

MODERN PENTATHLON

This is the only sport that was actually created especially for the Olympic Games. Baron De Coubertin, the founder of the modern Games backed its inclusion for 1912 in Stockholm. It appealed particularly to the military, the skills being likened to those required by a soldier of the late 19th century who might be needed to carry a message through enemy lines. Thus the five disciplines are riding, fencing, shooting, swimming, and cross-country running.

The event has now been part of every Games since 1912 with Sweden producing the individual champion on no fewer than nine occasions. Interestingly, they have never won the team gold medal which has been contested in addition, since 1952.

Britain in contrast has never produced an individual medallist, although several have come mighty close, but did win the team gold medal in Montreal in 1976 (Jim Fox, Danny Nightingale, and Adrian Parker).

THE COMPETITION

Both the individual and team gold medals went to Italy in 1984, but remember the Eastern Europeans did not take part. This time the Soviets and Hungarians will be the favourites, but the Italians are good and the strong Swedish tradition will make them medal hopefuls too.

Britain came third in the 1987 world championships, the first time ever a medal has been won. Hungary took the gold and silver to USSR. Britain's team was Dominic Mahoney, Graham Brookhouse and Richard Phelps.

In the individual competition, the gold went to Joel Bouzou of France. Mahony came sixth, Phelps seventh.

Phelps just missed a medal in the Los Angeles Olympics by a mere 16 points. He was fourth. So Britain have distinct medal chances in Seoul.

THE DISCIPLINES

The order of the disciplines is riding, fencing, swimming, shooting, and cross-country running competed in over five days.

RIDING

This in a sense is the 'lottery' discipline and has been responsible for many good and bad luck stories. Originally a cross-country test, rather like the third section of a three-day event, it is now more akin to show-jumping.

The problem for competitors is that unlike show-jumpers they do not compete on their own well-trained horses.

In this sport, they are obliged to ride horses unknown to them. Lots are drawn to decide which horse is ridden by which rider, and this, as you can imagine, creates many difficulties. As any horseman will tell you, no two animals are exactly alike, and much depends on the 'luck of the draw'.

Care is taken to exclude particularly 'feisty' beasts and efforts are made to make the overall standard as fair as possible. However, it continues to be difficult to produce suitable horses for this type of competition, and the sport's governing body has at times given thought to changing this discipline into canoeing or even cyclo-cross. The general feeling though is that any change would spoil the 'charisma' of modern pentathlon.

FENCING

The weapon used is the épée. The target area, unlike for the foil or sabre, is the whole body. Electronic scoring equipment is used.

In épée a direct hit is valid after the instruction 'play' unlike other fencing disciplines when the action has to follow prescribed movements before a score can be made. The winner of a bout is the first to score just one hit within the time limit. Competition is on a pool basis with everyone playing everyone else. Naturally, this takes a considerable time.

It was in this discipline at the 1976 Games that one of the great Olympic scandals took place. Boris Onishenko, a major in the Soviet Army, who had won every honour in the sport with the exception of the individual Olympic gold medal, was disqualified for cheating. The manner of it, though, was extraordinary.

His épée was found to be bugged with a device which would make the scoring equipment register a genuine hit.

As Onishenko lined up to play his old friend and foe, Britain's Jim Fox, the recording device suddenly lit as if the Russian had scored a hit. Onishenko left the 'piste' and was about to change weapons when Fox demanded that the épée be examined, believing it to be short-circuiting. It was then that the truth emerged. It was found that clever electrical engineering was giving Onishenko control over the registering device.

Onishenko was sent home in disgrace, leaving Fox remorseful that he had been the one to find him out, but wondering if the Russian had also been cheating when a victory over Fox in the 1972 Games had been responsible for depriving the British sportsman of an individual bronze medal.

SWIMMING

Any stroke may be employed, but naturally in order to score effectively, the front crawl is always used.

The distance is 300 metres – six lengths of the Olympic pool.

With due respect to the participants, this is when you realize just how good the 'real' swimmers are. The world-class freestylers would expect to cover 400 metres in the sort of time it takes most modern pentathletes to swim two lengths fewer – around 3 minutes 50 seconds. Mind you, as far as I know, Michael Gross is a lousy rider, fencer, runner, and shooter.

SHOOTING

The shooting is with pistol and the range is 25 metres. There are four rounds – 20 shots per round, with a maximum score of 200 per round, i.e. every shot scoring a bullseye of 10 points.

This discipline is in marked contrast to the others – requiring much self-control. Any flood of adrenalin, which may be of some assistance while controlling your horse or whilst running or swimming, is a distinct disadvantage here.

RUNNING

This is over 4000 metres cross-country and a real endurance test for non-specialist runners who've already completed four gruelling events. One of the quickest times ever was 12 minutes 9 seconds, recorded by Adrian Parker, a member of Britain's successful gold medal-winning team of 1976. Said Aouita has taken only around 50 seconds more to run an extra 1000 metres, but again, don't ever put him on a horse.

POINTS

Before 1956, competitors were placed in order of the lowest number of points gained (e.g. one for first in any event). Since then, an international points system has been employed which relates to performance in each discipline, rather like Daley Thompson's decathlon.

BRITISH SUCCESS

The only medal Britain has ever won in this event was the team gold in 1976 – the year of the 'Onishenko' affair.

After four disciplines, the team were lying fifth with the Czechs, Hungarians, Poles, and Americans ahead, but Adrian Parker's amazing run (he was the first to go – runners go at intervals and are timed, it is not a race) which was a full 17 seconds better than the next man, gave the team a great start. In fact the whole team ran brilliantly and, after much calculation, it was found that they had squeezed ahead of the Czechs for an unprecedented gold. It was one of the great stories of that year's Games.

THE STARS

Lars Hall (Sweden) is the only man to retain the individual Olympic title, winning in 1952 and '56.

András Balczó of Hungary was a member of the winning team in 1960 and '68, winning the individual silver on that second occasion and the individual gold in 1972.

Pavel Lednev of the Soviet Union won three individual bronze medals and a silver, plus two team gold medals and a silver between 1968 and '80.

Willie Grut (Sweden) may have been the greatest ever. In the 1948 Games he finished first in riding, fencing, and swimming, fifth in shooting, and eighth in running. He later became the secretary-general of the sport's governing body.

Not a lot of people know that

● Baron De Coubertin's original suggestion for the competition was that the order of events should be drawn on the day. This would have meant a competitor not knowing whether he would be, say, riding or shooting until the morning of the event. Thankfully, this idea was never taken up.

● There is no women's modern pentathlon in the Olympic Games. However women do compete in their own world championships and have been lobbying for Olympic recognition for some time.

● A certain George Patton (USA) came fifth in the 1912 Games. He was later to become famous as a general during the Second World War.

● The pentathlon of the ancient Olympics comprised javelin, discus, jumping, running, and wrestling.

VENUES

Riding: Seoul Equestrian Centre.
Fencing: Fencing Gymnasium.
Swimming: Olympic Pool
Shooting: Taenung International Shooting Range
Running: Special course in Olympic Park.

RESULTS

Individual

Gold	Silver	Bronze
1912 Gustaf Lilliehöök (SWE) 27	Gösta Asbrink (SWE) 28	Georg de Laval (SWE) 30
1920 Gustaf Dryssen (SWE) 18	Erik de Laval (SWE) 23	Gösta Rüno (SWE) 27
1924 Bo Lindman (SWE) 18	Gustaf Dryssen (SWE) 39.5	Bertil Uggla (SWE) 45
1928 Sven Thofelt (SWE) 47	Bo Lindman (SWE) 50	Helmuth Kahl (GER) 52
1932 Johan Gabriel Oxenstierna (SWE) 32	Bo Lindman (SWE) 35.5	Richard Mayo (USA) 38.5
1936 Gotthard Handrick (GER) 31.5	Charles Leonard (USA) 39.5	Silvano Abba (ITA) 45.5
1948 Willie Grut (SWE) 16	George Moore (USA) 47	Gösta Gärdin (SWE) 49
1952 Lars Hall (SWE) 32	Gábor Benedek (HUN) 39	István Szondi (HUN) 41
1956 Lars Hall (SWE) 4844	Olavi Nannonen (FIN) 4774.5	Väinö Korhonen (FIN) 4750
1960 Ferenc Németh (HUN) 5024	Imre Nagy (HUN) 4988	Robert Beck (USA) 4981
1964 Ferenc Török (HUN) 5116	Igor Novikov (URS) 5067	Albert Mokeyev (URS) 5039
1968 Björn Ferm (SWE) 4964	András Balczó (HUN) 4953	Pavel Lednev (URS) 4795
1972 András Balczó (HUN) 5412	Boris Onischenko (URS) 5335	Pavel Lednev (URS) 5328
1976 Janusz Pyciak-Peciak (POL) 5520	Pavel Lednev (URS) 5485	Jan Bartu (TCH) 5466
1980 Anatoily Starostin (URS) 5568	Tamás Szombathelyi (HUN) 5502	Pavel Lednev (URS) 5382
1984 Daniele Masala (ITA) 5469	Svante Rasmuson (SWE) 5456	Carlo Massullo (ITA) 5406

4. Richard Phelps (GBR) 5. Michael Storm (USA) 6. Paul Four (FRA)
7. Ivar Sisniega (MEX) 8. Jorge Quesada (ESP)

1988 Riding on 18 September
Fencing on 19 September
Swimming on 20 September
Shooting on 21 September
Cross-country running on 22 September

Team

	Gold	Silver	Bronze
1952	HUNGARY 166	SWEDEN 182	FINLAND 213
1956	USSR 13,690.5	UNITED STATES 13,482	FINLAND 13,185.5
1960	HUNGARY 14,863	USSR 14,309	UNITED STATES 14,192
1964	USSR 14,961	UNITED STATES 14,189	HUNGARY 14,173
1968	HUNGARY 14,325	USSR 14,248	FRANCE 13,289*
1972	USSR 15,968	HUNGARY 15,348	FINLAND 14,812
1976	GREAT BRITAIN 15,559	CZECHOSLOVAKIA 15,451	HUNGARY 15,395
1980	USSR 16,126	HUNGARY 15,912	SWEDEN 15,845
1984	ITALY 16,060	UNITED STATES 15,568	FRANCE 15,565
	Daniele Masala	Michael Storm	Paul Four
	Carlo Massullo	Robert Losey	Didier Boube
	Pierpaolo Cristofori	Dean Glenesk	Joel Bouzou

4. Switzerland 15,343 5. Mexico 15,283 6. West Germany 15,028
7. Great Britain 14,894 (Richard Phelps, Stephen Sowerby, Michael Mumford)
8. Spain 14,891

1988   From 18 to 22 September

* Sweden originally finished third but were disqualified when the level of alcohol found in one member was too high.

ROWING

Lord Mancroft once said of rowing, 'It is a sport the French rightly reserved for their convicts and the Romans for their slaves.' Despite this, the British engaged in rowing for pleasure and the rest of the world, as usual, have caught on.

Rowing was part of the second modern Games of 1900 and has been included ever since.

Women's rowing became part of the Olympics for the first time in 1976.

THE EVENTS

There are eight for men and six for women.

Men:
1. Single sculls – one rower with two oars

2. Doubles sculls – two rowers with two oars each

3. Coxless pairs – two rowers with one oar each (one on each side of the boat)

4. Coxed pairs – as above, with a cox to steer (three men in a boat)

5. Coxless fours – four rowers, with one oar each (two on each side of the boat)

6. Coxed fours – four rowers as above, with a cox to steer (five men in a boat)

7. Quadruple sculls – four rowers with two oars each

8. Eights – eight rowers with one oar each (usually four on each side, but not necessarily so), plus a cox (so, it is actually a 'nine')

Men race over 2000 metres.

Women:
1. Single sculls

2. Double sculls

3. Coxless pairs

4. Quadruple sculls

5. Coxed fours

6. Eights

Women have raced over 1000 metres since they began competing in the Games in 1976. In Seoul, however, they too will race over 2000 metres.

In the coxed events, the cox naturally steers the boat and shouts out the 'stroking rate', i.e. how many pulls to the minute.

In the coxless events, one of the rowers has rudder-lines attached to a pivoting shoe which he or she steers.

In the coxed boats, the cox may be placed at either the bow or, as in the Oxford v. Cambridge race, the stern.

It is interesting to note that if the cox falls overboard, a crew will be disqualified. If a rower falls overboard, the rest of the crew may continue. The thinking is that the loss of a rower would be a distinct disadvantage – the loss of a cox could even be an advantage.

This begs the question – why have a cox at all if crews can compete perfectly well without them? The answer is really historical. Rowing began with coxes and the practice is continued for tradition's sake. In the eights, however, a cox does keep the crew's momentum going, but a coxless four would nearly always beat a coxed four of the same standard.

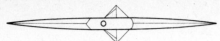

Single sculls length 8.2m

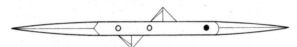

Double sculls length 10.4m

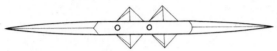

Coxless pair length 10.4m

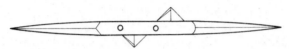

Coxed pair length 10.7m

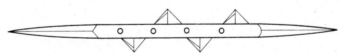

Coxless four length 13.4m

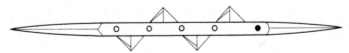

Coxed four length 13.7m

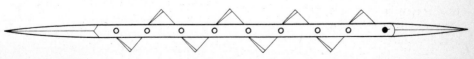

Eight length 18.9m

TERMINOLOGY AND EQUIPMENT

Canvas: the bow and stern sections of racing boats are covered with thin linen. A verdict of 'a canvas' indicates this as the winning margin.

Blade: the part of the oar that propels the boat. In the late 1950s the West Germans introduced shorter and wider blades and had considerable success with them.

'Catching a Crab': turning the blade while still in the water. By putting the blade into the water too deep, a rower loses momentum and rhythm and can even injure himself with the oar handle.

Rowlocks: called 'gates' in the eights, they support the oars.

Seats: these are fitted on rails and slide back and forth in unison with the rowing motion.

Shoes: are fixed in place, rather like a cyclist's toe-clip.

TECHNIQUE

The sport calls for both fitness and dexterity. Very heavy men who are not supple would not make good rowers.

The ideal oarsman is tall and supple with good lung capacity and a slow pulse rate. Indeed, it is an ideal 'aerobic' sport. Top class crews often average 90 kg. Women rowers are often of outstanding athletic proportions. Do not imagine they need to be musclebound heavyweights.

Smooth control of sliding seats is important.

In strong following winds, blades are kept vertical when out of the water in order to try to catch the wind. In a head wind, the blades are kept horizontal in order to reduce wind resistance.

Courses vary from Games to Games, so do conditions, therefore there are best times recorded but not Games' record times.

COMPETITION

Depending on number of entries, competition is usually based on heats, second round heats, and a final. If crews fail to qualify at their first attempt, they will usually get a second chance through repechage.

With the Eastern Bloc absent from the 1984 Games the gold medals in men's rowing were spread between eight countries. Rumania dominated the women's events, taking five of the six gold medals.

In Seoul, the Soviets and East Germans will once again be the crews the rest have to beat, and the East German women in particular could win every event.

Britain, with Andy Holmes and Steve Redgrave, will have great gold medal chances in either the coxed or coxless pairs (they have won the world championship in both events in their time).

THE BRITISH

Jack Beresford won three gold medals and two silvers between 1920 and 1936. But the first British gold medal since 1948 was won in the coxed fours in Los Angeles in 1984 by Martin Cross, Richard Budgett, Andy Holmes, and Steve Redgrave plus cox Adrian Ellison. Britain's 'eight' won the silver medal in 1976 and 1980.

THE STARS

The USA heads the medals' table with nearly twice as many gold medals as any other nation. East Germany and Rumania are the most successful nations in women's rowing.

Vyacheslav Ivanov (USSR) and Pertti Karppinen (FIN) have both won the singles' sculls on three consecutive occasions.

Not a lot of people know that

• Charles Burnell and his son Richard Burnell won gold medals for Great Britain in the 1908 and 1948 Games respectively.
• Jack Beresford, who won five medals (above), is the son of Julius Beresford who won a silver in 1912.
• 'Eights' can reach a speed of around 21 km.p.h.
• John Kelly, who won three gold medals for the USA, was the father of the famous film actress Grace Kelly, who became the Princess of Monaco. In 1956, his son, also John, won a bronze medal in the single sculls.

VENUE

Han River Regatta Course at Misa-ri.
10 km from the Olympic Village.
Capacity 25,000.

RESULTS

Single sculls/*Men*

	Gold	*Silver*	*Bronze*
1900	Henri Barrelet (FRA) 7:35.6	André Gaudin (FRA) 7:41.6	St George Ashe (GBR) 8:15.6
1904	Frank Greer (USA) 10.08.5	James Juvenal (USA) 2 lengths	Constance Titus (USA) 1 length
1906	Gaston Delaplane (FRA) 5:53.4	Joseph Larran (FRA) 6:07.2	—
1908	Harry Blackstaffe (GBR) 9:26.0	Alexander McCulloch (GBR) 1 length	Bernhard von Gaza (GER) d.n.a. Károly Levitzky (HUN) d.n.a.
1912	William Kinnear (GBR) 7:47.6	Polydore Veirman (BEL) 1 length	Everard Butter (CAN) d.n.a. Mikhail Kusik (URS) d.n.a.
1920	John Kelly (USA) 7:35.0	Jack Beresford (GBR) 7:36.0	Clarence Hadfield d'Arcy (NZL) 7:48.0
1924	Jack Beresford (GBR) 7:49.2	William Garrett-Gilmore (USA) 7:54.0	Josef Schneider (SUI) 8:01.1
1928	Henry Pearce (AUS) 7:11.0	Kenneth Myers (USA) 7:20.8	David Collet (GBR) 7:29.8
1932	Henry Pearce (AUS) 7:44.4	William Miller (USA) 7:45.2	Guillermo Douglas (URU) 8:13.6
1936	Gustav Schäfer (GER) 8:21.5	Josef Hasenöhrl (AUT) 8:25.8	Daniel Barrow (USA) 8:28.0
1948	Mervyn Wood (AUS) 7:24.4	Eduardo Risso (URU) 7:38.2	Romolo Catasta (ITA) 7:51.4
1952	Yuriy Tyukalov (URS) 8:12.8	Mervyn Wood (AUS) 8:14.5	Teodor Kocerka (POL) 8:19.4
1956	Vyacheslav Ivanov (URS) 8:02.5	Stuart Mackenzie (AUS) 8:07.7	John Kelly (USA) 8:11.8
1960	Vyacheslav Ivanov (URS) 7:13.96	Achim Hill (GER) 7:20.21	Teodor Kocerka (POL) 7:21.26
1964	Vyacheslav Ivanov (URS) 8:22.51	Achim Hill (GER) 8:26.24	Gottfried Kottmann (SUI) 8:29.68
1968	Henri Jan Wienese (HOL) 7:47:80	Jochen Meissner (FRG) 7:52.00	Alberto Demiddi (ARG) 7:57.19
1972	Yuriy Malishev (URS) 7:10.12	Alberto Demiddi (ARG) 7:11.53	Wolfgang Gueldenpfennig (GDR) 7:14.45

1976	Pertti Karppinen (FIN) 7:29.03	Peter Kolbe (FRG) 7:31.67	Joachim Dreifke (GDR) 7:38.03
1980	Pertti Karppinen (FIN) 7:09.61	Vasiliy Yakusha (URS) 7:11.66	Peter Kersten (GDR) 7:14.88
1984	Pertti Karppinen (FIN) 7:00.24	Peter Kolbe (FRG) 7:02.19	Robert Mills (CAN) 7:10.38

4. John Biglow (USA) 5. Ricardo Ibarra (ARG) 6. Kostantinos Kontomanolis (GRE)

1988 Final on 24 September

Double sculls/*Men*

	Gold	*Silver*	*Bronze*
1904	UNITED STATES 10:03.2 John Mulcahy William Varley	UNITED STATES d.n.a. John Hoben James McLoughlin	UNITED STATES d.n.a. John Wells Joseph Ravanack
1920	UNITED STATES 7:09.0 John Kelly Paul Costello	ITALY 7:19.0 Erminio Dones Pietro Annoni	FRANCE 7:21.0 Alfred Plé Gaston Giran
1924	UNITED STATES 6:34.0 John Kelly Paul Costello	FRANCE 6:38.0 Jean-Pierre Stock Marc Detton	SWITZERLAND 3 lengths Rudolf Bosshard Heini Thoma
1928	UNITED STATES 6:41.4 Charles McIlvaine Paul Costello	CANADA 6:51.0 Jack Guest Joseph Wright	AUSTRIA 6:48.8 Viktor Flessl Leo Losert
1932	UNITED STATES 7:17.4 William Garrett-Gilmore Kenneth Myers	GERMANY 7:22.8 Gerhard Boetzelen Herbert Buhtz	CANADA 7:27.6 Nöel de Mille Charles Pratt
1936	GREAT BRITAIN 7:20.8 Leslie Southwood Jack Beresford	GERMANY 7:26.2 Joachim Pirsch Willy Kaidel	POLAND 7:36.2 Jerzy Ustupski Roger Verey
1948	GREAT BRITAIN 6:51.3 Herbert Bushnell Richard D. Burnell	DENMARK 6:55.3 Aage Larsen Ebbe Parsner	URUGUAY 7:12.4 Juan Rodriguez William Jones
1952	ARGENTINA 7:32.2 Tranquilo Capozzo Eduardo Guerrero	USSR 7:38.3 Georgiy Zhilin Igor Emchuk	URUGUAY 7:43.7 Miguel Seijas Juan Rodriguez
1956	USSR 7:24.0 Aleksandr Berkutov Yuriy Tyukalov	UNITED STATES 7:32.2 Bernard Costello James Gardiner	AUSTRALIA 7:37.4 Murray Riley Mervyn Wood
1960	CZECHOSLOVAKIA 6:47.50 Václav Kozák Pavel Schmidt	USSR 6:50.49 Aleksandr Berkutov Yuriy Tyukalov	SWITZERLAND 6:50.59 Ernst Hürlimann Rolf Larcher
1964	USSR 7:10.66 Oleg Tyurin Boris Dubrovsky	UNITED STATES 7:13.16 Seymour Cromwell James Storm	CZECHOSLOVAKIA 7:14.23 Vladimir Andrs Pavel Hofmann
1968	USSR 6:51.82 Anatoliy Sass Aleksandr Timoshinin	NETHERLANDS 6:52.80 Henricus Droog Leendert van Dis	UNITED STATES 6:54.21 John Nunn William Maher
1972	USSR 7:01.77 Aleksandr Timoshinin Gennadiy Korshikov	NORWAY 7:02.58 Frank Hansen Svein Thogersen	EAST GERMANY 7:05.55 Joachim Böhmer Hans-Ulrich Schmied

1976	NORWAY 7:13.20	GREAT BRITAIN 7:15.26	EAST GERMANY 7:17.45
	Frank Hansen	Chris Baillieu	Hans-Ulrich Schmied
	Alf Hansen	Michael Hart	Jürgen Bertow
1980	EAST GERMANY 6:24.33	YUGOSLAVIA 6:26.34	CZECHOSLOVAKIA 6:29.07
	Joachim Dreifke	Zoran Pancic	Zdenek Pecka
	Klaus Kröppelien	Milorad Stanulov	Václav Vochoska
1984	UNITED STATES 6:36.87	BELGIUM 6:38.19	YUGOSLAVIA 6:39.59
	Bradley Lewis	Pierre-Marie Deloof	Zoran Pancic
	Paul Enquist	Dirk Crois	Milorad Stanulov

4. West Germany 5. Italy 6. Canada

1988   Final on 24 September

Coxless quadruple sculls/*Men*

	Gold	*Silver*	*Bronze*
1976	EAST GERMANY 6:18.65	USSR 6:19.89	CZECHOSLOVAKIA 6:21.77
1980	EAST GERMANY 5:49.81	USSR 5:51.47	BULGARIA 5:52.38
1984	WEST GERMANY 5:57.55	AUSTRALIA 5:57.98	CANADA 5:59.07
	Albert Hedderich	Paul Reedy	Doug Hamilton
	Raimund Hormann	Gary Gullock	Mikes Hughes
	Dieter Wiedenmann	Timothy McLaren	Phil Monckton
	Michael Dursch	Anthony Lovrich	Bruce Ford

4. Italy 5. France 6. Spain

1988   Final on 25 September

Coxless pairs/*Men*

	Gold	*Silver*	*Bronze*
1904	UNITED STATES 10:57.0	UNITED STATES	UNITED STATES
1908	GREAT BRITAIN 9:41.0	GREAT BRITAIN	—
	J. R. K. Fenning	2½ lengths	
	Gordon Thompson	George Fairbairn	
	(Leander I)	Philip Verdon	
		(Leander II)	
1924	NETHERLANDS 8:19.4	FRANCE 8:21.6	—
	Wilhelm Rösingh	Maurice Bouton	
	Antonie Beijnen	George Piot	
1928	GERMANY 7:06.4	GREAT BRITAIN 7:08.8	UNITED STATES 7:20.4
	Bruno Müller	Archibald Nisbet	John Schmitt
	Kurt Moeschter	Terence O'Brien	Paul McDowell
1932	GREAT BRITAIN 8:00.0	NEW ZEALAND 8:02.4	POLAND 8:08.2
	Arthur Edwards	Frederick Thompson	Janusz Mikolajczyk
	Lewis Clive	Cyril Stiles	Henryk Budzynski
1936	GERMANY 8:16.1	DENMARK 8:19.2	ARGENTINA 8:23.0
	Hugo Strauss	Harry Larsen	Julio Curatella
	Willi Eichhorn	Richard Olsen	Horacio Podestá
1948	GREAT BRITAIN 7:21.1	SWITZERLAND 7:23.9	ITALY 7:31.5
	John Wilson	Josef Kalt	Bruno Boni
	William Laurie	Hans Kalt	Felice Fanetti

1952	UNITED STATES 8:20.7 Charles Logg Thomas Price	BELGIUM 8:23.5 Michael Knuysen Robert Baetens	SWITZERLAND 8:32.7 Kurt Schmid Hans Kalt
1956	UNITED STATES 7:55.4 James Fifer Duvall Hecht	USSR 8:03.9 Igor Buldakov Viktor Ivanov	AUSTRIA 8:11.8 Josef Kloimstein Alfred Sageder
1960	USSR 7:02.01 Valentin Boreyko Oleg Golovanov	AUSTRIA 7:03.69 Josef Kloimstein Alfred Sageder	FINLAND 7:03.80 Veli Lehtelä Toimi Pitkänen
1964	CANADA 7:32.94 George Hungerford Roger Jackson	NETHERLANDS 7:33.40 Steven Blaisse Ernst Veenemans	GERMANY 7:38.63 Michael Schwan Wolfgang Hottenrott
1968	EAST GERMANY 7:26.56 Jörg Lucke Hans-Jürgen Bothe	UNITED STATES 7:26.71 Lawrence Hough Philip Johnson	DENMARK 7:31.84 Peter Christiansen Ib Ivan Larsen
1972	EAST GERMANY 6:53.16 Siegfried Brietzke Wolfgang Mager	SWITZERLAND 6:57.06 Heinrich Fischer Alfred Bachmann	NETHERLANDS 6:58.70 Roelof Luynenburg Rudolf Stokvis
1976	EAST GERMANY 7:23.31 Jörg Landvoigt Bernd Landvoigt	UNITED STATES 7:26.73 Calvin Coffey Michael Staines	WEST GERMANY 7:30.03 Peter Vanroye Thomas Strauss
1980	EAST GERMANY 6:48.01 Jörg Landvoigt Bernd Landvoigt	USSR 6:50.50 Juriy Pimenov Nikolai Pimenov	GREAT BRITAIN 6:51.47 Charles Wiggin Malcolm Carmichael
1984	ROMANIA 6:45.39 Petru Iosub Valer Toma	SPAIN 6:48.47 Fernando Climent Luis Lasurtegui	NORWAY 6:51.81 Hans Magnus Grepperud Sverre Loken

4. West Germany 5. Italy 6. United States

1988   Final on 24 September

Coxed pairs/*Men*

	Gold	*Silver*	*Bronze*
1900	NETHERLANDS 7:34.2	FRANCE I 7:34.4	FRANCE II 7:57.2
1906*	ITALY I 4:23.0	ITALY II 4:30.0	FRANCE d.n.a.
1906†	ITALY 7:32.4	BELGIUM 8:03.0	FRANCE 8:08.6
1920	ITALY 7:56.0	FRANCE 7:57.0	SWITZERLAND d.n.a.
1924	SWITZERLAND 8:39.0	ITALY 8:39.1	UNITED STATES 3 m
1928	SWITZERLAND 7:42.6	FRANCE 7:48.4	BELGIUM 7:59.4
1932	UNITED STATES 8:25.8	POLAND 8:31.2	FRANCE 8:41.2
1936	GERMANY 8:36.9	ITALY 8:49.7	FRANCE 8:54.0
1948	DENMARK 8:00.5	ITALY 8:12.2	HUNGARY 8:25.2
1952	FRANCE 8:28.6	GERMANY 8:32.1	DENMARK 8:34.9
1956	UNITED STATES 8:26.1	GERMANY 8:29.2	USSR 8:31.0
1960	GERMANY 7:29.14	USSR 7:30.17	UNITED STATES 7:34.58
1964	UNITED STATES 8:21.23	FRANCE 8:23.15	NETHERLANDS 8:23.42
1968	ITALY 8:04.81	NETHERLANDS 8:06.80	DENMARK 8:08.07

*Over 1000 m.
†Over 1600 m.

1972	EAST GERMANY 7:17.25	CZECHOSLOVAKIA 7:19.57	ROMANIA 7:21.36
1976	EAST GERMANY 7:58.99	USSR 8:01.82	CZECHOSLOVAKIA 8:03.28
1980	EAST GERMANY 7:02.54	USSR 7:03.35	YUGOSLAVIA 7:04.92
1984	ITALY 7:05.99	ROMANIA 7:11.21	UNITED STATES 7:12.81
	Carmine Abbagnale	Dimitrie Popescu	Kevin Still
	Giuseppe Abbagnale	Vasile Tomoiaga	Robert Espeseth
	Giuseppe DiCapua	Dumitru Raducanu	Douglas Herland

4. Brazil 5. Canada 6. West Germany

1988   Final on 25 September

Coxless fours/*Men*

	Gold	Silver	Bronze
1904	UNITED STATES 9:05.8	UNITED STATES d.n.a.	UNITED STATES d.n.a.
1908	GREAT BRITAIN 8:34.0	GREAT BRITAIN 1½ lengths	—
1924	GREAT BRITAIN 7:08.6	CANADA 7:18.0	SWITZERLAND 2 lengths
1928	GREAT BRITAIN 6:36.0	UNITED STATES 6:37.0	ITALY 6:37.6
1932	GREAT BRITAIN 6:58.2	GERMANY 7:03.0	ITALY 7:04.0
1936	GERMANY 7:01.8	GREAT BRITAIN 7:06.5	SWITZERLAND 7:10.6
1948	ITALY 6:39.0	DENMARK 6:43.5	UNITED STATES 6:47.7
1952	YUGOSLAVIA 7:16.0	FRANCE 7:18.9	FINLAND 7:23.3
1956	CANADA 7:08.8	UNITED STATES 7:18.4	FRANCE 7:20.9
1960	UNITED STATES 6:26.26	ITALY 6:28.78	USSR 6:29.62
1964	DENMARK 6:59.30	GREAT BRITAIN 7:00.47	UNITED STATES 7:01.37
1968	EAST GERMANY 6:39.18	HUNGARY 6:41.64	ITALY 6:44.01
1972	EAST GERMANY 6:24.27	NEW ZEALAND 6:25.64	WEST GERMANY 6:28.41
1976	EAST GERMANY 6:37.42	NORWAY 6:41.22	USSR 6:42.52
1980	EAST GERMANY 6:08.17	USSR 6:11.81	GREAT BRITAIN 6:16.58
1984	NEW ZEALAND 6:03.48	UNITED STATES 6:06.10	DENMARK 6:07.72
	Leslie O'Connell	David Clark	Michael Jessen
	Shane O'Brien	Jonathan Smith	Lars Nielsen
	Conrad Robertson	Philip Stekl	Per Rasmussen
	Keith Trask	Alan Forney	Erik Christiansen

4. West Germany 5. Switzerland 6. Sweden

1988   Final on 25 September

Coxed fours/*Men*

	Gold	Silver	Bronze
1900*	GERMANY 5:59.0	NETHERLANDS 6:33.0	GERMANY 6:35.0
1900*	FRANCE 7:11.0	FRANCE 7:18.0	GERMANY 7:18.2
1906	ITALY 8:13.0	FRANCE d.n.a.	FRANCE d.n.a.

*There were two separate finals in 1900.

1912	GERMANY 6:59.4	GREAT BRITAIN 2 lengths	NORWAY d.n.a. DENMARK d.n.a.
1920	SWITZERLAND 6:54.0	UNITED STATES 6:58.0	NORWAY 7:02.0
1924	SWITZERLAND 7:18.4	FRANCE 7:21.6	UNITED STATES 7:23.0
1928	ITALY 6:47.8	SWITZERLAND 7:03.4	POLAND 7:12.8
1932	GERMANY 7:19.0	ITALY 7:19.2	POLAND 7:26.8
1936	GERMANY 7:16.2	SWITZERLAND 7:24.3	FRANCE 7:33.3
1948	UNITED STATES 6:50.3	SWITZERLAND 6:53.3	DENMARK 6:58.6
1952	CZECHOSLOVAKIA 7:33.4	SWITZERLAND 7:36.5	UNITED STATES 7:37.0
1956	ITALY 7:19.4	SWEDEN 7:22.4	FINLAND 7:30.9
1960	GERMANY 6:39.12	FRANCE 6:41.62	ITALY 6:43.72
1964	GERMANY 7:00.44	ITALY 7:02.84	NETHERLANDS 7:06.46
1968	NEW ZEALAND 6:45.62	EAST GERMANY 6:48.20	SWITZERLAND 6:49.04
1972	WEST GERMANY 6:31.85	EAST GERMANY 6:33.30	CZECHOSLOVAKIA 6:35.64
1976	USSR 6:40.22	EAST GERMANY 6:42.70	WEST GERMANY 6:46.96
1980	EAST GERMANY 6:14.51	USSR 6:19.05	POLAND 6:22.52
1984	GREAT BRITAIN 6:18.64 Martin Cross Richard Budgett Andrew Holmes Steven Redgrave Adrian Ellison	UNITED STATES 6:20.28 Thomas Kiefer Gregory Springer Michael Bach Edward Ives John Stillings	NEW ZEALAND 6:23.68 Kevin Lawton Donald Symon Barrie Mabbott Ross Tong Brett Hollister

4. Italy 5. Canada 6. West Germany

1988 Final on 24 September

Eights/*Men*

	Gold	Silver	Bronze
1900	UNITED STATES 6:09.8	BELGIUM 6:13.8	NETHERLANDS 6:23.0
1904	UNITED STATES 7:50.0	CANADA d.n.a.	—
1908	GREAT BRITAIN I 7:52.0	BELGIUM 2 lengths	GREAT BRITAIN II d.n.a.
1912	GREAT BRITAIN I 6:15.0	GREAT BRITAIN II 6:19.0	GERMANY d.n.a.
1920	UNITED STATES 6:02.6	GREAT BRITAIN 6:05.0	NORWAY 6:36.0
1924	UNITED STATES 6:33.4	CANADA 6:49.0	ITALY ¾ length
1928	UNITED STATES 6:03.2	GREAT BRITAIN 6:05.6	CANADA 6:03.8
1932	UNITED STATES 6:37.6	ITALY 6:37.8	CANADA 6:40.4
1936	UNITED STATES 6:25.4	ITALY 6:26.0	GERMANY 6:26.4
1948	UNITED STATES 5:56.7	GREAT BRITAIN 6:06.9	NORWAY 6:10.3
1952	UNITED STATES 6:25.9	USSR 6:31.2	AUSTRALIA 6:33.1
1956	UNITED STATES 6:35.2	CANADA 6:37.1	AUSTRALIA 6:39.2
1960	GERMANY 5:57.18	CANADA 6:01.52	CZECHOSLOVAKIA 6:04.84
1964	UNITED STATES 6:18.23	GERMANY 6:23.29	CZECHOSLOVAKIA 6:25.11
1968	WEST GERMANY 6:07.00	AUSTRALIA 6:07.98	USSR 6:09.11
1972	NEW ZEALAND 6:08.94	UNITED STATES 6:11.61	EAST GERMANY 6:11.67

1976	EAST GERMANY 5:58.29	GREAT BRITAIN 6:00.82	NEW ZEALAND 6:03.51
1980	EAST GERMANY 5:49.05	GREAT BRITAIN 5:51.92	USSR 5:52.66
1984	CANADA 5:41.32	UNITED STATES 5:51.74	AUSTRALIA 5:43.40
	Pat Turner	Walter Lubsen Jr	Craig Muller
	Kevin Neufield	Andrew Sudduth	Clyde Hefer
	Mark Evans	John Terwilliger	Sam Patten
	Grant Main	Christopher Penny	Timothy Willoughby
	Paul Steele	Thomas Darling	Ian Edmunds
	Mike Evans	Earl Borchelt	James Battersby
	Dean Crawford	Charles Clapp	Ion Popa
	Blake Horm	Bruce Ibbetson	Steve Evans
	Brian McMahon	Robert Jaugstetter	Gavin Thredgold

4. New Zealand 5. Great Britain 6. France 7. China

1988   Final on 25 September

Single sculls/*Women*

	Gold	Silver	Bronze
1976	Christine Scheiblich (GDR) 4:05.56	Joan Lind (USA) 4:06.21	Elena Antonova (URS) 4:10.24
1980	Sandra Toma (ROM) 3:40.69	Antonina Makhina (URS) 3:41.65	Martina Schröter (GDR) 3:43.54
1984	Valeria Racila (ROM) 3:40.68	Charlotte Geer (USA) 3:43.89	Ann Haesebrouck (BEL) 3:45.72

4. Andrea Schreiner (CAN) 5. Lise Justesen (DEN) 6. Beryl Mitchell (GBR)

1988   Final on 25 September

Double sculls/*Women*

	Gold	Silver	Bronze
1976	BULGARIA 3:44.36	EAST GERMANY 3:47.86	USSR 3:49.93
	Svetla Otzetova	Sabine Jahn	Leonora Kaminskaite
	Zdravka Yordanova	Petra Boesler	Genovate Ramoshkene
1980	USSR 3:16.27	EAST GERMANY 3:17.63	ROMANIA 3:18.91
	Elena Khloptseva	Cornelia Linse	Olga Homeghi
	Larisa Popova	Heidi Westphal	Valeria Rosca-Racila
1984	ROMANIA 3:26.75	NETHERLANDS 3:29.13	CANADA 3:29.82
	Marioara Popescu	Greet Hellemans	Daniele Laumann
	Elizabeta Oleniuc	Nicolette Hellemans	Silken Laumann

4. Sweden 5. Norway 6. United States

1988   Final on 24 September

Coxless pairs/*Women*

	Gold	Silver	Bronze
1976	BULGARIA 4:01.22 Siika Kelbetcheva Stoyanka Grouitcheva	EAST GERMANY 4:01.64 Angelika Noack Sabine Dahne	WEST GERMANY 4:02.35 Edith Eckbauer Thea Einöder
1980	EAST GERMANY 3:30.49 Ute Steindorf Cornelia Klier	POLAND 3:30.95 Malgorzata Dluzewska Czeslawa Koscianska	BULGARIA 3:32.39 Siika Barboulova (née Kelbetcheva) Stoyanka Kubatova (née Grouitcheva)
1984	ROMANIA 3:32.60 Rodica Arba Elena Horvat	CANADA 3:36.06 Betty Craig Tricia Smith	WEST GERMANY 3:40.50 Ellen Becker Iris Volkner

4. Netherlands 5. United States 6. Great Britain

1988   Final on 24 September

Coxed quadruple sculls/*Women*

	Gold	Silver	Bronze
1976	EAST GERMANY 3:29.99	USSR 3:32.49	ROMANIA 3:32.76
1980	EAST GERMANY 3:15.32	USSR 3:15.73	BULGARIA 3:16.10
1984	ROMANIA 3:14.11 Titie Taran Anisoara Sorohan Ioana Badea Sofia Corban Ecaterina Oancia	UNITED STATES 3:15.57 Anne Marden Lisa Rohde Joan Lind Virginia Gilder Kelly Rickon	DENMARK 3:16.02 Hanne Eriksen Birgitte Hanel Charlotte Koefoed Bodil Rasmussen Jette Soeresen

4. West Germany 5. France 6. Italy

1988   Not being held

Coxless quadruple sculls/*Women*

1988   Final on 25 September

Coxed fours/*Women*

	Gold	Silver	Bronze
1976	EAST GERMANY 3:45.08	BULGARIA 3:48.24	USSR 3:49.38
1980	EAST GERMANY 3:19.27	BULGARIA 3:20.75	USSR 3:20.92
1984	ROMANIA 3:19.30 Florica Lavric Maria Fricioiu Chira Apostol Olga Bularda Viorica Ioja	CANADA 3:21.55 Marilyn Brain Angie Schneider Barbara Armbrust Jane Tregunno Lesley Thompson	AUSTRALIA 3:23.29 Robyn Grey-Gardner Karen Brancourt Susan Chapman Margot Foster Susan Lee

4. United States 5. Netherlands 6. West Germany

1988   Final on 24 September

Eights/*Women*

Gold	*Silver*	*Bronze*
1976 EAST GERMANY 3:33.32	USSR 3:36.17	UNITED STATES 3:38.68
1980 EAST GERMANY 3:03.32	USSR 3:04.29	ROMANIA 3:05.63
1984 UNITED STATES 2:59.80	ROMANIA 3:00.87	NETHERLANDS 3:02.92
Shyril O'Steen	Doina Balan	Nicolette Hellemans
Harriet Metcalf	Marioara Trasca	Lynda Cornet
Caroll Bower	Aurora Plesca	Harriet Van Ettekoven
Carie Graves	Aneta Mihaly	Greet Hellemans
Jeanne Flanagan	Adriana Chelariu	Marieke Van Drogenbroek
Kristine Norellus	Mihaela Armasescu	Anne Marie Quist
Kristen Thorsness	Carmelia Diaconescu	Catharina Neelissen
Kathryn Keeler	Lucia Sauca	Willemien Vaandrager
Betsy Beard	Viorica Ioja	Martha Laurijsen

4. Canada 5. Great Britain 6. West Germany

1988 Final on 25 September

SHOOTING

This sport was introduced into the first of the modern celebrations in 1896. Baron Pierre De Coubertin, the founder of the modern Games was a crack shot himself.

The various events have changed much down the years. Nowadays there are no live targets.

This is one of only three current Olympic sports where men and women compete together in some events. (The others are Equestrianism and Yachting.)

The terminology used in shooting is often quite complicated and confusing but the following should enable you to understand the various events without necessarily turning you into a small bore.

MEN'S EVENTS

PISTOL

There are three pistol events as follows:

Rapid fire pistol

Competitors may use any type of pistol with a .22 calibre (bore of 5.6 mm). There are five targets at a range of 25 metres. The targets turn from sideways on. A competitor has a limited time to hit all five targets. First it is eight seconds, then six seconds, and finally four seconds. This process is repeated four times over two days, making 60 shots in all with a maximum possible score of 600 (10 for bullseye, reducing to one for outer ring). In previous Games, that decided the medals. In Seoul, the top eight shooters from that process will compete again to decide medals. They take 10 more shots. This rule is not popular with the competitors (although it is with TV companies). Scores are carried forward.

Free pistol

Modern weapons used do not look like the familiar pistols. They have long barrels and no casing. The butt is more of a grip. This is a slow precision event. Again weapons are .22 calibre. The shooter has 2½ hours to fire six lots of 10 shots at a target 50 metres distance. So once again, the maximum score is 600.

As in the Rapid Fire Pistol, the top eight will progress to a final.

Air pistol

This weapon works on compressed air. The target is set at 10 metres and the '10 ring' is a mere quarter of an inch wide. 60 shots are fired with 1½ hours. Maximum score 600. The top eight compete in the final for 10 shots.

RIFLE

Small-bore rifle (prone)

This is sometimes known in the Olympics as the English Match. Weapons used are .22 calibre. The marksman lies on his stomach. 60 shots in all are fired at a target 50 metres distant. Maximum score 600. Maximum time two hours. The top eight compete again over 10 further shots.

Small-bore rifle (three position)

The weapon used is as above, but is fired from the prone position, standing and kneeling. 40 shots from each position, making a possible maximum score of 1200. The top eight compete in a final – 10 shots standing position only.

Running game

The above type of rifle is used, but here unlike the above events, telescopic sights are allowed. The target is a cutout boar with a '10 ring' target printed on the head. It crosses on rails at a 'slow' speed – 5 seconds and fast speed 2.5 seconds. 30 shots are fired at each speed from 50 metres. Possible maximum score, again, 600. Here the best four scorers compete again, firing 10 shots at each speed, giving another maximum of 200, which will be added to the previous score.

Air rifle

Rules as per air pistol.

WOMEN'S EVENTS

PISTOL

Sports pistol

This is a combination of the free and rapid fire events for men. The first 30 shots are as per men's free pistol. The rapid fire part is different from the men's. Here, there is just one target which presents itself for three seconds before turning away for seven seconds. Six series of five shots. Again the total points possible is 600. The top eight shooters compete in the final in which they fire two lots of five shots rapid fire.

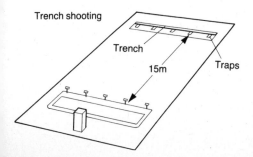

Trench shooting
Trench
15m
Traps

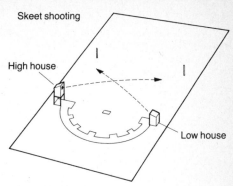

Skeet shooting
High house
Low house

Air pistol

A new event for women conducted on exactly the same basis as the men's, except that 40 shots are fired. Maximum possible score 400. Then the top eight shoot again.

RIFLE

Small bore rifle (three position)

As per men's. See above. Except maximum score of 600. Then top eight shoot again.

Air rifle

As per men's. See above. Except that women take 40 shots instead of 60. Maximum possible score 400. Again, best eight go forward for a final 10 shots.

OPEN EVENTS
(men and women)

SHOT-GUNS

Olympic trap

Weapon used – shotgun with single sight and double barrel. The barrels are 'over and under' unlike the sporting guns used for 'game' shooting when the barrels are often side by side.

The targets are clay discs. Competitors call for the release of targets into the air. Nowadays, the competitor's voice activates the release – known as acoustic release. Each trap has three different firing directions. One or both barrels can be used to hit the target. Over two days, 150 targets are released by each competitor. One point for a hit. After the first round, the top 24 have another 50 clays and then the best six a final 25, scores are carried forward – so the maximum score is 225 (200 at last Games).

Skeet

Same weapon, same targets, but there are eight shooting positions or stations (seven round a semicircle and the eighth where the centre of the circle would be – see diagram on page 157). At either end of the diameter are two 'houses' – a high one and a low one – from which the clays are released within three seconds of the call. They come in predetermined order from the high and low houses, but not the same number from each station. So the competitor receives either one or two targets on release.

THE COMPETITION

Medallists can come from almost anywhere. This is very much a universal sport and,

although nerve and control are vital, no real athletic prowess is required, so competitors can go on to a ripe old age. It has produced the oldest medallist – Oscar Swahn of Sweden at 72 years 280 days.

USA are the leading medal winners over the years, but even on home territory in 1984, they won only three of the 11 available medals. Watch out for China this time. They are improving rapidly at this sport.

THE STARS

Carl Osburn (USA) won a grand total of 11 medals between 1912 and 1924, five of them gold.

THE BRITISH

In pistol shooting only one bronze medal has been won. However, in other departments, Britain's record is good although most of the medals came before the First World War. Malcolm Cooper is the most recent gold

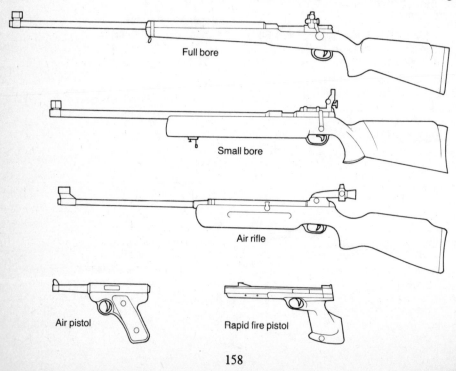

Full bore

Small bore

Air rifle

Air pistol

Rapid fire pistol

medallist ('Cooperman', he calls himself). His wife, Sarah, is also a leading competitor. Cooper's event is small-bore rifle shooting (three position). He will certainly be part of Britain's team in Seoul.

Not a lot of people know that

• Karoly Takacs of Hungary was in his country's world championship pistol team in 1938. However, while serving in the army, a grenade exploded in his right hand – his shooting hand – and shattered it completely. He taught himself to shoot lefthanded and 10 years later in the 1948 Olympics, won the rapid-fire pistol gold medal with a world record score. He retained the title in 1952.

• In the 1932 Games, Antonius Lemberkovits (HUN) hit a bullseye, except he had been aiming at the wrong target. Nobody else had noticed, but honest Antonius admitted his mistake. Had he not, he would have won the gold medal. As it was he did not finish in the top eight.

• One of the 'live' events of early Games was pigeon shooting. Crittenden Robinson won the bronze medal for Britain in 1900. He shot 18 of the birds

• Lt. Col. Philip Neame, who was a member of the British team at the 1924 Games, is the only Olympic competitor to have been awarded the Victoria Cross.

VENUE

Taenung International Range. 15 km from Olympic Village. Capacity 3000.

RESULTS

Free pistol/Men

	Gold	Silver	Bronze
1896	Sumner Paine (USA) 442	Viggo Jensen (DEN) 285	Holger Nielsen (DEN) d.n.a.
1900	Karl Röderer (SUI) 503	Achille Paroche (FRA) 466	Konrad Stäheli (SUI) 453
1906	Georgios Orphanidis (GRE) 221	Jean Fouconnier (FRA) 219	Aristides Rangavis (GRE) 218
1912	Alfred Lane (USA) 499	Peter Dolfen (USA) 474	Charles Stewart (GBR) 470
1920	Karl Frederick (USA) 496	Afranio da Costa (BRA) 489	Alfred Lane (USA) 481
1936	Torsten Ullmann (SWE) 559 WR	Erich Krempel (GER) 544	Charles des Jammonières (FRA) 540
1948	Edwin Vazquez Cam (PER) 545	Rudolf Schnyder (SUI) 539	Torsten Ullmann (SWE) 539
1952	Huelet Benner (USA) 553 OR	Angel Léon de Gozalo (ESP) 550	Ambrus Balogh (HUN) 549
1956	Pentti Linnosvuo (FIN) 556 OR	Makhmud Oumarov (URS) 556 OR	Offutt Pinion (USA) 551
1960	Aleksey Gushchin (URS) 560 OR	Makhmud Oumarov (URS) 552	Yoshihisa Yoshikawa (JPN) 552
1964	Väinö Markkanen (FIN) 560 = OR	Franklin Green (USA) 557	Yoshihisa Yoshikawa (JPN) 554
1968	Grigory Kossykh (URS) 562 OR	Heinz Mertel (FRG) 562 OR	Harald Vollmar (GDR) 560
1972	Ragnar Skanakar (SWE) 567 OR	Dan Iuga (ROM) 562	Rudolf Dollinger (AUT) 560

1976	Uwe Potteck (GDR) 573 WR	Harald Vollmar (GDR) 567	Rudolf Dollinger (AUT) 560
1980	Aleksandr Melentyev (URS) 581 WR	Harald Vollmar (GDR) 568	Lubcho Diakov (URS) 565
1984	Haifen Xu (CHN) 566	Ragnar Skanaker (SWE) 565	Yiju Wang (CHN) 564

4. Jurgen Hartmann (FRG) 5. Vincenzo Tondo (ITA) 6. Philippe Cola (FRA)
7. Hector DeLima Carrillo (VEN) 8. Paavo Palokangas (FIN)

1988   On 18 September

Rapid fire pistol/*Men*

	Gold	*Silver*	*Bronze*
1896	Jean Phrangoudis (GRE) 344	Georgios Orphanidis (GRE) 249	Holger Nielsen (DEN) d.n.a.
1900	Maurice Larrouy (FRA) 58	Léon Moreaux (FRA) 57	Eugene Balme (FRA) 57
1906	Maurice Lecoq (FRA) 250	Léon Moreaux (FRA) 249	Aristides Rangavis (GRE) 245
1908	Paul van Asbroeck (BEL) 490	Réginald Storms (BEL) 487	James Gorman (USA) 485
1912	Alfred Lane (USA) 287	Paul Palén (SWE) 286	Johan von Holst (SWE) 283
1920	Guilherme Paraense (BRA) 274	Raymond Bracken (USA) 272	Fritz Zulauf (SUI) 269
1924	Henry Bailey (USA) 18	Vilhelm Carlberg (SWE) 18	Lennart Hannelius (FIN) 18
1932	Renzo Morigi (ITA) 36	Heinz Hax (GER) 36	Domenico Matteucci (ITA) 36
1936	Cornelius van Oyen (GER) 36	Heinz Hax (GER) 35	Torsten Ullmann (SWE) 34
1948	Károly Takács (HUN) 580 WR	Carlos Diaz Sáenz Valiente (ARG) 571	Sven Lundqvist (SWE) 569
1952	Károly Takács (HUN) 579	Szilárd Kun (HUN) 578	Gheorghe Lichiardopol (ROM) 578
1956	Stefan Petrescu (ROM) 587 OR	Evgeniy Shcherkasov (URS) 585	Gheorghe Lichiardopol (ROM) 581
1960	William McMillan (USA) 587 = OR	Pentti Linnosvuo (FIN) 587 = OR	Aleksandr Zabelin (URS) 587 = OR
1964	Pentti Linnosvuo (FIN) 592 OR	Ion Tripsa (ROM) 591	Lubomir Nacovsky (TCH) 590
1968	Jozef Zapedzki (POL) 593 OR	Marcel Rosca (ROM) 591	Renart Suleimanov (URS) 591
1972	Jozef Zapedzki (POL) 595 OR	Ladislav Faita (TCH) 594	Victor Torshin (URS) 593
1976	Norbet Klaar (GDR) 597 OR	Jürgen Wiefel (GDR) 596	Roberto Ferraris (ITA) 595
1980	Corneliu Ion (ROM) 596*	Jürgen Wiefel (GDR) 596	Gerhard Petrisch (AUT) 596
1984	Takeo Kamachi (JPN) 595	Corneliu Ion (ROM) 593	Rauno Bies (FIN) 591

4. Delival Nobre (BRA) 5. Choong-Yull Yang (KOR) 6. Alfred Radke (FRG)
7. Jong-Gil Park (KOR) 8. Bernardo Tobar (COL)

1988   22 and 23 September

*Required three shoot-offs.

Small bore rifle – three positions/*Men*

Gold	*Silver*	*Bronze*
1952 Erling Kongshaug (NOR) 1164	Vihlo Ylönen (FIN) 1164	Boris Andreyev (URS) 1163
1956 Anatoliy Bogdanov (URS) 1172 OR	Otakar Hořinek (TCH) 1172 OR	Nils Sundberg (SWE) 1167
1960 Viktor Shamburkin (URS) 1149 =WR	Marat Niyasov (URS) 1145	Klaus Zähringer (GER) 1139
1964 Lones Wigger (USA) 1164 WR	Velitchko Khristov (BUL) 1152	László Hammerl (HUN) 1151
1968 Bernd Klingner (FRG) 1157	John Writer (USA) 1156	Vitaly Parkhimovich (URS) 1154
1972 John Writer (USA) 1166 WR	Lanny Bassham (USA) 1157	Werner Lippoldt (GDR) 1153
1976 Lanny Bassham (USA) 1162	Margaret Murdock (USA) 1162	Werner Seibold (FRG) 1160
1980 Viktor Vlasov (URS) 1173 WR	Bernd Hartstein (GDR) 1166	Sven Johansson (SWE) 1165
1984 Malcolm Cooper (GBR) 1173 =WR	Daniel Nipkow (SUI) 1163	Alister Allan (GBR) 1162

4. Kurt Hillenbrand (FRG) 6. Bo Arne Lilja (DEN) 6. Glenn Dubis (USA)
7. Jean Pierre Amat (FRA) 8. Peter Heinz (FRG)

1988 Final on 22 September

Skeet shooting/*Men*

Gold	*Silver*	*Bronze*
1968 Evgeny Petrov (URS) 198 =WR	Romano Garagnani (ITA) 198 =WR	Konrad Wirnhier (FRG) 198 =WR
1972 Konrad Wirnhier (FRG) 195	Evgeny Petrov (URS) 195	Michael Buchheim (GDR) 195
1976 Josef Panacek (TCH) 198 = OR	Eric Swinkels (HOL) 198 = OR	Wieslaw Gawlikowski (POL) 196
1980 Hans Kjeld Rasmussen (DEN) 196	Lars-Goran Carlsson (SWE) 196	Roberto Garcia (CUB) 196
1984 Matthew Dryke (USA) 198 = OR	Ole Riber Rasmussen (DEN) 196	Luca Scribani Rossi (ITA) 196

4. Johannes Pierik (HOL) 5. Anders Berglind (SWE) 6. Norbert Hofmann (FRG)
7. Jorge Molina (COL) 8. Ian Hale (AUS)

1988 Final on 24 September

Running game target/*Men*

	Gold	Silver	Bronze
1900	Louis Debray (FRA) 20	P. Nivet (FRA) 20	Comte de Lambert (FRA) 19
1972	Lakov Zhelezniak (URS) 569 WR	Helmut Bellingrodt (COL) 565	John Kynoch (GBR) 562
1976	Aleksandr Gazov (URS) 579 WR	Aleksandr Kedyarov (URS) 576	Jerzy Greszkiewicz (POL) 571
1980	Igor Sokolov (URS) 589 WR	Thomas Pfeffer (GDR) 589 WR	Aleksandr Gazov (URS) 587
1984	Yuwei Li (CHN) 587	Helmut Bellingrodt (COL) 584	Shiping Huang (CHN) 581

4. Uew Schroder (FRG) 5. David Lee (CAN) 6. Kenneth Skoglund (NOR) 7. Jorma Lievonen (FIN) 8. Ezio Cini (ITA)

1988   Final on 23 September

Olympic trap shooting/*Men*

	Gold	Silver	Bronze
1900	Roger de Barbarin (FRA) 17	René Guyot (FRA) 17	Justinien de Clary (FRA) 17
1906*	Gerald Merlin (GBR) 24	Ioannis Peridis (GRE) 23	Sidney Merlin (GBR) 21
1906*	Sidney Merlin (GBR) 15	Anastasios Metaxas (GRE) 13	Gerald Merlin (GBR) 12
1908	Walter Ewing (CAN) 72	George Beattie (CAN) 60	Alexander Maunder (GBR) 57 Anastasios Metaxas (GRE) 57
1912	James Graham (USA) 96	Alfred Goeldel-Bronikowen (GER) 94	Harry Blau (URS) 91
1920	Mark Arie (USA) 95	Frank Troeh (USA) 93	Frank Wright (USA) 87
1924	Gyula Halasy (HUN) 98 OR	Konrad Huber (FIN) 98 OR	Frank Hughes (USA) 97
1952	George Généreux (CAN) 192	Knut Holmquist (SWE) 191	Hans Liljedahl (SWE) 190
1956	Galliano Rossini (ITA) 195 OR	Adam Smelczynski (POL) 190	Alessandro Ciceri (ITA) 188
1960	Ion Dumitrescu (ROM) 192	Galliano Rossini (ITA) 191	Sergey Kalinin (URS) 190
1964	Ennio Mattarelli (ITA) 198 OR	Pavel Senichev (URS) 194	William Morris (USA) 194
1968	Robert Braithwaite (GBR) 198 =WR	Thomas Garrigus (USA) 196	Kurt Czekalla (GDR) 196
1972	Angelo Scalzone (ITA) 199 WR	Michel Carrega (FRA) 198	Silvano Basagni (ITA) 195
1976	Don Haldeman (USA) 190	Armando Marques (POR) 189	Ubaldesco Baldi (ITA) 189
1984	Luciano Giovanetti (ITA) 192	Rustam Yambulatov (URS) 196	Jörg Damme (GDR) 196
1984	Luciano Giovanetti (ITA) 192	Francisco Boza (PER) 192	Daniel Carlisle (USA) 192

4. Timo Nieminen (FIN) 5. Michel Carrega (FRA) 6. Eli Ellis (AUS) 7. Terry Rumbel (AUS) 8. Johnny Pahlsson (SWE)

1988   Final on 20 September

*Single shot.   †Double shot.

Small bore rifle* (prone) English Match at 50 metres/*Men*

	Gold	Silver	Bronze
1908	A. A. Carnell (GBR) 387	Harry Humby (GBR) 386	George Barnes (GBR) 385
1912	Frederick Hird (USA) 194	William Milne (GBR) 193	Harry Burt (GBR) 192
1920	Lawrence Nuesslein (USA) 391	Arthur Rothrock (USA) 386	Dennis Fenton (USA) 385
1924	Pierre Coquelin de Lisle (FRA) 398	Marcus Dinwiddie (USA) 396	Josias Hartmann (SUI) 394
1932	Bertil Rönnmark (SWE) 294	Gustavo Huet (MEX) 294	Zoltán Hradetsky-Soós (HUN) 293
1936	Willy Rögeberg (NOR) 300 WR	Ralph Berzsenyi (HUN) 296	Wlasyslaw Karăs (POL) 296
1948	Arthur Cook (USA) 599 WR	Walter Tomsen (USA) 599 WR	Jonas Jonsson (SWE) 597
1952	Josif Sarbu (ROM) 400 =WR	Boris Andreyev (URS) 400 =WR	Arthur Jackson (USA) 399
1956	Gerald Ouellette (CAN) 600†	Vasiliy Borissov (URS) 599	Gilmour Boa (CAN) 598
1960	Peter Kohnke (GER) 590	James Hill (USA) 589	Enrico Pelliccione (VEN) 587
1964	László Hammerl (HUN) 597 WR	Lones Wigger (USA) 597 WR	Tommy Pool (USA) 596
1968	Jan Kurka (TCH) 598 =WR	László Hammerl (HUN) 598 =WR	Ian Ballinger (NZL) 597
1972	Ho Jun Li (PRK) 599 WR	Victor Auer (USA) 598	Nicolae Rotaru (ROM) 598
1976	Karlheinz Smieszek (FRG) 599 =WR	Ulrich Lind (FRG) 597	Gennadiy Lushchikov (URS) 595
1980	Karoly Varga (HUN) 599 =WR	Hellfried Heilfort (GDR) 599 =WR	Petar Zapianov (BUL) 598
1984	Edward Etzel (USA) 599 =WR	Michel Bury (FRA) 596	Michael Sullivan (GBR) 596

4. Alister Allan (GBR) 5. Francesco Nanni (SMR) 6. Hans Strand (SWE)
7. John Duus (NOR) 8. Ulrich Lind (FRG)

1988   On 19 September

*In 1908 and 1912 any position was allowed but only standing in 1920. Since then it has been prone.
†Record was not allowed as the range was found to be marginally short.

Air rifle shot at 10 metres/*Men*

	Gold	Silver	Bronze
1984	Philippe Herberle (FRA) 589 OR	Andreas Kronthaler (AUT) 587	Barry Dagger (GBR) 587

4. Nicholas Berthelot (FRA) 5. Peter Heinz (FRG) 6. John Rost (USA)
7. Harald Stenvaag (NOR) 8. Itzchak Yonassi (ISR)

1988   Final on 20 September

Air pistol shot at 10 metres/*Men*

1988   Final on 24 September

Sport pistol shot at 25 metres/*Women*

	Gold	Silver	Bronze
1984	Linda Thom (CAN) 585 OR	Ruby Fox (USA) 585 OR	Patricia Dench (AUS) 583

4. Haiying Liu (CHN) 5. Kristine Fries (SWE) 6. Zhifang Wen (CHN)
7. Debora Srour (BRA) 8. Maria Macovei (ROM)

1988 Final on 19 September

Standard rifle – three positions shot at 50 metres/*Women*

	Gold	Silver	Bronze
1984	Xiaoxuan Wu (CHN) 581 OR	Ulrike Holmer (FRG) 578	Wanda Jewell (USA) 578

4. Gloria Parmentier (USA) 5. Anne Grethe Jeppesen (NOR) 6. Dongxiang Jin (CHN)
7. Biserka Vrbek (YUG) 8. Mirjana Jovovic (YUG)

1988 Final on 21 September

Air rifle shot at 10 metres/*Women*

	Gold	Silver	Bronze
1984	Pat Spurgin (USA) 393 OR	Edith Gufler (ITA) 391	Xiaoxuan Wu (CHN) 389

4. Sharon Bowes (CAN) 5. Yvette Courault (FRA) 6. Gisela Sailer (FRG)
7. Siri Landsem (NOR) 8. Sirpa Ylonen (FIN)

1988 Final on 18 September

Air pistol shot at 10 metres/*Women*

1988 Final on 21 September

SWIMMING

The sport has been part of every celebration in modern times. For the first four Games, the events took place in natural surroundings, twice in the sea, once in a lake, and once in the River Seine. It was not until 1908 that a pool was first used, at the White City Stadium, London.

The now established 50-metre pool was first used in 1924. The first indoor pool was at Wembley for the 1948 Games. However, outdoor pools are often used where the climate is suitable, as in Los Angeles.

In 1900, underwater swimming was one of the events. Not very pleasant one would have thought, as this was the year the swimming was held in the River Seine. Mind you, golf, cricket, croquet, fishing, and motorboat racing were all part of the extraordinary 1900 Olympics in Paris.

THE COMPETITION

There is no doubt at all that the USA are the world's best in men's swimming with the East Germans dominant in the women's events.

At the 1984 Olympics, when the Eastern European countries did not take part and the Americans were on home water, as it were, they won 24 of the 36 available gold medals. Back in 1976, the last time *all* the major swimming nations took part, the Americans were confined to 15 Olympic titles. Having said that, they did win every event in the men's competition bar one, the 200-metres breaststroke in which good old David Wilkie scored a notable British success. But in the women's competition the East Germans won 11 gold medals. With one or two notable exceptions, the East German women swimmers put their men in the shade. Just why is not abundantly clear, but it also happens in track and field. In the 1980 Games, they won all but three events.

Apart from the Americans and East Germans, the Soviets, Canadians and West Germans will provide a second-tier strength with the odd medal going to elsewhere in Western Europe, Australia, and the Far East. The African countries rarely take part and seem to be physiologically unsuited to the sport.

Note: Both men and women will race over 50 metres (just one lap) of the pool for the first time in the Olympics. This will be for freestyle swimmers only. There was a 50 yard race for men in the 1904 Games.

Men and women take part in identical events except that only women take part in synchronized swimming while only men compete in water polo. The men's longest event is the 1500-metre freestyle while for women it is 800 metres.

THE STROKES

FREESTYLE

This is the fastest of the four recognized strokes. All swimmers now use crawl, which was fashioned into a racing style by the Australians at the turn of the century. In early modern Games the sidestroke was quite often used.

50 metres
Men
New Olympic event
WR: 22.23 (Tom Jager USA, 1987)

Women
New Olympic event
WR: 25.28 (Tamara Costache ROM, 1986)

100 metres
Men
WR: 48.74 (Matt Biondi USA, 1986)
OR: 49.80 (Rowdy Gaines USA, 1984)

Women
WR: 54.73 (Kristin Otto GDR, 1986)
OR: 54.79 (Barbara Krause GDR, 1980)

200 metres
Men
WR: 1:47.44 (Michael Gross FRG, 1984)
OR: 1:47.44 (Michael Gross FRG, 1984)

Women
WR: 1:57.55 (Heike Friedrich GDR, 1986)
OR: 1:58.33 (Barbara Krause GDR, 1984)

400 metres
Men
WR: 3:47.38 (Artur Wojdat POL, 1988)
OR: 3:50.91 (Thomas Fahner FRG, 1984)

Women
WR: 4:05.45 (Janet Evans USA, 1987)
OR: 4:07.10 (Tiffany Cohen USA, 1984)

800 metres
Women
WR: 8:17.12 (Janet Evans USA, 1988)
OR: 8:24.95 (Tiffany Cohen USA, 1984)

1500 metres
Men
WR: 14:54.76 (Vladimir Salnikov URS, 1983)
OR: 14:58.27 (Vladimir Salnikov URS, 1980)

4 × 100 metre relay
Men
WR: 3:17.08 (United States, 1985)
OR: 3:19.03 (United States, 1984)

Women
WR: 3:40.57 (East Germany, 1986)
OR: 3:42.71 (East Germany, 1980)

4 × 200 metre relay
Men
WR: 7:13.10 (West Germany, 1987)
OR: 7:15.69 (United States, 1984)

BACKSTROKE

This is the only stroke for which swimmers begin the race in the water (difficult to dive in and turn on to your back).

100 metres
Men
WR: 55.19 (Rick Carey USA, 1983)
OR: 55.41 (Rick Carey USA, 1984) (in relay)

Women
WR: 1:00.59 (Ina Kleber GDR, 1984)
OR: 1:00.86 (Rica Reinisch GDR, 1980)

200 metres
Men
WR: 1:58.14 (Igor Poljanski URS, 1985)
OR: 1:58.99 (Rick Carey USA, 1984) (in heat)

Women
WR: 2:08.60 (Betsy Mitchell USA, 1986)
OR: 2:11.77 (Rica Reinisch GDR, 1980)

BREASTSTROKE

The slowest of the four strokes. Hands and feet are kept wide apart in a sweeping movement which propels the body forward. This stroke often poses disqualification problems. In principle, arms and legs should remain underwater, while part of the head must remain above water (underwater swimming was employed for a time; it is fast, but now outlawed). On turning, both hands must touch together.

100 metres
Men
WR: 1:01.65 (Steve Lindquist USA, 1984)
OR: 1:01.65 (Steve Lindquist USA, 1984)

Women
WR: 1:07.91 (Silke Horner GDR, 1987)
OR: 1:09.88 (Petra Van Staveren HOL, 1984)

200 metres
Men
WR: 2:13.34 (Victor Davis CAN, 1984)
OR: 2:13.34 (Victor Davis CAN, 1984)

Women
WR: 2:27.40 (Silke Horner GDR, 1986)
OR: 2:29.54 (Lina Kachushite URS, 1980)

BUTTERFLY

This stroke came to be used as a direct result of a loophole in the breaststroke rules. In the 1930s, both the Americans and the Germans found that quicker breaststroke styles could be developed if they took their arms out of the water. By 1952, the butterfly stroke had been formally adopted as a separate technique and event and was used at the Olympic Games that year in Helsinki.

As in breaststroke, swimmers must keep their shoulders in line with the surface of the water and may not swim underwater except for the first and last strokes into and out of the turn. Again, at turns or at the finish of a race, both hands must touch together.

100 metres
Men
WR: 52.84 (Pablo Pedro Morales USA, 1986)
OR: 53.08 (Michael Gross FRG, 1984)

Women
WR: 57.93 (Mary T. Meagher USA, 1981)
OR: 59.05 (Mary T. Meagher USA, 1984) (in a heat)

200 metres
Men
WR: 1:56.24 (Michael Gross FRG, 1986)
OR: 1:57.04 (John Sieben AUS, 1984)

Women
WR: 2:05.96 (Mary T. Meagher USA, 1981)

OR: 2:06.90 (Mary T. Meagher USA, 1984)

MEDLEY RACES

This is a race in which all four swimming strokes are combined. In the individual events (where one swimmer employs all four strokes) they are swum in the following order): butterfly, backstroke, breaststroke, freestyle.

In medley relays, teams of four swimmers compete, each a specialist at a given stroke. The order of strokes for the relay is: backstroke (since no dive is required), followed by breaststroke, butterfly, and freestyle.

200 metre individual medley
Men
WR: 2:00.56 (Tamas Darnyi HUN, 1987)
OR: 2:01.41 (Alex Baumann CAN, 1984)

Women
WR: 2:11.73 (Ute Geweniger GDR, 1981)
OR: 2:12.64 (Tracy Caulkins USA, 1984)

400 metre individual medley
Men
WR: 4:15.42 (Tamas Darnyi HUN, 1987)
OR: 4:17.41 (Alex Baumann CAN, 1984)

Women
WR: 4:36.10 (Petra Schneider GDR, 1982)
OR: 4:36.29 (Petra Schneider GDR, 1980)

4 × 100 medley relay
Men
WR: 3:38.28 (United States, 1985)
OR: 3:39.30 (United States, 1984)

Women
WR: 4:03.69 (East Germany, 1984)
OR: 4:06.67 (East Germany, 1980)

THE COURSE

The pool is 50 metres in length. 50-metre races will be held for the first time in these Olympics. Freestyle only – a real swimmers' sprint to find the 'Ben Johnson' of the sport.

The longest event, the mens' 1500-metre freestyle is the swimmers' 'marathon' and covers 30 lengths of the pool.

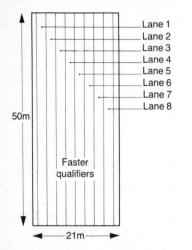

50m

Faster qualifiers

←—— 21m ——→

Lane 1
Lane 2
Lane 3
Lane 4
Lane 5
Lane 6
Lane 7
Lane 8

THE RULES

LANE ORDERS

There are eight lanes and the two swimmers with the best previous times swim in the 'centre' lanes – four and five. The next fastest swim to the right and left of the first two and so on, with the slowest swimmers in the two outside lanes, one and eight.

Qualifying times in the heats will dictate the draw for finals in exactly the same way.

FALSE STARTS

Two false starts are permitted, but whoever causes a subsequent false start is disqualified whether or not they were responsible for either of the previous false starts. The rule here is different from athletics where an individual has to be personally responsible for a second false start to be disqualified.

SYNCHRONIZED SWIMMING

Synchro swimming entered the Olympics for the first time in Los Angeles in 1984 and created quite a stir. Television viewers either loved or hated it. It is a sport for women only at Olympic level, although I hear that there is active male participation in California (where else?).

Even if you do not like the idea of this event, you must concede the athleticism, dedication and training needed to excel at it. Many of the sequences involve being underwater for well over half a minute. The perpetual smile is a prerequisite to success (not easy underwater and the effect somewhat spoiled by the necessary nose-clips).

Like diving, synchro swimming is marked by a set of judges giving marks up to a maximum of 10 for a programme in which some movements are voluntary and others compulsory. The voluntary section is, in effect, a water ballet set to music. Competitors equate their sport with figure-skating or gymnastics. Don't mention Esther Williams even if you are old enough to remember her.

There are two events – solo and duet. If you are wondering with what a solo swimmer 'synchronizes' – the answer is the music.

DIVING

SPRINGBOARD

Performed from a board three metres above the water. Divers take part in an elimination series which will reduce the field to 12 finalists. These 12 have another 11 dives – five compulsory and six voluntary. (For women it's five voluntary and five compulsory, making 10 in all.)

PLATFORM OR HIGHBOARD

Performed from a rigid platform 10 metres above the water. Again 12 finalists will qualify, but the men will have 10 dives (four compulsory, six voluntary) and the women eight dives (four compulsory, four voluntary).

There are more than 80 dives officially recognized by the sport's governing body – forward, backward, reverse, inward, twisting, and handstand, all with or without pikes, tucks, somersaults, and other combinations.

The degree of difficulty tariff goes from 1.2 marks for the easiest dive to 3.5 for the most difficult.

SCORING

There are seven judges. They mark each dive from nil for a complete failure up to a 10-point maximum for perfection. The highest and lowest marks are discarded and the remaining five added together and multiplied by the 'degree of difficulty' tariff. For example, if a diver goes for a forward three-and-a-half somersault which has a tariff of 3.5 and the judges score as follows 7.2, 7.4, 6.9, 6.7, 7.0, 7.2, and 7.3, the highest and lowest (7.4 and 6.7) would be discarded, the rest, adding up to 35.6, is multiplied by 3.5 and would give a points total of 124.6. Complicated stuff.

No dives are ever repeated by a contestant and the less splash you make the better.

WATER-POLO

One of the toughest sports physically. It is played between teams of 11, seven of which can be in the pool at any one time. Goals are scored by propelling the ball one-handed

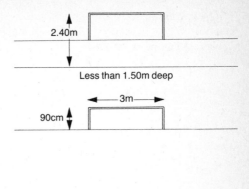

into the opponent's goal net. A goal may be scored only provided that at least two players, other than the goalkeeper, have touched the ball in the process. Play lasts for four periods of five minutes each.

Hungary has a fine tradition, having been Olympic champions on six occasions. The only time they have been out of the medals since 1924, was in 1984 when they did not take part. The defending Olympic champion, Yugoslavia, the Soviet Union and the United States will pose the greatest threat to the Hungarians winning in Seoul.

Sadly, Britain, who dominated the early modern Games in this sport, will not qualify.

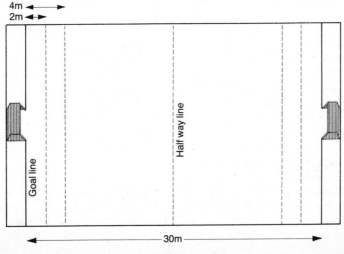

Some nations have direct entry based on world-ranking positions. The last time a British team finished in the top eight was in Melbourne in 1956 (seventh).

BRITISH SUCCESSES

The gold medal won by David Wilkie in the 200-metre breaststroke at Montreal in 1976 was the first by a British male swimmer at the Olympics since before the First World War. Duncan Goodhew did the trick again in 1980 with a gold in the 100-metre breast-stroke in Moscow.

British women have won three Olympic gold medals over the years. Lucy Morton won the 200-metre breaststroke at the 1924 Games in Paris. 36 years on, Anita Lons-borough reclaimed that Olympic title for Britain in Rome. And at the 1956 Games in Melbourne, Judy Grinham won the 100-metre backstroke.

In 1984, Britain's only individual medal in men's swimming was a bronze won by Neil Cochrane in the 200-metre individual medley. There was also a bronze in the 4 × 200 metre freestyle relay.

For the women, Sarah Hardcastle gained silver at 400-metre freestyle and bronze at 800 metres, while June Croft took the bronze behind Sarah in the 400.

The most recent Olympic medals won in diving by British competitors were a bronze by Brian Phelps (highboard) and a bronze by Liz Ferris (springboard) both at the Rome Olympics of 1960.

THE STARS

The number one star of men's Olympic swimming in its history so far is Mark Spitz of the United States who won nine gold medals, a silver, and a bronze. Seven of the gold medals were won in the 1972 Games, four years after his initial Olympic successes in Mexico. No competitor in any Olympic sport can match his record. Four of the gold medals in Munich were won in individual

events, the 100- and 200-metre freestyle and the 100- and 200-metre butterfly. The other three came from the relays.

Probably the greatest backstroke swimmer ever was the East German, Roland Matthes who took the 100- and 200-metre titles in Mexico in 1968 and defended both championships successfully in Munich.

In women's swimming, another great East German star Kornelia Ender (now Mrs Matthes) won three individual gold medals at the 1976 Games, in the 100- and 200-metre freestyle and the 100-metre butterfly plus another in the medley relay. Ender also won a host of silver medals.

Australia's Dawn Fraser is the only swimmer to have won a gold medal in the same event at three separate Games, in 1956, '60 and '64, in the 100-metre freestyle.

Best all-rounder of the 1984 Games was the Canadian, Alex Baumann. A world record holder at both the 200 and 400 individual medley events, he won gold medals in both. But the outstanding character of those last Games was undoubtedly Michael Gross, the 6 ft 7 ins West German. Known as the 'Albatross', he picked up gold medals in freestyle and butterfly events, and he added plenty of much-needed charisma to a sport in which the personalities of the competitors can often become, quite literally, submerged. Unlike the majority of world-class swimmers of our times, whose training is long and systematic, Gross is prepared to spare himself. 'I am a racing car, not a lorry,' he said. 'I don't believe in working too hard.' With an armspan of 7 ft 5 ins, he took just 29 strokes to cover a length, with his competitors taking as many as five more.

Klaus Dibiasi of Italy can claim to be the 'Mark Spitz' of diving. He won the highboard silver medal at the 1964 Games and then proceeded to win the gold at the three following Games, from '68 to '76. He also won the springboard silver in Tokyo at his first Olympics. Second to Dibiasi in the highboard event, as a 16-year-old at the 1976 Games, was Greg Louganis of the United

States, who was then deprived of competing in the Moscow Games because of the American withdrawal. In Los Angeles, however, he took both the springboard and highboard titles.

In women's diving, Pat McCormick won both springboard and highboard in 1952 and defended both championships successfully four years later.

Not a lot of people know that

• Don Schollander of the United States who won four gold medals in the 1964 Games would have finished only fifth in the 1980 Games at his best event, the 400-metre freestyle – in the *women's* race – such are the dramatic improvements in the sport in recent years.

• Swimming is definitely a young person's sport. The average age of Olympic male swimmers is just over 19 – and just over 16 for women.

• Johnny Weissmuller of the United States held the 100-metre freestyle record for 17 years. He won five gold medals 1924–28 and then went on to a film and acting career, becoming one of the most famous screen 'Tarzans'. He also won a bronze medal as a member of the USA water-polo team in 1924.

• At the first modern Games in 1896 – there was a special event for sailors – not any sailors but members of the Greek navy.

• In 1900, there was a swimming obstacle race. Competitors had to negotiate a pole, scramble over a row of boats and swim *under* a row of boats.

• Jean Boiteux of France unexpectedly won the 1952 400-metre gold medal. Rather more unexpected was the reaction of his father, Monsieur Boiteux senior, who fully clothed and wearing a beret duly leapt into the pool to congratulate his son.

• Oliver Halassey of Hungary won two golds and a silver medal in water polo despite losing one leg below the knee from a childhood accident.

VENUE

Prelims of water polo and diving at Chamsil Pool in the Seoul Sports Complex.
Swimming, water polo finals, Synchro and modern pentathlon swimming in new Olympic Pool at Olympic Park.

RESULTS

50 metres freestyle/*Men*

WR: 22.23 Tom Jager (USA) 1987
OR: 28.0 Zoltan Halmay (HUN) 1904

	Gold	Silver	Bronze
1904	Zoltan Halmay (HUN) 28.0	Scott Leary (USA) 28.6	Charles Daniels (USA) n.t.a.
1988	Final on 24 September		

100 metres freestyle/*Men*

WR: 48.74 Matt Biondi (USA) 1986
OR: 49.80 Rowdy Gaines (USA) 1984

	Gold	*Silver*	*Bronze*
1896	Alfred Hajos (HUN) 1:22.2 OR	Efstathios Choraphas (GRE) 1:23.0	Otto Herschmann (AUT) d.n.a.
1904	Zoltan v Halmay (HUN) 1:02.8	Charles Daniels (USA) d.n.a.	Scott Leary (USA) d.n.a.
1906	Charles Daniels (USA) 1:13.4 WR	Zoltan v Halmay (HUN) 1:14.2	Cecil Healy (AUS) d.n.a.
1908	Charles Daniels (USA) 1:05.6 WR	Zoltan v Halmay (HUN) 1:06.2	Harald Julin (SWE) 1:08.0
1912	Duke Kahanamoku (USA) 1:03.4	Cecil Healy (AUS) 1:04.6	Kenneth Huszagh (USA) 1:05.6
1920	Duke Kahanamoku (USA) 1:01.4	Pua Kealoha (USA) 1:02.2	William Harris (USA) 1:03.0
1924	Johnny Weissmuller (USA) 59.0 OR	Duke Kahanamoku (USA) 1:01.4	Sam Kahanamoku (USA) 1:01.8
1928	Johnny Weissmuller (USA) 58.6 OR	Istvan Barany (HUN) 59.8	Katsuo Takaishi (JPN) 1:00.0
1932	Yasuji Miyazaki (JPN) 58.2	Tatsugo Kawaishi (JPN) 58.6	Albert Schwartz (USA) 58.8
1936	Ferenc Csik (HUN) 57.6	Masanori Yusa (JPN) 57.9	Shigeo Arai (JPN) 58.0
1948	Walter Ris (USA) 57.3 OR	Alan Ford (USA) 57.8	Geza Kadas (HUN) 58.1
1952	Clarke Scholes (USA) 57.4	Hiroshi Suzuki (JPN) 57.4	Goran Larsson (SWE) 58.2
1956	Jon Henricks (AUS) 55.4 OR	John Devitt (AUS) 55.8	Gary Chapman (AUS) 56.7
1960	John Devitt (AUS) 55.2 OR	Lance Larson (USA) 55.2 OR	Manuel dos Santos (BRA) 55.4
1964	Don Schollander (USA) 53.4 OR	Bobbie McGregor (GBR) 53.5	Hans-Joachim Klein (GER) 54.0
1968	Mike Wenden (AUS) 52.2 WR	Ken Walsh (USA) 52.8	Mark Spitz (USA) 53.0
1972	Mark Spitz (USA) 51.22 WR	Jerry Heidenreich (USA) 51.65	Vladimir Bure (URS) 51.77
1976	Jim Montgomery (USA) 49.99 WR	Jack Babashoff (USA) 50.81	Peter Nocke (FRG) 51.31
1980	Jorg Woithe (GDR) 50.40	Per Holmertz (SWE) 50.91	Per Johansson (SWE) 51.29
1984	Rowdy Gaines (USA) 49.80 OR	Mark Stockwell (AUS) 50.24	Per Johansson (SWE) 50.31

4. Michael Heath (USA) 5. Dano Halsall (SUI) 6. Alberto Mestre Sosa (VEN) & Stephan Caron (FRA) 8. Dirk Korthals (FRG)

1988 Final on 22 September

200 metres freestyle/*Men*

WR: 1:47.44 Michael Gross (FRG) 1984
OR: 1:47.44 Michael Gross (FRG) 1984

	Gold	Silver	Bronze
1900	Frederick Lane (AUS) 2:25.2 OR	Zoltan Halmay (HUN) 2:31.4	Karl Ruberl (AUT) 2:32.0
1904	Charles Daniels (USA) 2:44.2	Francis Gailey (USA) 2:46.0	Emil Rausch (GER) 2:56.0
1968	Mike Wenden (AUS) 1:55.2 OR	Don Schollander (USA) 1:55.8	John Nelson (USA) 1:58.1
1972	Mark Spitz (USA) 1:52.78 WR	Steven Genter (USA) 1:53.73	Werner Lampe (FRG) 1:53.99
1976	Bruce Furniss (USA) 1:50.29 WR	John Naber (USA) 1:50.50	Jim Montgomery (USA) 1:50.58
1980	Sergey Kopliakov (URS) 1:49.81 OR	Andrej Krylov (URS) 1:50.76	Graeme Brewer (AUS) 1:51.60
1984	Michael Gross (FRG) 1:47.44 WR	Michael Heath (USA) 1:49.10	Thomas Fahrner (FRG) 1:49.69

4. Jeffrey Float (USA) 5. Alberto Mestre Sosa (VEN) 6. Frank Drost (HOL)
7. Marco Dell'Uomo (ITA) 8. Peter Dale (AUS)

1988 Final on 19 September

400 metres freestyle/*Men*

WR: 3:47.38 Artur Wojdat (POL) 1988
OR: 3:50.91 Thomas Fahrner (FRG) 1984 (in 'B' final)

	Gold	Silver	Bronze
1896	Paul Neumann (AUT) 8:12.6	Antonios Pepanos (GRE) 30 m	Efstathois Choraphas (GRE) d.n.a.
1904	Charles Daniels (USA) 6:16.2	Francis Gailey (USA) 6:22.0	Otto Wahle (AUT) 6:39.0
1906	Otto Scheff (AUT) 6:23.8	Henry Taylor (GBR) 6:24.4	John Jarvis (GBR) 6:27.2
1908	Henry Taylor (GBR) 5:36.8	Frank Beaurepaire (AUS) 5:44.2	Otto Scheff (AUT) 5:46.0
1912	George Hodgson (CAN) 5:24.4	John Hatfield (GBR) 5:25.8	Harold Hardwick (AUS) 5:31.2
1920	Norman Ross (USA) 5:26.8	Ludy Langer (USA) 5:29.0	George Vernot (CAN) 5:29.6
1924	Johnny Weissmuller (USA) 5:04.2 OR	Arne Borg (SWE) 5:05.6	Andrew Charlton (AUS) 5:06.6
1928	Alberto Zorilla (ARG) 5:01.6 OR	Andrew Charlton (AUS) 5:03.6	Arne Borg (SWE) 5:04.6
1932	Buster Crabbe (USA) 4:48.4 OR	Jean Taris (FRA) 4:48.5	Tsutomu Oyokota (JPN) 4:52.3
1936	Jack Medica (USA) 4:44.5 OR	Shumpei Uto (JPN) 4:45.6	Shozo Makino (JPN) 4:48.1
1948	William Smith (USA) 4:41.0 OR	James McLane (USA) 4:43.4	John Marshall (AUS) 4:47.7
1952	Jean Boiteux (FRA) 4:30.7 OR	Ford Konno (USA) 4:31.3˙	Per-Olof Ostrand (SWE) 4:35.2

1956	Murray Rose (AUS) 4:27.3 OR	Tsuyoshi Yamanaka (JPN) 4:30.4	George Breen (USA) 4:32.5
1960	Murray Rose (AUS) 4:18.3 OR	Tsuyoshi Yamanaka (JPN) 4:21.4	John Konrads (AUS) 4:21.8
1964	Don Schollander (USA) 4:12.2 WR	Frank Weigand (GER) 4:14.9	Allan Wood (AUS) 4:15.1
1968	Mike Burton (USA) 4:09.0 OR	Ralph Hutton (CAN) 4:11.7	Alain Mosconi (FRA) 4:13.3
1972	Brad Cooper (AUS) 4:00.27 OR	Steven Genter (USA) 4:01.94	Tom McBreen (USA) 4:02.64
1976	Brian Goodell (USA) 3:51.93 OR	Tim Shaw (USA) 3:52.54	Vladimir Raskatov (URS) 3:55.76
1980	Vladimir Salnikov (URS) 3:51.31 OR	Andrei Krylov (URS) 3:53.24	Ivar Stokolkin (URS) 3:53.95
1984	George Dicarlo (USA) 3:51.23 OR	John Mykkanen (USA) 3:51.49	Justin Lemberg (AUS) 3:51.79

4. Stefan Pfeiffer (FRG) 5. Franck Iacono (FRA) 6. Darjan Petric (YUG)
7. Marco Dell'Uomo (ITA) 8. Ronald McKeon (AUS)

1988   Final on 23 September

1500 metres freestyle/*Men*

WR: 14:54.76 Vladimir Salnikov (URS) 1983
OR: 14:58.27 Vladimir Salnikov (URS) 1980

	Gold	*Silver*	*Bronze*
1896	Alfred Hajos (HUN) 18:22.2 OR	Jean Andreou (GRE) 21:03.4	Efstathois Choraphas (GRE) d.n.a.
1900	John Jarvis (GBR) 13:40.2	Otto Wahle (AUT) 14:53.6	Zolton von Halmay (HUN) 15:16.4
1904	Emil Rausch (GER) 27:18.2	Géza Kiss (HUN) 28:28.2	Francis Gailey (USA) 28:54.0
1906	Henry Taylor (GBR) 28:28.0	John Jarvis (GBR) 30:13.0	Otto Scheff (AUT) 30:59.0
1908	Henry Taylor (GBR) 22:48.4 WR	Sydney Battersby (GBR) 22:51.2	Frank Beaurepaire (AUS) 22:56.2
1912	George Hodgson (CAN) 22:00.0 WR	John Hatfield (GBR) 22:39.0	Harold Hardwick (AUS) 23:15.4
1920	Norman Ross (USA) 22:23.2	George Vernot (CAN) 22:36.4	Frank Beaurepaire (AUS) 23:04.0
1924	Andrew Charlton (AUS) 20:06.6 WR	Arne Borg (SWE) 20:41.4	Frank Beaurepaire (AUS) 21:48.4
1928	Arne Borg (SWE) 19:51.8 OR	Andrew Charlton (AUS) 20:02.6	Buster Crabbe (USA) 20:28.8
1932	Kusuo Kitamura (JPN) 19:12.4 OR	Shozo Makino (JPN) 19:14.1	James Christy (USA) 19:39.5
1936	Norboru Terada (JPN) 19:13.7	Jack Medica (USA) 19:34.0	Shumpei Uto (JPN) 19:34.5
1948	James McLane (USA) 19:18.5	John Marshall (AUS) 19:31.3	György Mitró (HUN) 19:43.2
1952	Ford Konno (USA) 18:30.0 OR	Shiro Hashizune (JPN) 18:41.4	Tetsuo Okamoto (JPN) 18:51.3

1956	Murray Rose (AUS) 17:58.9	Tsuyoshi Yamanaka (JPN) 18:00.3	George Breen (USA) 18:08.2
1960	John Konrads (AUS) 17:19.06 OR	Murray Rose (AUS) 17:21.7	George Breen (USA) 17:30.6
1964	Bob Windle (AUS) 17:01.7 OR	John Nelson (USA) 17:03.0	Allan Wood (AUS) 17:07.7
1968	Mike Burton (USA) 16:38.9 OR	John Kinsella (USA) 16:57.3	Greg Brough (AUS) 17:04.7
1972	Mike Burton (USA) 15:52.58 WR	Graham Windeatt (AUS) 15:58.48	Doug Northway (USA) 16:09.25
1976	Brian Goodell (USA) 15:02.40 WR	Bobby Hackett (USA) 15:03.91	Steve Holland (AUS) 15:04.66
1980	Vladimir Salnikov (URS) 14:58.27 WR	Aleksandr Chaev (URS) 15:14.30	Max Metzker (AUS) 15:14.49
1984	Michael O'Brien (USA) 15:05.20	George Dicarlo (USA) 15:10.59	Stefan Pfeiffer (FRG) 15:12.11

4. Rainer Henkel (FRG) 5. Franck Iacono (FRA) 6. Stefano Grandi (ITA)
7. David Shemilt (CAN) 8. Wayne Shillington (AUS)

1988   Final on 25 September

100 metres backstroke/*Men*

WR: 55.19 Rick Carey (USA) 1983
OR: 55.41 Rick Carey (USA) 1984 (in relay)

	Gold	*Silver*	*Bronze*
1904	Walter Brack (GER) 1:16.8	Georg Hoffmann (GER) 1:18.0	Georg Zacharias (GER) 1:19.6
1908	Arno Bieberstein (GER) 1:24.6 WR	Ludvig Dam (DEN) 1:26.6	Herbert Haresnape (GBR) 1:27.0
1912	Harry Hebner (USA) 1:21.2	Otto Fahr (GER) 1:22.4	Paul Kellner (GER) 1:24.0
1920	Warren Kealoha (USA) 1:15.2	Ray Kegeris (USA) 1:16.2	Gérard Blitz (BEL) 1:19.0
1924	Warren Kealoha (USA) 1:13.2 OR	Paul Wyatt (USA) 1:15.4	Károly Bartha (HUN) 1:17.8
1928	George Kojac (USA) 1:08.2 WR	Walter Laufer (USA) 1:10.0	Paul Wyatt (USA) 1:12.0
1932	Masaji Kiyokawa (JPN) 1:08.6	Toshio Irie (JPN) 1:09.8	Kentaro Kawatsu (JPN) 1:10.0
1936	Adolf Keifer (USA) 1:05.9 OR	Albert Van de Weghe (USA) 1:07.7	Masaji Kiyokawa (JPN) 1:08.4
1948	Allen Stack (USA) 1:06.4	Robert Cowell (USA) 1:06.5	Georges Vallerey (FRA) 1:07.8
1952	Yoshinobu Oyakawa (USA) 1:05.4 OR	Gilbert Bozon (FRA) 1:06.2	Jack Taylor (USA) 1:06.4
1956	David Thiele (AUS) 1:02.2 OR	John Monckton (AUS) 1:03.2	Frank McKinney (USA) 1:04.5
1960	David Thiele (AUS) 1:01.9 OR	Frank McKinney (USA) 1:02.1	Robert Bennett (USA) 1:02.3
1968	Roland Matthes (GDR) 58.7 OR	Charles Hickcox (USA) 1:00.2	Ronnie Mills (USA) 1:00.5

1972	Roland Matthes (GDR) 56.58 OR	Mike Stamm (USA) 57.70	John Murphy (USA) 58.35
1976	John Naber (USA) 55.49 WR	Peter Rocca (USA) 56.34	Roland Matthes (GDR) 57.22
1980	Bengt Baron (SWE) 56.53	Viktor Kuznetsov (URS) 56.99	Vladimir Dolgov (URS) 57.63
1984	Rick Carey (USA) 55.79	David Wilson (USA) 56.35	Mike West (CAN) 56.49

4. Gary Hurring (NZL) 5. Mark Kerry (AUS) 6. Bengt Baron (SWE)
7. Sandy Goss (CAN) 8. Hans Kroes (HOL)

1988   Final on 24 September

200 metres backstroke/*Men*

WR: 1:58.14 Igor Poljanski (URS) 1985
OR: 1:58.99 Rick Carey (USA) 1984 (in heat)

	Gold	Silver	Bronze
1900	Ernst Hoppenberg (GER) 2:47.0	Karl Ruberl (AUT) 2:56.0	Johannes Drost (HOL) 3:01.0
1964	Jed Graef (USA) 2:10.3 WR	Gary Dilley (USA) 2:10.5	Robert Bennett (USA) 2:13.1
1968	Roland Matthes (GDR) 2:09.6 OR	Mitchell Ivey (USA) 2:10.6	Jack Horsley (USA) 2:10.9
1972	Roland Matthes (GDR) 2:02.82 =WR	Mike Stamm (USA) 2:04.09	Mitchell Ivey (USA) 2:04.33
1976	John Naber (USA) 1:59.19 WR	Peter Rocca (USA) 2:00.55	Don Harrigan (USA) 2:01.35
1980	Sándor Wladár (HUN) 2:01.93	Zóltán Verrasztó (HUN) 2:02.40	Mark Kerry (AUS) 2:03.14
1984	Rick Carey (USA) 2:00.23	Frederic Delcourt (FRA) 2:01.75	Cameron Henning (CAN) 2:02.37

4. Ricardo Prado (BRA) 5. Gary Hurring (NZL) 6. Nicolai Klapkarek (FRG)
7. Ricardo Aldabe (ESP) 8. David Orbell (AUS)

1988   Final on 22 September

100 metres breaststroke/*Men*

WR: 1:01.65 Steve Lundquist (USA) 1984
OR: 1:01.65 Steve Lundquist (USA) 1984

	Gold	Silver	Bronze
1968	Don McKenzie (USA) 1:07.7 OR	Vladimir Kossinsky (URS) 1:08.0	Nikolai Pankin (URS) 1:08.0
1972	Nobutaka Taguchi (JPN) 1:04.94 WR	Tom Bruce (USA) 1:05.43	John Hencken (USA) 1:05.61
1976	John Hencken (USA) 1:03.11	David Wilkie (GBR) 1:03.43	Arvidas Iuozaytis (URS) 1:04.23
1980	Duncan Goodhew (GBR) 1:03.34	Arsen Miskarov (URS) 1:03.82	Peter Evans (AUS) 1:03.96

| 1984 | Steve Lundquist (USA) 1:01.65 WR | Victor Davis (CAN) 1:01.99 | Peter Evans (AUS) 1:02.97 |

4. Adrian Moorhouse (GBR) 5. John Moffet (USA) 6. Brett Stocks (AUS)
7. Gerald Morken (FRG) 8. Raffaele Avagnano (ITA)

1988 Final on 19 September

200 metres breaststroke/*Men*

WR: 2:13.34 Victor Davis (CAN) 1984
OR: 2:13.34 Victor Davis (CAN) 1984

	Gold	*Silver*	*Bronze*
1908	Frederick Holman (GBR) 3:09.2 WR	William Robinson (GBR) 3:12.8	Pontus Hansson (SWE) 3:14.6
1912	Walter Barthe (GER) 3:01.8 OR	Wilhelm Lützow (GER) 3:05.2	Kurt Malisch (GER) 3:08.0
1920	Häken Malmroth (SWE) 3:04.4	Thor Henning (SWE) 3:09.2	Arvo Aaltonen (FIN) 3:12.2
1924	Robert Skelton (USA) 2:56.6	Joseph de Combe (BEL) 2:59.2	William Kirschbaum (USA) 3:01.0
1928	Yoshiyuki Tsuruta (JPN) 2:48.8 OR	Erich Rademacher (GER) 2:50.6	Teofilo Yldefonzo (PHI) 2:56.4
1932	Yoshiyuki Tsurata (JPN) 2:45.4	Reizo Koike (JPN) 2:46.4	Teofilo Yldefonzo (PHI) 2:47.1
1936	Tetsuo Hamuro (JPN) 2:41.5	Erwin Sietas (GER) 2:42.9	Reizo Koike (JPN) 2:44.2
1948	Joseph Verdeur (USA) 2:39.3 OR	Keith Carter (USA) 2:40.2	Robert Sohl (USA) 2:43.9
1952	John Davies (AUS) 2:34.4 OR	Bowen Stassforth (USA) 2:34.7	Herbert Klein (GER) 2:35.9
1956	Masaru Furukawa (JPN) 2:34.7 OR	Masahiro Yoshimura (JPN) 2:36.7	Charis Yunitschev (URS) 2:36.8
1960	William Mulliken (USA) 2:37.4	Yoshihiko Osaki (JPN) 2:38.0	Weiger Mensonides (HOL) 2:39.7
1964	Ian O'Brien (AUS) 2:27.8 WR	Georgy Prokopenko (URS) 2:28.2	Chester Jastremski (USA) 2:29.6
1968	Felipe Munoz (MEX) 2:28.7	Vladimir Kossinsky (URS) 2:29.2	Brian Job (USA) 2:29.9
1972	John Hencken (USA) 2:21.55 WR	David Wilkie (GBR) 2:23.67	Nobutaka Taguchi (JPN) 2:23.88
1976	David Wilkie (GBR) 2:15.11 WR	John Hencken (USA) 2:17.26	Rick Colella (USA) 2:19.20
1980	Robertas Zulpa (URS) 2:15.85	Alban Vermes (HUN) 2:16.93	Arsen Miskarov (URS) 2:17.28
1984	Victor Davis (CAN) 2:13.34 WR	Glenn Beringen (AUS) 2:15.79	Etienne Dagon (SUI) 2:17.41

4. Richard Schroeder (USA) 5. Ken Fitzpatrick (CAN) 6. Pablo Restrepo (COL)
7. Alexandre Yokochi (POR) 8. Marco DelPrete (ITA) disq.

1988 Final on 23 September

100 metres butterfly/*Men*

WR: 52.84 Pablo Pedro Morales (USA) 1986
OR: 53.08 Michael Gross (FRG) 1984

	Gold	Silver	Bronze
1968	Doug Russell (USA) 55.9 OR	Mark Spitz (USA) 56.4	Ross Wales (USA) 57.2
1972	Mark Spitz (USA) 54.27 WR	Bruce Robertson (CAN) 55.56	Jerry Heidenreich (USA) 55.74
1976	Matt Vogel (USA) 54.35	Joe Bottom (USA) 54.50	Gary Hall (USA) 54.65
1980	Pär Arvidsson (SWE) 54.92	Roger Pyttel (GDR) 54.94	David Lopez (ESP) 55.13
1984	Michael Gross (FRG) 53.08 WR	Pedro Pablo Morales (USA) 53.23	Glenn Buchanan (AUS) 53.85

4. Rafael Vidal Castro (VEN) 5. Andrew Jameson (GBR) 6. Anthony Mosse (NZL)
7. Andreas Behrend (FRG) Bengt Baron (SWE)

1988   Final on 21 September

200 metres butterfly/*Men*

WR: 1:56.24 Michael Gross (FRG) 1986
OR: 1:57.04 Jon Sieben (AUS) 1984

	Gold	Silver	Bronze
1956	William Yorzyk (USA) 2:19.3 OR	Takashi Ishimoto (JPN) 2:23.8	György Tumpek (HUN) 2:23.9
1960	Mike Troy (USA) 2:12.8 WR	Neville Hayes (AUS) 2:14.6	David Gillanders (USA) 2:15.3
1964	Kevin Berry (AUS) 2:06.6 WR	Carl Robie (USA) 2:07.5	Fred Schmidt (USA) 2:09.3
1968	Carl Robie (USA) 2:08.7	Martyn Woodruff (GBR) 2:09.0	John Ferris (USA) 2:09.3
1972	Mark Spitz (USA) 2:00.7 WR	Gary Hall (USA) 2:02.86	Robin Backhaus (USA) 2:03.23
1976	Mike Bruner (USA) 1:59.23 WR	Steven Gregg (USA) 1:59.54	William Forrester (USA) 1:59.96
1980	Sergey Fesenko (URS) 1:59.76	Phil Hubble (GBR) 2:01.20	Roger Pyttel (GDR) 2:01.39
1984	Jon Sieben (AUS) 1:57.04 WR	Michael Gross (FRG) 1:57.40	Rafael Vidal Castro (VEN) 1:57.51

4. Pedro Pablo Morales (USA) 5. Anthony Mosse (NZL) 6. Tom Ponting (CAN)
7. Peter Ward (CAN) 8. Patrick Kennedy (USA)

1988   Final on 24 September

200 metres individual medley/*Men*

WR: 2:00.56 Tamas Darnyi (HUN) 1987
OR: 2:01.41 Alex Baumann (CAN) 1984

	Gold	Silver	Bronze
1968	Charles Hickcox (USA) 2:12.0 OR	Greg Buckingham (USA) 2:13.0	John Ferris (USA) 2:13.3
1972	Gunnar Larsson (SWE) 2:07.17 WR	Tim McKee (USA) 2:08.37	Steve Furniss (USA) 2:08.45
1984	Alex Baumann (CAN) 2:01.42 WR	Pedro Pablo Morales (USA) 2:03.05	Neil Cochran (GBR) 2:04.38

4. Robin Brew (GBR) 5. Steve Lundquist (USA) 6. Andrew Phillips (JAM)
7. Nicolai Klapkarek (FRG) 8. Ralf Diegel (FRG)

1988   Final on 25 September

400 metres individual medley/*Men*

WR: 4:15.42 Tamas Darnyi (HUN) 1987
OR: 4:17.41 Alex Baumann (CAN) 1984

	Gold	Silver	Bronze
1964	Richard Roth (USA) 4:45.4	Roy Saari (USA) 4:47.1	Gerhard Hetz (GER) 4:51.0
1968	Charles Hickcox (USA) 4:48.4	Gary Hall (USA) 4:48.7	Michael Holthaus (FRG) 4:51.4
1972	Gunnar Larsson (SWE) 4:31.98 OR	Tim McKee (USA) 4:31.98 OR	András Hargitay (HUN) 4:32.70
1976	Rod Strachan (USA) 4:23.68 WR	Tim McKee (USA) 4:24.62	Andrei Smirnov (URS) 4:26.90
1980	Aleksandr Sidorenko (URS) 4:22.89 OR	Sergey Fesenko (URS) 4:23.43	Zóltán Verrasztó (HUN) 4:24.24
1984	Alex Baumann (CAN) 4:17.41 WR	Ricardo Prado (BRA) 4:18.45	Robert Woodhouse (AUS) 4:20.50

4. Jesus Vassallo (USA) 6. Maurizio Divano (ITA) 6. Jeffrey Kostoff (USA)
7. Stephen Poulter (GBR) 8. Giovanni Franceschi (ITA)

1988   Final on 21 September

4 × 100 metres freestyle relay/*Men*

WR: 3:17.08 UNITED STATES 1985
OR: 3:19.03 UNITED STATES 1984

	Gold	Silver	Bronze
1964	UNITED STATES 3:33.2 WR	GERMANY 3:37.2	AUSTRALIA 3:39.1
1968	UNITED STATES 3:31.7 WR	USSR 3:34.2	AUSTRALIA 3:34.7
1972	UNITED STATES 3:26.42 WR	USSR 3:29.72	EAST GERMANY 3:32.42

Not held in 1976 & 1980

1984	UNITED STATES 3:19.03 WR	AUSTRALIA 3:19.68	SWEDEN 3:22.69
	Christopher Cavanaugh	Greg Fasala	Thomas Leidstrom
	Michael Heath	Neil Brooks	Bengt Baron
	Matthew Biondi	Michael Delany	Mikael Orn
	Rowdy Gaines	Mark Stockwell	Per Johansson

4. West Germany 5. Great Britain (David Lowe, Roland Lee, Paul Easter, Richard Burrell)
6. France 7. Canada 8. Italy

1988   Final on 23 September

4 × 100 metres medley relay/*Men*
(order of strokes: backstroke, breaststroke, butterfly, freestyle)

WR: 3:38.28 UNITED STATES 1985
OR: 3:39.30 UNITED STATES 1984

	Gold	*Silver*	*Bronze*
1960	UNITED STATES 4:05.4 WR	AUSTRALIA 4:12.0	JAPAN 4:12.2
1964	UNITED STATES 3:58.4 WR	GERMANY 4:01.6	AUSTRALIA 4:02.3
1968	UNITED STATES 3:54.9 WR	EAST GERMANY 3:57.5	USSR 4:00.7
1972	UNITED STATES 3:48.16 WR	EAST GERMANY 3:52.12	CANADA 3:52.26
1976	UNITED STATES 3:42.22 WR	CANADA 3:45.94	WEST GERMANY 3:47.29
1980	AUSTRALIA 3:45.70	USSR 3:45.92	GREAT BRITAIN 3:47.71
1984	UNITED STATES 3:39.30 WR	CANADA 3:43.23	AUSTRALIA 3:43.25
	Rick Carey	Mike West	Mark Kerry
	Steve Lundquist	Victor Davis	Peter Evans
	Pedro Pablo Morales	Tom Ponting	Glenn Buchanan
	Rowdy Caines	Sandy Goss	Mark Stockwell

4. West Germany 5. Sweden 6. GBR (Neil Harper, Adrian Moorhouse, Andrew Jameson,
Richard Burrell) 7. Switzerland 8. Japan

1988   Final on 25 September

4 × 200 metres freestyle relay/*Men*

WR: 7:13.10 WEST GERMANY 1987
OR: 7:15.69 UNITED STATES 1984

	Gold	*Silver*	*Bronze*
1906	HUNGARY 16:52.4	GERMANY 17:16.2	GREAT BRITAIN n.t.a.
1908	GREAT BRITAIN 10:55.6 WR	HUNGARY 10:59.0	UNITED STATES 11:02.8
1912	AUSTRALASIA 10:11.6 WR	UNITED STATES 10:20.2	GREAT BRITAIN 10:28.2

1920	UNITED STATFS 10:04.4 WR	AUSTRALIA 10:25.4	GREAT BRITAIN 10:37.2
1924	UNITED STATES 9:53.4 WR	AUSTRALIA 10:02.2	SWEDEN 10:06.8
1928	UNITED STATES 9:36.2 WR	JAPAN 9:41.4	CANADA 9:47.8
1932	JAPAN 8:58.4 WR	UNITED STATES 9:10.5	HUNGARY 9:31.4
1936	JAPAN 8:51.5 WR	UNITED STATES 9:03.0	HUNGARY 9:12.3
1948	UNITED STATES 8:46.0 WR	HUNGARY 8:48.4	FRANCE 9:08.0
1952	UNITED STATES 8:31.1 OR	JAPAN 8:33.5	FRANCE 8:45.9
1956	AUSTRALIA 8:23.6 WR	UNITED STATES 8:31.5	USSR 8:34.7
1960	UNITED STATES 8:10.2 WR	JAPAN 8:13.2	AUSTRALIA 8:13.8
1964	UNITED STATES 7:52.1 WR	GERMANY 7:59.3	JAPAN 8:03.8
1968	UNITED STATES 7:52.33	AUSTRALIA 7:53.77	USSR 8:01.66
1972	UNITED STATES 7:35.78 WR	WEST GERMANY 7:41.69	USSR 7:45.76
1976	UNITED STATES 7:23.22 WR	USSR 7:27.97	GREAT BRITAIN 7:32.11
1980	USSR 7:23.50	EAST GERMANY 7:28.60	BRAZIL 7:29.30
1984	UNITED STATES 7:15.69 WR Michael Heath David Larson Jeffrey Float Lawrence Bruce Hayes	WEST GERMANY 7:15.73 Thomas Fahrner Dirk Korthals Alexander Schowtka Michael Gross	GREAT BRITAIN 7:24.78 Neil Cochran Paul Easter Paul Howe Andrew Astbury

4. Australia 5. Canada 6. Sweden 7. Holland 8. France

1988   Final on 21 September

Diving – springboard/*Men*

	Gold	*Silver*	*Bronze*
1908	Albert Zurner (GER) 85.5	Kurt Behrens (GER) 85.3	George Gaidzik (USA) 80.8 Gottlob Walz (GER) 80.8
1912	Paul Günther (GER) 79.23	Hans Luber (GER) 76.78	Kurt Behrens (GER) 73.73
1920	Louis Kuehn (USA) 675.4	Clarence Pinkston (USA) 655.3	Louis Balbach (USA) 649.5
1924	Albert White (USA) 696.4	Peter Desjardins (USA) 693.2	Clarence Pinkston (USA) 653.0
1928	Peter Desjardins (USA) 185.04	Michael Galitzen (USA) 174.06	Farid Simaika (EGY) 172.46
1932	Michael Galitzen (USA) 161.38	Harold Smith (USA) 158.54	Richard Degener (USA) 151.82
1936	Richard Degener (USA) 163.57	Marshall Wayne (USA) 159.56	Al Greene (USA) 146.29

1948	Bruce Harlan (USA) 163.64	Miller Anderson (USA) 157.29	Samuel Lee (USA) 145.52
1952	David Browning (USA) 205.29	Miller Anderson (USA) 199.84	Robert Clotworthy (USA) 184.92
1956	Robert Clotworthy (USA) 159.56	Donald Harper (USA) 156.23	Joaquin Capilla Péres (MEX) 150.69
1960	Gary Tobian (USA) 170.00	Samuel Hall (USA) 167.08	Juan Botella (MEX) 162.30
1964	Kenneth Sitzberger (USA) 159.90	Francis Gorman (USA) 157.63	Larry Andreasen (USA) 143.77
1968	Bernard Wrightson (USA) 170.15	Klaus Dibiasi (ITA) 159.74	James Henry (USA) 158.09
1972	Vladimir Vasin (URS) 594.09	Franco Cagnotto (ITA) 591.63	Craig Lincoln (USA) 577.29
1976	Philip Boggs (USA) 619.05	Franco Cagnotto (ITA) 570.48	Aleksandr Kosenkov (URS) 567.24
1980	Aleksandr Portnov (URS) 905.025	Carlos Giron (MEX) 892.140	Franco Cagnotto (ITA) 871.500
1984	Greg Louganis (USA) 754.41	Liangde Tan (CHN) 662.31	Ronald Merriott (USA) 661.32

4. Hongping Li (CHN) 5. Chris Snode (GBR) 6. Piero Italiani (ITA)

1988　Final on 20 September

Diving – platform/*Men*

	Gold	Silver	Bronze
1904*	George Sheldon (USA) 12.66	Georg Hoffmann (GER) 11.66	Frank Kehoe (USA) 11.33
1906	Gottlob Walz (GER) 156.00	Georg Hoffmann (GER) 150.20	Otto Satzinger (AUT) 147.40
1908	Hjalmar Johansson (SWE) 83.75	Karl Malström (SWE) 78.73	Arvid Spångberg (SWE) 74.00
1912	Erik Adlerz (SWE) 73.94	Albert Zürner (GER) 72.60	Gustaf Blomgren (SWE) 69.56
1920	Clarence Pinkston (USA) 100.67	Erik Adlerz (SWE) 99.08	Haig Prieste (USA) 93.73
1924	Albert White (USA) 97.46	David Fall (USA) 97.30	Clarence Pinkston (USA) 94.60
1928	Peter Desjardins (USA) 98.74	Farid Simaika† (EGY) 99.58	Michael Galitzen (USA) 92.34
1932	Harold Smith (USA) 124.80	Michael Galitzen (USA) 124.28	Frank Kurtz (USA) 121.98
1936	Marshall Wayne (USA) 113.58	Elbert Root (USA) 110.60	Hermann Stork (GER) 110.31
1948	Samuel Lee (USA) 130.05	Bruce Harlan (USA) 122.30	Joaquin Capilla Pérez (MEX) 113.52
1952	Samuel Lee (USA) 156.28	Joaquin Capilla Perez (MEX) 145.21	Günther Haase (GER) 141.31
1956	Joaquin Capilla Perez (MEX) 152.44	Gary Tobian (USA) 152.41	Richard Connor (USA) 149.79
1960	Robert Webster (USA) 165.56	Gary Tobian (USA) 165.25	Brian Phelps (GBR) 157.13

*Platform and springboard combined event.
†Placed second because his ordinals were not as good as Desjardins although his marks were better.

1964	Robert Webster (USA) 148.58	Klaus Dibiasi (ITA) 147.54	Thomas Gompf (USA) 146.57
1968	Klaus Dibiasi (ITA) 164.18	Alvaro Gaxiola (MEX) 154.49	Edwin Young (USA) 153.93
1972	Klaus Dibiasi (ITA) 504.12	Richard Rydze (USA) 480.75	Franco Cagnotto (ITA) 475.83
1976	Klaus Dibiasi (ITA) 600.51	Greg Louganis (USA) 576.99	Vladimir Aleynik (URS) 548.61
1980	Falk Hoffmann (GDR) 835.650	Valdimir Aleynik (URS) 819.705.	David Ambartsumyan (URS) 817.440
1984	Greg Louganis (USA) 710.91	Bruce Kimball (USA) 643.50	Kongzheng Li (CHN) 638.28
	Chris Snode (GBR) 7th		
1988	Final on 29 September		

Water polo

	Gold	Silver	Bronze
1900	GREAT BRITAIN	BELGIUM	FRANCE
1904	UNITED STATES	UNITED STATES	UNITED STATES
1908	GREAT BRITAIN	BELGIUM	SWEDEN
1912	GREAT BRITAIN	SWEDEN	BELGIUM
1920	GREAT BRITAIN	BELGIUM	SWEDEN
1924	FRANCE	BELGIUM	UNITED STATES
1928	GERMANY	HUNGARY	FRANCE
1932	HUNGARY	GERMANY	UNITED STATES
1936	HUNGARY	GERMANY	BELGIUM
1948	ITALY	HUNGARY	NETHERLANDS
1952	HUNGARY	YUGOSLAVIA	ITALY
1956	HUNGARY	YUGOSLAVIA	USSR
1960	ITALY	USSR	HUNGARY
1964	HUNGARY	YUGOSLAVIA	USSR
1968	YUGOSLAVIA	USSR	HUNGARY
1972	USSR	HUNGARY	UNITED STATES
1976	HUNGARY	ITALY	NETHERLANDS
1980	USSR	YUGOSLAVIA	HUNGARY
1984	YUGOSLAVIA	UNITED STATES	WEST GERMANY
1988	Final on 1 October		

50 metres freestyle/*Women*

WR: 25.28 Tamara Costache (ROM) 1986
OR: None – not held before

1988 Final on 25 September

100 metres freestyle/*Women*

WR: 54.73 Kristin Otto (GDR) 1986
OR: 54.79 Barbara Krause (GDR) 1980

	Gold	Silver	Bronze
1912	Fanny Durack (AUS) 1:22.2	Wilhelmina Wylie (AUS) 1:25.4	Jennie Fletcher (GBR) 1:27.0
1920	Ethelda Bleibtrey (USA) 1:13.6 WR	Irene Guest (USA) 1:17.0	France Schroth (USA) 1:17.2
1924	Ethel Lackie (USA) 1:12.4	Mariechen Wehselau (USA) 1:12.8	Gertrude Ederle (USA) 1:14.2
1928	Albina Osipowich (USA) 1:11.0 OR	Eleanor Garatti (USA) 1:11.4	Joyce Cooper (GBR) 1:13.6
1932	Helene Madison (USA) 1:06.8	Willemijntje den Ouden (HOL) 1:07.8	Eleanor Garatti-Saville (USA) 1:08.2
1936	Henrika Mastenbroek (HOL) 1:05.9 OR	Jeanette Campbell (ARG) 1:06.4	Gisela Arendt (GER) 1:06.6
1948	Greta Anderson (DEN) 1:06.3	Ann Curtis (USA) 1:06.5	Marie-Louise Vaessen (HOL) 1:07.6
1952	Katalin Szoke (HUN) 1:06.8	Johanna Termeulen (HOL) 1:07.0	Judit Temmes (HUN) 1:07.1
1956	Dawn Fraser (AUS) 1:02.0 WR	Lorraine Crapp (AUS) 1:02.3	Faith Leech (AUS) 1:05.1
1960	Dawn Fraser (AUS) 1:01.2 OR	Chris van Saltza (USA) 1:02.8	Natalie Steward (GBR) 1:03.1
1964	Dawn Fraser (AUS) 59.5 OR	Sharon Stouder (USA) 59.9	Kathleen Ellis (USA) 1:00.8
1968	Jan Henne (USA) 1:00.0	Susan Pedersen (USA) 1:00.3	Linda Gustavson (USA) 1:00.3
1972	Sandra Neilson (USA) 58.59 OR	Shirley Babashoff (USA) 59.02	Shane Gould (AUS) 59.06
1976	Kornelia Ender (GDR) 55.65 WR	Petra Priemer (GDR) 56.49	Enith Brigitha (HOL) 56.65
1980	Barbara Krause (GDR) 54.79 WR	Caren Metschuck (GDR) 55.16	Ines Diers (GDR) 55.65
1984	Carrie Steinseifer (USA) Nancy Hogshead (USA) 55.92	—	Annemarie Verstappen (HOL) 56.08

4. Conny Van Bentum (HOL) 5. Michele Pearson (AUS) 6. June Croft (GBR)
7. Suzanne Schuster (FRG) 8. Angela Russel (AUS)

1988 Final on 19 September

200 metres freestyle/*Women*

WR: 1:57.55 Heike Friedrich (GDR) 1986
OR: 1:58.33 Barbara Krause (GDR) 1980

	Gold	Silver	Bronze
1968	Debbie Meyer (USA) 2:10.5 OR	Jan Henne (USA) 2:11.0	Jane Barkman (USA) 2:11.2
1972	Shane Gould (AUS) 2:03.56 WR	Shirley Babashoff (USA) 2:04.33	Keena Rothhammer (USA) 2:04.92

184

1976	Kornelia Ender (GDR) 1:59.26 WR	Shirley Babashoff (USA) 2:01.22	Enith Brigitha (HOL) 2:01.40
1980	Barbara Krause (GDR) 1:58.33 OR	Ines Diers (GDR) 1:59.64	Carmela Schmidt (GDR) 2:01.44
1984	Mary Wayte (USA) 1:59.23	Cynthia Woodhead (USA) 1:59.50	Annemarie Verstappen (HOL) 1:59.69

4. Michele Pearson (AUS) 5. Conny Van Bentum (HOL) 6. June Croft (GBR)
7. Ina Beyermann (FRG) 8. Anna McVann (AUS)

1988 Final on 21 September

400 metres freestyle/*Women*

WR: 4:05.45 Janet Evans (USA) 1987
OR: 4:07.10 Tiffany Cohen (USA) 1984

	Gold	*Silver*	*Bronze*
1920	Ethelda Bleibtrey (USA) 6:34.0 WR	Margaret Woodbridge (USA) 6:42.8	Frances Schroth (USA) 6:52.0
1924	Martha Norelius (USA) 6:02.2 OR	Helen Wainwright (USA) 6:03.8	Gertrude Ederle (USA) 6:04.8
1928	Martha Norelius (USA) 5:42.8 WR	Marie Braun (HOL) 5:57.8	Josephine McKim (USA) 6:00.2
1932	Helen Madison (USA) 5:28.5 WR	Lenore Kight (USA) 5:28.6	Jennie Maakal (SAF) 5:47.3
1936	Hendrika Mastenbroek (HOL) 5:26.4 OR	Ragnhild Hveger (DEN) 5:27.5	Lenore Kight-Wingard (USA) 5:29.0
1948	Ann Curtis (USA) 5:17.8 OR	Karen Harup (DEN) 5:21.2	Cathy Gibson (GBR) 5:22.5
1952	Valéria Gyenge (HUN) 5:12.1 OR	Eva Nowák (HUN) 5:13.7	Evelyn Kawamoto (USA) 5:14.6
1956	Lorraine Crapp (AUS) 4:54.6 OR	Dawn Fraser (AUS) 5:02.5	Sylvia Ruuska (USA) 5:07.1
1960	Chris von Saltza (USA) 4:50.6 OR	Jane Cederquist (SWE) 4:53.9	Catharina Lagerberg (HOL) 4:56.9
1964	Virginia Duenkel (USA) 4:43.3 OR	Marilyn Ramenofsky (USA) 4:44.6	Terri Stickles (USA) 4:47.2
1968	Debbie Meyer (USA) 4:31.8 OR	Linda Gustavson (USA) 4:35.5	Karen Moras (AUS) 4:37.0
1972	Shane Gould (AUS) 4:19.04 WR	Novella Calligaris (ITA) 4:22.44	Gudrun Wegner (GDR) 4:23.11
1976	Petra Thuemer (GDR) 4:09.89 WR	Shirley Babashoff (USA) 4:10.46	Shannon Smith (CAN) 4:14.60
1980	Ines Diers (GDR) 4:08.76 OR	Petra Schneider (GDR) 4:09.16	Carmela Schmidt (GDR) 4:10.86
1984	Tiffany Cohen (USA) 4:07.10 OR	Sarah Hardcastle (GBR) 4:10.27	June Croft (GBR) 4:11.49

4. Kimberley Linehan (USA) 5. Anne McVann (AUS) 6. Jolande Van Der Meer (HOL)
7. Birgit Kowalczik (FRG) 8. Julie Daigneault (CAN)

1988 Final on 22 September

800 metres freestyle/*Women*

WR: 8:17.2 Janet Evans (USA) 1988
OR: 8:24.95 Tiffany Cohen (USA) 1984

Gold	*Silver*	*Bronze*
1968 Debbie Meyer (USA) 9:24.0 OR	Pamela Kruse (USA) 9:35.7	Maria Ramirez (MEX) 9.38.5
1972 Keena Rothhammer (USA) 8:53.68 WR	Shane Gould (AUS) 8:56.39	Novella Calligaris (ITA) 8:57.46
1976 Petra Thuemer (GDR) 8:37.14 WR	Shirley Babashoff (USA) 8:37.59	Wendy Weinberg (USA) 8:42.60
1980 Michelle Ford (AUS) 8:28.90 OR	Ines Diers (GDR) 8:32.55	Heike Dähne (GDR) 8:33.48
1984 Tiffany Cohen (USA) 8:24.95 OR	Michele Richardson (USA) 8:30.73	Sarah Hardcastle (GBR) 8:32.60

4. Anna McVann (AUS) 5. Carla Lasi (ITA) 6. Jolande Van Der Meer (HOL)
7. Monica Olmi (ITA) Karen Ward (CAN)

1988 Final on 24 September

100 metres backstroke/*Women*

WR: 1:00.59 Ina Kleber (GDR) 1984
OR: 1:00.86 Rica Reinisch (GDR) 1980

Gold	*Silver*	*Bronze*
1924 Sybil Bauer (USA) 1:23.2 OR	Phyllis Harding (GBR) 1:27.4	Aileen Riggin (USA) 1:28.2
1928 Marie Braun (HOL) 1:22.0	Ellen King (GBR) 1:22.2	Joyce Cooper (GBR) 1:22.8
1932 Eleanor Holm (USA) 1:19.4	Philomena Mealing (AUS) 1:21.3	Elizabeth Davies (GBR) 1:22.5
1936 Dina Senff (HOL) 1:18.9	Hendrika Mastenbroek (HOL) 1:19.2	Alice Bridges (USA) 1:19.4
1948 Karen Harup (DEN) 1:14.4 OR	Suzanne Zimmermann (USA) 1:16.0	Judy Davies (AUS) 1:16.7
1952 Joan Harrison (SAF) 1:14.3	Geertje Wielema (HOL) 1:14.5	Jean Stewart (NZL) 1:15.8
1956 Judy Grinham (GBR) 1:12.9 OR	Carin Cone (USA) 1:12.9	Margaret Edwards (GBR) 1:13.1
1960 Lynn Burke (USA) 1:09.3 OR	Natalie Steward (GBR) 1:10.8	Satoko Tanaka (JPN) 1:11.4
1964 Cathy Ferguson (USA) 1:07.7 WR	Christine Caron (FRA) 1:07.9	Virginia Duenkel (USA) 1:08.0
1968 Kaye Hall (USA) 1:06.2 WR	Elaine Tanner (CAN) 1:06.7	Jane Swaggerty (USA) 1:08.1
1972 Melissa Belote (USA) 1:05.78 OR	Andrea Gyarmati (HUN) 1:06.26	Susie Atwood (USA) 1:06.34
1976 Ulrike Ritcher (GDR) 1:01.83 OR	Birgit Treiber (GDR) 1:03.41	Nancy Garapick (CAN) 1:03.71
1980 Rica Reinisch (GDR) 1:00.86 WR	Ina Kleber (GDR) 1:02.07	Petra Reidel (GDR) 1:02.64

| 1984 | Theresa Andrews (USA) 1:02.55 | Betsy Mitchell (USA) 1:02.63 | Jolanda de Rover (HOL) 1:02.91 |

4. Carmen Bunaciu (ROM) 5. Aneta Patrascoiu (ROM) 6. Svenja Schlicht (FRG)
7. Beverley Rose (GBR) 8. Carmel Clark (NZL)

1988   Final on 22 September

200 metres backstroke/*Women*

WR: 2:08.60 Betsy Mitchell (USA) 1986
OR: 2:11.77 Rica Reinisch (GDR) 1980

	Gold	*Silver*	*Bronze*
1968	Lillian 'Pokey' Watson (USA) 2:24.8 OR	Elaine Tanner (CAN) 2:27.4	Kaye Hall (USA) 2:28.9
1972	Melissa Belote (USA) 2:19.19 WR	Susie Atwood (USA) 2:20.38	Donna Marie Gurr (CAN) 2:23.22
1976	Ulrike Richter (GDR) 2:13.43 OR	Birgit Treiber (GDR) 2:14.97	Nancy Garapick (CAN) 2:15.60
1980	Rica Reinisch (GDR) 2:11.77 WR	Cornelia Pilot (GDR) 2:13.75	Birgit Treiber (GDR) 2:14.14
1984	Jolanda de Rover (HOL) 2:12.38	Amy White (USA) 2:13.04	Aneta Patrascoiu (ROM) 2:13.29

4. Georgina Parkes (AUS) 5. Tori Trees (USA) 6. Svenja Schlicht (FRG)
7. Carmen Bunaciu (ROM) 8. Carmel Clark (NZL)

1988   Final on 25 September

100 metres breaststroke/*Women*

WR: 1:07.91 Silke Horner (GDR) 1987
OR: 1:09.88 Petra Van Staveren (HOL) 1984

	Gold	*Silver*	*Bronze*
1968	Djurdjica Bjedov (YUG) 1:15.8 OR	Galina Prozumenshchikova (URS) 1:15.9	Sharon Wichman (USA) 1:16.1
1972	Catherine Carr (USA) 1:13.58 WR	Galina Stepanova (née Prozumenshchikova) (URS) 1:14.99	Beverley Whitfield (AUS) 1:15.73
1976	Hannelore Anke (GDR) 1:11.16	Lubov Rusanova (URS) 1:13.04	Marina Koshevaya (URS) 1:13.30
1980	Ute Geweniger (GDR) 1:10.22	Elvira Vasilkova (URS) 1:10.41	Susanne Nielsson (DEN) 1:11.16
1984	Petra Van Staveren (HOL) 1:09.88 OR	Anne Ottenbrite (CAN) 1:10.69	Catherine Poirot (FRA) 1:10.70

4. Tracy Caulkins (USA) 5. Eva-Marie Hakansson (SWE) 6. Hiroko Nagasaki (JPN)
7. Susan Rapp (USA) 8. Jean Hill (GBR)

1988   Final on 23 September

200 metres breaststroke/*Women*

WR: 2:27.40 Silke Horner (GDR) 1986
OR: 2:29.54 Lina Kachushite (URS) 1980

	Gold	Silver	Bronze
1924	Lucy Morton (GBR) 3:33.2 OR	Agnes Geraghty (USA) 3:34.0	Gladys Carson (GBR) 3:35.4
1928	Hilde Schrader (GER) 3:12.6	Mietje Baron (HOL) 3:15.2	Lotte Mühe (GER) 3:17.6
1932	Claire Dennis (AUS) 3:06.3 OR	Hideko Maehata (JPN) 3:06.4	Else Jacobsen (DEN) 3:07.1
1936	Hideko Maehata (JPN) 3:03.6	Martha Genenger (GER) 3:04.2	Inge Sörensen (DEN) 3:07.8
1948	Petronella van Vliet (HOL) 2:57.2	Beatrice Lyons (AUS) 2:57.7	Eva Novák (HUN) 3:00.2
1952	Eva Székely (HUN) 2:51.7 OR	Eva Novák (HUN) 2:54.4	Helen Gordon (GBR) 2:57.6
1956	Ursula Happe (GER) 2:53.1 OR	Eva Székely (HUN) 2:54.8	Eva-Maria ten Elsen (GER) 2:55.1
1960	Anita Lonsbrough (GBR) 2:49.5 WR	Wiltrud Urselmann (GER) 2:50.0	Barbara Göbel (GER) 2:53.6
1964	Galina Prozumenshchikova (URS) 2:46.4 OR	Claudia Kolb (USA) 2:47.6	Svetlana Babanina (URS) 2:48.6
1968	Sharon Wichman (USA) 2:44.4 OR	Djurdjica Bjedov (YUG) 2:46.4	Galina Prozumenshchikova (URS) 2:47.0
1972	Beverley Whitfield (AUS) 2:41.71 OR	Dana Schoenfield (USA) 2:42.05	Galina Stepanova (née Prozumenshchikova) (URS) 2:42.36
1976	Marina Koshevaya (URS) 2:33.35 WR	Marina Yurchenia (URS) 2:36.08	Lubov Rusanova (URS) 2:36.22
1980	Lina Kachushite (URS) 2:29.54 OR	Svetlana Varganova (URS) 2:29.61	Yulia Bogdanova (URS) 2:32.39
1984	Anne Ottenbrite (CAN) 2:30.38	Susan Rapp (USA) 2:31.15	Ingrid Lempereur (BEL) 2:31.40

4. Hiroko Nagasaki (JPN) 5. Sharon Kellett (AUS) 6. Ute Hasse (FRG)
7. Susannah Brownsdon (GBR) 8. Kimberly Rhodenbaugh (USA)

1988 Final on 21 September

100 metres butterfly/*Women*

WR: 57.93 Mary T. Meagher (USA) 1981
OR: 59.05 Mary T. Meagher (USA) 1984 (in a heat)

	Gold	Silver	Bronze
1956	Shelley Mann (USA) 1:11.0 OR	Nancy Ramey (USA) 1:11.9	Mary Sears (USA) 1:14.4
1960	Carolyn Schuler (USA) 1:09.5 OR	Marianne Heemskerk (HOL) 1:10.4	Janice Andrew (AUS) 1:12.2
1964	Sharon Stouder (USA) 1:04.7 WR	Ada Kok (HOL) 1:05.6	Kathleen Ellis (USA) 1:06.0

1968	Lynette McClements (AUS) 1:05.5	Ellie Daniel (USA) 1:05.8	Susan Shields (USA) 1:06.2
1972	Mayumi Aoki (JPN) 1:03.34 WR	Roswitha Beier (GDR) 1:03.61	Andrea Gyarmati (HUN) 1:03.73
1976	Kornelia Ender (GDR) 1:00.13 =WR	Andrea Pollack (GDR) 1:00.98	Wendy Boglioli (USA) 1:01.17
1980	Caren Metschuck (GDR) 1:00.42	Andrea Pollack (GDR) 1:00.90	Christiane Knacke (GDR) 1:01.44
1984	Mary T. Meagher (USA) 59.26	Jenna Johnson (USA) 1:00.19	Karin Seick (FRG) 1:01.36

4. Annemarie Verstappen (HOL) 5. Michelle MacPherson (CAN) 6. Janet Tibbits (AUS)
7. Conny Van Bentum (HOL) 8. Ina Beyermann (FRG)

1988   Final on 23 September

200 metres butterfly/*Women*

WR: 2:05.96 Mary T. Meagher (USA) 1981
OR: 2:06.90 Mary T. Meagher (USA) 1984

	Gold	*Silver*	*Bronze*
1968	Ada Kok (HOL) 2:24.7 OR	Helga Lindner (GDR) 2:24.8	Ellie Daniel (USA) 2:25.9
1972	Karen Moe (USA) 2:15.57 WR	Lynn Colella (USA) 2:16.34	Ellie Daniel (USA) 2:16.74
1976	Andrea Pollack (GDR) 2:11.41 OR	Ulrike Tauber (GDR) 2:12.50	Rosemarie Gabriel (GDR) 2:12.86
1980	Ines Geissler (GDR) 2:10.44 OR	Sybille Schönrock (GDR) 2:10.45	Michelle Ford (AUS) 2:11.66
1984	Mary T. Meagher (USA) 2:06.90 OR	Karen Phillips (AUS) 2:10.56	Ina Beyermann (FRG) 2:11.91

4. Nancy Hogshead (USA) 5. Samantha Purvis (GBR) 6. Naoko Kume (JPN)
7. Sonja Hausladen (AUT) 8. Conny Van Bentum (HOL)

1988   Final on 25 September

200 metres individual medley/*Women*

WR: 2:11.73 Ute Geweniger (GDR) 1981
OR: 2:12.64 Tracy Caulkins (USA) 1984

	Gold	*Silver*	*Bronze*
1968	Claudia Kolb (USA) 2:24.7 OR	Susan Pedersen (USA) 2:28.8	Jan Henne (USA) 2:31.4
1972	Shane Gould (AUS) 2:23.07 WR	Kornelia Ender (GDR) 2:23.59	Lynn Vidali (USA) 2:24.06
1984	Tracy Caulkins (USA) 2:12.64 OR	Nancy Hogshead (USA) 2:15.17	Michele Pearson (AUS) 2:15.92

4. Lisa Curry (AUS) 5. Christiane Pielke (FRG) 6. Manuela Dalle Valle (ITA)
7. Petra Zindler (FRG) 8. Katrine Bomstad (NOR)

1988   Final on 24 September

400 metres individual medley/*Women*

WR: 4:36.10 Petra Schneider (GDR) 1982
OR: 4:36.29 Petra Schneider (GDR) 1980

	Gold	*Silver*	*Bronze*
1964	Donna De Varona (USA) 5:18.7 OR	Sharon Finneran (USA) 5:24.1	Martha Randall (USA) 5:24.2
1968	Claudia Kolb (USA) 5:08.5 OR	Lynn Vidali (USA) 5:22.2	Sabine Steinbach (GDR) 5:25.3
1972	Gail Neall (AUS) 5:02.97 WR	Leslie Cliff (CAN) 5:03.57	Novella Calligaris (ITA) 5:03.99
1976	Ulrike Tauber (GDR) 4:42.77 WR	Cheryl Gibson (CAN) 4:48.10	Becky Smith (CAN) 4:50.48
1980	Petra Schneider (GDR) 4:36.29 WR	Sharron Davies (GBR) 4:46.83	Agnieszka Czopek (POL) 4:48.17
1984	Tracy Caulkins (USA) 4:39.24	Suzanne Landells (AUS) 4:48.30	Petra Zindler (FRG) 4:48.57

4. Susan Heon (USA) 5. Nathalie Gingras (CAN) 6. Donna McGinnis (CAN)
7. Gaynor Stanley (GBR) 8. Katrine Bomstad (NOR)

1988 Final on 19 September

4 × 100 metres freestyle relay/*Women*

WR: 3:40.57 East Germany 1986
OR: 3:42.71 East Germany 1980

	Gold	*Silver*	*Bronze*
1912	GREAT BRITAIN 5:52.8 WR	GERMANY 6:04.6	AUSTRIA 6:17.0
1920	UNITED STATES 5:11.6 WR	GREAT BRITAIN 5:40.8	SWEDEN 5:43.6
1924	UNITED STATES 4:58.8 WR	GREAT BRITAIN 5:17.0	SWEDEN 5:35.6
1928	UNITED STATES 4:47.6 WR	GREAT BRITAIN 5:02.8	SOUTH AFRICA 5:13.4
1932	UNITED STATES 4:38.0 WR	NETHERLANDS 4:47.5	GREAT BRITAIN 4:52.4
1936	NETHERLANDS 4:36.0 OR	GERMANY 4:36.8	UNITED STATES 4:40.2
1948	UNITED STATES 4:29.2 OR	DENMARK 4:29.6	NETHERLANDS 4:31.6
1952	HUNGARY 4:24.4 WR	NETHERLANDS 4:29.0	UNITED STATES 4:30.1
1956	AUSTRALIA 4:17.1 WR	UNITED STATES 4:19.2	SOUTH AFRICA 4:25.7
1960	UNITED STATES 4:08.9 WR	AUSTRALIA 4:11.3	GERMANY 4:19.7
1964	UNITED STATES 4:03.8 WR	AUSTRALIA 4:06.9	NETHERLANDS 4:12.0
1968	UNITED STATES 4:02.5 OR	EAST GERMANY 4:05.7	CANADA 4:07.2

1972	UNITED STATES 3:55.19 WR	EAST GERMANY 3:55.55	WEST GERMANY 3:57.93
1976	UNITED STATES 3:44.82 WR	EAST GERMANY 3:45.50	CANADA 3:48.81
1980	EAST GERMANY 3:42.71 WR	SWEDEN 3:48.93	NETHERLANDS 3:49.51
1984	UNITED STATES 3:43.43 Jenna Johnson Carrie Steinseifer Dara Torres Nancy Hogshead	NETHERLANDS 3:44.40 Annemarie Verstappen Elles Voskes Desi Reijers Conny Van Bentum	WEST GERMANY 3:45.56 Iris Zscherpe Suzanne Schuster Christiane Pielke Karin Seick

4. Australia 5. Canada 6. Great Britain 7. Sweden 8. France

1988   Final on 22 September

4 × 100 metres medley relay/*Women*
(order of strokes: backstroke, breaststroke, butterfly, freestyle)

WR: 4:03.69 East Germany 1984
OR: 4:06.67 East Germany 1980

	Gold	*Silver*	*Bronze*
1960	UNITED STATES 4:41.1 WR	AUSTRALIA 4:45.9	GERMANY 4:47.6
1964	UNITED STATES 4:33.9 WR	NETHERLANDS 4:37.0	USSR 4:39.2
1968	UNITED STATES 4:28.3 OR	AUSTRALIA 4:30.0	WEST GERMANY 4:36.4
1972	UNITED STATES 4:20.75 WR	EAST GERMANY 4:24.91	WEST GERMANY 4:26.46
1976	EAST GERMANY 4:07.95 WR	UNITED STATES 4:14.55	CANADA 4:15.22
1980	EAST GERMANY 4:06.67 WR	GREAT BRITAIN 4:12.24	USSR 4:13.61
1984	UNITED STATES 4:08.34 Theresa Andrews Tracy Caulkins Mary T. Meagher Nancy Hogshead	WEST GERMANY 4:11.97 Svenja Schlicht Ute Hasse Ina Beyermann Karin Seick	CANADA 4:12.98 Reema Abdo Anne Ottenbrite Michelle MacPherson Pamela Rai

4. Great Britain 5. Italy 6. Switzerland (Japan and Sweden were disqualified)

1988   Final on 24 September

Diving – springboard/*Women*

	Gold	Silver	Bronze
1920	Aileen Riggin (USA) 539.9	Helen Wainwright (USA) 534.8	Thelma Payne (USA) 534.1
1924	Elizabeth Becker (USA) 474.5	Aileen Riggin (USA) 460.4	Caroline Fletcher (USA) 434.4
1928	Helen Meany (USA) 78.62	Dorothy Poynton (USA) 75.62	Georgia Coleman (USA) 73.38
1932	Georgia Coleman (USA) 87.52	Katherine Rawls (USA) 82.56	Jane Fauntz (USA) 82.12
1936	Marjorie Gestring (USA) 89.27	Katherine Rawls (USA) 88.35	Dorothy Poynton-Hill (USA) 82.36
1948	Victoria Draves (USA) 108.74	Zoe Ann Olsen (USA) 108.23	Patricia Elsener (USA) 101.30
1952	Patricia McCormick (USA) 147.30	Madeleine Moreau (FRA) 139.34	Zoe Ann Jensen (née Olsen) (USA) 127.57
1956	Patricia McCormick (USA) 142.36	Jeanne Stunyo (USA) 125.89	Irene Macdonald (CAN) 121.40
1960	Ingrid Krämer (GER) 155.81	Paula Myers-Pope (USA) 141.24	Elizabeth Ferris (GBR) 139.09
1964	Ingrid Krämer-Engel (GER) 145.00	Jeanne Collier (USA) 138.36	Mary Willard (USA) 138.18
1968	Sue Gossick (USA) 150.77	Tamara Pogozheva (URS) 145.30	Keala O'Sullivan (USA) 145.23
1972	Micki King (USA) 450.03	Ulrika Knape (SWE) 434.19	Marina Janicke (GDR) 430.92
1976	Jennifer Chandler (USA) 506.19	Christa Kohler (GDR) 469.41	Cynthia McIngvale (USA) 466.83
1980	Irina Kalinina (URS) 725.910	Martina Proeber (GDR) 698.895	Karin Guthke (GDR) 685.245
1984	Sylvie Bernier (CAN) 530.70	Kelly McCormick (USA) 527.46	Christina Seufert (USA) 517.62
1988	Final on 27 September		

Diving – platform/*Women*

	Gold	Silver	Bronze
1912	Greta Johansson (SWE) 39.9	Lisa Regnell (SWE) 36.0	Isabelle White (GBR) 34.0
1920	Stefani Fryland-Clausen (DEN) 34.6	Eileen Armstrong (GBR) 33.3	Eva Ollivier (SWE) 33.3
1924	Caroline Smith (USA) 33.2	Elizabeth Becker (USA) 33.4	Hjördis Töpel (SWE) 32.8
1928	Elisabeth Becker-Pinkston (USA) 31.6	Georgia Coleman (USA) 30.6	Lala Sjöqvist (SWE) 29.2
1932	Dorothy Poynton (USA) 40.26	Georgia Coleman (USA) 35.56	Marion Roper (USA) 35.22
1936	Dorothy Poynton-Hill (USA) 33.93	Velma Dunn (USA) 33.63	Käthe Köhler (GER) 33.43
1948	Victoria Draves (USA) 68.87	Patricia Elsener (USA) 66.28	Birte Christoffersen (DEN) 66.04
1952	Patricia McCormick (USA) 79.37	Paula Myers (USA) 71.63	Juno Irwin (USA) 70.49
1956	Patricia McCormick (USA) 84.85	Juno Irwin (USA) 81.64	Paula Myers (USA) 81.58

1960	Ingrid Krämer (GER) 91.28	Paula Myers-Pope (USA) 88.94	Ninel Krutova (URS) 86.99
1964	Lesley Bush (USA) 99.80	Ingrid Krämer-Engel (GER) 98.45	Galina Alekseyeva (URS) 97.60
1968	Milena Duchková (TCH) 109.59	Natalia Lobanova (URS) 105.14	Ann Peterson (USA) 101.11
1972	Ulrika Knape (SWE) 390.00	Milena Duchková (TCH) 370.92	Marina Janicke (GDR) 360.54
1976	Elena Vaytsekhovskaya (URS) 406.59	Ulrika Knape (SWE) 402.60	Deborah Wilson (USA) 401.07
1980	Martina Jäschke (GDR) 596.250	Servard Emirzyan (URS) 576.465	Liana Tsotadze (URS) 575.925
1984	Jihong Zhou (CHN) 435.51	Michele Mitchell (USA) 431.19	Wendy Wyland (USA) 422.07

1988 Final on 18 September

Synchronized swimming – solo/*Women*

	Gold	Silver	Bronze
1984	Tracie Ruiz (USA) 198.467	Carolyn Waldo (CAN) 195.300	Miwako Motoyoshi (JPN) 187.050

4. Marijke Engelen (HOL) 5. Gudrun Hanisch (FRG) 6. Caroline Holmyard (GBR)
7. Muriel Hermine (FRA) 8. Karin Singer (SUI)

1988 Final on 30 September

Synchronized swimming – duet/*Women*

	Gold	Silver	Bronze
1984	UNITED STATES 195.584 Candy Costie Tracie Ruiz	CANADA 194.234 Sharon Hambrook Kelly Kryczka	JAPAN 187.992 Saeko Kimura Miwako Motoyoshi

4. Great Britain (Caroline Holmyard, Carolyn Wilson) 5. Switzerland 6. Netherlands
7. France 8. Mexico

1988 Final on 1 October

TABLE TENNIS

The sport is included in the Games for the first time.

Like almost every sport, the British claim to be its inventors. Cambridge undergraduates played a form of the game, supposedly with small rubber balls, and books. A certain James Gibb introduced the idea of a length of string across the middle of the table and games up to 21 points. At this point the sport was called 'Gossima', but on the introduction of the celluloid ball it became known as ping-pong and the Ping-Pong Association was formed in 1902. The English Table Tennis Association was formed in 1927.

The Europeans dominated the sport until the Japanese took over in the fifties. Since then, the Chinese have become the top nation.

THE COMPETITION

There will be four Olympic titles won – men's singles and doubles and women's singles and doubles. There is no 'mixed' competition.

The inclusion of the sport coincides with the Games being held in the Orient for the first time since 1964 and the Chinese will strongly contest each major prize. The Chinese women have won the last seven world championships and the men six out of seven. They have six in the top ten in both the men's and women's game. The South Koreans will have a good medal chance in the women's competition, while of the Euro-

peans, Sweden could pick up a medal in the men's.

Each country can send a maximum of four men and three women. The men's singles will have 64, the doubles, 32 pairs. The women's singles will have 32 with 16 pairs in the doubles.

The competitors for the men's singles are selected as follows: 16 from the world rankings to include no more than two from any country plus 44 to qualify. Also, four selected by the sports governing body (ITTF) to include at least two South Koreans, if they have not otherwise qualified.

The women's qualifying is exactly half of the men's.

Desmond Douglas is Britain's only player gaining direct entry. He is ranked 12 in the world. Alan Cooke has qualified but Carl Prean, who beat the world number one from China, Jiang Jialiang early in 1988, will not take part unless there is a withdrawal.

No British women players have qualified.

THE TOURNAMENT

In the men's singles, eight groups of eight play on a round-robin basis. The eight group winners then compete in play-off matches for the final places.

In the women's singles, there will be four groups of eight, again playing on a round-robin basis. The first two in each group play off for further progression.

The men's doubles is in four groups of

eight pairs and is conducted as the women's singles above.

The women's doubles is in two groups of eight pairs, with the best four pairs in each group playing off for further progression.

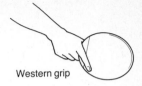

Western grip

THE MATCHES

Singles are the best of five games. Doubles, the best of three games. A game is won by the player who is the first to accumulate 21 points. If the score is 20-all, the first player to be two clear points ahead will win.

Each player serves for five points and then transfers service to the opponent. In doubles, the service changes every five points among the four players.

At 20-all in singles or doubles, the service changes at every point.

The 'expedite' rule has been introduced to stop interminable rallies and stonewalling. If a game is unfinished (a game, not a match) after 15 minutes, the rule is introduced for the rest of the *match*. Under the rule, the server is allowed his service plus 12 strokes in which to win the point. If he fails, the opponent wins the point. The players serve alternately.

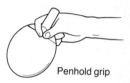

Penhold grip

'penhold' grip is employed all the strokes are much the same, and speed of footwork becomes even more essential.

EQUIPMENT

Table

2.7 m long by 1.5 m wide. It is 76 cm above the ground with a net 15 cm high. The net is 1.83 m in length and extends either side of the table. The doubles table is divided from end to end.

THE PLAY

When serving, the ball must bounce on the server's side of the net first (unlike tennis). The service must be made from the palm of the free hand. It must not be cupped or pinched by the fingers. It should then be tossed in the air in as near a vertical plain as possible without spin. Spin can only be induced by the bat.

Two types of grip are used, the 'western' where the bat is held as in a 'shake the hands' grip, and the 'penhold', which is favoured, among others, by the Chinese. In the western style, strokes used are akin to tennis, forehand, backhand, etc. When the

Bats

These may be of any size or shape or weight, but the blade must be made of wood. The covering may be plain or pimpled. 'Sandwich' bats are allowed, where a layer of cellular rubber (sponge) is used underneath the plain or pimpled surface. Since their introduction, play has become much faster with even more emphasis on spin.

Balls

Made of celluloid with a diameter of between 37.2 and 38.3 mm and weigh between 2.4 and 2.53 g.

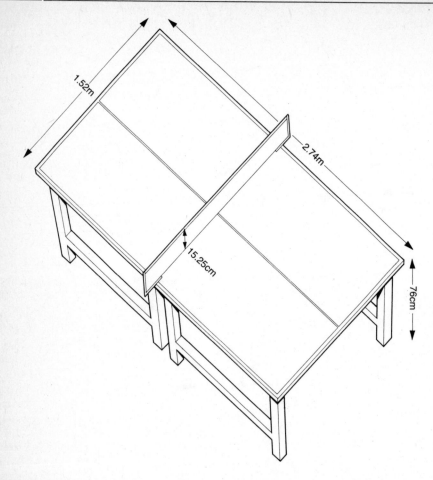

1.52m

2.74m

15.25cm

76cm

Not a lot of people know that

• Fred Perry, Britain's triple Wimbledon tennis champion of the 1930s, was also the world table tennis champion in 1929.
• Another famous Wimbledon champion, Ann Jones, was also a fine table tennis player. In 1957 she was runner-up in the singles, doubles and mixed doubles in the world championships. The following year she was the beaten finalist in the European championship singles.

• When smashed, the table tennis ball reaches speeds of over 100 mph.

VENUE

Seoul National University Gymnasium. 20 km from Olympic Village. Capacity 5000.

No previous results – a new Olympic sport.

TENNIS

The sport was part of every modern Games from 1896 to 1924. It now returns in an era when some of the competitors are multi-millionaires from tennis alone – a far cry from the original amateur Olympic ideal.

Many Wimbledon champions of those earlier times were also Olympic champions. The list includes the British Docherty brothers who won eight Wimbledon doubles' titles around the turn of the century, Suzanne Lenglen (France), and Helen Wills (Moody) (USA).

Kitty McKane won five Olympic medals in all for Great Britain and was Wimbledon singles' champion in 1924, beating Helen Wills in the final. At the time of writing, Kitty Godfree, as she is now, is still a regular visitor to the Wimbledon championships and was actively playing the game into her 90th year.

THE COMPETITION

There will be four titles at stake, men's singles and doubles and women's singles and doubles. Although there were mixed doubles competitions in those earlier tennis Olympics, there will be none on this occasion.

Ivan Lendl will not be taking part – Czechoslovakia will not select him because he has not made himself available for Davis Cup ties, and he cannot play for the United States.

John McEnroe is almost certain not to be part of the United States team. To find the eventual singles gold medallist, you may have to look no further than Sweden who, in

Stefan Edberg and Mats Wilander have two of the favourites.

In the women's competition, Martina Navratilova, who does qualify for the United States, has said, at the time of writing, that she does not wish to take part. It is almost certain that Chris Evert will not play either. Steffi Graf of West Germany is the hot tip for the women's singles title.

THE TOURNAMENT

64 players will compete for the men's singles. No more than three players from any one country.

32 will qualify as follows: two players from each nation that reached the quarter-finals of the Davis Cup World Group; two players from each nation that won their play-off tie in the world group; one player from each nation that lost their play-off tie in the world group; one player from each nation that won their zonal competition.

Wild Cards. Players are also eligible if they are in the top 200 and their nation did not take part in the Davis Cup. So are two players who have earned a junior singles' ranking in 1987, provided they are from countries who do not already have two contestants.

Qualifying competitions are for those nations who did not compete in the 1987 Davis Cup or who did not reach the stages above.

48 players will compete for the women's singles. 32 will qualify direct, as in the men's competition, except that the results will be based on the 1987 Federation Cup.

Wild cards are the same as for men, except ranking must be in top 100. Plus one junior ranked player.

Qualifying competitions are as per men's, except based on the Federation Cup.

32 pairs compete for the men's doubles (20 direct entries). Qualification is similar to men's singles.

A minimum of eight pairs compete for the women's doubles (eight direct entries).

SEEDING

There will be seeding as in all tennis competitions, based on current world-computer rankings. There will be 16 in men's singles, 12 in women's singles, eight in men's doubles. In women's doubles, it will depend on the size of the draw.

THE MATCHES

Men's singles and doubles will be the best of five sets with a tie-break operating at six games all in every set except the fifth.

Women's singles and doubles will be the best of three sets with a tie-break operating at six games all in every set except the third.

Not a lot of people know that

• In Los Angeles, tennis was a demonstration sport. No medals were awarded but the men's singles was won by Stefan Edberg (Sweden) who beat Francisco Maciel (Mexico) in the final. Steffi Graf (West Germany) won the women's final beating Sabrina Goles (Yugoslavia). Graf is favourite to make it a gold medal this time.

• This is the only sport in the Olympics in which Britain heads the list of gold medals. That won't last very long if the sport stays in the Games for the foreseeable future, unless there is a radical improvement in the British game.

• The 1912 Olympic tennis tournament was a trifle disappointing owing to the fact that the organizers in their infinite wisdom failed to notice that they had arranged play on exactly the same days as Wimbledon.

• In 1920, a match between Gordon Lowe (Great Britain) and a Greek called Zerlindi went on so long, the ballboys left the court and went to lunch forcing the match to be suspended. It had started the day before. (No tie-breaks then.)

RESULTS

Singles/*Men*

	Gold	Silver	Bronze
1896	John Boland (GBR)	Demis Kasdaglis (GRE)	—
1900	Hugh Doherty (GBR)	Harold Mahony (GBR)	Reginald Doherty (GBR)
			A. B. Norris (GBR)
1904	Beals Wright (USA)	Robert LeRoy (USA)	Alonzo Bell (USA)
			Edgar Leonard (USA)
1906	Max Decugis (FRA)	Maurice Germot (FRA)	Zdenek Zemla (BOH)
1908	Josiah Ritchie (GBR)	Otto Froitzheim (GER)	Wilberforce Eves (GBR)
1908*	Arthur Wentworth Gore (GBR)	George Caridia (GBR)	Josiah Ritchie (GBR)
1912	Charles Winslow (SAF)	Harold Kitson (SAF)	Oscar Kreuzer (GER)
1912*	André Gobert (FRA)	Charles Dixon (GBR)	Anthony Wilding (NZL)
1920	Louis Raymond (SAF)	Ichiya Kumagae (JPN)	Charles Winslow (SAF)
1924	Vincent Richards (USA)	Henri Cochet (FRA)	Umberto De Morpurgo (ITA)

1988 Starts on 20 September and the final is on 30 September

*Indoor tournaments.

Doubles/*Men*

	Gold	Silver	Bronze
1896	John Boland (GBR)	Demis Kasdaglis (GRE)	—
	Fritz Traun (GER)	Demetrios Petrokokkinos (GRE)	
1900	Hugh Doherty (GBR)	Max Decugis (FRA)	G. de la Chapelle (FRA)
	Reginald Doherty (GBR)	Spalding de Garmendia (USA)	A. Prevost (FRA)
1904	Edgar Leonard (USA)	Alonzo Bell (USA)	Joseph Wear (USA)
	Beals Wright (USA)	Robert LeRoy (USA)	Allen West (USA)
			Clarence Gamble (USA)
			Arthur Wear (USA)
1906	Max Decugis (FRA)	Ioannis Ballis (GRE)	Zdenek Zemla (BOH)
	Maurice Germot (FRA)	Zenophon Kasdaglis (GRE)	Ladislav Zemla (BOH)
1908	Reginald Doherty (GBR)	James Parke (IRL)	Charles Cazalet (GBR)
	George Hillyard (GBR)	Josiah Ritchie (GBR)	Charles Dixon (GBR)
1908*	Arthur Wentworth Gore (GBR)	George Caridia (GBR)	Wollmar Boström (SWE)
	Herbert Roper Barrett (GBR)	George Simond (GBR)	Gunnar Setterwall (SWE)
1912	Harold Kitson (SAF)	Felix Pipes (AUT)	Albert Canet (FRA)
	Charles Winslow (SAF)	Arthur Zborzil (AUT)	Marc Meny de Marangue (FRA)
1912*	Maurice Germot (FRA)	Carl Kempe (SWE)	Arthur Beamish (GBR)
	André Gobert (FRA)	Gunnar Setterwall (SWE)	Charles Dixon (GBR)

*Indoor tournament.

1920	Noel Turnbull (GBR)	Seiichiro Kashio (JAP)	Pierre Albarran (FRA)
	Max Woosnam (GBR)	Ichiya Kumagae (JAP)	Max Decugis (FRA)
1924	Frank Hunter (USA)	Jacques Brugnon (FRA)	Jean Borotra (FRA)
	Vincent Richards (USA)	Henri Cochet (FRA)	René Lacoste (FRA)

1988 Starts on 23 September with the final on 1 October

Singles/*Women*

	Gold	*Silver*	*Bronze*
1900	Charlotte Cooper (GBR)	Hélène Prévost (FRA)	Marion Jones (USA)
			Hedwiga Rosenbaumova (BOH)
1906	Esmeé Simiriotou (GRE)	Sophia Marinou (GRE)	Euphrosine Paspati (GRE)
1908	Dorothea Chambers (GBR)	Dorothy Boothby (GBR)	Joan Winch (GBR)
1908*	Gwen Eastlake-Smith (GBR)	Angela Greene (GBR)	Märtha Adlerstrahle (SWE)
1912	Marguerite Broquedis (FRA)	Dora Köring (GER)	Molla Bjurstedt (NOR)
1912*	Ethel Hannam (GBR)	Thora Castenschiold (DEN)	Mabel Parton (GBR)
1920	Suzanne Lenglen (FRA)	Dorothy Holman (GBR)	Kitty McKane (GBR)
1924	Helen Wills (USA)	Julie Vlasto (FRA)	Kitty McKane (GBR)

1988 Starts on 23 September with the final on 1 October

*Indoor tournament.

Doubles/*Women*

	Gold	*Silver*	*Bronze*
1920	Kitty McKane (GBR)	Geraldine Beamish (GBR)	Elisabeth d'Ayen (FRA)
	Winifred McNair (GBR)	Dorothy Holman (GBR)	Suzanne Lenglen (FRA)
1924	Hazel Wightman (USA)	Edith Covell (GBR)	Evelyn Colyer (GBR)
	Helen Wills (USA)	Kitty McKane (GBR)	Dorothy Shepherd-Barron (GBR)

1988 Starts on 24 September with the final on 30 September

VOLLEYBALL

The game in something like its current form was devised by William G. Morgan, a physical training instructor, at Holyoke YMCA in Massachusetts, just outside Boston. (Young Men's Christian Associations have played quite a part in producing Olympic sports – see chapter on *Basketball* (page 62.)

The game spread in two directions, via American teachers to the Far East, and via US troops stationed there to Europe.

A world body, the FIVB – the Fédération Internationale de Volleyball was founded in Paris only after the Second World War in 1947. The first men's world championship took place in 1949 and women's in 1952.

The sport has been part of the Olympics since the 1964 Games in Tokyo.

THE COMPETITION

The Olympic tournament consists of 12 men's teams and eight women's teams.

Both the men's and women's competitions are run on a two-group basis with the top two teams from each group after the 'round robin' matches, qualifying for semifinals. Group winners will then meet the second country in the other qualifying group to produce finalists. The losing semifinalists will play off for bronze medals.

USA are the defending men's champions and while most people thought their gold medal in Los Angeles was only won because so many of the top nations were absent, the Americans confounded their critics by going on to win the world championships in 1986. So they are the reigning Olympic and world

champions. The Soviets, current European champions and three times Olympic champions since 1964, will be another of the main contenders for the gold medal and the French, who have put a great deal of effort into producing a top team (they are second in Europe) are exciting and will also contest the medals.

In the women's competition, China, the defending champions, and Cuba (who did not compete in Los Angeles) are joint number one, but the East Germans are also outstanding, with the Americans and Japanese next best.

THE GAME

Teams consist of six players with up to six substitutes.

The teams play either side of a net and the idea in simple terms is for the attacking team to 'ground' the ball in the defenders' court or to make them put the ball out of court or fail to return it.

In order to do this, one team 'serves' the ball, like tennis, from the back of the court, over the net to the receivers. They are then allowed three touches of the ball, but the third must be a scoring attempt, i.e. returned over the net. The ball can be returned on the first or second touch, but, in practice, the first and second 'plays' are usually used to set up a smash or 'spike' of the ball to the server's court on the third touch. The server's team try to intercept and then endeavour to set up their own attack. If the receivers do manage to take advantage, then the serve goes to them. Only the serving team can win a point. The service rotates amongst all team members. The whole team rotates one position, although as play continues, they may assume more specialized roles, i.e. attackers or defenders. Sets continue up to 15 points, with a difference of at least two; matches are the best of five sets.

The court measures 18 metres by 9 metres. For the men's game, the net is 2.43 metres and 2.21 metres for the women. The ball used is marginally smaller than the ball used for soccer, but it is lighter.

Players wear padding on knees and elbows, because the sport is highly athletic and it protects them as they hurl themselves about.

THE BRITISH

While the game is highly popular in gymnasia and sports halls around the country, the standard is not high enough to produce a team capable of Olympic qualification for either men or women.

THE STARS

Volleyball is very much a team sport, so not many individuals stand out. Teams have

though. In the 1976 Games, the Soviets got to the men's final as expected and without dropping a game. Their opponents, Poland, had dropped seven sets. However, in an absolute thriller they beat the Soviets 19–17 in the fifth set. The Polish training methods were unbelievable. Every day they had to jump 392 times over a 4 ft 6 ins barrier, wearing weights of between 20 and 30 lbs on legs and body. Agonizing, but obviously effective.

Horofumi Daimatsu, coach to the Japanese women's team of 1964, would have thought the Poles were softies. Ten of Daimatsu's squad were workers at the Nichibo spinning mill in Osaka. Mr Daimatsu also worked there and his methods of training included hitting his players on the head, kicking them on their hips, insulting and goading them. They were forced to practise a minimum of six hours a day, seven days a week, 51 weeks a year. The Japanese women did however win the Olympic title that year. After the Games, Mr Daimatsu quit coaching and eventually ended up in the Japanese parliament.

At the 1984 Olympics, one player did stand out: Flo Hyman from Inglewood,

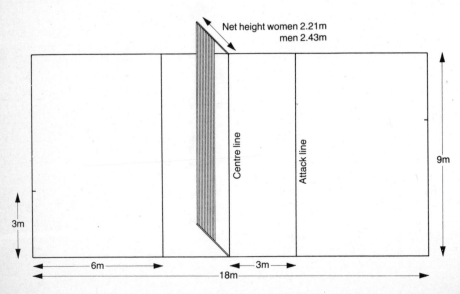

Net height women 2.21m
men 2.43m

Centre line

Attack line

9m

3m

6m

3m

18m

California at 6 ft 5 ins was the most exciting player in the women's game. Standing head and shoulders above the rest of the US team, the whole nation got behind her as she 'spiked' them to the silver medal behind China.

Not a lot of people know that

● At the Munich Games in 1972, the Japanese coach, Jiji Kojima, was the recipient of a writ issued by a West German viewer for 'Inhumane Treatment' to his players.

● While the standard of play in Britain is not high enough to do well in the Olympics, Britain never actually enters, because the sport is administered by four home unions, England, Wales, etc. Hockey has overcome this problem, why not volleyball?

RESULTS

Men

	Gold	Silver	Bronze
1964	USSR	CZECHOSLOVAKIA	JAPAN
1968	USSR	JAPAN	CZECHOSLOVAKIA
1972	JAPAN	EAST GERMANY	USSR
1976	POLAND	USSR	CUBA
1980	USSR	BULGARIA	ROMANIA
1984	UNITED STATES	BRAZIL	ITALY

1988 Final on 2 October (3rd and 4th place match also on 2 October)

Women

	Gold	Silver	Bronze
1964	JAPAN	USSR	POLAND
1968	USSR	JAPAN	POLAND
1972	USSR	JAPAN	NORTH KOREA
1976	JAPAN	USSR	SOUTH KOREA
1980	USSR	EAST GERMANY	BULGARIA
1984	CHINA	UNITED STATES	JAPAN

1988 Final on 29 September (3rd and 4th place match also on 29 September)

WEIGHTLIFTING

Strongman contests go back to ancient times, but the sport began formally in Germany in the latter half of the last century.

Weightlifting formed part of the first modern Games in 1896 when one-arm and two-arm lifts were included. There was no weightlifting in the Games of 1900, 1908 or 1912 but it returned in 1920 and has remained an Olympic sport ever since.

THE COMPETITION

The Chinese won four gold medals in the four lightest weight categories in the 1984 Games. However the quality of the competition was much reduced by the absence of the Eastern European countries with the exception of Rumania who won eight medals, including two gold. Nicu Vlad was a very worthy winner of the 90 kg gold medal for Rumania. He broke the Olympic record in both the snatch and the clean and jerk.

Like boxing, there is most interest in the biggest men of all, the super-heavyweights. Here Dino Lukin of Australia became champion in Los Angeles, the first time that title had gone outside the Soviet Union.

Currently, Bulgaria is the leading nation in the sport, with the Soviets a close second. Britain's top hope for a medal is Andrew Davies in the 110 kg category.

THE RULES

A lifter is allowed only three attempts at any given weight. If successful on his first lift, he must add at least 4.5 kg to the bar for the next attempt. If successful again, he must add at least 2.25 kg. A man in good form may add even more.

Because weightlifters can join the competition at any weight they choose, a popular but risky strategy is to worry the opposition by leaving one's entry until late. A lifter may then decide to attempt a weight near his personal best. There will be tremendous psychological advantage if successful, however, three failures and you are out of the competition. In the 1972 Games, the United States' top medal prospect in the super-heavyweights, Ken Patera attempted this ploy, and failed. In 1980, the gold medallist of the '72 and '76 Games, the great Soviet super-heavyweight, Vasiliy Alexeyev, attempting a comeback, failed to lift his opening weight. There is much 'jockeying' for mental advantage and there is much more to the sport than sometimes meets the eye.

Weightlifting makes superb television. The strain, concentration, the 'psyching up', the elation of success, the suffering of failure, plus the many idiosyncrasies of the competitors make it compulsive viewing for many.

THE LIFTS

Up to and including the 1972 Games, the sport was judged on three lifts, the press, the snatch, and the clean and jerk. However, judging the press became difficult and controversial and the sport's governing body decided that it should be abandoned. In each

Games since, the aggregate of the snatch and the clean and jerk has decided the result.

THE SNATCH

The bar must be lifted from the floor to the maximum arm extension above the head in one continuous motion. Lifters employ one of two methods, the squat or the split technique. In the latter, the lifter places one leg in front of the other at the start of the lift but, from either position, the feet must end in a straight line.

THE CLEAN AND JERK

This is a two-part lift as the name might imply. The 'clean' is where the bar is lifted to a temporary position at the shoulders while the lifter moves from a crouching position to a standing one. The jerk is the movement of the bar from the shoulders to maximum arm extension above the head.

JUDGING

Three referees are involved. Each has a white and a red light. If they are satisfied that a lift is valid, the white light is indicated. Red is for a failure or an illegal lift. Majority decisions can be taken.

If two or more competitors have tied for the same weight lifted, their own body weight will be taken into consideration. The lightest man will be deemed to have won.

No lifter can attempt a weight lower than a weight already successfully lifted by another competitor.

EQUIPMENT

The Bar: 2.2 metres long and 2.8 cm in diameter. The weights are attached to the ends of the bar and must be the same at each end for balance.

Supports: shoes are specially designed to give maximum support for ankles and Achilles' tendons. Belts to aid support of the back and stomach are usually of leather with a maximum width of 12 cm. Bandages can be used on the wrist and knee for additional support.

Powder: Most lifters wouldn't be seen dead without their baby powder. They use it on thighs, neck and elsewhere in order to ease the movement of the bar over the skin.

WEIGHT CATEGORIES

The various categories for contestants used to be defined by name, as in boxing, e.g.

The jerk

The snatch

welterweight, middleweight, etc. This changed in 1984 and the divisions are now simply referred to in kilograms. Competitions must be below the weights shown.

1 Up to 52	6 Up to 82.5
2 Up to 56	7 Up to 90
3 Up to 60	8 Up to 100
4 Up to 67.5	9 Up to 110
5 Up to 75	10 Over 110

BRITISH SUCCESSES

The only gold medal won by a British competitor was awarded to heavyweight Launceston Eliot in the very first modern Games of 1896. That was in the one-armed lift. He won a silver medal in the two-armed lift at the following Games. Since then the medals have been very sparse indeed.

The best British performance of more recent times was by Louis Martin. Jamaican-born Martin won a bronze medal in the 90 kg category at the 1960 Games and a silver in 1964. In addition he won no fewer than four world titles.

In 1984, David Mercer, a 23-year-old engineer from Manchester picked up the bronze medal in the same category.

THE STARS

Most famous of modern lifters must be the aforementioned Vassiliy Alexeyev of the Soviet Union. He broke no fewer than 87 world records between 1970 and 1977 in addition to gaining his two Olympic titles.

A typical Alexeyev diet during that period was:
Breakfast: 36 egg omelette
Lunch: six large steaks washed down with 20 pints of beer
Dinner: A repeat of lunch.
Vassiliy listed his hobby as . . . cooking!

Not a lot of people know that

• The best bantamweights (56 kg) of the present day lift heavier weights than the heavyweights (110 kg) of the pre-Second World War Olympics.
• The silver medallist in the 82.5 kg category in 1948, Harold Sakata of the USA, later became an actor. You may remember him best as 'Oddjob' in the James Bond Film, *Goldfinger*.
• Until the seventies, weightlifters trained at the most every other day. The Bulgarians, however, created something of a revolution in the sport, asking their top competitors to train as much as three times every day. The rest of the world followed.

VENUE

Olympic Weightlifting Gymnasium, Olympic Park. Capacity 4000.

RESULTS

Flyweight up to 52 kg (8 st 3 lb)

	Gold	Silver	Bronze
1972	Zygmunt Smalcerz (POL) 337.5 kg	Lajos Szuecs (HUN) 330 kg	Sandor Holczreiter (HUN) 327.5 kg
1976	Aleksandr Voronin (URS) 242.5 kg =WR	Gyorgy Koszegi (HUN) 237.5 kg	Mohammad Nassiri (IRN) 235 kg
1980	Kanybek Osmonaliev (URS) 245 kg OR	Bong Chol Ho (PRK) 245 kg OR	Gyong Si Han (PRK) 245 kg OR
1984	Guoqiang Zeng (CHN) 235 kg	Peishun Zhou (CHN) 235 kg	Kazushito Manabe (JPN) 232.5 kg
1988	Final on 18 September		

Bantamweight up to 56 kg (8 st 12 lb)

Gold	Silver	Bronze
1948 Joseph di Pietro (USA) 307.5 kg WR	Julian Creus (GBR) 297.5 kg	Richard Tom (USA) 295 kg
1952 Ivan Udodov (URS) 315 kg OR	Mahmoud Namdjou (IRN) 307.5 kg	Ali Mirzai (ROM) 300 kg
1956 Charles Vinci (USA) 342.5 kg	Vladimir Stogov (URS) 337.5 kg	Mahmoud Namdjou (IRN) 332.5 kg
1960 Charles Vinci (USA) 345 kg =WR	Yoshinobu Miyake (JPN) 337.5 kg	Esmail Khan (IRN) 330 kg
1964 Aleksey Vakhonin (URS) 357.5 kg WR	Imre Földi (HUN) 355 kg	Shiro Ichinoseki (JPN) 347.5 kg
1968 Mohammad Nassiri (IRN) 367.5 kg =WR	Imre Földi (HUN) 367.5 kg =WR	Henryk Trebicki (POL) 357.5 kg
1972 Imre Földi (HUN) 377.5 kg WR	Mohammad Nassiri (IRN) 370 kg	Gennadiy Chetin (URS) 367.5 kg
1976 Norair Nurikyan (BUL) 262.5 kg WR	Grzegorz Cziura (POL) 252.5 kg	Kenkichi Ando (JPN) 250 kg
1980 Daniel Nunez (CUB) 275 kg WR	Yurik Sarkisian (URS) 270 kg	Tadeusz Dembonczyk (POL) 265 kg
1984 Shude Wu (CHN) 267.45 kg	Runming Lai (CHN) 265 kg	Masahiro Kotaka (JPN) 252.5 kg
1988 Final on 19 September		

Featherweight up to 60 kg (9 st 8 lb)

Gold	Silver	Bronze
1920 Frans de Haes (BEL) 220 kg	Alfred Schmidt (EST) 212.5 kg	Eugène Ryther (SUI) 210 kg
1924* Pierino Gabetti (ITA) 402.5 kg	Andreas Stadler (AUT) 385 kg	Arthur Reinmann (SUI) 382.5 kg
1928 Franz Andrysek (AUT) 287.5 kg OR	Pierino Gabetti (ITA) 282.5 kg	Hans Wölpert (GER) 282.5 kg
1932 Raymond Suvigny (FRA) 287.5 kg =OR	Hans Wölpert (GER) 282.5 kg	Anthony Terlazzo (USA) 280 kg
1936 Anthony Terlazzo (USA) 312.5 kg WR	Saleh Mohammed Soliman (EGY) 305 kg	Ibrahim Shams (EGY) 300 kg
1948 Mahmoud Fayad (EGY) 332.5 kg WR	Rodney Wilkes (TRI) 317.5 kg	Jaffar Salmassi (IRN) 312.5 kg
1952 Rafael Chimishkyan (URS) 337.5 kg WR	Nikolai Saksonov (URS) 332.5 kg	Rodney Wilkes (TRI) 332.5 kg
1956 Isaac Berger (USA) 352.5 kg WR	Yevgeniy Minayev (URS) 342.5 kg	Marian Zielinski (POL) 335 kg
1960 Yevgeniy Minayev (URS) 372.5 kg =WR	Isaac Berger (USA) 362.5 kg	Sebastiano Mannironi (ITA) 352.5 kg
1964 Yoshinobu Miyake (JPN) 397.5 kg WR	Isaac Berger (USA) 382.5 kg	Mieczyslaw Nowak (POL) 377.5 kg

* Total of five lifts.

1968	Yoshinobu Miyake (JPN) 392.5 kg	Dito Shanidze (URS) 387.5 kg	Yoshiyuki Miyake (JPN) 385 kg
1972	Norair Nurikyan (BUL) 402.5 kg =WR	Dito Shanidze (URS) 400 kg	Janos Benedek (HUN) 390 kg
1976	Nikolai Kolesnikov (URS) 285 kg =WR	Georgi Todorov (BUL) 280 kg	Kazumasa Hirai (JPN) 275 kg
1980	Viktor Mazin (URS) 290 kg OR	Stefan Dimitrov (BUL) 287.5 kg	Marek Seweryn (POL) 282.5 kg
1984	Weiqiang Chen (CHN) 282.5 kg	Gelu Radu (ROM) 280 kg	Wen-Yee Tsai (TPE) 272.5 kg
1988	Final on 20 September		

Lightweight up to 67.5 kg (10 st 9 lb)

	Gold	*Silver*	*Bronze*
1920	Alfred Neuland (EST) 257.5 kg	Louis Williquet (BEL) 240 kg	Florimond Rooms (BEL) 230 kg
1924*	Edmond Decottignies (FRA) 440 kg	Anton Zwerina (AUT) 427.5 kg	Bohumil Durdis (TCH) 425 kg
1928†	Kurt Helbig (GER) 322.5 kg Hans Haas (AUT) 322.5 kg	—	Fernand Arnout (FRA) 302.5 kg
1932	René Duverger (FRA) 325 kg =WR	Hans Haas (AUT) 307.5 kg	Gastone Pierini (ITA) 302.5 kg
1936†	Anwar Mohammed Misbah (EGY) 342.5 kg WR Robert Fein (AUT) 342.5 kg WR	—	Karl Jansen (GER) 327.5 kg
1948	Ibrahim Shams (EGY) 360 kg OR	Attia Hamouda (EGY) 360 kg OR	James Halliday (GBR) 340 kg
1952	Tommy Kono (USA) 362.5 kg OR	Yevgeniy Lopatin (URS) 350 kg	Verne Barberis (AUS) 350 kg
1956	Igor Rybak (URS) 380 kg OR	Ravil Khabutdinov (URS) 372.5 kg	Chang-Hee Kim (KOR) 370 kg
1960	Viktor Bushuyev (URS) 397.5 kg WR	Howe-Liang Tan (SIN) 380 kg	Abdul Wahid Aziz (IRQ) 380 kg
1964	Waldemar Baszanowski (POL) 432.5 kg WR	Vladimir Kaplunov (URS) 432.5 kg WR	Marian Zielinski (POL) 420 kg
1968	Waldemar Baszanowski (POL) 437.5 kg OR	Parviz Jalayer (IRN) 422.5 kg	Marian Zielinski (POL) 420 kg
1972	Mukharbi Kirzhinov (URS) 460 kg WR	Mladen Koutchev (BUL) 450 kg	Zbigniev Kaczmarek (POL) 437.5 kg
1976**	Pyotr Korol (URS) 305 kg	Daniel Senet (FRA) 300 kg	Kazimierz Czarnecki (POL) 295 kg
1980	Yanko Roussev (BUL) 342.5 kg WR	Joachim Kunz (GDR) 335 kg	Mintcho Pachov (BUL) 435 kg
1984	Jingyuan Yao (CHN) 320 kg	Andrei Socaci (ROM) 312.5 kg	Jouni Gronman (FIN) 312.5 kg
1988	Final on 21 September		

* Aggregate of five lifts.
† Prior to the bodyweight tie-breaker.
** Kaczmarek (POL) finished first but was disqualified.

Middleweight up to 75 kg (11 st 11 lb)

	Gold	Silver	Bronze
1920	Henri Gance (FRA) 245 kg	Pietro Bianchi★ (ITA) 237.5 kg	Albert Pettersson (SWE) 237.5 kg
1924†	Carlo Galimberti (ITA) 492.5 kg	Alfred Neuland (EST) 455 kg	Jaan Kikas (EST) 450 kg
1928	Roger François (FRA) 335 kg WR	Carlo Galimberti (ITA) 332.5 kg	August Scheffer (HOL) 327.5 kg
1932	Rudolf Ismayr (GER) 345 kg WR	Carlo Galimberti (ITA) 340 kg	Karl Hipfinger (AUT) 337.5 kg
1936	Khadr El Thouni (EGY) 387.5 kg WR	Rudolf Ismayr (GER) 352.5 kg	Adolf Wagner (GER) 352.5 kg
1948	Frank Spellman (USA) 390 kg OR	Peter George (USA) 382.5 kg	Sung-Jip Kim (KOR) 380 kg
1952	Peter George (USA) 400 kg OR	Gerard Gratton (CAN) 390 kg	Sung-Jip Kim (KOR) 382.5 kg
1956	Fyodor Bogdanovski (URS) 420 kg WR	Peter George (USA) 412.5 kg	Ermanno Pignatti (ITA) 382.5 kg
1960	Aleksandr Kurinov (URS) 437.5 kg WR	Tommy Kono (USA) 427.5 kg	Gyözö Veres (HUN) 405 kg
1964	Hans Zdrazila (TCH) 445 kg =WR	Viktor Kurentsov (URS) 440 kg	Masashi Ouchi (JPN) 437.5 kg
1968	Viktor Kurentsov (URS) 475 kg OR	Masashi Ouchi (JPN) 455 kg	Károly Bakos (HUN) 440 kg
1972	Yordan Bikov (BUL) 485 kg WR	Mohamed Trabulsi (LIB) 472.5 kg	Anselmo Silvino (ITA) 470 kg
1976	Yordan Mitkov (BUL) 335 kg OR	Vartan Militosyan (URS) 330 kg	Peter Wenzel (GDR) 327.5 kg
1980	Asen Zlatev (BUL) 360 kg WR	Aleksandr Pervy (URS) 357.5 kg	Nedeltcho Kolev (BUL) 345 kg
1984	Karl-Heinz Radschinsky (FRG) 340 kg	Jacques Demers (CAN) 335 kg	Dragomir Cioroslan (ROM) 332.5 kg

1988   Final on 22 September

★ Drew lots for silver and bronze.
† Total of five lifts.

Light heavyweight up to 82.5 kg (13 st)

	Gold	Silver	Bronze
1920	Ernest Cadine (FRA) 290 kg	Fritz Hünenberger (SUI) 275 kg	Erik Pettersson (SWE) 272.5 kg
1924★	Charles Rigoulot (FRA) 502.5 kg	Fritz Hünenberger (SUI) 490 kg	Leopold Friedrich (AUT) 490 kg
1928	Said Nosseir (EGY) 355 kg WR	Louis Hostin (FRA) 352.5 kg	Johannes Verheijen (HOL) 337.5 kg
1932	Louis Hostin (FRA) 365 kg WR	Svend Olsen (DEN) 360 kg	Henry Duey (USA) 330 kg

★ Total of five lifts.

	Gold	Silver	Bronze
1936	Louis Hostin (FRA) 372.5 kg OR	Eugen Deutsch (GER) 365 kg	Ibrahim Wasif (EGY) 360 kg
1948	Stanley Stanczyk (USA) 417.5 kg OR	Harold Sakata (USA) 380 kg	Gösta Magnusson (SWE) 375 kg
1952	Trofim Lomakin (URS) 417.5 kg = OR	Stanley Stanczyk (USA) 415 kg	Arkadiy Vorobyev (URS) 407.5 kg
1956	Tommy Kono (USA) 447.5 kg WR	Vassiliy Stepanov (URS) 427.5 kg	James George (USA) 417.5 kg
1960	Ireneusz Palinski (POL) 442.5 kg	James George (USA) 430 kg	Jan Bochenek (POL) 420 kg
1964	Rudolf Plukfelder (URS) 475 kg OR	Géza Toth (HUN) 467.5 kg	Gyözö Veres (HUN) 467.5 kg
1968	Boris Selitsky (URS) 485 kg = WR	Vladimir Belyayev (URS) 485 kg = WR	Norbert Ozimek (POL) 472.5 kg
1972	Leif Jenssen (NOR) 507.5 kg OR	Norbert Ozimek (POL) 497.5 kg	György Horvath (HUN) 495 kg
1976†	Valeriy Shary (URS) 365 kg OR	Trendafil Stoichev (BUL) 360 kg	Peter Baczako (HUN) 345 kg
1980	Yurik Vardanyan (URS) 400 kg WR	Blagoi Blagoyev (BUL) 372.5 kg	Dusan Poliacik (TCH) 367.5 kg
1984	Petre Becheru (ROM) 355 kg	Robert Kabbas (AUS) 342.5 kg	Ryoji Isaoka (JPN) 340 kg

1988   Final on 24 September

† Blagoyev originally finished in second place but was disqualified.

Middle heavyweight up to 90 kg (14 st 2 lb)

	Gold	Silver	Bronze
1952	Norbert Schemansky (USA) 445 kg WR	Grigoriy Nowak (URS) 410 kg	Lennox Kilgour (TRI) 402.5 kg
1956	Arkadiy Vorobyev (URS) 462.5 kg WR	David Sheppard (USA) 442.5 kg	Jean Debuf (FRA) 425 kg
1960	Arkadiy Vorobyev (URS) 472.5 kg WR	Trofim Lomakin (URS) 457.5 kg	Louis Martin (GBR) 445 kg
1964	Vladimir Golovanov (URS) 487.5 kg WR	Louis Martin (GBR) 475 kg	Ireneusz Palinski (POL) 467.5 kg
1968	Kaarlo Kangasniemi (FIN) 517.5 kg	Jan Talts (URS) 507.5 kg	Marek Golab (POL) 495 kg
1972	Andon Nikolov (BUL) 525 kg OR	Atanas Chopov (BUL) 517.5 kg	Hans Bettembourg (SWE) 512.5 kg
1976	David Rigert (URS) 382.5 kg OR	Lee James (USA) 362.5 kg	Atanas Chopov (BUL) 360 kg
1980	Peter Baczako (HUN) 377.5 kg	Rumen Alexandrov (BUL) 375 kg	Frank Mantek (GDR) 370 kg
1984	Nicu Vlad (ROM) 392.5 kg OR	Dumitru Petre (ROM) 360 kg	David Mercer (GBR) 352.5 kg

1988   Final on 25 September

First heavyweight up to 100 kg (15 st 10 lb)

	Gold	Silver	Bronze
1980	Ota Zaremba (TCH) 395 kg OR	Igor Nitikin (URS) 392.5 kg	Alberto Blanco (CUB) 385 kg
1984	Rolf Milser (FRG) 385 kg	Vasile Gropa (ROM) 382.5 kg	Pekka Niemi (FIN) 367.5 kg
1988	Final on 26 September		

Second heavyweight up to 110 kg (17 st 4 lb)

From 1896 until 1920 the rules were different. Lifts were either with one hand, two hands or dumb-bell. Only two handed lifts are listed below

	Gold	Silver	Bronze
1896	Viggo Jensen (DEN)* 111.5 kg	Launceston Eliot (GBR) 111.5 kg	Sotirios Versis (GRE) 100 kg
1904	Perikles Kakousis (GRE) 111.58 kg	Oscar Osthoff (USA) 84.36 kg	Frank Kungler (USA) 79.83
1906	Dimitrios Tofalos (GRE) 142.5 kg	Josef Steinbach (AUT) 136.5 kg	Alexandre Maspoli (FRA) 129.5 kg Heinrich Rondi (GER) 129.5 kg Heinrich Schneidereit (GER) 129.5 kg
1920	Filippo Bottino (ITA) 270 kg	Joseph Alzin (LUX) 255 kg	Louis Bernot (FRA) 250 kg
1924†	Giuseppe Tonani (ITA) 517.5 kg	Franz Aigner (AUT) 515 kg	Harald Tammer (EST) 497.5 kg
1928	Josef Strassberger (GER) 372.5 kg WR	Arnold Luhaäär (EST) 360 kg	Jaroslav Skobla (TCH) 357.5 kg
1932	Jaroslav Skobla (TCH) 380 kg OR	Václav Psenicka (TCH) 377.5 kg	Josef Strassberger (GER) 377.5 kg
1936	Josef Manger (AUT) 410 kg WR	Václav Psenicka (TCH) 402.5 kg	Arnold Luhaäär (EST) 400 kg
1948	John Davis (USA) 452.5 kg OR	Norbert Schemansky (USA) 425 kg	Abraham Charité (HOL) 412.5 kg
1952	John Davis (USA) 460 kg OR	James Bradford (USA) 437.5 kg	Humberto Selvetti (ARG) 432.5 kg
1956	Paul Anderson (USA) 500 kg OR	Humberto Selvetti (ARG) 500 kg OR	Alberto Pigaiani (ITA) 452.5 kg
1960	Yuriy Vlasov (URS) 537.5 kg WR	James Bradford (USA) 512.5 kg	Norbert Schemansky (USA) 500 kg
1964	Leonid Zhabotinsky (URS) 572.5 kg OR	Yuriy Vlasov (URS) 570 kg	Norbert Schemansky (USA) 537.5 kg
1968	Leonid Zhabotinsky (URS) 572.5 kg = OR	Serge Reding (BEL) 555 kg	Joseph Dube (USA) 555 kg
1972	Jan Talts (URS) 580 kg OR	Alexandre Kraitchev (BUL) 562.5 kg	Stefan Grützner (GDR) 555 kg

* Jensen awarded gold as his style was judged to be better.
† Total of five lifts.

1976**	Yuriy Zaitsev (URS) 385 kg	Krastio Semerdiev (BUL) 385 kg	Tadeusz Rutkowski (POL) 377.5 kg
1980	Leonid Taranenko (URS) 422.5 kg WR	Valentin Christov (BUL) 405 kg	György Sealai (URS) 390 kg
1984	Noberto Oberburger (ITA) 390 kg	Stefan Tasnadi (ROM) 380 kg	Guy Carlton (USA) 377.5 kg

1988   Final on 27 September

**Christov (BUL) finished first but was later disqualified.

Super heavyweight over 110 kg (17 st 4 lb)

	Gold	*Silver*	*Bronze*
1972	Vasiliy Alexeyev (URS) 640 kg OR	Rudolf Mang (GDR) 610 kg	Gerd Bonk (GDR) 572.5 kg
1976	Vasiliy Alexeyev (URS) 440 kg OR	Gerd Bonk (GDR) 405 kg	Helmut Losch (GDR) 387.5 kg
1980	Sultan Rakhmanov (URS) 440 kg = OR	Jürgen Heuser (GDR) 410 kg	Tadeusz Rutkowski (POL) 407.5 kg
1984	Dinko Lukim (AUS) 412.5 kg	Mario Martinez (USA) 410 kg	Manfred Nerlinger (FRG) 397.5 kg

1988   Final on 29 September

WRESTLING

What you must put out of your mind immediately is the grappling you may occasionally watch by pressing the wrong switch on your television on a Saturday afternoon. That is strictly showbiz and has nothing whatsoever to do with Olympic wrestling.

The sport goes back as far as time, probably the oldest of the 23 in these Games.

There are two types of wrestling in the Olympics: freestyle and Greco-Roman. Greco-Roman was included in the first modern celebration in 1896, with no weight categories, while freestyle was introduced with weight divisions in 1904.

THE STYLES

Greco-Roman: This form prohibits any holds below the waist.

Freestyle: In this form, more varied tactics are allowed.

In both styles, however, there are many restrictions as to kind of holds that may be used. For example throat holds or armlocks applied to the forearm are against the rules. There are many more.

THE COMPETITION

The Soviet Union is the most successful nation in the sport at both Greco-Roman and freestyle and is likely to be so once again in Seoul.

In their absence, the United States dominated in Los Angeles in 1984 with seven gold medals in freestyle and two in Greco-Roman.

As in other sports, the Koreans on home territory will be likely to do well, despite the increased competition from four years ago when they won a good crop of medals including two gold. Look out, too, for the Bulgarians and Rumanians. Turkey, who were a very strong wrestling nation, seem to have faded.

WEIGHT CATEGORIES

There are ten categories and the limits are exactly the same for both styles. They are as follows:

Up to
48 kg	(Light-flyweight)
52 kg	(Flyweight)
57 kg	(Bantamweight)
62 kg	(Featherweight)
68 kg	(Lightweight)
74 kg	(Welterweight)
82 kg	(Middleweight)
90 kg	(Light-heavyweight)
100 kg	(Heavyweight)
	Unlimited

THE RULES

Bouts last six minutes with a rest of one minute after the first three minutes.

The object is to 'pin' the opponent's shoulders on the mat for two seconds, to the satisfaction of the officials. The bout is then terminated. In practice, at Olympic level where most of the competitors are of a very high standard, the number of bouts won this way are few. Most are won on points on the

Freestyle

Greco-Roman

and judo, just one bronze medal is awarded in each weight category. Original opponents are drawn by lot. Depending on the number of wrestlers, competition can be based on two or more 'pools'. You could be forgiven for thinking that learning the rules is more difficult than learning to wrestle.

Three officials control the bout, a mat chairman, a referee and judge. The referee wears a red band on one arm and blue on the other. He signals the number of points awarded at any time to the wrestler concerned. The judge is there for confirmation and is overall scorer.

THE EQUIPMENT

The Mat

This equates with the 'ring' in boxing. There is a one-metre diameter circle in the centre where the bout begins or resumes.

Dress

Tight-fitting one-piece suit (the garment must not be used to provide grip, as in judo, for example).

Footwear is similar to boxing-style boots and knee supports are allowed.

THE STARS

Three men have won three gold medals in the sport. Carl Westergren (SWE), Ivan Johannson (SWE) and Alexandr Medved (URS). Johannson and Kristjan Palusalu (Estonia) won gold medals in both styles at the same Games, Johannson in 1932, Palusalu in 1936.

basis of between one and four points awarded for various holds and throws.

And just to make it more complicated, these points are converted into 'penalty' points. The highest penalty mark is zero. That would be awarded to a competitor who had won by pinning his opponent to the mat (equivalent to a knockout in boxing). If a wrestler wins the bout by, say, between eight and 11 points, i.e. an emphatic win, he receives half a penalty point. If for example he loses by that sort of points margin he receives 3.5 penalty points. There are various stages in between.

The object of the exercise is, of course, to win as well as possible, thus incurring as few penalty points as possible.

The penalty points are accrued after each bout and when a wrestler acquires a total of six, he drops out of the competition. Eventually competition is reduced to the final three medallists who wrestle each other to decide who actually receives the gold, silver or bronze. If they have already met each other, penalty points from those earlier bouts are carried forward. Unlike boxing

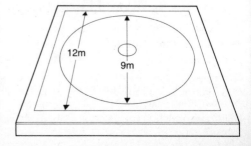

12m

9m

THE BRITISH

Way back in 1908 when the games were held in London, Britain won three gold medals and four silver. Since then medals have been few and far between and never better than bronze. The last was won by Noel Loban in Los Angeles in 1984.

All the British medals were won in freestyle wrestling. None have been won in Greco-Roman.

Not a lot of people know that

● While there are now time limits on bouts, it was not always so. In the Greco-Roman middleweight class in 1912, Alpo Asikainen (FIN) and Martin Klein (URS) were still locked in combat after 11 hours and 40 minutes. Klein won, but was so exhausted by his endeavours he could not compete in the final.

● In 1948, Turkey won six gold, four silver and a bronze and their government was so pleased they rewarded their competitors with gifts and money, thus disbarring them from future Olympic competition.

● Noel Loban, Britain's last medallist in the sport was a member of the USA team for the 1980 Games. The Americans of course pulled out and Loban, who was born in Britain and who was eligible for a British passport, offered himself to the British team. His offer was ignored then, but by 1984 he had established himself in England.

● Ken Richmond, who won a bronze medal in 1952, was the man who struck the gong for Rank films.

VENUE

Sangmu Gymnasium. 4 km from Olympic village. Capacity 5000.

RESULTS

Freestyle – light flyweight up to 48 kg (7 st 7 lb)

	Gold	Silver	Bronze
1904	Robert Curry (USA)	John Heim (USA)	Gustav Thiefenthaler (USA)
1972	Roman Dmitriev (URS)	Ognian Nikolov (BUL)	Ebrahim Javadpour (IRN)
1976	Khassan Issaev (BUL)	Roman Dmitriev (URS)	Akira Kudo (JPN)
1980	Claudio Pollio (ITA)	Se Hong Jang (PRK)	Sergey Kornilayev (URS)
1984	Robert Weaver (USA)	Takashi Irie (JPN)	Gab-Do Son (KOR)
1988	Final on 29 September		

Freestyle – flyweight up to 52 kg (8 st 2½ lb)

	Gold	Silver	Bronze
1904	George Mehnert (USA)	Gustave Bauer (USA)	William Nelson (USA)
1948	Lennart Viitala (FIN)	Halit Balamir (TUR)	Thure Johansson (SWE)
1952	Hasan Gemici (TUR)	Yushu Kitano (JPN)	Mahmoud Mollaghassemi (IRN)
1956	Mirian Tsalkalamanidze (URS)	Mohamad-Ali Khojastehpour (IRN)	Hüseyin Akbas (TUR)
1960	Ahmet Bilek (TUR)	Masayuki Matsubara (JPN)	Mohamad Saifpour Saidabadi (IRN)

1964	Yoshikatsu Yoshida (JPN)	Chang-sun Chang (KOR)	Said Aliaakbar Haydari (IRN)
1968	Shigeo Nakata (JPN)	Richard Sanders (USA)	Surenjav Sikhbaatar (MGL)
1972	Kiyomi Kato (JPN)	Arsen Alakhverdiev (URS)	Hyong Kim Gwong (PRK)
1976	Yuji Takada (JPN)	Aleksandr Ivanov (URS)	Hae-Sup Jeon (KOR)
1980	Anatoliy Beloglazov (URS)	Wladyslaw Stecyk (POL)	Nermedin Selimov (BUL)
1984	Saban Trstena (YUG)	Jong-Kyu Kim (KOR)	Yuji Takada (JPN)
1988	Final on 30 September		

Freestyle – bantamweight up to 57 kg (9 st)

	Gold	*Silver*	*Bronze*
1904	Isidor Niflot (USA)	August Wester (USA)	Z. B. Strebler (USA)
1908	George Mehnert (USA)	William Press (GBR)	Aubert Côté (CAN)
1924	Kustaa Pihlajamäki (FIN)	Kaarlo Mäkinen (FIN)	Bryant Hines (USA)
1928	Kaarlo Mäkinen (FIN)	Edmond Spapen (BEL)	James Trifunov (CAN)
1932	Robert Pearce (USA)	Ödön Zombori (HUN)	Aatos Jaskari (FIN)
1936	Ödön Zombori (HUN)	Ross Flood (USA)	Johannes Herbert (GER)
1948	Nasuh Akar (TUR)	Gerald Leeman (USA)	Charles Kouyos (FRA)
1952	Shohachi Ishii (JPN)	Rashid Mamedbekov (URS)	Kha-Shaba Jadav (IND)
1956	Mustafa Dagistanli (TUR)	Mohamad Yaghoubi (IRN)	Mikhail Chakhov (URS)
1960	Terrence McCann (USA)	Nejdet Zalev (BUL)	Tadeusz Trojanowski (POL)
1964	Yojiro Uetake (JPN)	Hüseyin Akbas (TUR)	Aidyn Ibragimov (URS)
1968	Yojiro Uetake (JPN)	Donald Behm (USA)	Abutaleb Gorgori (IRN)
1972	Hideaki Yanagide (JPN)	Richard Sanders (USA)	László Klinga (HUN)
1976	Vladimir Yumin (URS)	Hans-Dieter Brüchert (GDR)	Masao Arai (JPN)
1980	Sergey Beloglazov (URS)	Ho Pyong Li (PRK)	Dugarsuren Ouinbold (MGL)
1984	Hideaki Tomiyama (JPN)	Barry Davis (USA)	Eui-Kon Kim (KOR)
1988	Final on 1 October		

Freestyle – featherweight up to 62 kg (9 st 10 lb)

	Gold	*Silver*	*Bronze*
1904	Benjamin Bradshaw (USA)	Theodore McLear (USA)	Charles Clapper (USA)
1908	George Dole (USA)	James Slim (GBR)	William McKie (GBR)
1920	Charles Ackerly (USA)	Samuel Gerson (USA)	P. W. Bernard (GBR)
1924	Robin Reed (USA)	Chester Newton (USA)	Katsutoshi Naito (JPN)
1928	Allie Morrison (USA)	Kustaa Pihlajamäki (FIN)	Hans Minder (SUI)
1932	Hermanni Pihlajamäki (FIN)	Edgar Nemir (USA)	Einar Karlsson (SWE)
1936	Kustaa Pihlajamäki (FIN)	Francis Millard (USA)	Gösta Jönsson (SWE)
1948	Gazanfer Bilge (TUR)	Ivar Sjölin (SWE)	Adolf Müller (SUI)
1952	Bayram Sit (TUR)	Nasser Guivehtchi (IRN)	Josiah Henson (USA)
1956	Shozo Sasahara (JPN)	Joseph Mewis (BEL)	Erkki Penttilä (FIN)
1960	Mustafa Dagistanli (TUR)	Stantcho Kolev (BUL)	Vladimir Rubashvili (URS)

1964	Osamu Watanabe (JPN)	Stantcho Kolev (BUL)	Nodar Khokhashvili (URS)
1968	Masaaki Kaneko (JPN)	Enyu Todorov (BUL)	Shamseddin Seyed-Abbassi (IRN)
1972	Zagalav Abdulbekov (URS)	Vehbi Akdag (TUR)	Ivan Krastev (BUL)
1976	Jung-Mo Yang (KOR)	Zeveg Oidov (MGL)	Gene Davis (USA)
1980	Magomedgasan Abushev (URS)	Mikho Doukov (BUL)	Georges Hadjiioannidis (GRE)
1984	Randy Lewis (USA)	Kosei Akaishi (JPN)	Jung-Keun Lee (KOR)
1988	Final on 29 September		

Freestyle – lightweight up to 68 kg (10 st 10 lb)

	Gold	Silver	Bronze
1904	Otto Roehm (USA)	Rudolph Tesing (USA)	Albert Zirkel (USA)
1908	George de Relwyskow (GBR)	William Wood (GBR)	Albert Gingell (GBR)
1920	Kalle Anttila (FIN)	Gottfrid Svensson (SWE)	Peter Wright (GBR)
1924	Russell Vis (USA)	Volmart Wickström (FIN)	Arvo Haavisto (FIN)
1928	Osvald Käpp (EST)	Charles Pacôme (FRA)	Eino Leino (FIN)
1932	Charles Pacôme (FRA)	Károly Kárpáti (HUN)	Gustaf Klarén (SWE)
1936	Károly Kárpáti (HUN)	Wolfgang Ehrl (GER)	Hermanni Pihlajamäki (FIN)
1948	Celál Atik (TUR)	Gösta Frandfors (SWE)	Hermann Baumann (SUI)
1952	Olle Anderberg (SWE)	Thomas Evans (USA)	Djahanbakte Tovfighe (IRN)
1956	Emamali Habibi (IRN)	Shigeru Kasahara (JPN)	Alimberg Bestayev (URS)
1960	Shelby Wilson (USA)	Viktor Sinyavskiy (URS)	Enyu Dimov (BUL)
1964	Enyu Valtchev (formerly Dimov) (BUL)	Klaus-Jürgen Rost (GER)	Iwao Horiuchi (JPN)
1968	Abdollah Movahed Ardabili (IRN)	Enyu Valtchev (formerly Dimov) (BUL)	Sereeter Danzandarjaa (MGL)
1972	Dan Gable (USA)	Kikuo Wada (JPN)	Ruslan Ashuraliev (URS)
1976	Pavel Pinigin (URS)	Lloyd Keaser (USA)	Yasaburo Sugawara (JPN)
1980	Saipulla Absaidov (URS)	Ivan Yaknov (BUL)	Saban Sejdi (YUG)
1984	In-Tak You (KOR)	Andrew Rein (USA)	Jukka Rauhala (FIN)
1988	Final on 1 October		

Freestyle – welterweight up to 74 kg (11 st 9 lb)

	Gold	Silver	Bronze
1904	Charles Erickson (USA)	William Beckmann (USA)	Jerry Winholtz (USA)
1924	Hermann Gehri (SUI)	Eino Leino (FIN)	Otto Müller (SUI)
1928	Arvo Haavisto (FIN)	Lloyd Appleton (USA)	Maurice Letchford (CAN)
1932	Jack van Bebber (USA)	Daniel MacDonald (CAN)	Eino Leino (FIN)
1936	Frank Lewis (USA)	Ture Andersson (SWE)	Joseph Schleimer (CAN)
1948	Yasar Dogu (TUR)	Richard Garrard (AUS)	Leland Merrill (USA)
1952	William Smith (USA)	Per Berlin (SWE)	Abdullah Modjtabavi (IRN)

1956	Mitsuo Ikeda (JPN)	Ibrahim Zengin (TUR)	Vaktang Balavadze (URS)
1960	Douglas Blubaugh (USA)	Ismail Ogan (TUR)	Mohammed Bashir (PAK)
1964	Ismail Ogan (TUR)	Guliko Sagaradze (URS)	Mohamad-Ali Sanatkaran (IRN)
1968	Mahmut Atalay (TUR)	Daniel Robin (FRA)	Dagvasuren Purev (MGL)
1972	Wayne Wells (USA)	Jan Karlsson (SWE)	Adolf Seger (FRG)
1976	Jiichiro Date (JPN)	Mansour Barzegar (IRN)	Stanley Dziedzic (USA)
1980	Valentin Raitchev (BUL)	Jamtsying Davaajav (MGL)	Dan Karabin (TCH)
1984	David Schultz (USA)	Martin Knosp (FRG)	Saban Sejdi (YUG)
1988	Final on 30 September		

Freestyle – middleweight up to 82 kg (12 st 12 lb)

	Gold	*Silver*	*Bronze*
1908	Stanley Bacon (GBR)	George de Relwyskow (GBR)	Frederick Beck (GBR)
1920	Eino Leino (FIN)	Väinö Penttala (FIN)	Charles Johnson (USA)
1924	Fritz Hagmann (SUI)	Pierre Ollivier (BEL)	Vilho Pekkala (FIN)
1928	Ernst Kyburz (SUI)	Donald Stockton (CAN)	Samuel Rabin (GBR)
1932	Ivar Johansson (SWE)	Kyösti Luukko (FIN)	József Tunyogi (HUN)
1936	Emile Poilvé (FRA)	Richard Voliva (USA)	Ahmet Kireiççi (TUR)
1948	Glen Brand (USA)	Adil Candemir (TUR)	Erik Lindén (SWE)
1952	David Tsimakuridze (URS)	Gholam-Reza Takhti (IRN)	György Gurics (HUN)
1956	Nikola Stantschev (BUL)	Daniel Hodge (USA)	Georgiy Skhirtladze (URS)
1960	Hansan Güngör (TUR)	Georgiy Skhirtladze (URS)	Hans Antonsson (SWE)
1964	Prodan Gardschev (BUL)	Hasan Güngör (TUR)	Daniel Brand (USA)
1968	Boris Gurevitch (URS)	Munkbat Jigjid (MGL)	Prodan Gardschev (BUL)
1972	Levan Tediashvili (URS)	John Peterson (USA)	Vasile Jorga (ROM)
1976	John Peterson (USA)	Viktor Novojilov (URS)	Adolf Seger (FRG)
1980	Ismail Abilov (BUL)	Magomedhan Aratsilov (URS)	Istvan Kovacs (HUN)
1984	Mark Schultz (USA)	Hideyuki Nagashima (JPN)	Chris Rinke (CAN)
1988	Final on 1 October		

Freestyle – light-heavyweight up to 90 kg (14 st 2 lb)

	Gold	*Silver*	*Bronze*
1920	Anders Larsson (SWE)	Charles Courant (SUI)	Walter Maurer (USA)
1924	John Spellman (USA)	Rudolf Svensson (SWE)	Charles Courant (SUI)
1928	Thure Sjöstedt (SWE)	Anton Bögli (SUI)	Henri Lefèbre (FRA)
1932	Peter Mehringer (USA)	Thure Sjöstedt (SWE)	Eddie Scarf (AUS)
1936	Knut Fridell (SWE)	August Neo (EST)	Erich Seibert (GER)
1948	Henry Wittenberg (USA)	Fritz Stöckli (SUI)	Bengt Fahlkvist (SWE)
1952	Wiking Palm (SWE)	Henry Wittenberg (USA)	Adil Atan (TUR)

1956	Gholam-Reza Tahkti (IRN)	Boris Kulayev (URS)	Peter Blair (USA)
1960	Ismet Atli (TUR)	Gholam-Reza Tahkti (IRN)	Anatoliy Albuı (URS)
1964	Aleksandr Medved (URS)	Ahmet Ayik (TUR)	Said Mustafov (BUL)
1968	Ahmet Ayik (TUR)	Shota Lomidze (URS)	József Csatári (HUN)
1972	Ben Peterson (USA)	Gennadiy Strakhov (URS)	Karoly Bajko (HUN)
1976	Levan Tediashvili (URS)	Ben Peterson (USA)	Stelica Morcov (ROM)
1980	Sanasar Oganesyan (URS)	Uwe Neupert (GDR)	Aleksandr Cichon (POL)
1984	Ed Banach (USA)	Akira Ohta (JPN)	Noel Loban (GBR)

1988   Final on 29 September

Freestyle – heavyweight up to 100 kg (15 st 10 lb)

	Gold	*Silver*	*Bronze*
1904	Bernhuff Hansen (USA)	Frank Kungler (USA)	Fred Warmbold (USA)
1908	George O'Kelly (GBR)	Jacob Gundersen (NOR)	Edmond Barrett (GBR)
1920	Robert Roth (SUI)	Nathan Pendleton (USA)	Ernst Nilsson (SWE) Frederick Meyer (USA)
1924	Harry Steele (USA)	Henry Wernli (SUI)	Andrew McDonald (GBR)
1928	Johan Richthoff (SWE)	Aukusti Sihovla (FIN)	Edmond Dame (FRA)
1932	Johan Richthoff (SWE)	John Riley (USA)	Nikolaus Hirschl (AUT)
1936	Kristjan Palusalu (EST)	Josef Klapuch (TCH)	Hjalmar Nyström (FIN)
1948	Gyula Bóbis (HUN)	Bertil Antonsson (SWE)	Joseph Armstrong (AUS)
1952	Arsen Mekokishvili (URS)	Bertil Antonsson (SWE)	Kenneth Richmond (GBR)
1956	Hamit Kaplan (TUR)	Hussein Mechmedov (BUL)	Taisto Kangasniemi (FIN)
1960	Wilfried Dietrich (GER)	Hamit Kaplan (TUR)	Savkus Dzarassov (URS)
1964	Aleksandr Ivanitsky (URS)	Liutvi Djiber (BUL)	Hamit Kaplan (TUR)
1968	Aleksandr Medved (URS)	Osman Duraleiv (BUL)	Wilfried Dietrich (FRG)
1972	Ivan Yarygin (URS)	Khorloo Baianmunkh (MGL)	József Csatári (HUN)
1976	Ivan Yarygin (URS)	Russell Hellickson (USA)	Dimo Kostov (BUL)
1980	Ilya Mate (YUG)	Slavtcho Tchervenkov (BUL)	Julius Strnisko (TCH)
1984	Lou Banach (USA)	Joseph Atiyeh (SYR)	Vasile Puscasu (ROM)

1988   Final on 30 September

Freestyle – super heavyweight over 100 kg (15 st 10 lb)

	Gold	*Silver*	*Bronze*
1972	Aleksandr Medved (URS)	Osman Duraliev (BUL)	Chris Taylor (USA)
1976	Soslan Andiev (URS)	Jozsef Balla (HUN)	Ladislau Simon (ROM)
1980	Soslan Andiev (URS)	Jozsef Balla (HUN)	Adam Sandurski (POL)
1984	Bruce Baumgartner (USA)	Bob Molle (CAN)	Ayhan Taskin (TUR)

1988   Final on 1 October

Greco-Roman light flyweight up to 48 kg (7 st 7 lb)

	Gold	Silver	Bronze
1972	Gheorghe Berceanu (ROM)	Rahim Aliabadi (IRN)	Stefan Anghelov (BUL)
1976	Aleksey Shumakov (URS)	Gheorghe Berceanu (ROM)	Stefan Anghelov (BUL)
1980	Zaksylik Ushkempirov (URS)	Constantin Alexandru (ROM)	Ferenc Seres (HUN)
1984	Vincenzo Maenza (ITA)	Markus Scherer (FRG)	Ikuzo Saito (JPN)

1988 Final on 20 September

Greco-Roman flyweight up to 52 kg (8 st 2½ lb)

	Gold	Silver	Bronze
1948	Pietro Lombardi (ITA)	Kenan Olcay (TUR)	Reino Kangasmäki (FIN)
1952	Boris Gurevich (URS)	Ignazio Fabra (ITA)	Leo Honkala (FIN)
1956	Nikolai Solovyov (URS)	Ignazio Fabra (ITA)	Durum Ali Egribas (TUR)
1960	Dumitru Pirvulescu (ROM)	Osman Sayed (UAR)	Mohamad Paziraye (IRN)
1964	Tsutomu Hanahara (JPN)	Angel Kerezov (BUL)	Dumitru Pirulescu (ROM)
1968	Petar Kirov (BUL)	Vladimir Bakulin (URS)	Miroslav Zeman (TCH)
1972	Petar Kirov (BUL)	Koichiro Hirayama (JPN)	Giuseppe Bognanni (ITA)
1976	Vitaliy Konstantinov (URS)	Nicu Ginga (ROM)	Koichiro Hirayama (JPN)
1980	Vakhtang Blagidze (URS)	Lajos Racz (HUN)	Mladen Mladenov (BUL)
1984	Atsuji Miyahara (JPN)	Daniel Aceves (MEX)	Dae-Du Bang (KOR)

1988 Final on 21 September

Greco-Roman – bantamweight up to 57 kg (9 st)

	Gold	Silver	Bronze
1924	Eduard Pütsep (EST)	Anselm Ahlfors (FIN)	Väinö Ikonen (FIN)
1928	Kurt Leucht (GER)	Jindrich Maudr (TCH)	Giovanni Gozzi (ITA)
1932	Jakob Brendel (GER)	Marcello Nizzola (ITA)	Louis François (FRA)
1936	Márton Lörincz (HUN)	Egon Svensson (SWE)	Jakob Brendel (GER)
1948	Kurt Pettersén (SWE)	Aly Mahmoud Hassan (EGY)	Habil Kaya (TUR)
1952	Imre Hódos (HUN)	Zakaria Chihab (LIB)	Artem Teryan (URS)
1956	Konstantin Vyrupayev (URS)	Evdin Vesterby (SWE)	Francisc Horvat (ROM)
1960	Oleg Karavayev (URS)	Ion Cernea (ROM)	Petrov Dinko (BUL)
1964	Masamitsu Ichiguchi (JPN)	Vladlen Trostiansky (URS)	Ion Cernea (ROM)
1968	János Varga (HUN)	Ion Baciu (ROM)	Ivan Kochergin (URS)
1972	Rustem Kazakov (URS)	Hans-Jürgen Veil (FRG)	Risto Björlin (FIN)
1976	Pertti Ukkola (FIN)	Ivan Frgic (YUG)	Farhat Mustafin (URS)
1980	Shamil Serikov (URS)	Jozef Lipien (POL)	Benni Ljungbeck (SWE)
1984	Pasquale Passarelli (FRG)	Masaki Eto (JPN)	Haralambos Holidis (GRE)

1988 Final on 22 September

Greco-Roman – featherweight up to 62 kg (9 st 10 lb)

	Gold	*Silver*	*Bronze*
1912	Kaarlo Koskelo (FIN)	Georg Gerstacker (GER)	Otto Lasanen (FIN)
1920	Oskari Friman (FIN)	Hekki Kähkönen (FIN)	Fridtjof Svensson (SWE)
1924	Kalle Antila (FIN)	Aleksanteri Toivola (FIN)	Erik Malmberg (SWE)
1928	Voldemar Väli (EST)	Erik Malmberg (SWE)	Giacomo Quaglia (ITA)
1932	Giovanni Gozzi (ITA)	Wolfgang Ehrl (GER)	Lauri Koskela (FIN)
1936	Yasar Erkan (TUR)	Aarne Reini (FIN)	Einar Karlsson (SWE)
1948	Mehmet Oktav (TUR)	Olle Anderberg (SWE)	Ferenc Tóth (HUN)
1952	Yakov Punkin (URS)	Imre Polyák (HUN)	Abdel Rashed (EGY)
1956	Rauno Mäkinen (FIN)	Imre Polyák (HUN)	Roman Dzneladze (URS)
1960	Müzahir Sille (TUR)	Imre Polyák (HUN)	Konstantin Vyrupayev (URS)
1964	Imre Polyák (HUN)	Roman Rurua (URS)	Branko Martinovič (YUG)
1968	Roman Rurua (URS)	Hideo Fujimoto (JPN)	Simeon Popescu (ROM)
1972	Gheorghi Markov (BUL)	Heinz-Helmut Wehling (GDR)	Kazimierz Lipien (POL)
1976	Kazimierz Lipien (POL)	Nelson Davidian (URS)	Laszlo Reczi (HUN)
1980	Stilianos Migiakis (GRE)	Istvan Toth (HUN)	Boris Kramorenko (URS)
1984	Weon-Kee Kim (KOR)	Kentolle Johansson (SWE)	Hugo Dietsche (SUI)
1988	Final on 20 September		

Greco-Roman lightweight up to 68 kg (10 st 10 lb)

	Gold	*Silver*	*Bronze*
1906	Rudolf Watzl (AUT)	Karl Karlsen (DEN)	Ferenc Holuban (HUN)
1908	Enrico Porro (ITA)	Nikolay Orlov (URS)	Avid Lindén-Linko (FIN)
1912	Eemil Wäre (FIN)	Gustaf Malmström (SWE)	Edvin Matiasson (SWE)
1920	Eemil Wäre (FIN)	Taavi Tamminen (FIN)	Fritjof Andersen (NOR)
1924	Oskari Friman (FIN)	Lajos Keresztes (HUN)	Kalle Westerlund (FIN)
1928	Lajos Keresztes (HUN)	Eduard Sperling (GER)	Eduard Westerlund (FIN)
1932	Erik Malmberg (SWE)	Abraham Kurland (DEN)	Eduard Sperling (GER)
1936	Lauri Koskela (FIN)	Josef Herda (TCH)	Voldemar Väli (EST)
1948	Gustaf Freij (SWE)	Aage Eriksen (NOR)	Károly Ferencz (HUN)
1952	Shazam Safin (URS)	Gustaf Freij (SWE)	Mikuláš Athanasov (TCH)
1956	Kyösti Lehtonen (FIN)	Riza Dogan (TUR)	Gyul Tóth (HUN)
1960	Avtandil Koridze (URS)	Branislav Martinovic (YUG)	Gustaf Freij (SWE)
1964	Kazim Ayvaz (TUR)	Valeriu Bularca (ROM)	David Gvantseladze (URS)
1968	Munji Mumemura (JPN)	Stevan Horvat (YUG)	Petros Galaktopoulos (GRE)
1972	Shamil Khisamutdinov (URS)	Stoyan Apostolov (BUL)	Gian Matteo Ranzi (ITA)
1976	Suren Nalbandyan (URS)	Stefan Rusu (ROM)	Heinz-Helmut Wehling (GDR)
1980	Stefan Rusu (ROM)	Andrzej Supron (POL)	Lars-Erik Skiold (SWE)
1984	Vlado Lisjak (YUG)	Tapio Sipila (FIN)	James Martinez (USA)
1988	Final on 22 September		

Greco-Roman – welterweight up to 74 kg (11 st 9 lb)

	Gold	Silver	Bronze
1932	Ivar Johansson (SWE)	Väinö Kajander (FIN)	Ercole Gallegatti (ITA)
1936	Rudolf Svedberg (SWE)	Fritz Schäfer (GER)	Eino Virtanen (FIN)
1984	Gösta Andersson (SWE)	Miklós Szilvási (HUN)	Henrik Hansen (DEN)
1952	Miklós Szilvási (HUN)	Gösta Andersson (SWE)	Khalil Taha (LIB)
1956	Mithat Bayrak (TUR)	Vladimir Maneyev (URS)	Per Berlin (SWE)
1960	Mithat Bayrak (TUR)	Günther Maritschnigg (GER)	René Schiermeyer (FRA)
1964	Anatoliy Kolesov (URS)	Cyril Todorov (BUL)	Bertil Nyström (SWE)
1968	Rudolf Vesper (GDR)	Daniel Robin (FRA)	Károly Bajkó (HUN)
1972	Vitezslav Macha (TCH)	Petros Galaktopoulos (GRE)	Jan Karlsson (SWE)
1976	Anatoliy Bykov (URS)	Vitezslav Macha (TCH)	Karlheinz Helbing (FRG)
1980	Ferenc Kocsis (HUN)	Anatoliy Bykov (URS)	Mikko Huhtala (FIN)
1984	Jouko Salomaki (FIN)	Roger Tallroth (SWE)	Stefan Rusu (ROM)
1988	Final on 21 September		

Greco-Roman middleweight up to 82 kg (12 st 2 lb)

	Gold	Silver	Bronze
1906	Verner Weckman (FIN)	Rudolf Lindmayer (AUT)	Robert Bebrens (DEN)
1908	Frithiof Märtensson (SWE)	Mauritz Andersson (SWE)	Anders Andersen (DEN)
1912	Claes Johansson (SWE)	Martin Klein (URS)	Alfred Asikainen (FIN)
1920	Carl Westergren (SWE)	Artur Lindfors (FIN)	Matti Perttila (FIN)
1924	Eduard Westerlund (FIN)	Artur Lindfors (FIN)	Roman Steinberg (EST)
1928	Väinö Kokkinen (FIN)	László Papp (HUN)	Albert Kusnetz (EST)
1932	Väinö Kokkinen (FIN)	Jean Földeák (GER)	Axel Cadier (SWE)
1936	Ivar Johansson (SWE)	Ludwig Schweikert (GER)	József Palotás (HUN)
1948	Axel Grönberg (SWE)	Muhlis Tayfur (TUR)	Ercole Gallegatti (ITA)
1952	Axel Grönberg (SWE)	Kalervo Rauhala (FIN)	Nikolai Belov (URS)
1956	Givi Kartoziya (URS)	Dimiter Dobrev (BUL)	Rune Jansson (SWE)
1960	Dimiter Dobrev (BUL)	Lothar Metz (GER)	Ion Taranu (ROM)
1964	Branislav Simič (YUG)	Jiri Kormanik (TCH)	Lothar Metz (GER)
1968	Lothar Metz (GDR)	Valentin Olenik (URS)	Branislav Simič (YUG)
1972	Czaba Hegedus (HUN)	Anatoliy Nazarenko (URS)	Milan Nenadic (YUG)
1976	Momir Petkovic (YUG)	Vladimir Cheboksarov (URS)	Ivan Kolev (BUL)
1980	Gennadiy Korban (URS)	Jan Dolgowicz (POL)	Pavel Pavlov (BUL)
1984	Ion Draica (ROM)	Dimitrios Thanopoulos (GRE)	Soren Claeson (SWE)
1988	Final on 22 September		

Greco-Roman light heavyweight up to 90 kg (14 st 2 lb)

	Gold	Silver	Bronze
1908	Verner Weckman (FIN)	Yrjö Saarela (FIN)	Carl Jensen (DEN)
1912	*	Anders Ahlgren (SWE) Ivar Böhling (FIN)	Béla Varga (HUN)
1920	Claes Johansson (SWE)	Edil Rosenqvist (FIN)	Johannes Eriksen (DEN)
1924	Carl Westergren (SWE)	Rudolf Svensson (SWE)	Onni Pellinen (FIN)
1928	Ibrahim Moustafa (EGY)	Adolf Rieger (GER)	Onni Pellinen (FIN)
1936	Rudolf Svensson (SWE)	Onni Pellinen (FIN)	Mario Gruppioni (ITA)
1936	Axel Cadier (SWE)	Edwins Bietags (LIT)	August Néo (EST)
1948	Karl-Erik Nilsson (SWE)	Kaelpo Gröndahl (FIN)	Ibrahim Orabi (EGY)
1952	Kaelpo Gröndahl (FIN)	Shalva Shikhladze (URS)	Karl-Erik Nilsson (SWE)
1956	Valentin Nikolayev (URS)	Petko Sirakov (BUL)	Karl-Erik Nilsson (SWE)
1960	Tevfik Kis (TUR)	Krali Bimbalov (BUL)	Givi Kartoziya (URS)
1964	Boyan Radev (BUL)	Per Svensson (SWE)	Heinz Kiehl (GER)
1968	Boyan Radev (BUL)	Nikolai Yakovenko (URS)	Nicolae Martinescu (ROM)
1972	Valeriy Rezantsev (URS)	Josip Corak (YUG)	Czeslaw Kwiecinski (POL)
1976	Valeriy Rezantsev (URS)	Stoyan Ivanov (BUL)	Czeslaw Kwiecinski (POL)
1980	Norbert Nottny (HUN)	Igor Kanygin (URS)	Petre Dicu (ROM)
1984	Steven Fraser (USA)	Illie Matei (ROM)	Frank Andersson (SWE)

1988 Final on 20 September

*After nine hours of wrestling Ahlgren and Bohling declared joint second.

Greco-Roman heavyweight up to 100 kg (15 st 10 lb)

	Gold	Silver	Bronze
1896	Carl Schuhmann (GER)	Georgios Tsitas (GRE)	Stephanos Christopoulos (GRE)
1906	Sören Jensen (DEN)	Henri Baur (AUT)	Marcel Dubois (BEL)
1908	Richard Weisz (HUN)	Aleksandr Petrov (URS)	Sören Jensen (DEN)
1912	Yrjö Saarela (FIN)	Johan Olin (FIN)	Sören Jensen (DEN)
1920	Adolf Lindfors (FIN)	Poul Hansen (DEN)	Martti Nieminen (FIN)
1924	Henri Deglane (FRA)	Edil Rosenqvist (FIN)	Raymund Badó (HUN)
1928	Rudolf Svensson (SWE)	Hjalmar Nyström (FIN)	Georg Gehring (GER)
1932	Carl Westergren (SWE)	Josef Urban (TCH)	Nikolaus Hirschl (AUT)
1936	Kristjan Palusalu (EST)	John Nyman (SWE)	Kurt Hornfischer (GER)
1948	Ahmet Kireççi (TUR)	Tor Nilsson (SWE)	Guido Fantoni (ITA)
1952	Johannes Kotkas (URS)	Josef Ružička (TCH)	Tauno Kovanen (FIN)
1956	Anatoliy Parfenov (URS)	Wilfried Dietrich (GER)	Adelmo Bulgarelli (ITA)
1960	Ivan Bogdan (URS)	Wilfried Dietrich (GER)	Bohumil Kubat (TCH)
1964	István Kozma (HUN)	Anatoliy Roschin (URS)	Wilfried Dietrich (GER)
1968	István Kozma (HUN)	Anatoliy Roschin (URS)	Petr Kment (TCH)
1972	Nicolae Martinescu (ROM)	Nikolai Yakovenko (URS)	Ferenc Kiss (HUN)

1976	Nikolai Bolboshin (URS)	Kamen Goranov (BUL)	Andrzej Skrzylewski (POL)
1980	Gheorghi Raikov (BUL)	Roman Bierla (POL)	Vasile Andrei (ROM)
1984	Vasile Andrei (ROM)	Greg Gibson (USA)	Jozef Tertelje (YUG)

1988 Final on 21 September

Greco-Roman super heavyweight over 100 kg (15 st 10 lb)

	Gold	*Silver*	*Bronze*
1972	Anatoliy Roschin (URS)	Alexandre Tomov (BUL)	Victor Dolipschi (ROM)
1976	Aleksandr Kolchinsky (URS)	Alexandre Tomov (BUL)	Roman Codreanu (ROM)
1980	Aleksandr Kolchinsky (URS)	Alexandre Tomov (BUL)	Hassan Bchara (LIB)
1984	Jeffrey Blatnick (USA)	Refik Memisevic (YUG)	Victor Dolipschi (ROM)

1988 Final on 22 September

YACHTING

The first Olympic regatta was scheduled for the first modern Games in 1896 but the weather was so bad it was cancelled and the first medals were won four years later in 1900. In that year, the boats sailed were huge. There was a 10–20 ton class and an 'open' class where the size of the vessel was left up to you.

Over the years, the classes of boat sailed have changed constantly.

Also, while most classes are open to women, the '470' class, which has previously been for men only, now has a separate women's race. So there are six open classes, one for men only and one for women only – eight Olympic titles at stake in all.

THE BOATS

Finn

At only 4.47 metres long, this is one of the smallest boats raced. It is a centre-board single-sail dinghy operated by a single crewman (or woman). It has been an Olympic class boat since 1952.

470

4.7 metres long centre-board dinghy with mainsail, foresail and spinnaker. Operated by two-man crew. Olympic class since 1976. This class will have a separate race for women, unlike all the other classes, which are for open competition.

Flying Dutchman

Another two-crew centre-board dinghy 6.05 metres in length. Mainsail, foresail plus spinnaker used. This has been Britain's most successful class in recent years.

Star

This is a two-crew racer. Spinnaker not allowed. This craft has a permanent keel. Sailed in the Olympics since 1932, it is the oldest class still used.

Soling

Another keel boat. Spinnakers used. Operated by a three-person crew. An Olympic class since 1972. With a length of 8.16 metres it is the largest yacht used in the Olympics.

Tornado

This is a catamaran (twin-hulled boat). Length is just 6.09 metres. Operated by two-person crew. Very fast.

Division Two

This class replaces the winglider or sailboard class used in the 1984 Games. It is little more than a name change.

Note: Spinnakers are billowing large foresails used in addition to the two existing sails to produce more speed when a craft is sailing downwind or 'on a run'.

A keelboat is one where the finlike blade protruding from the bottom of the boat, which produces the balance to the sail, is fixed in contrast to the craft with centreboards which can be withdrawn into the boat as necessary while sailing.

THE EVENTS

Each class takes part in seven races over seven days. Their best six performances count.

The courses are standard Olympic courses – basically a combination of triangles plus windward and leeward legs.

A low-point Olympic scoring system is used as follows:

Finishing place	Points
1st	0
2nd	3
3rd	5.7
4th	8
5th	10
6th	11.7
7th and thereafter	Place plus 6

Lowest total score wins.

THE COMPETITION

In 1984, the United States were in the medals in every class, winning three gold medals in the process. The medals, however, can come from anywhere. For example, in 1980, Brazil won both the 470 and Tornado classes. The Soviets can pick up gold medals while not being as dominant in this sport as in so many others. Western Europeans do well, including Britain. And Ireland, too, has some outstanding yachtsmen – they won silver in the Flying Dutchman class in 1980.

THE STARS

Paul Elvström (DEN) is the most successful yachtsman in Olympic history. He won the single-handed class four times in succession – 1948 to 1960. He was still competing in 1984, partnering his daughter Trine in the Tornado class. They came fourth.

King Constantine of Greece won a gold medal at the 1960 Games in the Dragon Class (discontinued).

THE BRITISH

Rodney Pattison is Britain's most successful Olympic sailor with two gold medals and

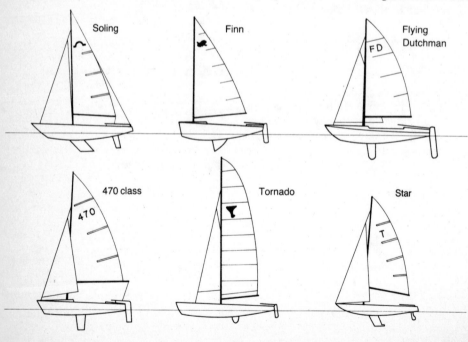

one silver. All were won in the Flying Dutchman class. In 1968 he was partnered by Iain McDonald-Smith to gold, despite being disqualified in the first race after finishing first. They subsequently had five wins and a second place for the record score in Olympic yachting – three points (remember – lowest means best). In 1972 he defended his title successfully, partnered by Christopher Davies, and in 1976 Pattison won a silver medal along with Julian Brooke-Houghton.

In 1984 Jo Richard and Peter Allam were third in this class.

Not a lot of people know that

● The Dragon class, in which King Constantine of Greece won a gold medal in 1960, was superseded by the Soling Class.

● USA, Britain and Norway head the list of gold medals won in Olympic yachting so far – each country has 14.

● For the 1900 Olympics, apart from the huge 20 tonners that were raced in the English Channel, other classes competed in the River Seine.

● At a regatta held in the Bay of Pusan in 1987, yachtsmen complained that they had to sail out through sewage to reach the start. Olympic races will take place in – yes you have it – the Bay of Pusan.

VENUE

Bay of Pusan Yachting Centre. 450 km southeast of Seoul.

RESULTS

Division-2 class windglider/*Open*

	Gold	Silver	Bronze
1984	Stephan Van Den Berg (HOL)	Randall Steele (USA)	Bruce Kendall (NZL)
1988	20–28 September		

Finn class/*Open*

	Gold	Silver	Bronze
1920*	NETHERLANDS Franciscus Hin Johannes Hin	NETHERLANDS Arnoud van der Biesen Petrus Beikers	—
1920†	GREAT BRITAIN Francis Richards T. Hedberg	—	—
1924	Leon Huybrechts (BEL)	Henrik Robert (NOR)	Hans Dittmar (FIN)
1928	Sven Thorell (SWE)	Henrik Robert (NOR)	Bertil Broman (FIN)
1932	Jacques Lebrun (FRA)	Adriaan Maas (HOL)	Santiago Cansino (ESP)
1936	Daniel Kagchelland (HOL)	Werner Krogmann (GER)	Peter Scott (GBR)
1948	Paul Elvström (DEN)	Ralph Evans (USA)	Jacobus de Jong (HOL)

* 12 ft dinghy, two handed.
† The only entry, 18 ft and two handed.

1952	Paul Elvström (DEN)	Charles Currey (GBR)	Rickard Sarby (SWE)
1956	Paul Elvström (DEN)	André Nelis (BEL)	John Marvin (USA)
1960	Paul Elvström (DEN)	Aleksandr Chuchelov (URS)	André Nelis (BEL)
1964	Willi Kuhweide (GER)	Peter Barrett (USA)	Henning Wind (DEN)
1968	Valentin Mankin (URS)	Hubert Raudaschl (AUT)	Fabio Albarelli (ITA)
1972	Serge Maury (FRA)	Ilias Hatzipavlis (GRE)	Viktor Potapov (URS)
1976	Jochen Schümann (GDR)	Andrei Balashov (URS)	John Bertrand (AUS)
1980	Esko Rechardt (FIN)	Wolfgang Mayrhofer (AUT)	Andrei Balashov (URS)
1984	Russell Coutts (NZL)	John Bertrand (USA)	Terry Neilson (CAN)

1988   20–28 September

470 class/*Men*

	Gold	*Silver*	*Bronze*
1976	WEST GERMANY Frank Hübner Harro Bode	SPAIN Antonio Gorostegui Pedro Millet	AUSTRALIA Ian Brown Ian Ruff
1980	BRAZIL Marcos Soares Eduardo Penido	EAST GERMANY Jörn Borowski Edberg Swensson	FINLAND Jouko Lindgren Georg Tallberg
1984	SPAIN Luis Doreste Roberto Molina	UNITED STATES Stephen Benjamin Christopher Steinfeld	FRANCE Thierry Peponnet Luc Pillot

1988   20–28 September

Tornado/*Open*

	Gold	*Silver*	*Bronze*
1976	GREAT BRITAIN Reg White John Osborn	UNITED STATES David McFaull Michael Rothwell	WEST GERMANY Jörg Spengler Jörg Schmall
1980	BRAZIL Alexandre Welter Lars Björkström	DENMARK Peter Due Per Kjergard	SWEDEN Göran Marström Jörgen Ragnarsson
1984	NEW ZEALAND Rex Sellers Christopher Timms	UNITED STATES Randy Smyth Jay Glaser	AUSTRALIA Chris Cairns John Anderson

1988   20–28 September

Star class/*Open*

	Gold	Silver	Bronze
1932	UNITED STATES Gilbert Gray Andrew Libano Jr	GREAT BRITAIN Colin Ratsey Peter Jaffe	SWEDEN Gunnar Asther Daniel Sunden-Cullberg
1936	GERMANY Peter Bischoff Hans-Joachim Weise	SWEDEN Arved Laurin Uno Wallentin	NETHERLANDS Adriaan Maas Willem de Vries Lentsch
1948	UNITED STATES Hilary Smart Paul Smart	CUBA Carlos de Cardenas Carlos de Cardenas Jr	NETHERLANDS Adriaan Maas Edward Stutterheim
1952	ITALY Agostino Straulino Nicolo Rode	UNITED STATES John Reid John Price	PORTUGAL Francisco de Andrade Joaquim Fiuza
1956	UNITED STATES Herbert Williams Lawrence Low	ITALY Agostino Straulino Nicolo Rode	BAHAMAS Durward Knowles Sloan Farrington
1960	USSR Timir Pinegin Fedor Shutkov	PORTUGAL Mario Quina José Quina	UNITED STATES William Parks Robert Halperin
1964	BAHAMAS Durward Knowles Cecil Cooke	UNITED STATES Richard Stearns Lyn Williams	SWEDEN Pelle Pettersson Holger Sundström
1968	UNITED STATES Lowell North Peter Barrett	NORWAY Peder Lunder Per Olav Wiken	ITALY Franco Cavallo Camillo Gargano
1972	AUSTRALIA David Forbes John Anderson	SWEDEN Pelle Pettersson Stellan Westerdahl	WEST GERMANY Willi Kuhweide Karsten Meyer
1976	Not held		
1980	USSR Valentin Mankin Aleksandr Muzychenko	AUSTRIA Hubert Raudaschl Karl Ferstl	ITALY Giorgio Gorla Alfio Peraboni
1984	UNITED STATES William Buchan Stephen Erickson	WEST GERMANY Joachim Griese Michael Marcour	ITALY Giorgio Gorla Alfio Peraboni
1988	20–28 September		

Flying Dutchman/*Open*

	Gold	Silver	Bronze
1956*	NEW ZEALAND Peter Mander John Cropp	AUSTRALIA Roland Tasker John Scott	GREAT BRITAIN Jasper Blackall Terence Smith
1960	NORWAY Peder Lunde Jr Bjorn Bergvall	DENMARK Hans Fogh Ole Erik Petersen	GERMANY Rolf Mulka Ingo von Bredow

* Sharpie class.

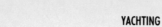

1964	NEW ZEALAND	GREAT BRITAIN	UNITED STATES
	Helmer Pedersen	Keith Musto	Harry Melges Jr
	Earle Wells	Arthur Morgan	William Bentsen
1968	GREAT BRITAIN	WEST GERMANY	BRAZIL
	Rodney Pattisson	Ullrich Libor	Reinaldo Conrad
	Iain Macdonald-Smith	Peter Naumann	Burkhard Cordes
1972	GREAT BRITAIN	FRANCE	WEST GERMANY
	Rodney Pattisson	Yves Pajot	Ullrich Libor
	Christopher Davies	Marc Pajot	Peter Naumann
1976	WEST GERMANY	GREAT BRITAIN	BRAZIL
	Jorg Diesch	Rodney Pattisson	Reinaldo Conrad
	Eckart Diesch	Julian Brooke Houghton	Peter Ficker
1980	SPAIN	IRELAND	HUNGARY
	Alejandro Abascal	David Wilkins	Szabolcs Detre
	Miguel Noguer	James Wilkinson	Zsolt Detre
1984	UNITED STATES	CANADA	GREAT BRITAIN
	Jonathan McKee	Terry McLaughlin	Jonathan Richards
	William Buchan	Evert Bastet	Peter Allam

1988   20–28 September

Soling class/*Open*

	Gold	*Silver*	*Bronze*
1972	UNITED STATES	SWEDEN	CANADA
	Harry Melges	Stig Wennerstrom	David Miller
	William Bentsen	Lennart Roslund	John Ekels
	William Allen	Bo Knape	Paul Cote
		Stefan Krook	
1976	DENMARK	UNITED STATES	EAST GERMANY
	Poul Jensen	John Kolius	Dieter Below
	Valemar Bandolowski	Walter Glagwo	Michael Zachries
	Erik Hansen	Richard Hoepfner	Olaf Engelhardt
1980	DENMARK	USSR	GREECE
	Poul Jensen	Boris Budnikov	Anastassios Boudouris
	Valdemar Bandolowski	Aleksandr Budnikov	Anastassios Gavrilis
	Erik Hansen	Nikolay Polyakov	Aristidis Rapanakis
1984	UNITED STATES	BRAZIL	CANADA
	Robert Haines Jr	Torben Grael	Hans Fogh
	Edward Trevelyan	Daniel Adler	John Kerr
	Roderick Davis	Ronaldo Senfft	Steve Calder

1988   20–28 September

470 Class/*Women*

1988   First time held, from 20–28 September

THE MOSTESTS, OLDESTS, YOUNGESTS, ETC

Men

Most gold medals	10 Ray Ewry (USA) 1900–8 athletics
Most medals	15 Nikolai Andrianov (URS) 1972–80 gymnastics
Oldest gold medallist	Oscar Swahn (SWE) 64 yr 258 days 1912 shooting
Oldest medallist	Oscar Swahn (SWE) 72 yr 280 days 1920 shooting
Youngest gold medallist	Anonymous French boy 7–10 yrs 1900 rowing
Youngest medallist	Anonymous French boy 7–10 yrs 1900 rowing
Most golds in one games	7 Mark Spitz (USA) 1972 swimming
Most medals in one games	8 Aleksandr Ditiatin (URS) 1980 gymnastics
Oldest competitor	Oscar Swahn (SWE) 72 yr 280 days 1920 shooting
Youngest competitor	Anonymous French boy 7–10 yrs 1900 rowing
Most games attended	8 Raimondo d'Inzeo (ITA) 1948–76 equestrianism
Longest span	40 years Ivan Osiier (DEN) 1908–48 fencing 40 years Magnus Konow (NOR) 1908–48 yachting

Women

Most gold medals	9 Larissa Latynina (URS) 1956–64 gymnastics
Most medals	18 Larissa Latynina (URS) 1956–64 gymnastics
Oldest gold medallist	Maud Van Rosen (SWE) 46 yr 258 days 1972 equestrianism
Oldest medallist	Maud Van Rosen (SWE) 46 yr 258 days 1972 equestrianism
Youngest gold medallist	Marjorie Gestring (USA) 13 yr 267 days 1936 diving
Youngest medallist	Inge Sorensen (DEN) 12 yr 24 days 1936 swimming
Most golds in one games	4 by 6 women
Most medals in one games	7 Maria Gorochowskaya (URS) 1952 gymnastics
Oldest competitor	Lorna Johnstone (GBR) 70 yr 5 days 1972 equestrianism
Youngest competitor	Cecilia Colledge (GBR) 11 yr 73 days 1932 skating
Most games attended	6 Janice York-Romary (USA) 1948–68 fencing 6 Lia Manoliu (ROM) 1952–72 athletics
Longest span	24 years Ellen Muller-Preis (AUT) 1932–56 fencing